Clashing Views in

Human Sexuality

TENTH EDITION

TAKING SIDES

Clashing Views in

Human Sexuality

TENTH EDITION

Selected, Edited, and with Introductions by

William J. Taverner

Consulting Editor

Ryan W. McKee
Fairleigh Dickinson University and Montclair State University

Contemporary Learning Series
2460 Kerper Blvd., Dubuque, IA 52001

Visit us on the Internet
http://www.mhcls.com

To Denise, Robert, and Christopher

Photo Acknowledgment
Cover image: Royalty-Free/CORBIS

Cover Acknowledgment
Maggie Lytle

Compositor: ICC Macmillan Inc.

Manufactured in the United States of America

Tenth Edition

123456789DOCDOC987

Library of Congress Cataloging-in-Publication Data
Main entry under title:
Taking sides: clashing views on controversial issues in human sexuality/selected,
edited, and with introductions by William J. Taverner.—10th ed.
Includes bibliographical references and index.
1. Sex. 2. Sexual ethics. I. Taverner, William J., *comp.*
612.6

MHID: 0-07-339719-9
ISBN: 978-0-07-339719-1
ISSN: 1098-5387

Printed on Recycled Paper

Preface

In few areas of American society today are clashing views more evident than in the area of human sexual behavior. Almost daily, in the news media, in congressional hearings, and on the streets, we hear about Americans of all ages taking completely opposite positions on such issues as abortion, contraception, fertility, homosexuality, teenage sexuality, and the like. Given the highly personal, emotional, and sensitive nature of these issues, sorting out the meaning of these controversies and fashioning a coherent position on them can be a difficult proposition. The purpose of this book, therefore, is to encourage meaningful critical thinking about current issues related to human sexuality, and the debates are designed to assist you in the task of clarifying your own personal values in relation to some common, and often polar, perspectives on the issues presented.

This tenth edition of *Taking Sides: Clashing Views in Human Sexuality* presents 36 lively and thoughtful statements by articulate advocates on opposite sides of a variety of sexuality related questions. Each issue includes:

- A *question* (e.g., Issue 1 asks, Could sex be addictive?);
- An *introduction* that presents background information helpful for understanding the context of the debate and information on the authors who will be contributing to the debate;
- *Essays* by two authors—one who responds yes, and one who responds no to the question; and
- A *postscript* that poses additional questions to help you further examine the issues raised (or not raised) by the authors, including bibliographical resources.

It is important to remember that for the questions debated in this volume, the essays represent only two perspectives on the issue. Remember that the debates do not end there—most issues have many shades of gray, and you may find your own values congruent with neither author. Since this book is a tool to encourage critical thinking, you should not feel confined to the views expressed in the articles. You may see important points on both sides of an issue and may construct for yourself a new and creative approach, which may incorporate the best of both sides or provide an entirely new vantage point for understanding.

As you read this collection of issues, try to respect other people's philosophical worldviews and beliefs and attempt to articulate your own. At the same time, be aware of the authors' potential biases and how they may affect the positions each author articulates. Be aware, too, of your own biases. We all have experiences that may shape the way we look at a controversial issue. Try to come to each issue with an open mind. You may find your values challenged—or strengthened—after reading both views. Although you may disagree with one or even both of the arguments offered for each issue, it is important that you read each statement carefully and critically.

Changes to This Edition

This edition of *Taking Sides: Clashing Views in Human Sexuality* includes substantial changes from the previous edition, including five brand new issues or issues with updated articles.

Brand New Issues

- Can Sex Be Addictive?
- Should Sex Ed Teach about Abstinence?
- Does the Availability of "Sexual Health Services" Make Some College Campuses Healthier than Others?
- Should Children Have an HPV Vaccination before They Enroll in School?
- Should Parents Be Allowed to Select the Sex of Their Baby?

Note that one issue, "Is the G Spot a Myth?", has new commentary by Beverly Whipple, who conducted much research on the G spot and other aspects of female sexuality. In all, 10 of the 36 essays are brand new, and many of the other issues have had introductions and postscripts edited to reflect new developments since the last edition of *Taking Sides: Clashing Views on Human Sexuality.*

A Word to the Instructor

An *Instructor's Manual,* with issue synopses, suggestions for classroom discussions, and test questions (multiple-choice and essay) is available from McGraw-Hill/Dushkin. This resource, authored by Ryan W. McKee, is a very useful accompaniment for this text. A general guidebook, *Using Taking Sides in the Classroom,* which discusses methods and techniques for integrating the pro/con approach into any classroom setting, is also available. An online version of *Using Taking Sides in the Classroom* and a correspondence service for *Taking Sides* adopters can be found at www.mhcls.com/usingts.

Taking Sides: Clashing Views in Human Sexuality is one of the many titles in the Taking Sides series. If you are interested in seeing the table of contents for any of the other titles, please visit the Taking Sides Web site at www.mhcls.com/takingsides.

For more information, please contact McGraw-Hill Contemporary Learning Series or visit www.mhcls.com, or www.mhhe.com, or by contacting the author at taverner@ptd.net. Ideas for new issues are *always welcome!*

Acknowledgments

First and foremost, I wish to thank my family. Putting together a collection of pro and con essays is no easy task, and the many hours I worked on this book were also hours that my wife spent patiently watching the kids, letting me bounce ideas off her, reviewing my selections and commentary, and helping me to temper my own biases. I thank my wife, Denise, and my children, Robert and Christopher, who always welcomed me with open arms whenever I was done working for the day. Thanks also to 8-year-old Robert for devising his "Yawn Scale." This started playfully the night before I was to speak at a Congressional Briefing in Washington, D.C. As I practiced my speech in the hotel room, Robert would yawn whenever things sounded too boring. He modified this empirical method for *Taking Sides,* ranking the title of each issue with a series of yawns from 0 to 5, to help me know when the titles sounded too boring. I am pleased to say there are very few 3+ yawn issues in this edition.

I thank my parents and family. As is probably true with many families, Thanksgiving at the Taverner's is very much like seeing *Taking Sides* in real life, especially following an election! I love them all for their support and for their help in making me think critically about all these issues.

For the hard work that goes into this book, I am indebted to the expert publishing skills of all my colleagues at McGraw-Hill Contemporary Learning Series. Thank you, Larry Loeppke, for your patience and support. Thanks to Lori Church for handling all the permissions requests. Thanks to Julie Keck and Alice Link for all your efforts in marketing. Most of all, thanks to Jill Peter and Susan Brusch. Both advised me on the new issues, carefully reviewing every article and giving me excellent feedback on what to keep and what to cut. I couldn't have done this edition without them.

Many thanks to Ryan W. McKee, author of the Instructor's Manual to *Taking Sides,* who also assisted with editing and researching many of the new issues, and fine-tuning them for publication. Ryan is a gifted researcher and writer, whose thoughtful analysis shines in the commentaries that precede and follow many of the selections.

Thanks to professional colleagues who reviewed parts of the manuscript, or who otherwise shared their expertise generously: Vern Bullough (whose passing in 2006 is a great loss to the field of sexology), Barbara Huberman (who checked my facts on emergency contraception), Sue Montfort (who is a role model for thoughtful analysis), Ricky Siegel (who offered new insights on emergency contraception, and whose enthusiasm for sexology is unmatched), Leonore Tiefer (who checked and rechecked my write-up on Intrinsa for accuracy), and Beverly Whipple (who checked my facts on the history of the G spot and generously offered to update her 2000 article). Thanks to Maggi Boyer and Nora Gelperin, expert reviewers who critically examined an essay on abstinence that I am contributing to this edition. Thanks also to Mark Eberle, my high school buddy, now a lawyer, who helped me navigate the legal arguments on sex and the Internet, so that I could better explain legal concepts to my readers. And speaking of high school buddies, I also thank my dear friend Tim Cummings, who passed away 5 years ago. I think Tim's knack for seeing the other side of arguments—often in sardonic terms—left a lasting impression on me.

Thanks to professional colleagues who suggested new issues, or pointed me in the direction of great articles: Linda Hendrickson, Lis Maurer, Irene Peters, Erika Pluhar, Deborah Roffman, Martha Roper, and Susie Wilson. Thanks also to students at Fairleigh Dickinson University who told me—sometimes in less kind terms than Robert—which issues are interesting, and which are not.

Finally, I wish to thank two colleagues who have been both mentors and friends for many years: Peggy Brick and Bob Francoeur. Peggy and I have collaborated on numerous sexuality education manuals, and I value her advice dearly. She is a generous mentor who constantly inspires me to think critically about all matters, not just those related to sexuality education. Bob edited or coedited the first seven editions of *Taking Sides: Clashing Views in Human Sexuality.* I have had the privilege of working with Bob on three previous editions of this book, and was introduced to both *Taking Sides* and Bob when I took his international studies course in Copenhagen, Denmark, 15 years ago. I am grateful for his kind guidance over the years, and honored to carry on his legacy. Everyone should be so lucky as to have such knowledgeable and caring mentors.

William J. Taverner

Contents In Brief

Contents

Patrick J. Carnes, considered by many to be an expert on sexual addiction, answers some common questions about this phenomenon, as featured on the Web site http://www.sexhelp.com. Carnes discusses the nature of sexual addiction, including ways in which it might be manifested, and offers suggestions for treatment. Sex therapist Lawrence A. Siegel and sex therapist/educator Richard M. Siegel counter that sexual addiction is grounded in "moralistic ideology masquerading as science." They argue that while some sexual behaviors may be dysfunctional, the term "sexual addiction" pathologizes many common forms of sexual expression that are not problematic.

Sexuality educator Rhonda Chittenden says that it is important for young people to expand their narrow definitions of sex and understand that oral sex *is* sex. Chittenden offers additional educational messages about oral sex. Sexuality trainer Nora Gelperin argues that adult definitions of oral sex are out of touch with the meaning the behavior holds for young people. Rather than impose adult definitions of intimacy, educators should be seeking to help young people clarify and understand their own values.

Stephanie Ann Sanders, a director and scientist with the Kinsey Institute and a contributing author to the *Encarta Online Encyclopedia*, summarizes

Masters and Johnson's Human Sexual Response Cycle. Paul Joannides, author of the popular book *The Guide to Getting It On!*, says that the Human Sexual Response Cycle is a "one-size-fits-all" model that does not account for individual variations.

Psychologist Terence M. Hines says that the widespread acceptance of the G Spot as real conflicts with available research. Hines explains that the existence of the G Spot has never been verified by empirical, objective means and that women may have been misinformed about their bodies and their sexuality. Sexuality researcher Beverly Whipple outlines historical and interdisciplinary research that has been conducted on female sexual response over the past 20 years, particularly on the anatomy and neurophysiology of the sensitive area known as the G Spot, which surrounds the urethra and is felt through the anterior vaginal wall.

Columnist Carolyn Susman comments favorably on Intrinsa, a testosterone patch intended to treat low female desire in women. Susman outlines research findings that say the patch could improve sexual desire in women. Iver Juster, a family practitioner, Gary Schubach, a sex researcher and educator, and Patricia Taylor, a sex researcher and sexual enhancement coach, reject the idea that female sexual desire is hormonally driven, and say that the testosterone patch should not be regarded as a cure-all.

David M. Hall, a graduate professor of human sexuality at Widener University, outlines and comments favorably on the "Sexual Health Report Card," a ranking of 100 universities in the United States by Trojan Condoms. Dr. Hall describes the various sexual health indicators for college campuses, as measured by the report, and argues for better sexuality education programs. Jens Alan Dana, a student and school newspaper editor at Brigham Young University, which was ranked lowest in the Trojan survey, argues that the rankings were unscientific, and based on a subjective set of criteria that were self-serving to Trojan's interests in marketing condoms.

William J. Taverner, sexuality educator and editor of *Taking Sides*, argues that sexuality education should teach about abstinence, and introduces a new model to replace problematic abstinence education models of the past. Sexuality educator Maureen Kelly argues that the framing of abstinence by conservatives has essentially made the term politically volatile, and that the one-size-fits-all definition has rendered the term useless to educators.

Cynthia Dailard, a senior public policy associate for the Alan Guttmacher Institute, outlines the potential for a new vaccination to prevent the spread of the human papillomavirus (HPV), a sexually transmitted infection that causes genital warts and most cases of cervical cancer. Dailard explains and summarizes the views of experts who believe that widespread vaccinations of preadolescent girls will dramatically reduce the incidence of HPV in the United States and abroad, especially in developing nations. *New York Times* columnist Roni Rabin acknowledges the potential for the HPV vaccination, but contends that cervical cancer can be staved off more economically by encouraging girls and women to have routine Pap smears.

Janice Weinman, executive director of the American Association of University Women (AAUW), states that, while there has been some progress since the AAUW published its study entitled *How Schools Shortchange Girls* in 1991, its 1998 review of 1,000 research studies entitled *Gender Gaps: Where Schools Still Fail Our Children* found that girls still face a gender gap in math, science, and computer science. Psychologist and author Judith Kleinfeld argues that despite appearances, girls still have an advantage over boys in terms of their future plans, teachers' expectations, and everyday school experiences. Furthermore, minority males in particular are at a disadvantage educationally.

Law professor John A. Robertson argues that preimplantation genetic diagnosis (PGD), a new technique that allows parents-to-be to determine the gender of their embryo before implantation in the uterus, should be permissible. Robertson argues that it is not sexist to want a baby of a particular gender, and that the practice should not be restricted. Marcy Darnovsky, associate director of the Center for Genetics and Society, argues that by allowing PGD for sex selection, governments are starting down a slippery slope that could create an era of consumer eugenics.

New York Times columnist Jane E. Brody believes that politics, not science, drove the FDA's decision not to allow emergency contraception to be made available over the counter. The Food and Drug Administration, responsible for regulating all drugs dispensed in the United States, says that its decision was not political, and that it would reconsider its decision if presented with evidence that girls under age 16 could take it safely without parental supervision.

President George W. Bush explains his decision to permit limited federal funding of embryonic stem cell research for the purpose of seeking treatments for serious diseases. Douglas F. Munch, a management consultant to the pharmaceutical and biotechnology industries, criticizes President Bush's decision for not fully reflecting the will of the people and for being too restrictive to have any meaningful impact on medical science and the lives of people affected by serious diseases.

UNIT 4   SEX AND SOCIETY   197

The Human Rights Campaign (HRC), America's largest gay and lesbian organization, explains why same-sex couples should be afforded the same legal right to marry as heterosexual couples. John Cornyn, United States senator from Texas, says a constitutional amendment is needed to define marriage as permissible only between a man and a woman. Senator Cornyn contends that the traditional institution of marriage needs to be protected from activist courts that would seek to redefine it.

Dorian Solot and Marshall Miller, founders of the Alternatives to Marriage Project (www.unmarried.org), describe some of the challenges faced by people who choose to live together without marrying, and offer practical advice for couples who face discrimination. David Popenoe and Barbara Dafoe Whitehead, directors of the National Marriage Project (marriage.rutgers.edu), contend that living together before marriage is not a good way to prepare for marriage or avoid divorce. They maintain that cohabitation weakens the institution of marriage and poses serious risks for women and children.

Radio commentator Laura Schlessinger denounces a study, published
by the American Psychological Association (APA), that reexamined the
results and conclusions from 59 earlier studies of child sexual abuse
(CSA) in more than 35,000 college students. Schlessinger views this
study as a "pseudo-scientific" attempt to convince people to accept
pedophilia as normal. Author David L. Riegel summarizes the major
findings of the research in question, and criticizes the dismissal of
scientific research that challenges common assumptions about CSA and
its effects on children.

Loretta M. Kopelman, a professor of medical humanities, argues that
certain moral absolutes apply to all cultures and that these, combined
with the many serious health and cultural consequences of female
circumcision, require that all forms of female genital mutilation be
eliminated. P. Masila Mutisya, a professor of multicultural education,
contends that we should allow the simplest form of female circumcision,
nicking the clitoral hood to draw a couple of drops of blood, as part of the
rich heritage of rite of passage for newborn and pubertal girls in those
cultures with this tradition.

The Federal Communications Commission (FCC), a U.S. government
agency charged with regulating the content of the broadcast airways,
including television and radio, outlines what it defines as "indecent"
broadcast material and describes its enforcement policy. Author Judith
Levine traces the history of censorship in the United States, and argues
that much of what the FCC has determined is "indecent" sexual speech
is not, in fact, harmful to children.

In a dissenting opinion, United States Supreme Court Justice Stephen
G. Breyer argues that the Child Online Protection Act does not impose

an unreasonable burden on free speech, and should have been upheld by the high court. Explaining the Supreme Court's decision to strike down the Child Online Protection Act, Justice Anthony M. Kennedy says that filtering software is a better and less restrictive alternative for protecting children from sexual content on the Internet.

Introduction

Sexual Attitudes in Perspective

America is one big divided country, with a blue northern and coastal perimeter, and a bright red center! At least that is the picture painted by television and print media's portrayal of American social attitudes. Are you from a "red state," perhaps Florida, or maybe Texas? Then surely you are a Republican who supported George W. Bush in the 2004 presidential election and conservative candidates in the 2006 midterm elections. You also oppose abortion and same-sex marriage, and you probably love hunting and NASCAR. Are you from a "blue state," perhaps California, or maybe Massachusetts? Then surely you are a Democrat who voted for John Kerry in 2004 and liberal candidates in the 2006 midterm elections. You support a woman's right to choose, are a staunch civil libertarian, and maybe have plans to attend a friend's same-sex wedding. Oh, and you are also a vegetarian who loves to drink lattes!

If you are scratching your head thinking that neither profile describes you, you are not alone. Texas and Florida may be "red states," but how do we reconcile the fact that more than 6 million Americans in these two states voted for Kerry, who has been called a "bleeding heart liberal"? Or that another 6 million people voted for "redneck conservative" Bush in "blue states" California and Massachusetts? Or that many more millions in other states voted in ways that were inconsistent with their assigned state color? Moreover, what do we know about the 40 percent of eligible voters who did not vote at all in 2004? It's an important question as these non-voters make up almost 100 million Americans! The reality is that our opinions, attitudes, and values on social and sexual issues are as diverse as we are. They are formed by numerous factors that we will explore in this introduction.

As you examine the 18 controversial issues in human sexuality in this volume, you will find yourself unavoidably encountering the values you have absorbed from our society, your ethnic background, your religious heritage and traditions, and your personal experiences. Because these values will influence your decisions, often without being consciously recognized, it is important to actively think about the role these undercurrent themes play in the positions you take on these issues.

Many thanks to Robert T. Francoeur for his insights on this Introduction, parts of which are repeated from previous editions of *Taking Sides* when Francoeur was editor. Dr. Francoeur is the editor of the award-winning *International Encyclopedia of Sexuality,* and there is no greater authority on global cultural differences related to understanding sexuality.

How Social and Ethnic Factors Influence Our Values

American society is not homogeneous, nor is it even red or blue! People who grow up in rural, suburban, and large urban environments sometimes have subtle differences in their values and attitudes when it comes to gender roles, marriage, and sexuality, or trends that may reflect the views of the majority of people in communities. Growing up in different areas of the United States can influence one's views of sex, marriage, and family. This is even more true for men and women who were born, and raised, in another country and culture.

Many studies have shown how values can be affected by one's family income level and socioeconomic status. Studies have also indicated that one's occupation, educational level, and income are closely related to one's values, attitudes, sex-role conceptions, child-rearing practices, and sexual identity. Our values and attitudes about sex are also influenced by whether we are brought up in a rural, suburban, or large urban environment. Our ethnic background can be an important influence on our values and attitudes. In contrast to the vehement debates among white, middle-class Americans about pornography, for instance, Robert Staples, a professor of sociology at the University of California, San Francisco, says that among African Americans, pornography is a trivial issue. "Blacks," Staples explains, "have traditionally had a more naturalistic attitude toward human sexuality, seeing it as the normal expression of sexual attraction between men and women. . . . Rather than seeing the depiction of heterosexual intercourse or nudity as an inherent debasement of women, as a fringe group of [white] feminists claims, the black community would see women as having equal rights to the enjoyment of sexual stimuli. . . . Since the double [moral] standard has never attracted many American blacks, the claim that women are exploited by exhibiting their nude bodies or engaging in heterosexual intercourse lacks credibility" (quoted in Philip Nobile and Eric Nadler, *United States of America vs. Sex* [Minotaur Press, 1986]). While some middle-class whites may be very concerned about pornography promoting sexual promiscuity, many African Americans are far more concerned about issues related to poverty and employment opportunities.

Similarly, attitudes toward homosexuality vary among white, African American, and Latino cultures. In the macho tradition of Latin America, male homosexual behavior may be considered a sign that one cannot find a woman and have sexual relationships like a "real" man. In some African American communities, a similar judgment prevails, and gay and lesbian relationships are often unrecognized. In his book, *On the Down Low: A Journey into the Lives of "Straight" Black Men Who Sleep with Men* (Broadway, 2004), J.L. King explains this cultural ethic, and how "straight" men live secret lives with their same-sex sexual encounters "on the down low," and not impacting their sexual orientation. Understanding this ethnic value becomes very important in appreciating the ways in which African Americans and Latinos respond to the crisis of AIDS and the presence of males with AIDS in their families. The family might deny that a son or husband has AIDS until the very end because others might interpret this admission as a confession that the person is homosexual. Or, a man on the "down low" might receive inadequate treatment from a doctor or health clinic who does not ask the right questions. A clinician who asks him if he is gay, will probably be told no. A clinician who asks a number of questions, including whether he sometimes has sex with men, might be able to get a better picture of his sexuality and needs.

Another example of differing ethnic values is the issue of single motherhood. In ethnic groups with a strong tradition of extended matrilineal families, the concept of an "illegitimate" child born "out-of-wedlock" may not even exist. Unmarried mothers in these cultures do not carry the same stigma often associated with single mothers in other, less-matrilineal cultures. When "outsiders" who do not share the particular ethnic values of a culture enter into such a subculture, they often cannot understand why contraception and sexuality education programs do not produce any substantial change in attitudes. They overlook the basic social scripting that has already taken place. Gender roles also vary from culture to culture. Muslim men and women who grow up in the Middle East and then emigrate to the United States have to adapt to the much greater freedom women have in the States. Similarly, American men and women who have served in the armed forces in Afghanistan, Iraq, Saudi Arabia, and other parts of the Middle East found they had to adapt to very different Muslim cultures that put many restrictions on the movement and dress of women in the military.

A boy who grows up among the East Bay Melanesians in the Southwestern Pacific is taught to avoid any social contact with girls from the age of three or four, even though he may run around naked and masturbate in public. Adolescent Melanesian boys and girls are not allowed to have sex with each other, but boys are expected to have sex both with an older male and with a boy of his own age. Their first heterosexual experiences come with marriage. In the Cook Islands, Mangaian boys are expected to have sex with many girls after an older woman teaches them about the art of sexual play. Mangaians also accept and expect both premarital and extramarital sex.

But one does not have to look to exotic anthropological studies to find evidence of the importance of ethnic values. Even within the United States, subtle but important differences in sexual attitudes and values exist among its diverse population of its native people, and of those who immigrated from all over the world.

Religious Factors in Attitudes Toward Sex

In the Middle Ages, Christian theologians divided sexual behaviors into two categories: behaviors that were "natural" and those that were "unnatural." Since they believed that the natural function and goal of all sexual behavior and relations was reproduction, masturbation was unnatural because it frustrated the natural goal of conception and continuance of the species. Rape was certainly considered illicit because it was not within the marital bond, but since it was procreative, rape was also considered a natural use of sex. The same system of distinction was applied to other sexual relations and behaviors. Premarital sex, adultery, and incest were natural uses of sexuality, while oral sex, anal sex, and contraception were unnatural. Homosexual relations were both illicit and unnatural. These religious values were based on the view that God created man and woman at the beginning of time and laid down certain rules and guidelines for sexual behavior and relations. This view is still very influential in our culture, even for those who are not active in any religious tradition.

In recent years, several analysts have highlighted two philosophical or religious perspectives that appear throughout Judeo-Christian tradition and Western civilization. Understanding these two perspectives is important in any attempt to debate controversial issues in human sexuality.

Judeo-Christian tradition allows us to examine two distinct worldviews: the *fixed worldview* and the *process worldview*. The fixed worldview says that morality is unchanging. Right and wrong are always right and wrong, regardless of the situation or circumstances. The fixed worldview relies on a literal interpretation of its religious or ethical teachings, without regard for context. The process worldview examines issues of morality in an ever-changing world. What is right or wrong may require a contextual examination, and rules and ethics must constantly be re-examined in light of new information and the world's evolving context.

Take for example the question of masturbation. Where does the Christian prohibition of masturbation come from? If you search the Bible, the word is never mentioned! Yet much of what has been taught in Christianity regarding masturbation comes from the story of Onan:

> Then Judah said to Onan, "Go in to your brother's wife and perform the duty of a brother-in-law to her, and raise up offspring for your brother." But Onan knew that the offspring would not be his. So whenever he went in to his brother's wife he would waste the semen on the ground, so as not to give offspring to his brother. And what he did was wicked in the sight of the Lord, and he put him to death also. (Genesis 38:8–10, English Standard Version)

The passage describes how Judah asked his brother Onan to help him to bear a child, and how Onan would have sexual intercourse with his sister-in-law, but "waste the semen." This phrase has been interpreted literally by fundamentalist Christians to say that semen must never be wasted. Indeed, Catholic theologians in the middle ages even examined whether or not sperm cells had souls![1] This literal interpretation led to prohibitions on masturbation and other sexual behaviors that do not produce pregnancy. The fixed worldview is that God did not want any semen wasted—what Onan did was "wicked," and so masturbation will always be wicked.

Process worldview Christians may read the same passage differently. They might ask, What was the thing Onan did that was 'wicked in the sight of

---

[1] Under the belief that the sperm cell might have a soul, consider that there are at least 300 million sperm cells in the typical ejaculation. If a male masturbated just one time per month for 10 years, he alone would be responsible for the death of 36 billion ensouled individuals.

the Lord'? Was it really the wasting of semen? Or was it Onan's intentional failure to produce a child for his brother, as was his traditional obligation at the time? Further, was it his deceit as he apparently enjoyed the sexual interaction with his sister-in-law without fulfilling his obligation? A process worldview Christian might also wonder about the role of female masturbation, since there is no seed released in such an act. Or about the fact that masturbation is such a common behavior, from birth to death, that causes no harm. Or, how masturbation might be a healthy sexual alternative to teen sexual activity[2] or extramarital urges.

This example only serves to illustrate two possible values related to the sometimes controversial issue of masturbation. It may be tempting to stop there and look at only two perspectives, but consider that there are many other reasons people may support or oppose masturbation. The ancient Chinese Tao of love and sex advises that semen should be ejaculated very rarely, for reasons related to mental and physical (not moral) health. Masturbation aside, the Tao advises that males should only ejaculate one time per every 100 acts of intercourse, so that female—not male—pleasure is maximized! Another position on masturbation may be its functionality, as viewed by sex therapists, for treating sexual dysfunction. There are many perspectives on this one topic, and there are similarly many perspectives beyond the two articles presented for every issue in this book.

Consider a non-Western example from recent history—the Islamic cultures of the Middle East and the politics of Islamic fundamentalists. On the fixed worldview side are fundamentalist Muslims who believe that the Muslim world needs to return to the unchanging, literal words of Mohammed and the Koran (the sacred book of the teachings of Allah, or God). Again, there is no gray area in a fixed worldview—what Allah revealed through Mohammed is forever the truth, and the words of the Koran must be taken literally. There is no room for mitigating factors or new or unique circumstances that may arise. The literal interpretation of the Koran calls for purging all Western and modern influences that have assimilated into Islamic society. Consequently, about 25 years ago, Islamic fundamentalists overthrew the shah of Iran and assassinated the president of Egypt, who had encouraged modernization of their countries. More recently, the September 11, 2001, terrorist attacks against the U.S. World Trade Center and the Pentagon represented the rejection of Western influences at its ultimate, deadliest extreme.

On the other side are Muslims who view the world through a process worldview—an ever-changing scene in which they must struggle to reinterpret and apply the basic principles of the Koran to new situations. They consider as progress the new rights that women have earned in recent years, such as the right to education, the right to vote, the right to election of political office, the right to divorce their husbands, the right to contraception, and many other rights.

---

[2] Former U.S. Surgeon General Joycelyn Elders was fired in 1994 for suggesting this.

The fixed and process worldviews are evident throughout the history of American culture. Like Islamic fundamentalists, Christian fundamentalists believe that Americans need to return to traditional values. This worldview often shares a conviction that the sexual revolution, changing attitudes toward masturbation and homosexuality, a tolerance of premarital and extramarital sex, sexuality education in the schools, and the legality of abortion are contributing to a cultural decline and must be rejected. A classic expression of this value system surfaced in the aftermath of the September 11, 2001, terrorist attacks when former presidential candidate Pat Robertson and the Reverend Jerry Falwell agreed that the destruction of the towers of the World Trade Center and the Pentagon were caused by the immoral activism of the American Civil Liberties Union and advocates for abortion and gay rights.

At the same time, other Americans argue for legalized abortion, civil rights for homosexuals, decriminalization of prostitution, androgynous sex roles in child-rearing practices, and the abolition of all laws restricting the right to privacy for sexually active, consenting adults. For a time, the process worldview gained dominance in Western cultures, but renewed influences of such fixed world groups as the Moral Majority and Religious Right have manifested in the elections of President George W. Bush and other fundamentalist politicians.

The two worldviews described here characteristically permeate and color the way we look at everything in our lives. One or the other view will influence the way we approach a particular political, economic, or moral issue, and the way we reach decisions about sexual issues and relationships. However, one must keep in mind that no one is ever fully and always on one or the other end of the spectrum. The spectrum of beliefs, attitudes, and values proposed here is an intellectual abstraction. Real life is not that simple. You may find yourself holding fixed worldviews on some issues, and process worldviews on others. Your views may represent neither worldview. Just like there are no pure blue and red states, there are no absolutes when it comes to sexual values. There is a continuum of values, with the fixed worldview on one end, and the process worldview on the other. Your sexual values for each issue presented in this text will likely depend on the issue, your personal experiences with the subject matter, and the values and beliefs that you have accumulated by important sources within your own life.

Personal connection with an issue may be a strong indicator of one's sexual values. If you are among the millions of Americans who have had a sexually transmitted infection, that firsthand experience will likely affect what you believe about condom availability programs or sexuality education. If you are a woman who has experienced female ejaculation, you would be hardpressed to believe an author's rejection of the G-spot. A family member whom you love and respect, who taught you that pornography is wrong, will make it difficult for you to accept the proposition that it is okay. We are all sexual beings, so many of the issues presented here provide an opportunity for a personal connection to an issue, beyond a simple academic exercise.

As you plunge into the 18 controversial issues selected for this volume, try to be aware of your own predispositions toward certain topics, and try to be sensitive to the kinds of ethnic, religious, social, economic, and other factors that may be influencing the position a particular author takes on an issue. Understanding the roots that support a person's overt position on an issue will help you to decide whether or not you agree with that position. Take time to read a little bit about the authors' biographies, too, as their affiliations may reveal something about their potential biases. Understanding these same factors in your own thinking will help you to articulate more clearly and convincingly your own values and decisions.

Internet References . . .

SexHelp.com

SexHelp.com is a Web site that showcases resources championed by Patrick J. Carnes, authority on sexual addiction. The Web site provides links for further reading, self-assessments, discussion forums, and more.

http://www.sexhelp.com/

Sexual Intelligence

Sexual Intelligence provides information and commentary on contemporary sexual issues, written by sex therapist Dr. Marty Klein. The Web site also features a free monthly newsletter.

http://www.sexualintelligence.org

Goofyfoot Press

Visitors to this Web site will find links to chapters from the popular sex information resource, *The Guide to Getting It On,* and weekly commentary by author Paul Joannides.

http://www.goofyfootpress.com

FSD Alert

FSD Alert is an educational campaign that challenges myths promoted by the pharmaceutical industry and calls for research on the causes of women's sexual problems. Visitors will find developing information on Intrinsa at this Web site.

http://www.fsd-alert.org

The Nature of Sex

*R*obert T. Francoeur, author of The Complete Dictionary of Sexology, *calls sexuality a "bio-psycho-socio and cultural phenomenon."
Humans are sexual beings from birth through death, and our sexuality
is shaped by our physical makeup (biological), our thoughts, feelings,
and perceptions of our sexuality (psychological); and the way we interact with our environment (sociological and cultural). In many ways,
sexuality may be as subjective as the individual who expresses it.*

   *Defining "sex" is no more universal. One of my favorite classroom
activities is to ask students to take out their cell phones, call a few
friends and family members, and ask them what "sex" means. The
varied responses illustrate the many different viewpoints people have
about the nature of sex.*

   *This section examines the very nature of sex by presenting issues
that debate definitions related to sex—and competing viewpoints on
the way we interpret and understand sexual behavior—and how sexual
problems are treated.*

- Can Sex Be Addictive?

- Is Oral Sex Really Sex?

- Is Masters and Johnson's Model an Accurate Description of Sexual
  Response?

- Is the G Spot a Myth?

- Is the Testosterone Patch the Right Cure of Low Libido in Women?

ISSUE 1

Can Sex Be Addictive?

YES: Patrick J. Carnes, from "Sex Addiction Q & A," http://www. sexhelp.com/sa_q_and_a.cfm (November 11, 2006)

NO: Lawrence A. Siegel and Richard M. Siegel, from "Sex Addiction: Recovering from a Shady Concept," An Original Essay Written for This Volume (2006)

ISSUE SUMMARY

YES: Patrick J. Carnes, considered by many to be an expert on sexual addiction, answers some common questions about this phenomenon, as featured on the Web site http://www.sexhelp.com. Carnes discusses the nature of sexual addiction, including ways in which it might be manifested, and offers suggestions for treatment.

NO: Sex therapist Lawrence A. Siegel and sex therapist/educator Richard M. Siegel counter that sexual addiction is grounded in "moralistic ideology masquerading as science." They argue that while some sexual behaviors may be dysfunctional, the term "sexual addiction" pathologizes many common forms of sexual expression that are not problematic.

What is sex? Does it include masturbation? Does it include oral or anal intercourse, in addition to vaginal intercourse? Are nongenital touching behaviors, like kissing or massage, sexual in nature? And how about the viewing of erotic material or the reading of an erotic passage? Answers will depend on who you ask.

Similarly, people have very different opinions about how much sex is *too much* sex? Consider this exchange from the 1977 Woody Allen movie, *Annie Hall.* Two characters, Alvy and Annie, have just been asked by their therapists if they have sex "often."

> *Alvie* Hardly ever. Maybe three times a week.

> *Annie* Constantly. I'd say three times a week.

Whether or not one can (or is) having too much sex might be a matter of perspective, as it seems to be for Alvie (wanting more) and Annie (wanting less). On the other hand, some aspects of the sexological community will clearly tell you that there is a point at which sex can become too much. The Web site http://www.sexualaddiction.com declares, "SEXUAL ADDICTION: Yes, it's a real problem! And yes, there's real help for it!" and points the visitor to links for information, a self-test, and treatment.

Much of the modern understanding of sexual addiction comes from the work of Patrick J. Carnes, who authored *Don't Call It Love: Recovery from Sexual Addiction.* Carnes co-founded the Society for the Advancement of Sexual Health in 1987, an organization dedicated to "helping those who suffer from out of control sexual behavior." Today, Carnes is considered a leading authority on sexual addiction, in a field that includes prevention services, treatment services (including a 12-step recovery model), professional conferences, an academic journal *(Sexual Addiction and Compulsivity),* and more.

Other sexologists call the whole idea of sexual addiction nonsense, and say that the very term "sexual addiction" invites comparison to other addictions in which the object of addiction (heroin, nicotine, alcohol, gambling, etc.) is inherently harmful. They explain that sex, as a normal biological drive, should not be placed in the same category. Efforts to create an addiction out of sex do nothing more than feed a hungry new addiction treatment industry that is erotophobic at its core.

In the following passages, Patrick J. Carnes explains the nature of sexual addiction, signs of possible sexual addiction, codependency, and different types of treatment. Sex therapists Lawrence Siegel and Richard Siegel reject the notion of "sexual addiction" as unscientific and moralistic.

YES

Patrick J. Carnes

Sex Addiction Q & A

"Like an alcoholic unable to stop drinking, sexual addicts are unable to stop their self-destructive sexual behavior. Family breakups, financial disaster, loss of jobs, and risk to life are the painful themes of their stories.

Sex addicts come from all walks of life—they may be ministers, physicians, homemakers, factory workers, salespersons, secretaries, clerks, accountants, therapists, dentists, politicians, or executives, to name just a few examples. Most were abused as children—sexually, physically, and/or emotionally. The majority grew up in families in which addiction already flourished, including alcoholism, compulsive eating, and compulsive gambling. Most grapple with other addictions as well, but they find sex addiction the most difficult to stop.

Much hope nevertheless exists for these addicts and their families. Sex addicts have shown an ability to transform a life of self-destruction into a life of self-care, a life in chaos and despair into one of confidence and peace."

Sexual Dependency: What It Is

Sexual addiction is defined as any sexually-related, compulsive behavior which interferes with normal living and causes severe stress on family, friends, loved ones, and one's work environment.

Sexual addiction has been called sexual dependency and sexual compulsivity. By any name, it is a compulsive behavior that completely dominates the addict's life. Sexual addicts make sex a priority more important than family, friends, and work. Sex becomes the organizing principle of addicts' lives. They are willing to sacrifice what they cherish most in order to preserve and continue their unhealthy behavior.

No single behavior pattern defines sexual addiction. These behaviors, when they have taken control of addicts' lives and become unmanageable, include: compulsive masturbation, compulsive heterosexual and homosexual relationships, pornography, prostitution, exhibitionism, voyeurism, indecent phone calls, child molesting, incest, rape, and violence. Even the healthiest forms of human sexual expression can turn into self-defeating behaviors.

Recognition of Sexual Addiction by the Professional Health Care Community

Sexual addiction was first brought to the forefront in Dr. Patrick Carnes' 1983 book, *Out of the Shadows: Understanding Sexual Addiction* (CompCare Publishers).

Since then, thousands of people have come forward seeking help, and more and more professionals are being trained to identify and treat sexual addiction.

The National Council on Sexual Addiction (NCSA) was created in 1987 to serve as an independent clearing house for information on sexual addiction and treatment options. One of NCSA's missions is to decrease the stigma surrounding sexual addiction problems and treatment. They may be contacted at:

NATIONAL COUNCIL ON SEXUAL ADDICTION/COMPULSIVITY
1090 Northchase Parkway, Suite 100 South
Marietta, Georgia 30067, 1-770-989-9754

Sexual Dependency and Other Addictions

Sexual addiction can be understood by comparing it to other types of addictions. Individuals addicted to alcohol or other drugs, for example, develop a relationship with their "chemical(s) of choice"—a relationship that takes precedence over any and all other aspects of their lives. Addicts find they need drugs merely to feel *normal.*

In sexual addiction, a parallel situation exists. Sex—like food or drugs in other addictions—provides the "high" and addicts become dependent on this sexual high to feel normal. They substitute unhealthy relationships for healthy ones. They opt for temporary pleasure rather than the deeper qualities of "normal" intimate relationships.

Sexual addiction follows the same progressive nature of other addictions. Sexual addicts struggle to control their behaviors, and experience despair over their constant failure to do so. Their loss of self-esteem grows, fueling the need to escape even further into their addictive behaviors. A sense of powerlessness pervades the lives of addicts.

How Many People Are Affected by Sexual Addiction?

Estimates range from three to six percent of the population.

Multiple Addictions

National surveys revealed that most sexual addicts come from severely dysfunctional families. Usually at least one other member of these families has another addiction (87%).

Dual addictions include sexual addiction and:

- Chemical dependency 42%
- Eating disorder 38%
- Compulsive working 28%
- Compulsive spending 26%
- Compulsive gambling 5%

Sexual Addiction and Abuse

Research has shown that a very high correlation exists between childhood abuse and sexual addiction in adulthood.

Sexual addicts who have reported experiencing:

- Emotional abuse 97%
- Sexual abuse 83%
- Physical abuse 71%

Sexual Addicts: Male and Female

It remains unclear whether one gender has a higher incidence of sexual addiction than the other. Research by Dr. Carnes shows that approximately 20% of all patients seeking help for sexual dependency are women. (This same male-female ratio is found among those recovering from alcohol addiction.)

As once was the case with alcohol addiction, many people cannot accept the reality that women can become sexual addicts. One of the greatest problems facing female sexual addicts is convincing others that they have a legitimate problem.

Why Sexual Addicts Don't "Just Stop" Their Destructive Behavior

Sexual addicts feel tremendous guilt and shame about their out-of-control behavior, and they live in constant fear of discovery. Yet addicts will often act out sexually in an attempt to block out the very pain of their addiction. This is part of what drives the addictive cycle. We say that they are addicts because they are out of control and unable to stop their behaviors *despite* their self-destructive nature and potentially devastating consequences. Years of treating chemically dependent individuals have shown that successful intervention with an addict's extensive denial and repression system often requires professional help.

AIDS and the Sexual Addict

As a function of their denial system, sexual addicts often ignore the severe emotional, interpersonal, and physical consequences of their behavior. Addicts are so entrenched in maintaining their behaviors that environmental cues which would signal caution and danger to most non-addicted people are lost to them. Such has been the case with the HIV virus and other dangerous, sexually transmitted diseases (STDs).

Sexual addicts are focused on getting a sexual 'lix.' They may occasionally consider the possible consequences of their activities, but in the throes of the addictive cycle, rational thinking is seldom, if ever, present. Often dismissing the potential danger of their behavior, addicts will embrace an anxiety-laden situation to enhance their sexual high. Avoiding reality and disregarding personal safety and health are typical symptoms of sexual addiction, and they put sexual addicts at grave risk for contracting one of the many disabling STDS, including HIV.

Fear of being infected with the HIV virus and developing AIDS is not enough to stop an addict intent on being anonymously sexual, picking up prostitutes, or having multiple affairs with unsafe sex partners. Even the potential of infecting a loved one with an STD is often not enough to stop addicts from acting out. In fact, sexual addicts may find ways to act out even more intensely after such sexual practices in order to help drown out the shame and guilt of an overloaded and repressed emotional life.

Despite the frequency and range of their acting-out experiences, sexual addicts are often poorly informed about sexuality in general. An important part of their recovery process is learning about healthy sexual practices: behaviors which are connecting and affirming rather than shaming and guilt inducing. In addition, sexual addicts often need to be taught about safe sexual practices, basic self-care, and health concerns.

Diagnosing Sexual Addiction

Often sexual addicts don't know what is wrong with them. They may suffer from clinical depression or have suicidal tendencies. They may even think they are losing their minds.

There are, however, recognizable behavior patterns which indicate the presence of sexual addiction. Diagnosis should be done by a mental health professional trained in carrying out such diagnoses.

To help professionals determine whether a sexual addiction is present, Dr. Carnes has developed the Sexual Addiction Screening Test (SAST), an assessment tool specially designed for this purpose.

Behavior Patterns Which May Indicate Sexual Addiction

While an actual diagnosis for sexual addiction should be carried out by a mental health professional, the following behavior patterns can indicate the presence of sexual addiction. Individuals who see any of these patterns in their own life, or in the life of someone they care about, should seek professional help.

1. Acting Out, a Pattern of Out-of-Control Sexual Behavior
Examples may include:

- Compulsive masturbation
- Indulging in pornography
- Having chronic affairs
- Exhibitionism
- Dangerous sexual practices
- Prostitution
- Anonymous sex
- Compulsive sexual episodes
- Voyeurism

2. Experiencing Severe Consequences Due to Sexual Behavior, and an Inability to Stop Despite These Adverse Consequences

Some of the losses reported by sexual addicts include:

- Loss of partner or spouse 40%
- Severe marital or relationship problems 70%
- Loss of career opportunities 27%
- Unwanted pregnancies 40%
- Abortions 36%
- Suicidal obsession 72%
- Suicide attempts 17%
- Exposure to AIDS and venereal disease 68%
- Legal risks from nuisance offenses to rape 58%

3. Persistent Pursuit of Self-Destructive Behavior

Even understanding that the consequences of their actions will be painful or have dire consequences does not stop addicts from acting out. They often seem to have a willfulness about their actions, and an attitude that says, "I'll deal with the consequences when they come."

4. Ongoing Desire or Effort to Limit Sexual Behavior

Addicts often try to control their behavior by creating external barriers to it. For example, some move to a new neighborhood or city, hoping that a new environment removed from old affairs will help. Some think marriage will keep them from acting out. An exposer may buy a car in which it's difficult to act out while driving.

Others seeking control over their behavior try to immerse themselves in religion, only to find out that while religious compulsion may soothe their shame, it does not end their acting out.

Many go through periods of sexual anorexia during which they allow themselves no sexual expression at all. Such efforts, however, only fuel the addiction.

5. Sexual Obsession and Fantasy as a Primary Coping Strategy

Though acting out sexually can temporarily relieve addicts' anxieties, they still find themselves spending inordinate amounts of time in obsession and fantasy. By fantasizing, the addict can maintain an almost constant level of arousal. Together with obsessing, the two behaviors can create a kind of analgesic "fix." Just as our bodies generate endorphins, natural antidepressants, during vigorous exercise, our bodies naturally release peptides when sexually aroused. The molecular construction of these peptides parallels that of opiates like heroin or morphine, but are many times more powerful.

6. Regularly Increasing the Amount of Sexual Experience Because the Current Level of Activity is no Longer Sufficiently Satisfying

Sexual addiction is often progressive. While addicts may be able to control themselves for a time, inevitably their addictive behaviors will return and quickly escalate to previous levels and beyond. Some addicts begin adding additional acting out behaviors. Usually addicts will have three or more behaviors which play a key role in their addiction—masturbation, affairs, and anonymous sex, for instance.

In addition, 89% of addicts reported regularly "bingeing" to the point of emotional exhaustion. The emotional pain of withdrawal for sexual addicts can parallel the physical pain experienced by those withdrawing from opiate addiction.

7. Severe Mood Changes Related to Sexual Activity

Addicts experience intense mood shifts, often due to the despair and shame of having unwanted sex. Sexual addicts are caught in a crushing cycle of shame driven and shame-creating behavior. While shame drives the sexual addicts' actions, it also becomes the unwanted consequence of a few moments of euphoric escape into sex.

8. Inordinate Amounts of Time Spent Obtaining Sex, Being Sexual, and Recovering from Sexual Experiences

Two sets of activities organize sexual addicts' days. One involves obsessing about sex, time devoted to initiating sex, and actually being sexual. The second involves time spent dealing with the consequences of their acting out: lying, covering up, shortages of money, problems with their spouse, trouble at work, neglected children, and so on.

9. Neglect of Important Social, Occupational, or Recreational Activities Because of Sexual Behavior

As more and more of addicts' energy becomes focused on relationships which have sexual potential, other relationships and activities—family, friends, work, talents and values—suffer and atrophy from neglect. Long-term relationships are stormy and often unsuccessful. Because of sexual over-extension and intimacy avoidance, short-term relationships become the norm.

Sometimes, however, the desire to preserve an important long-term relationship with spouse or children, for instance, can act as the catalyst for addicts to admit their problem and seek help.

Getting Help: The First Step

The first step in seeking help is to admit to the problem. Though marital, professional, and societal consequences may follow, admission of the problems must come, no matter the cost. Fear of these consequences unfortunately keeps many sexual addicts from seeking help.

Many sources of help are available to provide information, support, and assistance for sexual addicts trying to regain control of their lives. These include inpatient and outpatient treatment, professional associations, self-help groups, and aftercare support groups.

Treating Sexual Addiction

Treatment programs for sexual addiction include patient, outpatient, and aftercare support, and self-help groups. Treatment programs also offer family counseling programs, support groups, and educational workshops for addicts and their families to help them understand the facets of belief and family life that are part of the addiction.

Unlike recovering alcoholics who must abstain from drinking for life, sexual addicts are led back into a normal, healthy sex life much in the way those suffering from eating disorders must relearn healthy eating patterns.

Dr. Carnes' program is based on the spiritual principals of the Twelve Step program of Alcoholics Anonymous, and it incorporates the expertise of the most knowledgeable health care professionals in the field of sexual addiction.

Recovery from sexual addiction is a lifelong journey. Dr. Carnes' program is designed to set addicts on the road to recovery, to provide relapse prevention techniques, and to help them stay in recovery with the help of aftercare and Twelve Step recovery support groups.

Are Sexual Addicts Ever Cured?

Like other types of addicts, some sexual addicts may never be "cured." Sexual addicts achieve a state of recovery, but maintaining that recovery can be a life-long, day-by-day process. The Twelve Step treatment approach teaches addicts to take their recovery "one day at a time"—concentrating on the present, not the future.

Sexual Codependency—The Co-Addict

Partners of sexual addicts, like partners of alcoholics, can also benefit from counseling and support groups. Normally these partners are codependents, and they, too, suffer from the extreme adverse effects of the addiction. Inpatient and outpatient programs, counseling, and support groups are all available to help them regain control of their lives and support the recovery of their partner.

Lawrence A. Siegel and
Richard M. Siegel

 **NO**

Sex Addiction: Recovering from a Shady Concept

It seems, more than ever, that many Americans are more comfortable keeping sex in the dark or, as sex addiction advocates might actually prefer, *in* the
shadows. We seem to have gotten no further than the Puritan claims of sex
being evil and pleasure being threatening. "The Devil made me do it" seems
to be something of a battle cry, especially when someone gets caught cheating
on their spouse, having inappropriate dalliances with congressional pages, or
visiting prostitutes. Even those not in relationships are easily targeted. We
constantly hear about the "dangers" of internet porn and how every internet
chat room is just teeming with predators just waiting to devour our children.
Daily masturbation is considered by these folks as being unhealthy and a
marked pathology. As a society, we seem able to be comfortable with sex only
as long as we make it uncomfortable. As one of the leading sexologists, Marty
Klein, once wrote:

> "If mass murderer Ted Bundy had announced that watching Cosby Show
> reruns had motivated his awful crimes, he would have been dismissed as a
> deranged sociopath. Instead, Bundy proclaimed that his 'pornography addic-
> tion' made him do it, and many Right-wing feminists and conservatives
> treated this as the conclusion of a thoughtful social scientist. Why?"[1]

The whole idea of "sex addiction" is borne out of a moralistic ideology
masquerading as science. It is a concept that seems to serve no other purpose
than to relegate sexual expression to the level of shameful acts, except within
the extremely narrow and myopic scope of a monogamous, heterosexual marriage. Sexual diversity? Interests in unusual forms or frequency of sexual
expression? Choosing not to be monogamous? Advocates of "sex addiction"
would likely see these as the uncontrollable acts of a sexually pathological
individual; one who needs curing.

To be clear, we do not deny the fact that, for some people, sexual
behavior can become problematic, even dysfunctional or unmanageable. Our
objection is with the use of the term "sexual addiction" to describe a virtually
unlimited array of—in fact, practically ANY—aspect of sexual expression that
falls outside of the typically Christian view of marriage. We believe that
the term contributes to a generally sex-negative, pleasure-phobic tone in

American society, and it also tends to "pathologize" most forms of sexual expression that fall outside of a narrow view of what "normal" sex is supposed to look like. This is a point made clear by sex addiction advocates" own rhetoric. Three of the guiding principles of Sexaholics Anonymous include the notion that (1) sex is most healthy in the context of a monogamous, heterosexual relationship; (2) sexual expression has "obvious" limits; and (3) it is unhealthy to engage in any sexual activity for the sole purpose of feeling better, either emotionally or to escape one's problems. These principles do not represent either science or most people's experience. They, in fact, represent a restrictive and repressive view of sex and sexuality and reflect an arrogance that sex addiction proponents are the keepers of the scepter of morality and normalcy. Moreover, the concept of "sex addiction" comes out of a shame-based, arbitrarily judgmental addiction model and does not speak to the wide range of sexual diversity; both in and outside the context of a committed relationship.

A primary objection to the use of the term "sex addiction," an objection shared with regard to other supposed behavioral "addictions," is that the term *addiction* has long ago been discredited. Back in 1964, the World Health Organization (WHO) declared the term "addiction" to be clinically invalid and recommended in favor of dependence, which can exist in varying degrees of severity, as opposed to an all-or-nothing disease entity (as it is still commonly perceived).[2] This is when we began to see the terms *chemical dependency* and *substance abuse*, terms considered to be much more appropriate and clinically useful. This, however, did not sit well with the addiction industry. Another objection to the concept of "sex addiction" is that it is a misnomer whose very foundation as a clinically significant diagnosis is built on flawed and faulty premises. For example, a common assertion put forth by proponents of sex addiction states that the chemical actions in the brain during sexual activity are the same as the chemical activity involved in alcohol and drug use. They, therefore, claim that both sexual activity and substance abuse share reward and reinforcement mechanisms that produce the "craving" and "addictive" behaviors. This assertion is flawed on several levels, not the least of which is that it is based on drawing conclusions from brain scan imaging that are devoid of any real interpretive foundation; a "leap of faith," so to speak. Furthermore, it is somewhat of a stretch to equate the neurophysiological mechanisms which underlie chemical dependency, tolerance, and withdrawal with the underlying mechanisms of what is most often obsessive-compulsive or anxiety-reducing behaviors like gambling, shopping, and sex. Another example often cited by sex addiction proponents is the assertion that, like alcohol and drugs, the "sex addict" is completely incapable of controlling his or her self-destructive behavior. Of course, this begs the question of how, then, can one change behavior they are incapable of controlling? More importantly, however, is the unique excuse this "disease" model provides for abdicating personal responsibility. "It's not my fault, I have a disease." Finally, a major assertion put out by sex addiction advocates is that anyone who is hypersexual in any way (e.g., frequent masturbation, anonymous "hook ups," infidelity, and cybersex) must have been abused as children or adolescents.

Again, the flaws here are obvious and serve to continue to relegate any type of frequent sexual engagement to the pathological and unseemly.

Every clinician knows that "addiction" is not a word that appears anywhere in the Diagnostic and Statistical Manual, or "DSM," the diagnostic guidebook used by psychiatrists and psychologists to make any psychopathological diagnosis. Nor does it appear in any of the International Classification of Diseases (ICD-10), codes used for classifying medical diagnoses. "Abuse" and "dependence" do appear in the DSM, relevant only to substance use patterns, but "addiction" does not. Similarly, there is an ICD-10 code for "substance dependence," but not addiction. Why? Perhaps because the word means different things to different people, especially when used in so many different contexts. Even without acknowledging the many trivial uses of the addiction concept, such as bumper stickers that proclaim, *"addicted to sports, not drugs,"* cookies that claim to be *"deliciously addicting,"* Garfield coffee mugs that warn *"don't talk to me until after my first cup,"* or T-shirts that say *"chocoholic,"* there aren't even consistent *clinical* definitions for the concept of addiction. A 1993 study, published in the American Journal of Drug and Alcohol Abuse, compared the diagnostic criteria for substance abuse and dependence between the DSM and ICD-10. The results showed very little agreement between the two.[3]

Pharmacologists, researchers who study the effects of drugs, define addiction primarily based on the presence of tolerance and withdrawal. Both of these phenomena are based on pharmacological and toxicological concepts of "cellular adaptation," wherein the body, at the very cellular level, becomes accustomed to the constant presence of a substance, and readjusts for "normal" function; in other words, whatever the "normal" response was before regular use of the substance began returns. This adaptation first accounts for tolerance, wherein an increasing dose of the substance to which the system has adapted is needed to maintain the same level of "normal." Then it results in withdrawal, wherein any discontinuation of the substance disrupts the "new" equilibrium the system has achieved and symptoms of "withdrawal sickness" ensue. This is probably most often attributed to addiction to opiates, such as heroin, because of its comparison to "having a monkey on one's back," with a constantly growing appetite, and its notorious "cold turkey" withdrawal. But perhaps it is most commonly observed with the chronic use of drugs with less sinister reputations, such as caffeine, nicotine or alcohol.

Traditional psychotherapists may typically define addiction as a faulty coping mechanism, or more accurately, the *result* of using a faulty coping mechanism to deal with some underlying issue. Another way to consider this is to see addiction as the symptom, rather than the disease, which is why the traditional therapist, of any theoretical orientation, is likely to want to find the causative issue or issues, and either teach the patient more effective coping mechanisms or resolve the unresolved issue(s) altogether.

Another definition of addiction has emerged, and seems to have taken center-stage, since the development of a pseudo-medical specialty known as "addictionology" within the last twenty or so years. Made up primarily of physicians, but including a variety of "addiction professionals," this field has helped to forge a treatment industry based on the disease model of addiction that is at the core of 12-Step "fellowships," such as Alcoholics Anonymous and Narcotics Anonymous. Ironically, despite the resistance to medical or psychiatric treatment historically expressed in AA or NA, their philosophy has become the mainstay of the addictionological paradigm.

If the concept of chemical addictions, which have a neurophysiological basis that can be measured and observed, yields no clinical consensus, how, then, can we legitimize the much vaguer notion that individuals can be "addicted" to behavior, people, emotions, or even one's own brain chemistry? Other than to undermine responsibility and self-determination, we really can't. It does a tremendous disservice to our clients and patients to brand them with a label so full of judgment, arbitrary opinion, and fatuous science. It robs individuals of the ability to find their own levels of comfort and, ultimately, be the determining force in directing their own lives. There is a significant and qualitative difference between the person who acts because he or she can't (not a choice, but a position of default) and the person who is empowered to choose not to. As clinicians, we should be loathe to send our clients and patients down such a fearful, shameful road.

In 1989, Patrick Carnes, founder of the sex addiction movement, wrote a book entitled "Contrary to Love." The book is rife with rhetoric and personal ideology that reveals Carnes's lack of training, knowledge, and understanding of sexuality and sexual expression; not surprising for someone whose background is solely in the disease model of alcoholism. This, while seemingly a harsh judgment, is clearly reflected in his Sex Addiction Screening Test (SAST). Even a cursory glance at the items on the SAST show a deep-seeded bias against most forms of sexual expression. Unlike other legitimate screening and assessment tools, there is no scientific foundation that would show this tool to be credible (i.e., tests of reliability and validity). Instead, Carnes developed this "test" by simply culling his own ideas from his book. Annie Sprinkle, America's first adult-film-star-turned-PhD-Sexologist, has written a very good web article on the myth of sex addiction. In it, she also describes some of the shortcomings of the SAST. While not describing the complete test here, a listing of some of the assessment questions are listed below, along with commentary.[4]

1. *Have you subscribed to sexually explicit magazines like Playboy or Penthouse?* This question is based on the assumption that it is unhealthy to view images of naked bodies. Does that mean that the millions of people who subscribe to or buy adult magazines are sex addicts? Are adolescent boys who look at the Sports Illustrated Swim Suit edition budding sex addicts? By extension, if looking at Playboy or Penthouse is unhealthy and pathological, then those millions of people who look at hardcore magazines or Internet porn should be hospitalized!
2. *Do you often find yourself preoccupied with sexual thoughts?* This is totally nebulous. What does "preoccupied" mean? How often does one have to think about sex in order to constitute preoccupation? Research has shown that men, on average, think about sex every eight seconds; does that mean that men are inherently sex addicts?
3. *Do you feel that your sexual behavior is not normal?* What is normal? What do they use as a comparison? As sexologists, we can state

unequivocally that the majority of people's sexual concerns relate, in one way or another, to the question "Am I normal?" This is incredibly vague, nebulous, and laughably unscientific.

4. *Are any of your sexual activities against the law?* This question is also steeped in a bias that there is only a narrowly acceptable realm of sexual expression. It assumes that any sexual behavior that is against the law is bad. Is being or engaging a prostitute a sign of pathology? What about the fact that oral sex, anal sex, and woman on top are illegal in several states?

5. *Have you ever felt degraded by your sexual behavior?* Again, there is a serious lack of quantification here. Does regretting a sexual encounter constitute feeling degraded? Does performing oral sex for your partner, even though you think it's degrading, constitute a pathology or compromise? What if one's partner does something during sex play that is unexpected and perceived as degrading (like ejaculating on someone's face or body)? What if someone enjoys feeling degraded? This question pathologizes at least half of the S/M and B/D communities. Moreover, anyone who has had a long and active sexual life may likely, at one point, to have felt degraded. It is important to note that this question does not ask if one consistently puts oneself in a position of being degraded but, rather, have you ever felt degraded. We suspect that most people can lay claim to that.

6. *Has sex been a way for you to escape your problems?* Is there a better way to escape one's problems temporarily? This is a common bias used against both sex and alcohol use: using sex or alcohol to provide relief from anxieties or problems is inherently problematic. It also begs the question: why are things like sex and alcohol not appropriate to change how one is feeling but Zoloft, Paxil, Xanax, and Klonopin are? The truth of the matter is that sex is often an excellent and healthy way to occasionally experience relief from life's stressors and problems.

7. *When you have sex, do you feel depressed afterwards?* Sex is often a great way to get in touch with one's feelings. Oftentimes, people do feel depressed after a sexual experience, for any number of reasons. Furthermore, this doesn't mean that sex was the depressing part! Perhaps people feel depressed because they had dashed expectations of the person they were involved with. Unfulfilled expectations, lack of communication, and inattentiveness to one's needs and desires often result in post-coital feelings of sadness and disappointment. In addition, asking someone if they "feel depressed" is arbitrary, subjective, and clinically invalid.

8. *Do you feel controlled by your sexual desire?* Again, we are being asked to make an arbitrary, subjective, and clinically invalid assessment. There is an undercurrent here that seems to imply that a strong sexual desire is somehow not normal. Human beings are biologically programmed to strongly desire sex. Our clients and patients might be better served if we addressed not their desires, but how and when they *act* upon them.

Again, it needs noting that the concept of "sex addiction" is one with very little clinical relevance or usefulness, despite it's popularity. Healthy sexual expression encompasses a wide array of forms, functions, and frequency, as well as myriad emotional dynamics and personal experiences. Healthy behavior, in general, and sexual behavior, in particular, exists on a continuum rather than a quantifiable point. Using the addiction model to describe sexual behavior simply adds to the shame and stigma that is already too often attached to various forms of sexual expression. Can sexual behaviors become problematic? Most certainly. However, we must be careful to not overpathologize even problematic sexual behaviors because, most often, they are symptomatic expressions rather than primary problems.

For many years, sexologists have described compulsive sexual behavior, where sexual obsessions and compulsions are recurrent, distressing, and interfere with daily functioning. The actual number of people suffering from this type of sexual problem is relatively small. Compulsive sexual behaviors are generally divided into two broad categories: *paraphilic* and *non-paraphilic*.[5] Paraphilias are defined as recurrent, intensely arousing fantasies, sexual urges, or behaviors involving non-human objects, pain and humiliation, or children.[6] Paraphilic behaviors are usually non-conventional forms of sexual expression that, in the extreme, can be harmful to relationships and individuals. Some examples of paraphilias listed in the DSM are pedophilia (sexual attraction to children), exhibitionism (exposing one's genitals in public), voyeurism (sexual excitement from watching an unsuspecting person), sexual sadism (sexual excitement from dominating or inflicting pain), sexual masochism (sexual excitement from being dominated or receiving pain), transvestic fetishism (sexual excitement from wearing clothes of the other sex), and frotteurism (sexual excitement from rubbing up against or fondling an unsuspecting person). All of these behaviors exist on a continuum of healthy fantasy play to dangerous, abusive, and illegal acts. A sexologist is able to view these behaviors in varying degrees, knowing the difference between teacher-student fantasy role play and cruising a playground for victims; between provocative exhibitionist displays (including public displays of affection) and illegal, abusive public exposure. For those with a "sex addiction" perspective, simply having paraphilic thoughts or desires of any kind is reason to brand the individual a "sex addict."

The other category of compulsive sexual behavior is non-paraphilic, and generally involves more conventional sexual behaviors which, when taken to the extreme, cause marked distress and interference with daily functioning. This category includes a fixation on an unattainable partner, compulsive masturbation, compulsive love relationships, and compulsive sexuality in a relationship. The most vocal criticism of the idea of compulsive sexual behavior as a clinical disorder appears to center on the overpathologizing of these behaviors. Unless specifically trained in sexuality, most clinicians are either uncomfortable or unfamiliar with the wide range of "normal" sexual behavior and fail to distinguish between individuals who experience conflict between their values and sexual behavior, and those with obsessive sexual behavior.[7] When diagnosing compulsive sexual behavior overall, there is little consensus even among sexologists. However, it still provides a more useful clinical framework for the professional trained in sexuality and sexual health.

To recognize that sexual behavior can be problematic is not the same as labeling the behaviors as "sexually compulsive" or "sexual addiction." The reality is that sexual problems are quite common and are usually due to non-pathological factors. Quite simply, people make mistakes (some more than others). People also act impulsively. People don't always make good sexual choices. When people do make mistakes, act impulsively, and make bad decisions, it often negatively impacts their relationships; sometimes even their lives. Moreover, people do often use sex as a coping mechanism or, to borrow from addiction language, medicating behavior that can become problematic. However, this is qualitatively different from the concept that problematic sexual behavior means the individual is a "sexual addict" with uncontrollable urges and potentially dangerous intent. Most problematic sexual behavior can be effectively redirected (and cured) through psycho-sexual education, counseling, and experience. According to proponents of "sex addiction," problematic sexual behavior cannot be cured. Rather, the "sex addict" is destined for a life of maintaining a constant vigil to prevent the behavior from reoccurring, often to the point of obsession, and will be engaged in a lifelong process of recovery. Unfortunately, this view often causes people to live in fear of the "demon" lurking around every corner: themselves.

References

1. Klein M. The myth of sex addiction. Sexual Intelligence: An Electronic Newsletter (Issue #1). March, 2000. . . .

2. Center for Substance Abuse Treatment (CSAT) and Substance Abuse and Mental Health Services Administration (SAMHSA). Substance use disorders: A guide to the use of language. 2004.

3. Rappaport M, Tipp J, Schuckit M. A comparison of ICD-10 and DSM-III criteria for substance abuse and dependence. American Journal of Drug and Alcohol Abuse. June, 1993.

4. Sprinkle, A. Sex addiction. Online article. . . .

5. Coleman E. What sexual scientists know about compulsive sexual behavior. Electronic series of the Society for the Scientific Study of Sexuality (SSSS). Vol 2(1). 1996. . . .

6. American Psychiatric Association. Diagnostic and Statistical Manual of Mental Disorders. 4th edition, TR. Washington: American Psychiatric Publishing. June, 2000.

7. Coleman E. What sexual scientists know about compulsive sexual behavior. Electronic series of the Society for the Scientific Study of Sexuality (SSSS). Vol 2(1). 1996. . . .

POSTSCRIPT

Can Sex Be Addictive?

The framing of sex as a compulsive and addictive behavior is nothing new. The idea that masturbation and frequent intercourse could send a person into a downward spiral of unhealthiness was presented in advice columns, "health" journals, and other periodicals during the Victorian Era and the early 1900s. Consider the following excerpt about masturbation from John Harvey Kellogg's *Plain Facts for Old and Young,* written in 1891:

> As a sin against nature, it has no parallel except in sodomy. It is known by the terms self-pollution, self-abuse, masturbation, onanism, voluntary pollution, and solitary or secret vice. The habit is by no means confined to boys; girls also indulge in it, though it is to be hoped, to a less fearful extent than boys, at least in this country. Of all the vices to which human beings are addicted, no other so rapidly undermines the constitution, and so certainly makes a complete wreck of an individual as this, especially when the habit is begun at an early age. It wastes the most precious part of the blood, uses up the vital forces, and finally leaves the poor victim a most utterly ruined and loathsome object.
>
> Suspicious signs are: bashfulness, unnatural boldness, round shoulders and a stooping position, lack of development of the breasts in females, eating chalk, acne, and the use of tobacco.

Nineteenth-century preacher Sylvester Graham also described a litany of ailments that would affect the masturbator or anyone who had "frequent" intercourse before age 30. If the names Kellogg and Graham ring a bell, it may be because they created cornflakes and graham crackers—food products that were thought to suppress the sexual urges of some of the earliest "sex addicts" (which could have been just about anyone)!

More recently, attempts at measuring sexual addiction have taken on a more scientific tone, although critics of this term pose that it is simply the same old Victorian idea, repackaged for a new century. At the heart of this controversy, however, is the true meaning of a word many have trouble defining: addiction.

Think of the many things that might be considered addictive—alcohol, caffeine, tobacco, other drugs—and assess whether or not they are part of your life, or the lives of your family or friends. What makes something addictive? Is it how often a person indulges in it? Is it the degree to which it seems recreational or compulsive? Is it how much control a person has in deciding whether or not to engage in it? Or, is addiction more about what might be considered a social vice?

How about non-chemical behaviors that some might consider compulsive? Are people who surf the Internet for hours "addicted"? How about a political "junkie" who constantly scours newspapers and blogs for new information? The person who never misses an episode of their favorite TV crime-fighting drama, or who has every episode of *The Family Guy* on DVD? What about the guy who spends every Sunday (and Monday night) glued to the TV watching football, or the woman who builds her life around her favorite soaps? The person who constantly checks and updates his MySpace or Face-Book account? Can a person be addicted to his or her artistic or musical pursuits? Are these harmless habits ways to relax and blow off steam? Which behaviors escape the realm of "addiction" because they are more socially functional?

Does something become addictive only when it is undesired or otherwise interferes with one's life? Does this apply to spending more time with one's hobbies than a significant other, family, or job might like? Does skipping class to play video games or engage in online gambling put one at the cusp of addiction?

Considering sexual behaviors, is it possible to be addicted to masturbation or other sexual behaviors, as Carnes asserts? Is looking at online porn for hours different than playing an online game for hours? Is skipping class to have intercourse with a partner a sign of addiction? Is there a line between healthy sexual expression and compulsion or addiction? And if so, where is that line drawn?

Did you agree with Carnes' examples of behaviors that may indicate sexual addiction? Do you agree or disagree with Siegel and Siegel's critiques of Carnes' assessment criteria? Is sex addiction a serious problem, as Carnes asserts? Or is the assigning of an "addiction" status to otherwise healthy and consensual activities simply adding to the modern trend of the medicalization of sexuality, while recalling an era when sexuality was simply demonized?

Suggested Readings

P. Carnes, *Don't Call It Love: Recovery from Sexual Addiction* (Bantam Books, 1992).

P. Carnes, *Out of the Shadows: Understanding Sexual Addiction* (Compcare Publications, 1992).

B.J. Dew & M.P. Chaney, "Sexual Addiction and the Internet: Implications for Gay Men," *Journal of Addictions & Offender Counseling* (vol. 24, 2004).

B. Dodge et al., "Sexual Compulsivity among Heterosexual College Students," *The Journal of Sex Research* (vol. 41, 2004).

R. Eisenman, "Sex Addicts: Do they Exist?" *Journal of Evolutionary Psychology* (2001).

M. Griffiths, "Sex on the Internet: Observations and Implications for Internet Sex Addiction," *The Journal of Sex Research* (vol. 38, 2001).

M. Klein, *America's War on Sex* (Praeger, 2006).

M.F. Schwartz, "Sexual Addiction: An Integrated Approach," *Archives of Sexual Behavior* (vol. 33, 2004).

ISSUE 2

Is Oral Sex Really Sex?

YES: Rhonda Chittenden, from "Oral Sex *Is* Sex: Ten Messages about Oral Sex to Communicate to Adolescents," *Sexing the Political* (May 2004)

NO: Nora Gelperin, from "Oral Sex and Young Adolescents: Insights from the 'Oral Sex Lady,'" *Educator's Update* (September 2004)

ISSUE SUMMARY

YES: Sexuality educator Rhonda Chittenden says that it is important for young people to expand their narrow definitions of sex and understand that oral sex *is* sex. Chittenden offers additional educational messages about oral sex.

NO: Sexuality trainer Nora Gelperin argues that adult definitions of oral sex are out of touch with the meaning the behavior holds for young people. Rather than impose adult definitions of intimacy, educators should be seeking to help young people clarify and understand their own values.

In 1998, President Bill Clinton famously stated, "I did not have sexual relations with that woman, Miss Lewinsky." As it later became evident that the president, in fact, did have *oral* sex with intern Monica Lewinsky, a national debate raged over the meaning of sex. What, people asked, does "sexual relations" mean? What about "sex?" Do these terms refer to vaginal intercourse only, or are other sexual behaviors, like oral sex, included?

Some welcomed this unprecedented opportunity to have an open, national discussion about sex in an otherwise erotophobic, sexually repressed culture. Sexuality education professionals lent their expertise, offering suggestions to help parents answer their children's questions about the new term, "oral sex," they might hear on the evening news or at family gatherings. Others feared such openness would inevitably lead to increased sexual activity among teens. Perhaps the media viewed this as a foregone conclusion when they began airing hyped reports indicating a rise in teen oral sex, based on anecdotal, rather than research-based, evidence.

Feature reports, often intended to alarm viewers, have introduced even more new terms into our sexual lexicon. "Friends with benefits" describes a partner pairing based on friendship and casual oral sex. "Rainbow parties" involve events where girls wear different colors of lipstick and boys try to get as many colored rings on their penises as they can. But how much of this is really happening, and how much of this just makes for good television?

Even if *some* of what the reports say is true, many adults—parents, teachers, public health officials, and others—are concerned. Some are worried about the potential rise in sexually transmitted infections that can be passed orally as well as vaginally or anally. Others lament the inequity of oral sex as young people may experience it—with females *giving* oral sex far more than they are *receiving* it. Still others may have religious or other moral reasons that drive their concerns.

The apprehension among many adults is rooted in the very meaning of sex and oral sex. Since many adults hold oral sex to be an intensely intimate act—one that is even more intimate than vaginal intercourse—it is difficult for them to observe what they interpret as casual attitudes toward this behavior.

In the following selections, sexuality education professionals Rhonda Chittenden and Nora Gelperin examine the meaning of sex and oral sex in the context of giving young people helpful educational messages. Chittenden articulates several reasons why it is important for young people to know that oral sex is sex, and offers several other important messages for adults to convey to young people. Gelperin argues that it is not for adults to decide the meaning of such terms for young people. Rather, educators can help young people critically examine the meaning of such words and activities for themselves. She further argues against having overly dramatized media accounts dictate public health approaches.

YES

Rhonda Chittenden

Oral Sex *Is* Sex: Ten Messages about Oral Sex to Communicate to Adolescents

As a teen in the early-80s, I was very naïve about oral sex. I thought oral sex meant talking about sex with one's partner in a very sexy way. A friend and I, trying to practice the mechanics, would move our mouths in silent mock-talk as we suggestively switched our hips from left to right and flirted with our best bedroom eyes. We wondered aloud how anyone could engage in oral sex without breaking into hysterical laughter. In our naïveté, oral sex was not only hilarious, it was just plain stupid.

Twenty years later, I doubt most teens are as naïve as my friend and I were. Although the prevalence of oral sex among adolescents has yet to be comprehensively addressed by researchers,[1] any adult who interacts with teens will quickly learn that, far from being stupid or hilarious, oral sex is a common place activity in some adolescent crowds.

Some teens claim, as teens have always claimed about sex, that "everyone is doing it." They tell of parties—which they may or may not have attended—where oral sex is openly available. They describe using oral sex as a way to relieve the pressure to be sexual with a partner yet avoid the risk of pregnancy. Some believe oral sex is an altogether risk-free behavior that eliminates the worry of sexually transmitted infections. There is a casualness in many teens' attitudes towards oral sex revealed in the term "friends with benefits" to describe a non-dating relationship that includes oral sex. In fact, many teens argue that oral sex really isn't sex at all, logic that, try as we might, defies many adults. Most pointedly, teens' anecdotal experiences of oral sex reveal the continuing imbalance of power prevalent in heterosexual relationships where the boys receive most of the pleasure and the girls, predictably, give most of the pleasure.

Not willing to wait until research confirms what many of us already know, concerned adults want to address the issue of adolescent oral sex *now*. We know that young people long for straightforward and honest conversations about the realities and complexities of human sexuality, including the practice of oral sex. But where do we start with such an intimidating topic? The following ten messages may help caring and concerned adults to initiate authentic conversations about oral sex with young people.

1. Oral sex *is* sex. Regardless of how casual the behavior is for some young people, giving and receiving oral sex are both sexual behaviors. This is made obvious simply by defining the act of oral sex: oral sex is the stimulation of a person's genitals by another person's mouth to create sexual pleasure and, usually, orgasm for at least one of the partners. It's that straightforward.

Even so, many young people—and even some adults—believe that oral sex is not "real sex." Real sex, they say, is penis-vagina intercourse only. Any other sexual behavior is something "other" and certainly not *real* sex. This narrow definition of sex, rooted in heterosexist attitudes, is problematic for several reasons.

First, such a narrow definition is ahistorical. Art and literature reveal human beings, across human history and culture, consensually engaging their bodies in loving, pleasurable acts of sex beyond penis-vagina intercourse.[2] In Western culture, our notions of sex are still shackled by religious teachings that say the only acceptable sex—in society and the eyes of God—is procreative sex. Of course, the wide accessibility of contraceptives, among other influences, has dramatically shifted our understanding of this.[3] Even still, many people are unaware that across centuries and continents, human beings have enjoyed many kinds of sex and understood those acts to be sex whether or not they involved a penis and a vagina.

Next, by defining sex in such narrow terms, we perpetuate a dangerous ignorance that places people at risk for sexually transmitted infections (STIs), including HIV. Many people, including teens, who define sex in such narrow terms incorrectly reason that they are safe from HIV if they avoid penis-vagina intercourse. Because saliva tends to inhibit HIV, it's true that one's chances of contracting HIV through oral sex with an infected partner are considerably small, compared to the risk of unprotected vaginal or anal sex. Of course, this varies with the presence of other body fluids as well as the oral health of the giver. However, if one chooses to avoid "real sex" and instead has anal sex, the risk for HIV transmission increases.[4] In reality, regardless of what orifice the penis penetrates, all of these sex acts are real sex. In this regard, the narrow definition of sex is troubling because it ignores critical sexual health information that all people deserve, especially those who are sexually active or intend to be in the future.

Finally, this narrow definition of sex invalidates the sexual practices of many people who, for whatever reasons, do not engage in penis-vagina intercourse. Obviously, these people include those who partner with lovers of the same sex. They also include people who, regardless of the sex of their partners, are physically challenged due to illness, accident, or birth anomaly. To suggest to these individuals that oral sex—or any other primary mode of shared sexual expression—is not real sex invalidates the range of accessible and sensual ways they can and do share their bodies with their partners.

Clearly, we must educate young people that there are many ways to enjoy sex, including the sensual placement of one's mouth on another person's genitals.

Oral sex may be practiced in casual, emotionally indifferent ways, but this does not disqualify it as a legitimate sex act. Oral sex *is* sex—and, in most states, the law agrees.

2. Without consent, oral sex may be considered sexual assault.   Adults who work with teens know that oral sex often takes place at parties where alcohol and other drugs are consumed. It's imperative, then, that when adults talk to teens about oral sex, we confront the legal realities of such situations. Of course, drinking and drug use are illegal for adolescents. In addition, according to Iowa law, if alcohol or drugs are used by either partner of any age, consent for oral sex (or any sex) cannot be given. Without consent, oral sex may be considered sexual assault.[5] Other states have similar laws.

While giving some adolescents reason to reflect on their substance use, this information may also help them to contextualize their past experiences of oral sex. It may affirm the often uneasy and unspoken feelings of some teens who feel they were pressured into oral sex, either as the giver or receiver. It may also illuminate other risks that often occur when sex and substance use are combined, especially the failure to use protection against pregnancy, and in the case of oral sex, sexually transmitted infections.

3. Practice safer oral sex to reduce the risk of sexually transmitted infections.   Because many young people don't consider oral sex to be real sex, they don't realize that sexually transmitted infections that are typically transmitted through genital-genital contact can also be transmitted through oral-genital contact. Although some are more easily transmitted through oral sex than others, these infections include chlamydia, gonorrhea, herpes, and, in some cases, even pubic lice. The lips, tongue, mouth cavity, and throat, are all vulnerable to various sexually transmitted bacteria and viruses.[6] With pubic lice, facial hair, including mustaches, beards and eyebrows, can be vulnerable.[7]

Aside from abstaining from oral sex, young people can protect themselves and their partners from the inconvenience, embarrassment, treatment costs, and health consequences of sexually transmitted infections by practicing safer oral sex. The correct and consistent use of latex condoms for fellatio (oral sex performed on a penis) and latex dental dams for cunnilingus (oral sex performed on a vulva) should be taught and encouraged. Manufacturers of condoms, dental dams, and pleasure-enhancing lubricants offer these safer sex supplies in a variety of flavors—including mint, mango, and banana—to increase the likelihood that people will practice safer oral sex.[8] Certainly, adolescents who engage in oral sex should be taught about the correct, pleasure-enhancing uses of these products, informed of the location of stores and clinics that carry them, and strongly encouraged to have their own supply at hand.

4. Oral sex is a deeply intimate and sensual way to give sexual pleasure to a partner.   Although casual references to oral sex abound in popular music, movies and culture, many young people have never heard an honest, age-appropriate description of the profoundly intimate and sensual nature of oral sex. Especially for the giver of oral sex, the experience of pleasuring a partner's genitals may be far from casual. Unlike most other sex acts, oral sex acutely engages all five senses of the giver.

As is suggested by the availability of flavored safer sex supplies, for the giver of oral sex, the sense of taste is clearly engaged. If safer sex supplies are not used, the giver experiences the tastes of human body fluids—perhaps semen, vaginal fluids, and/or perspiration. In addition, the tongue and lips feel the varied textures of the partner's genitals, and, depending on the degree of body contact, other touch receptors located elsewhere on the body may be triggered. With the face so close to their partner's genitals, the giver's nose can easily smell intimate odors while the eyes, if opened, get a very cozy view of the partner's body. Lastly, during oral sex the ears not only pick up sounds of voice, moaning, and any music playing in the background, they also hear the delicate sounds of caressing another's body with one's mouth. Obviously, if one is mentally engaged in the experience, it can be quite intense! Honest conversations with adolescents about the intimate and sensual nature of oral sex acknowledge this incredibly unique way human beings share pleasure with one another and elevate it from the casual references of popular culture.

5. Boys do not have to accept oral sex (or any sex) just because it is offered.   As I talked with a group of teenagers at a local alternative high school, it became painfully clear to me that some teen girls offer oral sex to almost any guy they find attractive. As a consequence of such easy availability, these teen boys, although they did not find a girl attractive nor did they desire oral sex from her, felt pressured to accept it simply because it was offered. After all, what real man would turn down sex? Popular music videos, rife with shallow depictions of both men and women, show swaggering males getting play right and left from eager, nearly naked women. These same performances of exaggerated male sexual bravado are mirrored on the streets, in the hall-ways, and in the homes of many boys who may, for various reasons, lack other more balanced models of male sexuality.

When I told the boys that they were not obligated to accept oral sex from someone to whom they were not attracted, it was clearly a message they had never heard. I saw open expressions of surprise and relief on more than a few young faces. This experience taught me that adults must give young men explicit permission to turn down oral sex—and any sex—they do not want. We must teach them that their manhood is not hinged on the number of sex part-ners they amass.

6. Making informed decisions that respect others and one's self is a true mark of manhood.   In May 2002, when Oprah Winfrey and Dr. Phil tried to tackle this subject on her afternoon talk show, they not only put the onus of curbing the trend of casual adolescent oral sex on the girls, they threw up their hands and said, "What do the guys have to lose in this situation? Nothing!"

Nothing? I would suggest otherwise. To leave teen boys off the hook in regard to oral sex fails them miserably as they prepare for responsible adult relationships. In doing so, we set up boys to miss out on developing skills that truly define manhood: healthy sexual decision making, setting and respecting personal boundaries, and being accountable for one's actions. We also leave them at risk for contracting sexually transmitted infections. In addition, although our culture rarely communicates this, men who accept oral sex whenever it is offered risk losing the respect of people who do not admire or appreciate men who have indiscriminate sex with large numbers of partners. Clearly, adults—and especially adult men—must be willing to teach boys, through words and actions, that authentic manhood is a complex identity that cannot be so simply attained as through casual sex, oral or otherwise.[9]

7. Giving oral sex is not an effective route to lasting respect, popularity or love.   For some teen girls, giving oral sex is weighted with hopes of further attention, increased likeability, and perhaps even a loving relationship.[10] For them, giving oral sex becomes a deceptively easy, if not short-term, way to feel worthy and loved. Adults who care about girls must empower them to see beyond the present social situation and find other routes to a sense of belonging and love.

One essential route to a sense of belonging and love is the consistent experience of non-sexual, non-exploitive touch. Some adolescent girls seek sex as a way to find the sense of love and belonging conveyed by touch. If a girl's touch needs go unfilled by parents or other caregivers, sex is often the most available means for fulfilling them.[11] Adults who work with girls must acknowledge the deeply human need for touch experienced by some adolescent girls. Although outside the scope of this discussion, girl-serving professionals can provide creative ways for girls to experience safe, non-sexual touch as part of their participation in programs without violating program restrictions on physical touch between staff and clients.

On the other hand, it is possible—and developmentally normal—for teen girls to experience sexual desire. Although our cultural script of adolescent sexuality contradicts this, it may be that some girls, especially older teens, authentically desire the kind of sensual and sexual intimacy oral sex affords. If this is the case, it is essential that adults do not shame girls away from these emergent desires. Instead, they should explore the ways oral sex may increase one's physical and emotional vulnerabilities and strategize ways that girls can stay healthy and safe while acknowledging their own sexual desires.

8. Girls can refuse to give oral sex.   Unlike Oprah and Dr. Phil, I do not believe the onus for curbing casual adolescent oral sex rests solely or even primarily on teen girls. Teen boys can and should assert firmer boundaries around participating in oral sex. The cultural attitudes that make girls and women the gatekeepers of heterosexual male sexual behavior, deciding when and if sex will happen, are unduly biased and burdensome. By perpetuating these attitudes, Oprah and Dr. Phil missed a grand opportunity to teach the value of mutuality in sexual decision-making and relationships, a message many young people—and adults—desperately need to hear.

That said, it is disturbing to hear stories of adolescent girls offering casual oral sex to teen boys. Again, the models of a balanced female sexuality in the media and in the lives of many girls are often few and far between.

This, coupled with the troubling rates of sexual abuse perpetrated against girls in childhood and adolescence, makes the establishment of healthy sexual boundaries a problem for many girls.

Therefore, adults must go beyond simply telling girls to avoid giving oral sex for reasons of reputation and health, as was stressed by Dr. Phil. We must empower girls, through encouragement, role plays, and repeated rehearsals, to establish and maintain healthy boundaries for loving touch in their friendships and dating relationships, an experience that may be new to some. Moreover, we must be frank about the sexual double-standards set up against girls and women that make them responsible for male sexual behavior. And, we must create safe spaces where girls can encourage and support each other in refusing to give boys oral sex, thus shifting the perceived norm that "everyone is doing it."

9. Young women may explore their own capacities for sexual pleasure rather than spending their energies pleasuring others.   Some girls will argue that oral sex is just another exchange of friendship, something they do with their male friends as "friends with benefits." I would argue, however, that, in most cases, the benefits are rather one-sided. Rarely do the teen boys give oral sex to the teen girls in exchange. Neither research nor anecdotal evidence indicates a trend of boys offering casual oral sex to girls. It seems that the attention the girls get *en route* to oral sex make it a worthwhile exchange for them, even as they are shortchanged on other "benefits."

If, indeed, girls are fulfilling their valid need for attention and acceptance through giving oral sex, and if they don't consider what they are doing to be "real sex," it stands to reason that many girls engaged in oral sex may not be experiencing genuine sexual desire or pleasure at all. It wouldn't be surprising if they're not. After all, few girls receive a truly comprehensive sexuality education, one that acknowledges the tremendous life-enhancing capacities for desire and pleasure contained in the female body. Our sex education messages are often so consumed by trying to prevent girls from getting pregnant and abused that we fail to notice how we keep them as the objects of other people's sexual behaviors. In doing so, we keep girls mystified about their own bodies and thus fail to empower them as the sexual subjects of their own lives.[12]

Adults can affirm girls' emerging capacities for desire and pleasure by, first, teaching them the names and functions of all of their sexual anatomy, including the pleasure-giving clitoris and G-spot. When discussing the benefits of abstinence, adults can suggest to girls that their growing sexual curiosity and desires may be fulfilled by learning, alone in the privacy of one's room, about one's own body—what touch is pleasing, what is not, how sexual energy builds, and how it is released through their own female bodies. If girls could regard themselves as the sexual subjects of their own lives rather than spending vast energies on being desirable objects of others, perhaps they would make healthier, firmer, more deliberate decisions about the sexual experiences and behaviors they want as adolescents.[13] Not only might girls make better decisions around oral sex, they may feel more empowered to negotiate the use of contraception and safer sex supplies, a skill that would serve them well through their adult years.[14]

10. Seek the support and guidance of adults who have your best interests at heart. Young people do not have to figure it all out on their own. Human sexuality is complicated, and most of us, adults and adolescents, do better by sometimes seeking out the support, guidance, and caring of others who want to see us enjoy our sexualities in healthy, life-enhancing ways. Adults can let young people know we are willing to listen to their concerns around issues of oral sex. We can offer teens support and guidance in their struggles to decide what's right for their lives. We can become skilled and comfortable in addressing risk-reduction and the enhancement of sexual pleasure together, as companion topics. And, finally, adults can use the topic of oral sex as a catalyst to dispel myths, discuss gender roles, and communicate values that affirm the importance of mutuality, personal boundaries, and safety in the context of healthy relationships.

References

1. L. Remez, "Oral Sex Among Adolescents: Is it Sex or Is It Abstinence?" *Family Planning Perspectives*, Nov/Dec 2000, p. 298.

2. R. Tannahill, *Sex in History* (New York: Stein and Day, 1980), pp. 58–346.

3. M. Carrera, *Sex: The Facts, The Acts, and Your Feelings* (New York: Crown, 1981), pp. 49–51.

4. Centers for Disease Control and Prevention, "Preventing the Sexual Transmission of HIV, the Virus that Causes AIDS, What You Should Know about Oral Sex," Dec. 2000. . . .

5. Iowa Code, Section 709.1, Sexual abuse defined (1999). . . .

6. S. Edwards and C. Carne, "Oral Sex and the Transmission of Viral STIs," *Sexually Transmitted Infections*, April 1998, pp. 95–100.

7. Centers for Disease Control and Prevention, "Fact Sheet: Pubic Lice or 'Crabs'," June 2000. . . .

8. Several online retailers sell safer sex supplies, including flavored condoms and lubricants. . . .

9. P. Kivel, *Boys Will Be Men: Raising Our Sons for Courage, Caring and Community.* (Gabriola Island B.C., Canada: New Society, 1999), pp. 177–184.

10. S. Thompson, *Going All the Way: Teenage Girls' Tales of Sex, Romance, and Pregnancy* (New York: Hill & Wang, 1995), pp. 17–46.

11. P. Davis, *The Power of Touch* (Carlsbad, CA: Hay House, 1999), p. 71.

12. M. Fine, "Sexuality, Schooling, and Adolescent Females: The Missing Discourse of Desire," *Disruptive Voices: The Possibilities of Feminist Research*, Ann Arbor: University of Michigan, 1992), pp. 31–59.

13. M. Douglass & L. Douglass, *Are We Having Fun Yet? The Intelligent Woman's Guide to Sex* (New York: Hyperion, 1997), pp. 170–171.

14. TARSHI (Talking About Reproductive and Sexual Health Issues), *Common Ground Sexuality: Principles for Working on Sexuality* (New Dehli, India: TARSHI, 2001), p. 13.

Nora Gelperin  **NO**

Oral Sex and Young Adolescents: Insights from the "Oral Sex Lady"

A Brief History

I've been the Director of Training at the Network for Family Life Education for three years, but recently I've become known as the "Oral Sex Lady." (My parents are so proud.) It all began when I started receiving more frequent calls from parents, teachers and the media concerning alleged incidents of 11–14 year-olds engaging in oral sex in school buses, empty classrooms or custodial closets, behind the gym bleachers and during "oral sex parties." People were beginning to panic that youth were "sexually out of control." Most people believe young teens should not engage in oral sex, but that's not our current reality. So in response, I developed a workshop about oral sex and young teens, which I have since delivered to hundreds of professionals throughout the country. This process has helped me refine my thinking about this so-called oral sex "problem." Now, when I arrive at a meeting or workshop I smile when I'm greeted with, "Hey, aren't you the Oral Sex Lady?!"

What's the "Problem"?

The 1999 documentary, "The Lost Children of Rockdale County," first chronicled a syphilis outbreak in suburban Conyers, Georgia due to a rash of sex parties. Since then, more anecdotal and media stories about middle school students having oral sex began to surface. Initially, a training participant would tell me about an isolated incident of a young girl caught performing oral sex on a boy in the back of the school bus. During a workshop in Minnesota, I was educated about "Rainbow Parties" in which girls wear different colored lipstick and the goal for guys is to get as many different colored rings on their penises by night's end. In Florida, there were stories of "chicken head" parties where girls supposedly gave oral sex to boys at the same time, thus bobbing their heads up and down like chickens. During a workshop in New Jersey, I learned that oral sex was becoming the ultimate bar mitzvah gift in one community, given under the table during the reception hidden by long tablecloths. (At one synagogue, the caterer was ultimately asked to shorten the tablecloths as a method of prevention!) The media began to pick up on these stories and run cover stories in local and national newspapers and magazines. One could conclude from the media buzz that the majority of early adolescents are frequently having oral sex at sex parties around the country. But what was *really* going on and what can the research tell us?

What is missing from the buzz is any recent scientific data to support or refute the claims of early adolescents having oral sex at higher rates than in previous years. Due to parental rights, research restrictions, and lack of funding, there is no rigorous scientific data conducted on the behavior of early adolescents to establish the frequency or incidence of oral sex. So we are left with anecdotal evidence, research conducted on older adolescents, media reports and cultural hype about this "new" phenomenon. We don't know how frequent this behavior is, at what ages it might begin, how many partners a young teen might have, whether any safer sex techniques are utilized or the reasoning behind a teen's decision to engage in oral sex. What is universal among the anecdotes is that girls are giving oral sex to boys without it generally being reciprocated and it's mostly the adults that find this problematic. But what can we learn from all this?

Major Questions to Consider

Is Oral Sex Really "Sex"?

One of the most common themes I hear during my workshop is that adults want to convince teens that oral sex is really "sex." The adult logic is that if we can just convince teens that oral sex is "really" sex, they will take it more seriously and stop engaging in it so recklessly. This perspective seeks to universally define oral sex from an adult perspective that is out of sync with how many teens may define it. Many teens view oral sex as a way to maintain their "virginity" and reduce their risk for pregnancy and infections. According to a recent Kaiser Family Foundation report, 33 percent of 15–17 year-old girls report having oral sex to avoid having intercourse. In the same report, 47 percent of 15–17 year-old girls and boys believe that oral sex is a form of safer sex. Most people believe that young adolescents should not engage in oral, anal or vaginal sex. As a back up, we should make sure teens understand that if they are going to engage in sexual behaviors, oral sex is less risky for many infections than vaginal or anal sex if latex barriers like flavored condoms and sheer glyde dams[1] are used, and it cannot start a pregnancy.

If You've Only Had Oral Sex, Are You Still a Virgin?

From my experience facilitating workshops on oral sex, professionals really struggle with this question and many of the 32,000 teens per day who come to our *SEX, ETC.* Web site . . . do too. The concept of virginity, while troublesome to many adults, is still central to the identity of many teens, particularly girls. Many adults and teens define virginity as not having had vaginal intercourse, citing the presence or absence of the hymen. Some adults then wrestle with the idea of what constitutes actual intercourse—penetration of a penis into a vagina, orgasm by one or both partners, oral sex, anal sex, penetration of any body opening? For heterosexual couples, virginity is something girls are often pressured to "keep" and boys are pressured to "lose." The issue also becomes much more volatile when a teen may not have given consent to have intercourse the first time—does this mean that he/she is no longer a virgin? Gay and lesbian teens are also left out when virginity is tied to penis-vagina intercourse, possibly meaning that a gay or lesbian teen might always be a "virgin" if it's defined that way. Educators can help teens think more critically about their definitions of sex, intercourse, and virginity and the meanings of these words in their lives.

How Intimate Is Oral Sex?

Many adults in my workshops express their belief that oral sex is just as intimate as other types of penetrative sexual behaviors. Some adults believe oral sex is even *more* intimate than vaginal or anal intercourse because one partner is considered very vulnerable, it involves all of the senses (smell, taste, touch, sight, and sound) and requires a lot of trust. Many teens, although certainly not all teens, believe oral sex is *less* intimate than vaginal intercourse. Through my experience as an on-line expert for our *SEX, ETC.* Web site, I hear from hundreds of teens every month who submit their most personal sexual health questions. Some of these teens believe oral sex is very intimate and acknowledge the same issues that adults raise while others find it less intimate than vaginal intercourse. From a teen's perspective, it is less intimate because:

- oral sex doesn't require that both partners be nude;
- oral sex can be done in a short amount of time (particularly if performed on adolescent boys);
- oral sex can maintain virginity;
- oral sex doesn't involve eye contact with a partner;
- oral sex doesn't require a method of contraception;
- oral sex doesn't require a trip to the gynecologist; and
- most teens believe oral sex doesn't carry as much of a risk for sexually transmitted infections as vaginal or anal intercourse.

Some girls even feel empowered during oral sex as the only sexual behavior in which they have complete control of their partner's pleasure. Others feel pressured to engage in oral sex and exploited by the experience. So while many adults view oral sex as extremely intimate, some teens do not.

This dichotomy presents challenges for an educator in a group that may assign a different value to oral sex than the educator. Oral sex also requires a conversation about sexual pleasure and sexual response, topics that many educators are not able to address with young teens. The salient issue is how teens define behaviors, not how adults define behaviors, since we are operating in their world when we deliver sexuality education. I believe our definitions and values should be secondary to those of teens because ultimately teens need to be able to operate in a teen culture, not our adult world.

What Can an Educator Do?

As sexual health educators, our role is to provide medically-accurate information and encourage all adolescents to think critically about decisions relating to their sexuality. We should ask middle school-age adolescents to sift through their own beliefs and hear from their peers, many of whom might not agree about oral sex, virginity, intimacy or the definition of sex. Finding ways to illuminate the variety of teens' opinions about oral sex will more accurately reflect the range of opinions instead of continuing to propagate the stereotype that "all teens are having oral sex." Additionally, instead of focusing exclusively on the ramifications of oral sex and infections, we should address the potential social consequences of having oral sex. Since early adolescents are not developmentally able to engage in long-term planning, focusing on the long-term consequences of untreated sexually transmitted infections (STIs) is not developmentally appropriate. Educators should be cognizant of what is developmentally appropriate for early adolescents and strive to include information about sexual coercion, correct latex condom and sheer glyde dam use, and infection prevention.

So Are They or Aren't They?

Without research, this question will remain unanswered and we must not rely on overly-dramatized media accounts to dictate public health approaches. Instead we should focus on giving young adolescents developmentally appropriate information, consider their reasoning for wanting to engage in oral sex, explore their definitions of sex, virginity and intimacy, and develop programs that incorporate all of these facets. We need to advocate for more research and reasoned media responses to what is likely a minority of early adolescents having oral sex before it becomes overly dramatized by our shock-culture media. Finally, we must not forget that the desire for early adolescents to feel sexual pleasure is normal and natural and should be celebrated, not censored. From my experience as the "Oral Sex Lady," teens are much more savvy than we adults think.

Note

1. Sheer glyde dams are squares of latex that are held in place of the vulva of a female during oral sex to help prevent sexually transmitted infections. They are the only brand of dental dam that is FDA approved for the prevention of infections.

POSTSCRIPT

Is Oral Sex Really Sex?

"Sex is more than sexual intercourse. This means teaching young people that there are many ways to be sexual with a partner besides intercourse and most of these behaviors are safer and healthier than intercourse. The word 'sex' often has a vague meaning. When talking about intercourse, the word 'intercourse' [should be] used."

This statement is taken from a list of principles for sexuality education developed by The Center for Family Life Education, included in the U.S. chapter of the *International Encyclopedia of Sexuality.* Do you agree or disagree with this principle? How does it compare with your own definition of "sex"? Do you agree with Chittenden that young people need to recognize oral sex as "really sex"? Or are you inclined to side with Gelperin as she asserts that adult values and definitions should be secondary, and that young people need to form their own meaning to oral sex?

Chittenden presents specific messages she believes young people need to hear about oral sex. What do you think about these messages? Are they messages you would want to give to a son or daughter, or to a younger sibling? What other advice would you want to give to a loved one who was thinking about having oral sex?

Whereas Chittenden identifies specific messages that need to be articulated to young people, Gelperin seems more inclined to advocate a values clarification process and educational strategies based on the developmental needs of a given audience. What merits do these different approaches have? Would you advocate a combination of these approaches? Or would your own educational approach be very different?

Gelperin expresses great concern about the hype surrounding media reports of oral sex. What do you think about such reports? How do they compare with the social climate in your schools or community as you were growing up?

Since both Chittenden and Gelperin are sexuality education professionals, you may have noticed several overlapping themes, such as the concern both expressed about condom use and protection from sexuality transmitted infections. What other similarities did you observe?

Is it more important to have a uniform definition of "sex," that includes (or does not include) oral sex, or for people to create their own personal definitions that have meaning for themselves and/or their partners? Some reproductive health professionals have ascertained that if you cannot define "sex," then you cannot define its supposed opposite, "abstinence." In other words, one needs to understand what sex is before she or he can determine what it is they are being encouraged to abstain from. How has a culturally vague notion of "sex" and "abstinence" contributed to the widespread failure of abstinence-only education programs?

Suggested Readings

C. Billhartz and C.M. Ostrom, "What's 'Real' Sex? Kids Narrow Definition, Put Themselves at Risk," *Seattle Times* (November 6, 2002).

S. Brown and B. Taverner, "Principles for Sexuality Education," in R.T. Francoeur and R. Noonan, eds., *The International Encyclopedia of Sexuality* (Continuum, 2004).

Centers for Disease Control and Prevention, "Preventing the Sexual Transmission of HIV, the Virus that Causes AIDS, What You Should Know about Oral Sex," (December 2000). Available at www.thebody.com/cdc/oralsex.html

14 and Younger: The Sexual Behaviors of Young Adolescents (National Campaign to Prevent Teen Pregnancy, 2003).

E. Marchetta, "Oral Sex = Safe Sex? No Way!" *SEX, ETC.* (Spring 2001).

National Survey of Adolescents and Young Adults: Sexual Health, Knowledge, Attitudes and Experience (Kaiser Family Foundation, 2003).

L. Remez, "Oral Sex Among Adolescents: Is It Sex or Is It Abstinence?" *Family Planning Perspectives* (November/December 2000).

J. Timpane, "No Big Deal: The Biggest Deal of All—Young Adults and the Oral Sex Code," *Philadelphia Inquirer* (October 28, 2002).

P. Wilson, "Talking with Youth about Oral Sex," *Family Life Matters* (Fall 2000).

ISSUE 3

Is Masters and Johnson's Model an Accurate Description of Sexual Response?

YES: Stephanie Ann Sanders, from "Physiology of Sex," *Microsoft Encarta Online Encyclopedia* (2004)

NO: Paul Joannides, from "The HSRC—Is Everything Better in Black & White?" An Original Essay Written for This Volume (2004)

ISSUE SUMMARY

YES: Stephanie Ann Sanders, a director and scientist with the Kinsey Institute and a contributing author to the *Encarta Online Encyclopedia,* summarizes Masters and Johnson's Human Sexual Response Cycle.

NO: Paul Joannides, author of the popular book *The Guide to Getting It On!,* says that the Human Sexual Response Cycle is a "one-size-fits-all" model that does not account for individual variations.

Scientific interest in the physiological changes that humans experience during sexual activity can be traced to the late nineteenth century. In 1876, the French physician Felix Roubaud wrote about sexual response and described his research on changes in penis size, vaginal lubrication, and other physiological changes. In the 1940s, while renowned sex research Alfred Kinsey was interviewing Americans about their sexual behavior, a lesser-known researcher, Robert Latou Dickinson, studied changes in the vagina when his female subjects masturbated with a glass tube resembling a penis. Dickinson reported his findings in *Human Sex Anatomy* in 1949, and so did others, describing changes that were visible to the naked eye.

William Masters and Virginia Johnson were the first scientists to study sexual response through systematic observation in a laboratory setting. They observed almost 700 subjects who engaged in sexual activity while the researchers measured and recorded their sexual responses with the aid of new technological developments, especially microphotography.

Masters and Johnson's primary interest in studying sexual response was to help therapists identify sources of sexual dysfunction and recommend effective treatment. However, their 1966 book, *Human Sexual Response,* was considered groundbreaking for both its popular insights and its political implications. Their research revealed and emphasized the many similarities in sexual response between men and women. This revelation came to signify equality for women and underscored the importance of regarding women's sexuality as equal to that of men.

Their model of sexual response, the Human Sexual Response Cycle (HSRC) describes four phases of sexual response in men and women— excitement, plateau, orgasm, and resolution. These changes are physiological in nature, as they describe changes in the size and color of sexual organs, as well as changes in blood pressure, heart rate, muscular tension, respiration, and other physical changes. Some researchers have found the focus on physiological changes too limiting. Helen Singer Kaplan added desire as a phase that preceded excitement, describing it as specific sensations that moved a person to seek out (or become receptive to) sexual activity, and suggesting that three phases (desire, excitement, and orgasm) were sufficient to illustrate sexual response.

Others who criticize the HSRC for being too centered on physical changes point to cultures in which sexual experience is intertwined with spirituality. Eastern Tantric traditions of Buddhism, Hinduism, Taoism, and yoga link sexual response with spiritual energy. Critics also charge that the HSRC places a Western emphasis on orgasm as the goal of sex, rather than the intimacy of the couple, or the sensuality of many different behaviors that do not necessarily lead to orgasm. The HSRC has also been criticized for being too medical or for trying to "fit" female sexual response into a mostly male-oriented model.

Despite its many critics, the HSRC remains the one model that can be found in every college textbook on sexuality. Even the texts that point out the limitations of the model still describe its four phases of sexual response in great detail.

In the following essays, Stephanie Ann Sanders, writing for the *Encarta Online Encyclopedia,* presents a concise illustration of the HSRC. Paul Joannides challenges the prominence the HSRC is given in sexuality textbooks, and criticizes it as a "one-size-fits-all" model.

YES

Stephanie Ann Sanders

Physiology of Sex

Understanding the processes and underlying mechanisms of sexual arousal and orgasm is important to help people become more familiar with their bodies and their sexual responses and to assist in the diagnosis and treatment of sexual dysfunctions. Nevertheless, it was not until the work of American gynecologist William H. Masters and American psychologist Virginia Johnson that detailed laboratory studies were conducted on the physiological aspects of sexual arousal and orgasm in a large number of men and women. Based on data from 312 men and 382 women and observations from more than 10,000 cycles of sexual arousal and orgasm, Masters and Johnson described the human sexual response cycle in four stages: excitement, plateau, orgasm, and resolution.

In men who are unaroused, the penis is relaxed, or flaccid. In unaroused women, the labia majora lie close to each other, the labia minora are usually folded over the vaginal opening, and the walls of the vagina lie against each other like an uninflated balloon.

A. Excitement

The excitement stage of sexual arousal is characterized by increased blood flow to blood vessels (vasocongestion), which causes tissues to swell. In men, the tissues in the penis become engorged with blood, causing the penis to become larger and erect. The skin of the scrotum thickens, tension increases in the scrotal sac, and the scrotum is pulled up closer to the body. Men may also experience nipple erection.

In women, vasocongestion occurs in the tissue surrounding the vagina, causing fluids to seep through the vaginal walls to produce vaginal lubrication. In a process similar to male erection, the glans of the clitoris becomes larger and harder than usual. Muscular contraction around the nipples causes them to become erect. However, as the excitement phase continues, vasocongestion causes the breasts to enlarge slightly so that sometimes the nipples may not appear erect. Vasocongestion also causes the labia majora to flatten and spread apart somewhat and the labia minora to swell and open. The upper two-thirds of the vagina expands in a "ballooning" response in which the cervix and the uterus pull up, helping to accommodate the penis during sexual intercourse.

Both women and men may develop "sex flush" during this or later stages of the sexual response cycle, although this reaction appears to be more common among women. Sex flush usually starts on the upper abdomen and spreads to the chest, resembling measles. In addition, pulse rate and blood pressure increase during the excitement phase.

B. Plateau

During the plateau stage, vasocongestion peaks and the processes begun in the excitement stage continue until sufficient tension is built up for orgasm to occur. Breathing rate, pulse rate, and blood pressure increase. The man's penis becomes completely erect and the glans swells. Fluid secreted from the Cowper's gland (located near the urethra, below the prostate) may appear at the tip of the penis. This fluid, which nourishes the sperm, may contain active sperm capable of impregnating a woman. In women, the breasts continue to swell, the lower third of the vagina swells, creating what is called the orgasmic platform, the clitoris retracts into the body, and the uterus enlarges. As the woman approaches orgasm, the labia majora darken.

C. Orgasm

Orgasm, or climax, is an intense and usually pleasurable sensation that occurs at the peak of sexual arousal and is followed by a drop in sexual tension. Not all sexual arousal leads to orgasm, and individuals require different conditions and different types and amounts of stimulation in order to have an orgasm. Orgasm consists of a series of rhythmic contractions in the genital region and pelvic organs. Breathing rate, pulse rate, and blood pressure increase dramatically during orgasm. General muscle contraction may lead to facial contortions and contractions of muscles in the extremities, back, and buttocks.

In men, orgasm occurs in two stages. First, the vas deferens, seminal vesicles, and prostate contract, sending seminal fluid to the bulb at the base of the urethra, and the man feels a sensation of ejaculatory inevitability—a feeling that ejaculation is just about to happen and cannot be stopped. Second, the urethral bulb and penis contract rhythmically, expelling the semen—a process called ejaculation. For most adult men, orgasm and ejaculation are closely linked, but some men experience orgasm separately from ejaculation.

In women, orgasm is characterized by a series of rhythmic muscular contractions of the orgasmic platform and uterus. These contractions can range in number and intensity. The sensation is very intense—more intense than the tingling or pleasure that accompany strong sexual arousal.

D. Resolution

During resolution, the processes of the excitement and plateau stages reverse, and the bodies of both women and men return to the unaroused state. The muscle contractions that occurred during orgasm lead to a reduction in muscular tension and release of blood from the engorged tissues.

The woman's breasts return to normal size during resolution. As they do, the nipples may appear erect as they stand out more than the surrounding breast tissue. Sex flush may disappear soon after orgasm. The clitoris quickly returns to its normal position and more gradually begins to shrink to its normal size, and the orgasmic platform relaxes and starts to shrink. The ballooning of the vagina subsides and the uterus returns to its normal size. Resolution generally takes from 15 to 30 minutes, but it may take longer, especially if orgasm has not occurred.

In men, erection subsides rapidly and the penis returns to its normal size. The scrotum and testes shrink and return to their unaroused position. Men typically enter a refractory period, during which they are incapable of erection and orgasm. The length of the refractory period depends on the individual. It may last for only a few minutes or for as long as 24 hours, and the length generally increases with age. Women do not appear to have a refractory period and, because of this, women can have multiple orgasms within a short period of time. Some men also experience multiple orgasms. This is sometimes related to the ability to have some orgasms without ejaculation.

Paul Joannides

The HSRC—Is Everything Better in Black & White?

Back in the 1950s and 1960s, there was a famous pair of sex researchers who were working on two charts that were to become the Rosetta Stone of sexual satisfaction. Known as the Human Sexual Response Cycle (HSRC), each chart consisted of "the" four phases of sexual response called excitement, plateau, orgasm, and resolution.

There is not a single college textbook on sex that does not devote several pages to the HSRC charts, and there have been few books written on sex since the 1960s that do not take the HSRC as fact. We regarded this famous pair of sex researchers in the same way that many psychoanalysts did Freud. Rather than viewing them as visionaries, we viewed them as prophets. Rather than looking at their findings through the lens of science, we enshrined them as the Ten Commandments of what human couples do when naked and breathing hard.

In case you weren't aware, the HSRC model is based on the experiences of recruits who were so uninhibited that they were able to get naked, have sex, and pop out easy orgasms in a university laboratory while researchers watched, listened, filmed and measured. As a result, the model is based on only three things: getting hard, getting wet, and coming. Nowhere in this model is there room for how qualities like intimacy, tenderness and even kink can impact, shape and change sex. Nowhere is there concern about desire, anticipation, fantasy, or what happened in the lives of the research subjects before they got naked in the lab and started fucking on command.

When you reduce human sexuality to just three parts—erect penis, lubricated vagina and orgasms—what you get is a mechanistic model of human sexual response. If the three parts are present and accounted for, then your sex life is said to be okay. If one of these "essential" elements is missing, then modern medicine has a pill, patch, or demeaning diagnosis to throw at it.

While the elements that are shown in the two HSRC charts can easily describe the human sexual response of some people, they fall short when describing the sexual response of others.

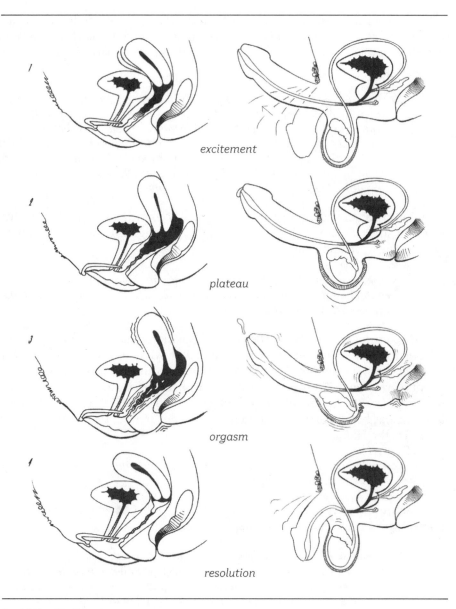

excitement

plateau

orgasm

resolution

Daerick Gross Sr., Illustrator

For instance, consider two situations brought up by Deborah Tolman, followed by three examples of my own:

1. *A young girl is in her gym class and discovers that she enjoys climbing up a rope and sliding down it. Her bare feet are extremely sensitive, so it feels sensual on the bottoms of her feet as the thick cotton rope slides through them. She also finds the feeling of the rope between her legs to be quite nice. She climbs up the rope and slides down several times. She never has an orgasm and was never thinking sexual thoughts.*

Many of us would consider this to be an innocent and delightful sexual experience—totally private and unlabeled. But according to the Human Sexual Response Cycle, there was no orgasm so it was not part of the human sexual response.

> 2. *An adult woman is in a competitive academic situation. She is overwhelmed with nervousness and anxiety. She excuses herself to the rest room and quickly masturbates to orgasm. There was not a sexual thought in her mind when she was masturbating and she had not felt any sexual arousal before going to the rest room to masturbate. For her, the masturbation provided relief from unbearable anxiety. Its effect was similar to downing a shot of whisky or popping a Valium.*

This woman had an orgasm, so it's Bingo according to the HSRC. Motivation and situation are irrelevant to the HSRC, as long as the woman's genitals swelled, quivered and convulsed.

> 3. *One couple makes out passionately for an hour but has no genital contact and no orgasms. Another couple doesn't make out, but has intercourse and orgasms.*

According to the HSRC, the first couple didn't have a complete sexual experience, while the second couple did. But what if you found that the couple who was kissing passionately for an hour had been married for twenty-five years? Even without an orgasm, making out for an hour is a pretty powerful statement about intimacy and sexual satisfaction when a couple has been married for a quarter of a century. Yet they didn't register a blip on the HSRC.

> 4. *A woman seldom has an orgasm with her husband, but looks forward to having intercourse with him.*

According to the HSRC, her husband is the only one who has a complete sexual experience when they are making love.

> 5. *A man who could have been Mr. HSRC hit a patch of black ice while riding his Harley. He is now a quadriplegic who has no feeling below his shoulders, yet he finds that having the top of his head stroked is as blissful and sexually satisfying as his former HSRC marathons.*

The head that this man used to receive was HSRC certified—now that it's lost its metaphorical quality, it's HSRC challenged.

Some therapists would say that the events listed below can be tremendously important elements of a satisfying sex life even if they are not immediately chased by throbbing crotches and pounding orgasms, yet it's difficult to figure where they fit on the charts of the Human Sexual Response Cycle:

- A woman receives a rose and a card saying "Just thinking of you" from her partner while she is at work.

- A woman finds it to be an incredible sexual experience when her lover sucks on her fingers. This is the sum of their sexual activity one night until she is so overwhelmed that she falls asleep in his arms, exhausted but ecstatic.
- A couple talks on the phone during the middle of the day, for no other reason than to connect emotionally.
- One partner lightly tickles, caresses and kisses the other's back for an hour.
- A man opens his briefcase at work and finds a box of condoms with a note from his lover "Hope you'll be ready to use these tonight!"
- One partner licks and kneads the nipples of the other, who then asks to have nipple clamps put on them. This couple never gets around to having orgasms in the traditional sense.
- One partner loves being tickled, so the other ties him up and tickles him mercilessly.
- After talking dirty together, one partner finds it to be a nearly mystical experience when the other probes or fists his or her anus.

The range of orgasmic experience can also be minimized by the HSRC. I know of a woman whose orgasms have unleashed such raw emotional torrents that it left her profoundly sad and sobbing in tears. Another woman wrote to me this week wanting to know if she was strange because after twenty years of having the usual "moaning" kind of orgasms, she now bursts into uncontrollable laughter as she starts to come—with the same husband. But according to the HSRC, an orgasm is an orgasm, who cares about the tears, laughter, moans, silence or whatever.

If you were to accept the HSRC as THE model of human sexual response, it's the sexual equivalent of throwing away color TV and going back fifty years when everything was in black and white. It's calling the smile on the Mona Lisa's face irrelevant, or showing the genitals on the statue of David while covering the rest of him with duct tape or a gunny sack.

The Human Sexuality Response Cycle does not differentiate between love and indifference. It does not explain how the freshly spanked bottom of a lover can be so sexually gratifying for a kinky couple. Forget relationship issues, forget intimacy, forget hopes and dreams. Sexual complexity outside of the three parameters of erection, lubrication and orgasm is irrelevant.

This can be a real problem if one of you is the poster child for the HSRC, but the other is non-compliant and values fun and intimacy more than whether you come.

The HSRC provides a one-size-fits-all approach. Either you wear the male size or the female size. There are no allowances for the way other things in your life shape your sexual experiences. No consideration is given to the influences of your work schedule, the demands of your family, the shadows of your sexual past, the pull of religion and gender roles, the impact of your ethnic background or the dictates of your social class or the demands of the culture you were raised in.

The Human Sexual Response Cycle is about a hard penis going into a very orgasmic and very wet vagina.

There wouldn't be a single thing wrong about the HSRC if it had been proposed as two charts out of ten, or at the very least, if it was layered with other charts. In this way, it could guide modern medicine in providing solutions for men who need help with certain types of erection problems or premature ejaculation, but it wouldn't limit the entirety of human sexual response to that which can be maintained with drugs or surgery. It would recognize that for a lot of people there are many different ways to have a sexual response.

POSTSCRIPT

Is Masters and Johnson's Model an Accurate Description of Sexual Response?

Masters and Johnson's Human Sexual Response Cycle (HSRC) has endured much criticism over the years. Nevertheless, it continues to be described in every college textbook on sexuality. As Paul Joannides says, "There is not a single college textbook on sex that does not devote several pages to the HSRC charts." How does your textbook handle the subject of sexual response? Does it present the HSRC as the *only* model? Is the HSRC model given more prominence than other models of sexual response, or are a variety of models presented with equal validity?

While the HSRC has been criticized for its emphasis on physiological responses, some researchers defend the model precisely for such an emphasis. Upon learning that the HSRC was to be examined in *Taking Sides,* one sexologist tersely commented that the model could not be refuted—it was biological fact. What could be disputed, he said, was how sexual response was "packaged" (e.g., as Kaplan's three-phase model, or with other labels to describe physiological changes that are universal). What do you make of this observation? Does the HSRC present a helpful model of human capacity for physiological sexual response, even if not everyone experiences excitement, plateau, orgasm, or resolution? What do you think of Masters and Johnson's "packaging" of the four phases? Are the physiological changes described in the model universal? Is the model necessary for its detailed descriptions of physiological sexual response?

Interestingly, the work of Masters and Johnson predates much of the research on female ejaculation and the G-spot (see Issue 6 of this *Taking Sides* edition). Do such responses fit into the HSRC?

Joannides illustrates a variety of examples that do not seem to fit within the HSRC, or within traditional understanding of "sexual response" as it is physiologically described. How would you classify the behaviors he described? What do you think about expanding the definition of "sex" beyond being associated with intercourse or orgasm?

Finally, how would you describe the phases of sexual response? Is the HSRC helpful as a model? A baseline? Would your model be entirely different? Would your model include emotional, spiritual, relational, or other characteristics?

Suggested Readings

R. Eisler, *Sacred Pleasure: Sex, Myth, and the Politics of the Body* (Harper-Collins, 1995).

P. Joannides, *The Guide to Getting It On* (Goofyfoot Press, 2004).

G. Kelly, *Sexuality Today: The Human Perspective* (McGraw-Hill, 2005).

G. Kelly, *Sources: Notable Selections in Human Sexuality* (McGraw-Hill/ Dushkin, 1998).

J. Kuriansky, *The Complete Idiot's Guide to Tantric Sex* (Alpha Books, 2002).

W. Masters and V. Johnson, *Human Sexual Response* (Lippincott Williams & Wilkins, 1966).

L. Tiefer, "Historical, Scientific, Clinical, and Feminist Criticisms of 'The Human Sexual Response Cycle' Model," *Annual Review of Sex Research* (vol. 2, 1991).

L. Tiefer, *Sex Is Not a Natural Act and Other Essays* (Westview Press, 2004).

ISSUE 4

Is the G Spot a Myth?

YES: Terence M. Hines, from "The G Spot: A Modern Gynecologic Myth," *American Journal of Obstetrics and Gynecology* (August 2001)

NO: Beverly Whipple, from "Beyond the G Spot: New Research on Human Female Sexual Anatomy and Physiology," *Scandinavian Journal of Sexology* (2000, and updated commentary, 2006)

ISSUE SUMMARY

YES: Psychologist Terence M. Hines says that the widespread acceptance of the G Spot as real conflicts with available research evidence. Hines explains that the existence of the G Spot has never been verified by empirical, objective means and that women may have been misinformed about their bodies and their sexuality.

NO: Sexuality researcher Beverly Whipple outlines historical and interdisciplinary research that has been conducted on female sexual response over the past 20 years, particularly on the anatomy and neurophysiology of the sensitive area known as the G Spot, which surrounds the urethra and is felt through the anterior vaginal wall.

$\mathbf{I}$n late 2001 Sexnet, an online discussion community of sexologists, was stirred by the news that the G Spot may not be real. For 20 years most sex researchers, educators, counselors, and therapists had accepted the existence of the G Spot, even while they acknowledged there were many unanswered questions. Female ejaculation has also been accepted as factual, widely documented by the work of Beverly Whipple and others. The article by Terence M. Hines, from which one of the following selections has been excerpted, led to much debate and discussion on Sexnet about a tenet that had been largely unchallenged.

The G Spot is named for Dr. Ernest Gräfenberg, who first described it in a 1950 article in the *International Journal of Sexology*. The term the Grafenberg spot or *G Spot* was coined in the late 1970s by Beverly Whipple and John D. Perry, and then described by them in a 1981 article in the *Journal of Sex Research*, and again in the 1982 best-selling book *The G Spot and Other Recent Discoveries about Human Sexuality*, by Alice Kahn Ladas, Beverly Whipple, and John D. Perry. The G Spot made its way into most modern college sexuality textbooks and dictionaries, described as being felt through the anterior wall of the vagina, with its stimulation leading to ejaculation from the urethra of a small amount of fluid in some women. That landmark book has since been translated into 19 languages, and was later updated and published as a classic by Holt Owl Books in 2005, as *The G Spot and Other Discoveries about Human Sexuality.*

Before the research of Whipple, Perry, and others, the expulsion of fluid during orgasm was believed to be the result of urinary stress incontinence. Sex educators and therapists have been concerned that this "dysfunctional" label might lead women to feel shameful about an experience that is intended to be pleasurable—and unrelated to urination. In fact, in over 5,000 letters, Whipple heard from men and women who reported that women had surgery for this perfectly normal phenomenon, or stopped having orgasm. Research in recent years has focused on the chemical consistency of female ejaculatory fluid to determine that the fluid is not urine. This is an important distinction for many women, and their partners, who do not believe themselves to be urinating at the height of orgasm. Most conclude that the fluid comes from the Skene's glands, or paraurethral glands, now officially referred to by the Federative International Committee on Anatomical Terminology as the female prostate. This decision was based on over 250 studies, many of which were conducted by and cited in Dr. Milan Zaviacic's book, *The Human Female Prostate Gland,* which demonstrates that this gland produces prostatic specific antigen (PSA) found in the female ejaculate.

In the following selections, Terence Hines critically examines some of the research on the G Spot, highlighting the limitations, methodological flaws, and inability of the research to conclusively determine the existence of the G Spot. In response, sexuality researcher Beverly Whipple, a scientist who conducted some of the research on the G Spot, and who was named "one of the 50 most influential scientists in the world" by the journal *New Scientist,* outlines and explains over 20 years of interdisciplinary research on female sexuality, the G Spot, and female ejaculation.

YES

Terence M. Hines

The G-Spot: A Modern Gynecologic Myth

The G-spot is an allegedly highly erogenous area on the anterior wall of the human vagina. Since the concept first appeared in a popular book on human sexuality in 1982, the existence of the spot has become widely accepted, especially by the general public. This article reviews the behavioral, biochemical, and anatomic evidence for the reality of the G-spot, which includes claims about the nature of female ejaculation. The evidence is far too weak to support the reality of the G-spot. Specifically, anecdotal observations and case studies made on the basis of a tiny number of subjects are not supported by subsequent anatomic and biochemical studies.

— (Am J Obstet Gynecol 2001; 185: 359–62.)

The term *G-spot* or *Grafenberg spot* refers to a small but allegedly highly sensitive area on the anterior wall of the human vagina, about a third of the way up from the vaginal opening. Stimulation of this spot is said to result in high levels of sexual arousal and powerful orgasms.[1] The term *G-spot* was coined by Addiego et al[2] in 1981 to recognize Dr Ernest Grafenberg who, they said, was the first to propose the existence of such an area in a 1950 paper.[3] The G-spot broke into public consciousness in 1982 with the publication of the popular book on human sexuality "The G Spot and Other Recent Discoveries About Human Sexuality."[1] One survey study[4, 11] suggests that the reality of the G-spot is widely accepted at least by professional women. A 192-item questionnaire on sexuality was mailed to "a random sample of 2350 professional women in health-related fields in the United States and Canada."[11] The response rate was 55% with a total of 1289 questionnaires being returned. Of this sample, 84% responded that they "believed that a highly sensitive area exists in the vagina."[4] Most popular books on sexuality take it for granted that the G-spot is real. Even a leading college-level sexuality text[5] uncritically reports that the spot is "located within the anterior (or front) wall of the vagina, about one centimeter from the surface and one-third to one-half the way in from the vaginal opening."

Given the widespread acceptance of the reality of the G-spot, one would expect to find a considerable body of research confirming the existence of such a structure. In fact, such supporting evidence is minimal at best. Two types of evidence have been used to argue for the existence of the G-spot and will be reviewed in turn. The first is behavioral, the second is based on claims of female ejaculation. This issue of female ejaculation is relevant to the G-spot for 2 reasons. First, the two are often considered together in the popular literature with the strong implication that the reality of ejaculation supports the reality of the G-spot. Second, some authors[4] mistake the presence of glands that may produce a female ejaculate with the G-spot, a topic discussed in detail later.

Behavioral Evidence

Ladas, Whipple, and Perry[1] reported anecdotes about women who had powerful orgasms when their G-spot was stimulated. Anecdotes aside, there are only 2 published studies of the effects of specific stimulation of this area. The first study[2] reported a single case of a woman who experienced "deeper" orgasms when her G-spot was stimulated. During one session with the subject during which digital stimulation of the anterior vaginal wall was administered, it was reported that the area "grew approximately 50%."

Two years later, Goldberg et al[6] examined 11 women, both to determine whether they had a G-spot and to examine the nature of any fluid they ejaculated during orgasm. The latter aspect of this article will be discussed later. To determine whether the subjects possessed G-spots, 2 gynecologists examined each subject. Both had been given a 3-hour training session on how to examine for the presence of a G-spot. This training consisted of "a special type of bimanual exam as well as a sexological exam where they palpated the entire vagina in a clockwise fashion." Using this technique, they judged that 4 of the 11 women had G-spots.

Even if a G-spot had been found by using techniques such as those described in a much larger sample, this would still have provided little real evidence for the existence of the spot. Almost any gentle, manual stimulation of any part of the vagina can, under the right circumstances, be sexually arousing, even to the level of orgasm.[7,8] The fact that manual stimulation of the putative G-spot resulted in real sexual arousal in no way demonstrates that the stimulated area is anatomically different from other areas in the vagina. The subjects in these studies knew that researchers were searching for an allegedly sexually sensitive area, as did the individuals who performed the stimulation. Under these conditions, it is highly likely that the demand characteristics of the situation played a major role in the responsiveness of the female subjects.

One might think that Grafenberg's original 1950 paper,[3] which is credited with introducing the concept, would contain significant evidence for the spot. It does not. In that paper, Grafenberg discusses no evidence for a G-spot. Rather, he reports anecdotes about some of his female patients. Some he terms *frigid*. Others, he says, derived sexual pleasure from inserting objects, such as hat pins, into their urethras. Just how later writers (i.e., 2) transformed these reports into evidence for a G-spot is unclear.

Grafenberg[3] does make some mention of the innervation of the vagina. He cites Hardenbergh[9] whom, he says, "mentions that nerves have been demonstrated only inside the vagina in the anterior wall, proximate to the head of the clitoris." Hardenbergh does indeed make this statement, but provides no citation. Hardenbergh then goes on to rather dismiss claims of vaginal sensitivity in the course of his discussion of his questionnaire study of female sexual experience, the actual topic of his paper.

Female Ejaculation

The second source of evidence for the existence of a G-spot is the claim that women sometimes ejaculate a non-urine fluid during orgasm. Initially, the relationship between female ejaculation and the G-spot was tenuous and nonanatomic. Grafenberg[3] noted the possible existence of such ejaculation. Ladas, Whipple, and Perry[1] devoted an entire chapter to the topic in their book. The chapter consists largely of anecdotes about ejaculation.

Belzer[10] concluded that "female ejaculation . . . is theoretically plausible" based on a brief literature review and interview-generated anecdotes. The interviews were conducted by students taking a graduate level course on sexuality. Six students interviewed "about 5" people each, male or female. Included in the interview was a question about female ejaculation. Of the 6 students, each "found at least 1 person who reported that she herself, or, in the case of a male informant, his female partner, had expelled fluid at orgasm." Three of these women were then interviewed at length about their ejaculation, and their comments are included in the paper in some detail. In the questionnaire study[4,11] discussed above, 40% of the respondents reported experiencing ejaculation.

Anecdotal and interview-generated reports such as those noted above are far from adequate to show that the ejaculated fluid is anything other than urine. Such evidence would be provided by chemical analysis of the ejaculated fluid. Addiego et al[2] were the first to perform such a chemical analysis. They obtained samples of urine and ejaculate from 1 female subject. They reported a higher level of prostatic acid phosphatase in the ejaculate than in the urine. Prostatic acid phosphatase is found in high levels in male ejaculate and originates in the prostate which, of course, produces components of the male ejaculate. This evidence could be taken, indirectly, as support for a "female prostate" and, more indirectly, for the G-spot. However, Belzer[12] later noted that the test used was "not entirely specific for acid phosphatase," citing a review to this effect by Stolorow, Hauncher, and Stuver.[13] In another study[6] of the chemical nature of female ejaculate, 11 subjects were studied. All produced preorgasmic urine samples. All then engaged in "some form of non-coital activity resulting in orgasm" and 6 collected some resulting ejaculate. The urine and ejaculate samples did not differ in levels.

Anatomic Considerations

Other researchers have taken a more anatomic approach to the issue of prostatelike components in female ejaculate. If women ejaculate a fluid that is not urine, or has non-urine constituents, it must be coming from someplace other than the bladder. Following Severly and Bennett,[15] Tepper et al[16] suggested that any non-urine female ejaculate would likely come from the female paraurethral glands, also known as Skene's glands or ducts. On anatomic grounds, these glands were considered analogous with the male prostate by Huffman[17] who also provided a detailed anatomic description and notes on the history of anatomic thought on the nature of these glands. If these glands are analogous to the male prostate, it might be expected that their secretions would be similar to those of the prostate. It was this hypothesis that Tespper et al[16] tested.

Eighteen autopsy specimens and 1 surgical specimen were obtained. These were sectioned and examined for immunologic reactions to prostate-specific acid phosphatase and prostate-specific antigen by using a peroxidase-antiperoxidase method. The results showed that "eighty-three percent (15/18) of the specimens had glands that stained with antibody to prostate-specific antigen and 67% (12/18) with PSAcPh (prostate-specific acid phosphatase)."[16] The authors concluded that "we have clearly demonstrated . . . that cells of the female paraurethral glands and adjacent urethral mucosa contain antigenic substances identical to those found in the prostate." Heath,[18] commenting separately on this finding, stated that the "homology between male and female prostate was shown."

More recent studies[14] have come to similar conclusions and have confirmed the presence of prostate-specific antigen reactivity in the paraurethral tissues. These studies, using immunohistochemical techniques to look for prostate-specific antigen expression, found the market in the "superficial layer of the female secretory (luminal) cells of the female prostatic glands and membranes of secretory and basal cells and membranes of cells of pseudo-stratified columnar epithelium of ducts."[14] On the basis of these findings, Zaviacic and Ablin[14] argued for dropping the term *Skene's glands* and replacing it with *female prostate*. Whatever term one favors, these results are in line with a view of female ejaculate in which "evacuation of the female prostate induced by orgasmic contractions of the muscles surrounding the female urethra may account for the increased PSA (prostate-specific antigen) values in urine after orgasm."[14]

It was the results of the study by Pepper et al[16] that led Crooks and Baur,[4] in their aforementioned college sexuality text, to confuse the concept of glands that release something with a sensitive area that would have to have a large number of nerve endings to support the reported heightened sensitivity. Specifically, Crooks and Baur stated that the G-spot consists of a "system of glands (Skene's glands) and ducts that surround the urethra."

If the G-spot does exist, it will certainly be more than a "system of glands and ducts." If an area of tissue is highly sensitive, that sensitivity must be mediated by nerve endings, not ducts. One can ask whether, on embryologic grounds, one would expect to find tissue with nerve endings inside the vagina. Heath[18] seems to have been the first to discuss this issue in light of the topics considered in this article. He criticized Kinsey, Pomeroy, and Martin[19] for stating that the entire vagina originates from the mesoderm, which is "poorly supplied with end organs of touch." Rather, Heath[18] cites Koff's[20] work, which is said to show that the upper 80% of the vagina is of mesodermal origin, but the lower 20% is of ectodermal origin, the ectoderm also giving rise to the skin.

A more modern view of the embryology of the vagina is that the vestibulum, bladder, and urethra are of endodermal origin, whereas the rest of the vagina, and the vulva, are of ectodermal origin.[21] This view leaves open at least the possibility that tissue with nerve endings sufficient for the function of a G-spot could be present in the lower portion of the anterior vaginal wall, where the G-spot is said to be.

There have, of course, been histologic studies of the vagina and surrounding tissue. In 1958, Krantz[22] reviewed the early literature, starting with Tiedman's 1822[23] treatise, and then reported the results of his own microscopic analysis. The various studies Krantz reviewed are difficult to evaluate in terms of the issue at hand because they used various methods and many different species. Krantz himself examined only human tissue. In the vagina itself, what he termed "ganglion cells" were found "along the lateral walls of the vagina adjacent to the vascular supply" that were thought to be "parasympathetic terminal neurons." Regarding the types of nerve cell endings that mediate sensations of touch, pressure, and pain in cutaneous tissue, "no corpuscles were observed in the muscularis tunica propria and epithelial areas" although "a very small number/of fibers/were found to penetrate the tunica propria and occasionally terminate in the epithelium as free nerve endings." As would be expected from their well-known high levels of sensitivity, tissues of the external genitals were rich in the various disks, corpuscles, and nerve endings found in other highly sensitive cutaneous tissue.

No further work on the innervation of the vagina seems to have been done after Krantz[22] until 1995 when Hilliges et al[24] published their results. Anatomic techniques had obviously advanced between 1958 and 1995 and these latter authors used immunohistochemical techniques to search for nerve cells in the vagina. Twenty-four vaginal biopsy specimens, 4 from each of 6 women undergoing operation for "benign gynecological disorders not including the vagina," were obtained. The 4 locations from which biopsy specimens were obtained were the "anterior and posterior fornices, the anterior vaginal wall at the bladder neck level, and the introitus vagina region."

Results generally showed a greater degree of innervation than previously reported by Krantz.[22] There was innervation of the introitus vaginae, with this are showing free nerve endings and a few structures that resembled Merkel's disk. The anterior vaginal wall showed more innervation than the posterior wall, but this was subepithelial, and there was "no evidence for intra-epithelial innervation of this part of the vagina." Such innervation would be expected if a sensitive G-spot existed in the area.

The failure of Hilliges et al[24] to find a richly innervated area on the anterior vaginal wall does not prove that the G-spot does not exist there. The authors did not specifically set out to search for the G-spot and did not sample the entire anterior vaginal wall. Thus, they might have simply missed it. Nonetheless, the existence of such a spot would presume a plexus of nerve fibers, and no trace of such appeared in the results.

Finally, it should be pointed out that the issue of the existence of the G-spot is not just a point of minor anatomic interest. As noted, the G-spot seems to be widely accepted as being real, at least within a sample of American and Canadian women.[4,11] If the G-spot does not exist, then many women have been seriously misinformed about their bodies and their sexuality. Women who fail to "find" their G-spot, because they fail to respond to stimulation as the G-spot myth suggests that they should, may end up feeling inadequate or abnormal.

Two conclusions emerge from this review. First, the widespread acceptance of the reality of the G-spot goes well beyond the available evidence. It is astonishing that examinations of only 12 women, of whom only 5 "had" G-spots, form the basis for the claim that this anatomic structure exists. Second, on the basis of the existing anatomic studies reviewed above, it seems unlikely that a richly innervated patch of tissue would have gone unnoticed for all these years. Until a thorough and careful histologic investigation of the relevant tissue is undertaken, the G-spot will remain a sort of gynecologic UFO: much searched for, much discussed, but unverified by objective means.

References

1. Ladas A.K., Whipple B., Perry J.D. *The G spot and other discoveries about human sexuality.* New York: Holt, Rinehart, and Winston; 1982.

2. Addiego F., Belzer E.G., Comolli J., Moger W., Perry J.D., Whipple B. Female ejaculation: a case study. *J Sex Res 1981;* 17: 1–13.

3. Grafenberg E. The role of the urethra in female orgasm. *Int J Sexology* 1950; 3: 145–8.

4. Davidson J.K., Darling C.A., Conway-Welch C. The role of the Grafenberg spot and female ejaculation in the female orgasmic response: an empirical analysis. *J Sex Marital Ther 1989;* 15: 102–20.

5. Crooks R., Baur K. *Our sexuality.* 7th ed. Pacific Grove (Calif): Brooks/Cole; 1999.

6. Goldberg D.C., Whipple B., Fishkin R.E., Waxman H., Fink P.J., Weisberg M. The Grafenberg spot and female ejaculation: a review of initial hypotheses. *J Sex Marital Ther 1983;* 9: 27–37.

7. Alzate H., Londono M. Vaginal erotic sensitivity. *J Sex Marital Ther 1984;* 14: 529–37.

8. Hardenbergh E.W. Psychology of the feminine sex experience. *Int J Sexology 1949;* 2: 224–8.

9. Belzer E.G. Orgasmic expulsion of females: a review and heuristic inquiry. *J Sex Res 1981;* 17: 1–12.

10. Darling C.A., Davidson J.K., Conway-Welch G. Female ejaculation: perceived origins, the Grafenberg spot/area, and sexual responsiveness. *Arch Sex Behav 1990;* 19: 29–47.

11. Belzer E.G. A review of female ejaculation and the Grafenberg spot. *Women's Health 1984;* 9: 5–16.

12. Stolorow M.D., Hauncher J.D., Stuver W.C. Identification of human seminal acid phosphatase by electrophoresis. *J Assoc Off Anal Chem 1976;* 59: 1352–6.

13. Zaviacic M., Ablin R.J. The female prostate and prostate-specific antigen. Immunohistochemical localization, implications for this prostate marker in

women, and reasons for using the term "prostate" in the human female. *Histol Histopathol 2000;* 15: 131–42.

14. Severly J.L., Bennett J.W. Concerning female ejaculation and the female prostate. *J Sex Res 1978;* 14: 1–20.

15. Tepper S.L., Jagirdar J., Heath D., Geller S.A. Homology between the female paraurethral (Skene's) glands and the prostate. *Arch Pathol Lab Med 1984;* 108: 423–5.

16. Huffman J.W. The detailed anatomy of the paraurethral ducts in the adult human female. *Am J Obstet Gynecol 1948;* 55: 86–101.

17. Heath D. An investigation into the origins of a copious vaginal discharge during intercourse: "enough to wet the bed"—that "is not urine." *J Sex Res 1984;* 108: 423–5.

18. Kinsey A.C., Pomeroy W.B., Martin C.E. *Sexual behavior in the human female.* Philadelphia: W.B. Saunders; 1948.

19. Koff A.K. Development of the vagina in the human fetus. *Contrib Embryol 1933;* 24: 59–90.

20. Westrom L.V., Willen R. Vestibular nerve fiber proliferation in vulvar vestibulitis syndrome. *Obstet Gynecol 1998;* 91: 572–6.

21. Krantz K. Innervation of the human vulva and vagina. *Obstet Gynecol 1959;* 12: 382–96. 2fs

22. Tiedman F. *Tabula nervorum utera.* Heidelberg; 1822.

23. Hilliges M., Falconer C., Ekman-Ordeberg G., Johansson O. Innervation of the human vaginal mucosa as revealed by PGP 9.5 immunohistochemistry. *Acta Anat 1995;* 153: 119–26.

Beverly Whipple  **NO**

Beyond the G Spot: New Research on Human Female Sexual Anatomy and Physiology

Introduction

I am honored to have the opportunity to discuss some of our interdisciplinary research concerning female sexual response and to talk about where do we go from here. I will be summarizing 20 years of research, from vaginal orgasm to PET scans of the brain during orgasm.

Before I can discuss research findings, it is important for me to put these findings into a context of how I view sexuality and sexual expression. In the past, sexuality was viewed as having one purpose and that purpose was reproduction. Today it is seen as an important aspect of health; it enhances the quality of life, fosters personal growth and contributes to human fulfillment. When the term sexuality is viewed holistically, it refers to the totality of a being. It refers to human qualities, not just to the genitals and their functions. It includes all the qualities—biological, psychological, emotional, cultural, social and spiritual—that make people who they are. And people have the capacity to express their sexuality in any of these areas, it doesn't have to be just through the genitals.

Goal and Pleasure Oriented Sexual Expression

It is important for sexual health care providers to consider what the person and/or the couple view as their goal of sexual expression. Whenever I discuss our research, I always present it in terms of Timmers' model (Timmers et al 1976). That is, I do not want to have people set up our findings as a goal that they or the individual or couple they are counseling must achieve. My objective has been to validate women's sexual experiences, not create new goals. According to Timmers et al (1976) there are two commonly held views. The most common view is goal-directed, which is analogous to climbing a flight of stairs. The first step is touch, the next step kissing, the next steps are caressing, then vagina/penis contact, which leads to intercourse and the top step of orgasm. There is a goal that both or one partner has in mind, and that goal is orgasm. If the sexual experience does not lead to the achievement of that goal, then the couple or the person who is goal-directed does not feel good about all that has been experienced.

The alternative view is pleasure-directed, which can be conceptualized as a circle, with each expression on the perimeter of the circle considered an end in itself. Whether the experience is kissing, oral sex, holding, etc, each is an end in itself and each is satisfying to the couple. There is no need to have this form of expression lead to anything else. If one person in a couple is goal-directed (and this is typically the male) and the other person is pleasure-directed (and this is typically the female, although it could be vice versa), problems may occur if they do not realize their goals or do not communicate their goals to their partner.

The Grafenberg Spot

It was with the concept of pleasure-directed sexual expression that John Perry and I listened to what women described as pleasurable to them. Listening to the reports of women who said they did not fit into the monolithic pattern of sexual response, i.e. they had sexual pleasure, orgasm and in some cases an expulsion of fluid from vaginal stimulation, not clitoral stimulation, led to our rediscovery of a sexually sensitive area felt through the anterior vaginal wall, which we called the Grafenberg or "G spot."

This sensitive area is usually located about halfway between the back of the pubic bone and the cervix, along the course of the urethra and near the neck of the bladder. It swells when it is stimulated, although it is difficult to palpate in an un-stimulated state (Perry & Whipple 1981, Ladas et al 1982).

The Grafenberg spot has not been found universally by all researchers who have conducted sexological examinations of the vagina. It may be that not all women have this distinct area, or the lack of universality may be due to the different methods of stimulating or different criteria for identifying this area.

Vaginal Orgasm

In addition to vaginal sensitivity, some women reported that they had orgasm from vaginal stimulation. Masters & Johnson (1966) and Kaplan (1974) reported that there is only one reflex pathway in sexual response. In women, the clitoris is reported to be the major source of sensory input, the pudendal nerve is its sensory pathway, and the "orgasmic platform" undergoes myotonic build-up and discharge during orgasm. Perry & Whipple (1982) described a second reflex pathway that included the Grafenberg spot as the major source of stimulation, the pelvic nerve and the hypogastric plexus as its major pathway and the musculature of the uterus, the bladder, the urethra, the contractile elements associated with the paraurethral glands, and the proximal portion of the pubococcygeus muscle as its major myotonic responder. We claimed that this double reflex concept could account for the reported ability of some women to selectively experience "vulva," "uterine" or "blended" orgasm, as described by Singer (1973).

Based on studies in laboratory rats, the pelvic nerve conveys afferent activity from the vagina and conveys efferent activity to the pubococcygeus muscle. This later study provides evidence that vaginal stimulation can produce pubococcygeus muscle contraction and indicates a possible reflex pathway (afferent and efferent) by which vaginal stimulation can produce an orgasmic response (Pacheco et al 1989).

I became interested in the phenomenon of female ejaculation, because I was teaching women to do Kegel exercises using biofeedback for stress urinary incontinence. However, we found that some of our clients were women who only lost fluid at orgasm and these women seemed to have very strong pubococcygeus muscles. So we designed a study that demonstrated a significant difference in the muscle strength of women who claimed to ejaculate, i.e. the women who ejaculated had stronger pelvic muscles than women who did not experience female ejaculation (Perry & Whipple 1981).

Female Ejaculation

The phenomenon of female ejaculation refers to expulsions of fluid from the urethra. Many women reported having surgery to correct this "problem" and others reported that they stopped having orgasm to prevent "wetting the bed." The fluid was described as looking like watered-down skim-milk, tasting sweet and usually about a teaspoon (3–5 cc) in volume.

Six studies have been published in which the fluid expelled from the urethra has been subjected to chemical analysis. In four of these studies, the ejaculated fluid was chemically significantly different from urine (Addiego et al 1981, Sensabaugh 1982, Belzer et al 1984, Zaviacic et al 1988), while in two studies, no significant difference was observed (Goldberg et al 1983, Alzate 1985). Others have reported an expulsion of fluid with and without chemical analysis. We reported a significant difference between urine and female ejaculate in terms of prostatic acid phosphatase, urea and creatinine. We have also found a significant elevation in glucose in the ejaculate and other researchers report a significant elevation in fructose (Belzer et al 1984, Zaviacic et al 1988). Cabello reported at the World Congress in Valencia that he tested the hypothesis that all women ejaculate, although some may have retrograde ejaculation. Using Microparticle Enzyme Immunoassay to detect prostate specific antigen (PSA), he found a significant difference in PSA between preorgasmic and postorgasmic urine specimens (Cabello 1998).

Based on these findings, it is evident that some women expel a fluid that is different from urine during sexual activities and orgasm and some women may expel a little urine. In some women G spot stimulation, orgasm and female ejaculation are related, while in other women they are not related (Whipple & Komisaruk 1991). Some women have reported experiencing ejaculation with orgasm from clitoral stimulation and some have reported experiencing ejaculation without orgasm. It is hoped that women and their partners can be counseled to feel more comfortable with the normal phenomenon of female ejaculation and therefore avoid surgery designed to eliminate it. This phenomenon is reported by most women experiencing it as extremely pleasurable.

Adaptive Significance of G Spot

Is the G spot just for pleasure or does it have adaptive significance? An extensive series of studies in laboratory rats demonstrated that vaginal mechanical stimulation produced a strong pain blocking effect, stronger than 10 mg of morphine per kg of bodyweight. However, the most convincing evidence that vaginocervical stimulation blocks pain requires a verbal confirmation from women. Consequently, we performed a series of studies in women, measuring pain thresholds during vaginal self-stimulation.

We found that the elevation in pain detection threshold (PD) increased by a mean of 47% when pressure was self-applied to the anterior vaginal wall (the Grafenberg spot). When stimulation was applied in a pleasurable manner, the pain threshold was greater (by 84%) than that in the resting control condition. The PD threshold increased by a mean of 107% when the women reported orgasm (Whipple & Komisaruk 1985). There were no increases in tactile (or touch) thresholds. This demonstrates that the effect was analgesic not an anesthetic effect and not a distracting effect. This analgesic effect was produced by pressure and by pleasurable self-stimulation applied to the anterior vaginal wall (G spot) but not pressure applied to other genital regions (Whipple & Komisaruk 1988).

It was then demonstrated that an analgesic effect also occurs naturally during labor. We believe that childbirth would be more painful without this natural pain blocking effect, which is activated when the pelvic and hypogastric nerves are stimulated as the cervix dilates and from pressure in the vagina produced by the emerging fetus (Whipple et al 1990).

Further animal studies revealed that when new-born rats are injected with the chemical capsaicin, they do not get this natural analgesia when they are adults. This led to a very interesting study that was based on my observations made of women during labor. That is, Spanish speaking women in my country seemed to express a harder time during labor, which I thought was cultural, until I learned of the studies with laboratory rats. I hypothesized that women who have chronically ingested a diet high in chili peppers (the main pungent ingredient of which is capsaicin) would have a diminished analgesic response to vaginal self-stimulation.

We conducted a study in Mexico, where we found women who fell into three different groups, depending on their dietary consumption of chili peppers. The results of this study supported my hypothesis, i.e. women who had diets high in chili peppers did not have the elevation in pain thresholds that women in Mexico had who did not eat chili peppers. The group of women who did not eat chili peppers had pain thresholds very similar to the women in the United States; i.e. they had the natural pain blocking effect (Whipple et al 1989).

Imagery-Induced Orgasm

Orgasm has been reported to occur in response to imagery in the absence of any physical stimulation. In another study, we documented orgasm from imagery alone in the laboratory. We measured heart rate, blood pressure, pupil diameter, and pain and tactile thresholds in women who had orgasm from genital self-stimulation and orgasm from imagery alone. Orgasm from self-induced imagery or genital self-stimulation generated significant increases in systolic blood pressure, heart rate, pupil diameter and pain thresholds over resting control conditions. In these women, there were no significant differences in the increases in the physiological and perceptual correlates of orgasm from genital self-stimulation and from imagery alone. Physical genital stimulation is evidently not necessary to produce a state that is reported to be an orgasm (Whipple et al 1992). We may have to re-look at our definition of orgasm and we have to believe women when they say they have had an orgasm, even if no one, including the women themselves, has physically stimulated her body.

Spinal Cord Injury

We are continuing our research program by validating the subjective reports of women with complete spinal cord injury (SCI) that they do indeed experience orgasm. These women have been told, based on the literature, that they could not experience orgasm, or if they did, it was "phantom orgasm." Based on extensive studies in laboratory rats concerning the neural pathways and neurotransmitters involved in the pain blocking and other effects of vaginal mechanical stimulation, we have documented that women with complete spinal cord injury do indeed experience orgasm from self-stimulation of the anterior wall of the vagina, the cervix, and a hypersensitive area of their body (Whipple et al 1996).

Because the fibers of the hypogastric nerve enter the spinal cord at T-10 and below, we hypothesized that in women with complete SCI below T-10, the hypogastric nerve could convey to the brain signals elicited by cervical stimulation. We also hypothesized that women with complete SCI above the level of entry of the hypogastric nerve would have no sexual response or analgesia from vaginal and cervical self-stimulation. However, we found that self-stimulation of the cervix or the vagina could produce orgasm and a significant elevation in pain thresholds in women with complete SCI as high as T-7. These women reported that they did not use imagery during this laboratory study (Whipple et al 1996, Komisaruk et al 1997).

Vagus Nerves

We then postulated the existence of a sensory pathway that bypasses the spinal cord, carrying sensory input from the vagina and cervix directly to the brain. We hypothesized that this pathway is the vagus nerve (Whipple et al 1996, Komisaruk et al 1997).

In the laboratory rat, after injection of the tracer, horseradish peroxidase, into the wall of the cervix and uterus, the tracer was found in cell bodies of the nodose ganglion, which is the sensory ganglion of the vagus nerve (Ortega-Villalobos et al 1990). To further test this hypothesis, we transected either the spinal cord or all nerves known to respond to genital stimulation (pelvic, hypogastric and pudendal) in the laboratory rat and tested for responses to vaginocervical stimulation. The transections reduced the magnitude of brain-mediated responses, leaving a significant residual response. Bilateral transection of the vagus nerves at the subdiaphragmatic level abolished these residual responses (Cueva-Rolon et al 1996).

To test whether the vagus nerve can convey afferent activity from the cervix to the brain in women with and without spinal cord injury, we are conducting PET scans of the brain to ascertain if cervical self-stimulation activates the region of the nucleus of the solitary tract (NTS), which receives the primary afferent terminals of the vagus nerve. In a pilot study with two women with complete SCI above T-10 and one woman without SCI, we have observed evidence of activation of the region of the NTS in response to cervical self-stimulation (Komisaruk et al 1997). These preliminary findings support our hypothesis that the vagus nerve can carry genital sensory information to the brain even if the major spinal cord pathways are interrupted. It is important to note, based on pilot data, that the sensory vagus nerve may be involved in sexual response in women with or without neurological impairment.

Based on these studies, we can conclude that vaginal and cervical stimulation clearly exert powerful perceptual and physiological effects. It may be possible to harness these responses for therapeutic benefit, for example in the control of pain and in the augmentation of sexual response. Further research on the vagus nerve could lead to methods of amplifying activity in this pathway by pharmacological means and/or by biofeedback, which could lead to improved prognosis for rehabilitation and quality of life in women with complete SCI at any level.

We are now extending the PET scan and fMRI studies to map the brain regions that mediate the responses to vaginal-cervical stimulation beyond the first synapse, in the case of pain blockage and sexual response, including orgasm. We anticipate that these studies will provide insight as to where in the brain pain is blocked and orgasm is generated.

I do not have space to go into our extensive research concerning vasoactive intestinal peptide (VIP), which is released into the spinal cord in response to vaginal stimulation in laboratory rats, and which produces a stronger analgesic effect than morphine. VIP is a vasodilator that seems to be involved in sexual response in women in terms of pelvic vasculature and the pelvic nerve. Nitric oxide may be involved in clitoral response (much more research is needed in this area).

Future Research

Let's now look at where we will be going with sexuality research in the future. First of all, I believe that we have to stop extrapolating research findings in men and applying them to women. There may be some similarities, but there are many differences as well. Women have to be the focus of specific studies.

We have to conduct more international studies and look at cross cultural similarities and differences. Laboratory research is very weak in its ability to understand how socio-cultural and partner variables affect sexual response.

In the future we will be conducting more research using newer technologies, such as in home transducers (although the Foxes used them back in the 1970s), to take some of the research out of basic physiology laboratories. We will continue to use state of the art methodology such as PET scans and fMRl's. And we will be making more use of the internet for qualitative research.

We have to determine if the basic physiological research we are conducting in our laboratories has meaning for sexual behavior under other conditions, such as with one's sexual partner.

We have to continue to be open to hearing what women and men say brings them sexual pleasure and then continue to validate their experiences, and not try to fit them into a monolithic model of only one way to respond sexually and only one way to have sexual pleasure.

Whatever the final outcome in terms of neural pathways and neurotransmitters involved in sexual response, it is important for you to be aware of the variety of sexual responses that women report and that have been documented in the laboratory. It is also important that women be aware of what is pleasurable to them, acknowledge this to themselves, and then communicate what they find pleasurable to their partners. People need to be encouraged to feel good about the variety of ways they may achieve sexual pleasure, without setting up specific goals, such as finding the G spot or experiencing female ejaculation. Healthy sexuality begins with acceptance of the self, in addition to an emphasis on the process, rather than only the goals, of sexual interactions.

References

Addiego F, Belzer EG, Comolli J, Moger W, Perry JD, Whipple B. Female ejaculation: A case study. *J Sex Res* 1981; 17:13–21.

Alzate H. Vaginal eroticism: A replication study. *Arch Sex Behav* 1985; 14:529–537.

Belzer E G, Whipple B, Moger W. On female ejaculation. *J Sex Res* 1984; 20:403–406.

Cabello F. Female ejaculation, myth and reality. In: Borras-Valls *JJ,* Parez-Conchillo M (eds) *Sexuality and Human Rights.* Valencia, Spain: XIII World Congress of Sexology, 1998.

Cueva-Rolon R, Sanson G, Bianca R, Gomez LE, Beyer C, Whipple B, Komisaruk BR. Vagotomy blocks responses to vaginocervical stimulation in genitospinal-neurectomized rats. *Physiol Behav* 1996; 60:19–24.

Goldberg DC, Whipple B, Fishkin RE, Waxman H, Fink J, Weisberg M. The Grafenberg spot and female ejaculation: A review of initial hypothesis. *J Sex Maritial Ther* 1983; 9:27–37.

Kaplan HS. *The New Sex Therapy.* New York: Brunner/Mazel 1974.

Komisaruk BR, Gerdes CA, Whipple B. Complete spinal cord injury does not block perceptual responses to genital self-stimulation in women. *Arch Neurol* 1997; 54: 1513–1520.

Komisaruk BR, Whipple B, Gerdes C, Harkness B, Keyes JW. Brainstem response to cervical self-stimulation: Preliminary PET scan analysis. *Neurosci Abstr* 1997; 23:1001.

Ladas AK, Whipple B, Perry JD. *The G Spot and Other Recent Discoveries about Human Sexuality.* New York: Holt, Rinehart and Winston, 1982.

Masters W, Johnson V. *Human Sexual Response.* Boston: Little, Brown & Co., 1966.

Ortega-Villalobos M, Garcia-Bazan M, Solano-Flores LP, Ninomiya-Alarcon JG, Guevara-Guzman R, Wayner MJ. Vagus nerve afferent and efferent innervation of the rat uterus: An electrophysiological and HRP study. *Brain Res Bull* 1990; 25:365–371.

Pacheco P, Martinez-Gomez M, Whipple B, Beyer C, Komisaruk BR. Somato-motor components of the pelvic and pudendal nerves of the female rat. *Brain Res* 1989; 490:85–94.

Perry JD, Whipple B. Pelvic muscle strength of female ejaculators: Evidence in support of a new theory of orgasm. *J Sex Res* 1981; 17:22–39.

Sensabaugh GR, Kahane D. Biochemical studies on "female ejaculates." Paper presented at the meeting of the California Association of Criminalists. Newport Beach, CA. 1982.

Singer I. *The Goals of Sexuality.* New York: Schocken, 1973.

Timmers et al. Treating goal-directed intimacy. *Social Work* 1976; 401–402.

Whipple B, Gerdes, CA, Komisaruk BR. Sexual response to self-stimulation in women with complete spinal cord injury. *J Sex Res* 1996; 33:231–240.

Whipple B, Josimovich JB, Komisaruk BR. Sensory thresholds during the antepartum, intrapartum, and postpartum periods. *Int J Nurs Stud* 1990; 27:213–221.

Whipple B, Komisaruk BR. Elevation of pain thresholds by vaginal stimulation in women. *Pain* 1985; 21:357–367.

Whipple B, Komisaruk BR. Analgesia produced in women by genital self-stimulation. *J Sex Res* 1988; 24:130–140.

Whipple B, Komisaruk BR. The G spot, orgasm and female ejaculation: Are they related? In: Kothari P (ed). *Proceedings: First International Conference on Orgasm.* Bombay: VRP Publishers, 1991, pp. 227–237.

Whipple B, Martinez-Gomez M, Oliva-Zarate L, Pacheco P, Komisaruk BR. Inverse relationship between intensity of vaginal self-stimulation-produced analgesia and level of chronic intake of a dietary source of capsaicin. *Physiol Behav* 1989; 46:247–252.

Whipple B, Ogden G, Komisaruk BR. Physiological correlates of imagery induced orgasm in women. *Arch Sex Behav* 1992; 21:121–133.

Zaviacic M, Dolezalova S, Holoman IK; Zaviacicova A, Mikulecky M, Bradzil V. Concentrations of fructose in female ejaculate and urine: A comparative biochemical study. *J Sex Res* 1988; 24:319–325.

Beverly Whipple, 2006  **NO**

Updated Commentary

More recent research by my colleagues and I can be found in the 2006 book, *The Science of Orgasm,* by Komisaruk, Beyer and Whipple, and published by Johns Hopkins University Press. In this book we explore the complex biological processes behind orgasm in men and women. We also discuss the various types of orgasm experienced by women, describe the genitalia-brain connection, how the brain produces orgasms, how aging affects orgasm, and the effects of prescription medications, street drugs, hormones, disorders, and diseases on orgasm.

We have documented the various types of orgasms experienced by women, have conducted PET scans and fMRI's of the brain during orgasm from vaginal (G spot) and cervical self-stimulation in women with and without complete spinal cord injury, as well as during orgasm from imagery alone. We have found that the same brain areas are activated in women with and without complete spinal cord injury and support our hypothesis about the different nerve pathways that are involved in orgasm, including the sensory vagus nerves. (Whipple et al, 1996; Whipple & Komisaruk, 2002; Komisaruk et al, 1997).

As documented by fMRI, the brain regions activated during vagino-cervical self-stimulation include the hypothalamus, the limbic system (including the amygdala, hippocampus, cingulate cortex, insular cortex, and the region of the accumbens-bed nucleus of the stria terminalis-preoptic area), the neocortex (including parietal and frontal cortices), the basal ganglia (especially putamen), and the cerebellum, in addition to the lower brainstem (central gray, mesencephalic reticular formation and the nucleus of the solitary tract (NTS)). During orgasm from imagery alone, the same regions are activated, except for the amygdala, suggesting that the amygdala is perhaps closer to having a genital sensory role in orgasm, while the other regions activated may be more cognitively related to orgasm (Komisaruk, Whipple, et al, 2004; Komisaruk & Whipple, 2005a, Komisaruk & Whipple, 2005b).

It is important for medical and sexuality professionals to listen to the reports of women concerning what they find pleasurable and then document these reports with physiological laboratory studies. Based on these data, my colleagues and I have concluded that orgasm is not just a reflex, it is a total body experience. And orgasm can be generated by many body regions, including imagery alone. To deny the experiences reported by women as pleasurable, including orgasmic experiences that do not fit into the male linear model, is to deny sensual and sexual pleasure to women world-wide. Let us be open to listening to and supporting women and their sensual and sexual pleasurable responses, including those who find stimulation of the G spot pleasurable.

References

Komisaruk, B.R., Gerdes, C., & Whipple, B. 1997. "Complete" spinal cord injury does not block perceptual responses to genital self-stimulation in women. *Archives of Neurology* 54: 1513–1520.

Komisaruk, B.R., & Whipple, B. 2005a Brain activity imaging during sexual response in women with spinal cord injury. In *Biological Substrates of Human Sexuality*. Ed J.S. Hyde. Washington, DC: American Psychological Association.

Komisaruk, B.R., & Whipple, B. 2005b Functional MRI of the brain during orgasm in women. *Annual Review of Sex Research* 16: 62–86.

Komisaruk, B.R., Whipple, B. Crawford, A., Grimes. S., Liu, W.-C., Kalnin, A., & Mosier, K. 2004. Brain activation during vaginocervical self-stimulation and orgasm in women with complete spinal cord injury: fMRI evidence of mediation by the vagus nerves. *Brain research*, 1024: 77–88.

Whipple, B., Gerdes, C., & Komisaruk, B.R. 1996. Sexual response to self-stimulation in women with complete spinal cord injury. *Journal of Sex Research,* 33: 231–240.

Whipple, B., & Komisaruk, B.R. (2002). Brain (PET) responses to vaginal-cervical self-stimulation in women with complete spinal cord injury: Preliminary findings. *Journal of Sex and Marital Therapy,* 28: 79–86.

POSTSCRIPT

Is the G Spot a Myth?

Hines concludes his selection by calling the G Spot a "gynecologic UFO"—something that is much searched for and much discussed but unverified by objective means. What do you think about his assessment? Were you impressed by the lack of empirical evidence he described? What do you make of two decades worth of sexologists acknowledging the existence of the G Spot, as identified anecdotally in their patients and supported by findings with research subjects, as described by Whipple?

In a letter to the editor responding to Hines's article, published in the *American Journal of Obstetrics and Gynecology*, Whipple and John D. Perry pointed out that Hines cited only 24 of the more than 250 published peer-reviewed research studies concerning the anatomy and neurophysiology of the G Spot. What do you think of Hines ignoring most of this published data?

Hines notes his concern about women who are unable to find their G Spots, when their textbooks, and research, are so definitive about saying they have one. On the other hand, not all women may enjoy stimulation of this area, just as not all women enjoy having their nipples stimulated. What does your textbook say about the G Spot? Do you think information about the G Spot could help alleviate negative feelings? Or does it present sexual performance pressures for women and their partners? In *The G Spot and Other Recent Discoveries about Human Sexuality,* Ladas, Whipple, and Perry devote the last chapter to not striving to find the G Spot or experience female ejaculation, but rather enjoy whatever feels pleasurable to the individual.

Finally, you may have taken note that one point of view on the G Spot was given by a man, Terence Hines. And, as the Introduction notes, the G Spot was named after Ernest Gräfenberg, a gynecologist who also developed the first intrauterine device (IUD). (Whipple declined to have the G Spot named after her, as had been suggested by her colleagues.) Further, the Skene's gland was named after a nineteenth-century gynecologist, Alexander Skene. What thoughts do you have about so many men examining a question of female sexuality and sexual response? In Whipple's commentary about future research, she says that we need to "stop extrapolating research findings on men and applying them to women." Do you agree? Do you think that research on female sexuality and sexual response should be conducted on women by women?

Suggested Readings

F. Addiego, E. G. Belzer, J. Comolli, W. Moger, J. D. Perry, & B. Whipple, "Female Ejaculation: A Case Study," *The Journal of Sex Research,* 1981, vol. 17.

R. T. Francoeur, et al., "Female Sexuality Today: Challenging Cultural Repression," *Cross Currents,* 2004, vol. 54.

E. Grafenberg, "The Role of the Urethra in Female Orgasm," *International Journal of Sexology,* 1950, vol. 3.

D. Heath, "An Investigation into the Origins of a Copious Vaginal Discharge during Intercourse: 'Enough to Wet the Bed,'—That Is 'Not Urine,'" *Journal of Sex Research,* 1984, vol. 20.

B. R. Komisaruk, C. Beyer-Flores, & B. Whipple, *The Science of Orgasm* (Johns Hopkins University Press, 2006).

A. K. Ladas, B. Whipple, & J. D. Perry, *The G Spot and Other Recent Discoveries about Human Sexuality* (Holt, Rinehart and Winston, 2002, Dell 2003).

A. K. Ladas, B. Whipple, & J. D. Perry, *The G Spot: And Other Discoveries about Human Sexuality* (Owl Books, 2005).

J. D. Perry & B. Whipple, "Pelvic Muscle Strength of Female Ejaculators: Evidence in Support of a New Theory of Orgasm," *The Journal of Sex Research,* 1981, vol. 17.

J. D. Perry & B. Whipple, "Multiple Components of the Female Orgasm," in B. Graber, ed., *Circumvaginal Musculature and Sexual Function* (S. Karger, 1982).

S. Reinberg, "The G Spot: A Gynecological UFO?" *Reuters Health* (August 29, 2001).

C. Winks, *The Good Vibrations Guide: The G Spot* (Down There Press, 1998).

M. Zaviacic, *The Human Female Prostate: From Vestigial Skene's Glands and Ducts to Woman's Functional Prostate* (Slovak Academic Press, 1999).

ISSUE 5

Is the Testosterone Patch the Right Cure for Low Libido in Women?

YES: Carolyn Susman, from "Look Who's Smiling Now: A New Patch Delivers to Menopausal Women a Dose of What the Guys Have: Sex-Drive-Revving Testosterone," *Palm Beach Post* (October 30, 2004)

NO: Iver Juster, Gary Schubach, and Patricia Taylor, from "Testosterone Patches—The Cure for Low Female Sexual Desire?" http://www.DoctorG.com/intrinsa.htm (2002)

ISSUE SUMMARY

YES: Columnist Carolyn Susman comments favorably on Intrinsa, a testosterone patch intended to treat low female desire in women. Susman outlines research findings that say the patch could improve sexual desire in women.

NO: Iver Juster, a family practitioner, Gary Schubach, a sex researcher and educator, and Patricia Taylor, a sex researcher and sexual enhancement coach, reject the idea that female sexual desire is hormonally driven, and say that the testosterone patch should not be regarded as a cure-all.

Most people have heard of Viagra, the little blue pill designed to treat erectile dysfunction in men. Prescribed to about 16 million men worldwide, Viagra has catapulted pharmaceutical manufacturer Pfizer into a giant in the business. The popularity of the little blue pill continues to soar. Its logo is emblazoned on a NASCAR race car, and it has even received endorsements from former presidential candidate Bob Dole, who has spoken candidly about his erectile dysfunction in Viagra commercials.

Some have hailed Viagra as a miracle pill that has revolutionized the treatment of sexual dysfunction and has improved the sex lives of millions of men. But many health professionals point to the far more common psychogenic causes of sexual dysfunction that cannot be treated by medication. They contend that non-medical treatments (improving partner communication, for example) would be far more effective.

In 2004, Proctor and Gamble announced their application to the U.S. Food and Drug Administration (FDA) seeking approval for Intrinsa, a drug to treat hypoactive sexual desire disorder, or low libido, in women. If approved, Intrinsa would be the first such treatment for women to have FDA approval.

The active ingredient in Intrinsa is testosterone, a hormone that contributes to sex drive in both men and women. After menopause, testosterone production levels drop in women. Supporters of the testosterone patch say that it will improve sexual libido by increasing testosterone levels in the bodies of menopausal and postmenopausal women.

Whereas the Viagra pill increases blood flow to the penis to enhance erection, Intrinsa dispenses a hormone—testosterone—continuously into a woman's body by means of a transdermal patch. This means that while Viagra can be stored in the medicine cabinet and used when the mood strikes, Intrinsa would need to be worn continuously, and could take weeks or even months before any effect is noticed. When sexual libido is enhanced, it could be at times when a woman is not interested in sexual activity.

Some sexologists wondered what took so long for this type of treatment to arrive. Viagra has been FDA approved for treating male erectile dysfunction since 1997, and other testosterone treatments have been available for men since 1953. Critics wonder if sexism might explain why these treatments for men have been available for so long while an estimated 15 million women who struggle with low libido have remained overlooked until now.

Other sexologists respond that this estimated number of cases is inflated, and that the vast majority of real cases of both female and male sexual dysfunction are caused by psychological or interpersonal factors that are better treated with non-medical intervention. They charge that pharmaceutical companies are making their billions through the "medicalization" of sexuality.

In the following essays, columnist Carolyn Susman describes the research findings that led to the FDA's approval of Intrinsa, while also outlining the possible risks and side effects. The team of Iver Juster, Gary Schubach, and Patricia Taylor express their concerns that Intrinsa will follow in Viagra's footsteps, and come to be regarded as a "magic pill" that will not solve underlying, non-hormonal factors related to sexual arousal and dysfunction.

YES

Carolyn Susman

Look Who's Smiling Now: A New Patch Delivers to Menopausal Women a Dose of What the Guys Have: Sex-Drive-Revving Testosterone

Let's be upfront: Sex, for women, takes work.

We have to relax, get in the mood and concentrate on something other than a grocery list or a crazed kid before we can come close to having an orgasm.

When Lynette on the ABC-TV show *Desperate Housewives* rolls her eyes and asks her husband, "Do you mind if I just lay here?," lots of us can relate. The woman has four children under 6 and hardly has time to brush her teeth. Wanting to have sex is a big part of enjoying the experience. But there are many women who can't even get that far. So drug companies have been researching like mad, trying to come up with a product that will put the oomph back.

For some women, the wait may be over.

While only time will heal the libido-deadening effect of a houseful of screaming youngsters, a new testosterone patch is just months from becoming the first federally approved product to treat low desire in menopausal women.

Procter & Gamble's patch, to be called Intrinsa, is expected to be the first product approved by the U.S. Food and Drug Administration to deal with what doctors call hypoactive sexual desire disorder (HSDD).

Naturally and surgically menopausal women may suffer from low sex drives because their hormone balances have changed. Menopause produces a decline in estrogen and testosterone (women produce small amounts of this "male" hormone nicknamed the "hormone of desire") and that can affect sex drive.

The good news is that studies showed women reported increases in desire, satisfaction with sex, orgasm, responsiveness and self-image while receiving a low, controlled dose of natural testosterone. The hormone is delivered via a thin, transparent patch on either the lower back, abdomen or arm.

Side effects didn't seem to curb their enthusiasm, either. Irritation at the patch site, and even excess facial hair, were reported. But researchers said the women kept using the patch anyway.

The catch is that the patch has been tested in, and will be prescribed for, women who have undergone surgical menopause. But it is expected that doctors will prescribe it also for women who complain of low sex drive and are going through natural menopause. The patch is now being studied on those women.

Younger women—like the exhausted Lynette—might also want it, but there is no data to support its use for them, and the package insert warns the patch shouldn't be used by women who might become pregnant.

The other catch is that the patch was tested while women were taking oral or transdermal estrogen—trials started in 2002—so women may be advised to take this hormone while on the patch.

The Women's Health Initiative concluded last year that estrogen increases the risk for blood clots and strokes, so women advised to use estrogen with the libido patch will have to discuss risk factors with their doctors.

But with no other approved products on the market right now for low libido in women, millions are anxious to give it a go. (There are over-the-counter products available, such as the herbal tablet, Avlimil, but none have undergone the clinical trials required to get FDA approval.)

"This can't be approved soon enough," says Dr. Maureen Whelihan, an obstetrician/gynecologist in West Palm Beach who is a member of Procter & Gamble's Florida Female Sexual Function Advisory Board. "It's extremely safe." And if one approved treatment is good, two must be even better.

Close on the heels of Intrinsa is LibiGel, a testosterone gel for treatment of female sexual dysfunction, being developed by BioSante Pharmaceuticals, also for surgically menopausal women.

How do they feel about the competition?

Stephen Simes, president and chief executive officer of BioSante, says his company is glad that the FDA seems to be taking testosterone seriously as a libido treatment for women and expects his product to apply for approval by the end of 2006.

"By that time we expect the market (demand) to be multibillion dollars."

LibiGel is applied to the upper arm from a metered-dose bottle and rubbed in. It takes about 30–60 seconds to dry with no residue. The dosing is once-per-day, while the Intrinsa patch is changed twice weekly.

Not all doctors are certain these products will break the low-sexual-desire cycle. "It's still premature to say what does or doesn't work in improving women's sexual libido, but researchers are learning more all the time," said Dr. Vivian M. Dickerson, president of the American College of Obstetricians and Gynecologists, in a statement released a month ago.

It's also true that some women may not care a hoot about either product.

After all, not all women consider low sexual desire a problem. And a study sponsored by Procter & Gamble proves the point.

Of 2,000 American women surveyed, one in three naturally menopausal women reported problems with sexual desire. But only one in 10 said it upset them.

Iver Juster, Gary Schubach,
and Patricia Taylor

 **NO**

Testosterone Patches—The Cure for Low Female Sexual Desire?

Proctor & Gamble is about to release a new drug, Intrinsa™, which is intended for women suffering from a loss of sexual desire as a result of medical or surgical menopause. The drug is being developed as a skin patch containing testosterone, a hormone that affects sexual desire in women. While there is considerable evidence that testosterone can impact sexual desire after menopause[1-3], we don't accept the idea that female sexual desire is totally or—even mostly—about hormones. A growing body of evidence—as well as most people's personal experience—tells us that emotional connection and good communication play key roles. Our fear is that Proctor & Gamble is about to spend $100,000,000 to convince all women that the cure for low sexual desire is Intrinsa™.

We fear that, since most people hope this is true, Intrinsa™ use will lead to preventable disappointments.

Let's start with some hormone science. Studies do show that testosterone can make a big difference for women who have had their ovaries removed. However, it won't do much good for post-menopausal women who don't have low free testosterone levels. While we're sure Procter and Gamble is not deliberately promoting the idea that sexual desire is about hormones and needs drugs to fix it, they are certainly capitalizing on the increasing public hope that sexual desire is basically a medical issue and can be fixed with drugs or surgery, and if not that, then a new partner. Because of this, people will take drugs or get surgery and not deal with issues of turn on, communication, and personal transformation. The most one could hope for is a return to the previous state of affairs, definitely an improvement, but, for most people in long term relationships, the previous state of affairs wasn't all that great.

In terms of using testosterone to stimulate sexual desire in women, the long-term effects are unknown and might prove to be dangerous. After years of promoting HRT (hormone replacement therapy—estrogen or estrogen/progesterone) to millions of women, United States health authorities have stopped clinical trials of various forms of HRT because of the dangerous nature of their findings[4,5] and the North American Menopause Society has recommended that these hormones not be prescribed except for short-term

---

Intrinsa™ is a registered trademark of Proctor and Gamble.

relief of severe symptoms of menopause[6]. In the case of declining levels of testosterone, just because a hormone is declining from levels achieved at age 25 doesn't imply that it should (in terms of healthy outcomes) be replaced back to those levels (or even higher).

The lessons from estrogen and estrogen/progesterone are quite relevant in this regard. It may be years before we know about the safety of testosterone replacement, especially after natural menopause. The first good studies will likely be completed after at least five years of use of the drug. These initial studies will likely be simple case-control studies (find two groups of people; one group of 'cases' has some disease you want to study like heart disease or some kind of cancer; the other group is a 'control' with those who don't have the disease; then you look back to get the odds of 'exposure,' to testosterone). Early case-control studies of estrogen and estrogen/progesterone suggested that these medications were beneficial or at least not harmful for preventing heart disease[7] and in combination even prevented uterine cancer[8]. Later more rigorous studies called 'retrospective cohort studies' often agreed with the case-control studies[9]. It was only when we had 'randomized prospective trials' that the truth (even though suggested by a few of the earlier studies) emerged[10,11]. It could be at least ten years until we get to that point with testosterone, if indeed anyone even decides to study it.

When Intrinsa™ is released, with its $100 million ad campaign, we strongly suspect that there will be enormous patient pressure on doctors to prescribe Intrinsa™ for all women who perceive themselves to have low sexual desire, regardless of their age or reproductive status. In order to be medically responsible, Intrinsa™ should not be prescribed for any woman until tests have been performed to determine whether she really has low testosterone levels. If the testosterone levels are low, our recommendation would be to replace testosterone at the lowest level of *free* testosterone in range for women in their late 30s; get tested for cancer and liver function as well as blood counts a couple of times a year; get screened for cancer as recommended; and live an extremely healthy lifestyle. And be aware that women using this patch are part of an uncontrolled experiment.

Even for women whose biochemical profile and history make a strong case for the patch, it's only a part of improving her sex life. We believe that the emotional and psychological components are still the most important aspects of female sexual desire. And let's distinguish between *sexual drive* and *sexual desire*. One can have profound levels of desire—for emotional connection, physical contact, and erotic arousal and adventure—with minimal levels of drive. We are not born knowing how to be sublime lovers, but the good news is that that can be learned, as a reflection of love and caring for another human being.

Sadly, in our culture, boys and girls are not given good information about human sexuality so as to be able to craft a rewarding sex life. We are a society full of contradictions about sex and young people are coming to sexual maturity full of fears and confusion and misunderstandings. Men are not taught how to pleasurably stimulate a woman sexually and function with beliefs that intercourse is the ultimate sexual goal and is the way to sexual satisfaction for both partners. Yet study after study shows how dissatisfied women are with intercourse alone as a path to sexual gratification, and how women's sexual response cycles are usually much longer than men's. It would make sense to be teaching men and women lovemaking techniques that will allow for—even celebrate—the differences in male and female physiology.

Just as Viagra has turned out not to be the universal panacea for male sexual issues, Intrinsa™ will not be the "magic pill" that resolves the problem of female low sexual desire, either pre- or post-menopause. The human issues, how to love and care for another human being and be aware of and satisfy their emotional as well as physical needs, are still the most important factors.

Notes

1. Davis SR. The use of testosterone after menopause. *Journal of the British Menopause Society.* 2004;10(2):65–69.

2. Goldstat R, Briganti E, Tran J, Wolfe R, Davis SR. Transdermal testosterone therapy improves well-being, mood, and sexual function in premenopausal women. *Menopause.* 2003;10(5):390–398.

3. Mazer NA, Shifren JL. Transdermal testosterone for women: a new physiological approach for androgen therapy. *Obstetrics and Gynecology Surveys.* 2003; 58(7):489–500.

4. Manson JE, Hsia j, Johnson KC, Women's Health Initiative. Estrogen plus progestin and the risk of coronary heart disease. *New England Journal of Medicine.* 2003;349:523–534.

5. Writing Group for the Women's Health Initiative Investigators. Risks and benefits of estrogen plus progestin in healthy menopausal women: A randomized, controlled trial. *JAMA.* 2002;288:321–333.

6. North American Menopause Society. Amended report from the NAMS Advisory Panel on Postmenopausal Hormone Therapy. *Menopause.* 2003;10:6–12.

7. Grodstein F, Stampfer MJ. The epidemiology of coronary heart disease and estrogen replacement in postmenopausal women. *Progress in Cardiovascular Disease.* 1995;38:199–210.

8. Grady D, Rubin SM, Penn DB. Hormone therapy to prevent disease and prolong life in postmenopausal women. *Archives of Internal Medicine.* 1992;116: 1016–1037.

9. Grodstein F, Stampfer MJ, Manson JE, et al. Postmenopausal Estrogen and Progestin Use and the Risk of Cardiovascular Disease. *N Engl J Med.* August 15, 1996 1996;335(7):453–461.

10. Grady D, Herrington D, Bittner B, The HERS Research Group. Cardiovascular disease outcomes during 6.8 years of hormone therapy. *JAMA.* 2002;288: 49057.

11. Hulley S, Furberg C, Barrett-Conner E, Group THR. Risk factors and secondary prevention in women with heart disease: The Heart and Estrogen/Progestin Replacement Study. *Annals of Internal Medicine.* 2003;138:81–89.

POSTSCRIPT

Is the Testosterone Patch the Right Cure for Low Libido in Women?

The Food and Drug Administration (FDA) convened an advisory committee of independent scientists to give expert advice on whether or not the FDA should approve Intrinsa to treat low libido in women. The 14-member committee voted unanimously against recommending approval, and urged additional research to ensure the safety of the patch. The FDA usually, but not always, follows the expert advice of its panel. (See Issue 5 on the FDA's decision on emergency contraception for a notable exception.) In this case, manufacturer Proctor and Gamble decided to withdraw their application and resubmit a new application to address the concerns the panel raised.

One wonders how the product will be marketed if and when it becomes available. The marketing strategy may reveal a great deal about the traditional views Americans hold regarding male and female sexuality. For example, a prominent marketing campaign for Viagra featured a man standing in front of the word "Viagra," blocking most of the V so that it appears that two horns are protruding from his head. The unmistakable reference to Viagra making a man "horny" is further confirmed by the logo that urges men to "get back to mischief." Might Intrinsa be marketed in the same way? Do you believe society would look favorably upon women as "horny little devils" in the same way male sexual urges are accepted and encouraged? Bob Dole's celebrity rose when he became a spokesman for Viagra. Will the public regard an older woman in the same way when she speaks openly about overcoming her low sex drive? What does this say about our collective social attitudes toward female and male sexuality?

Beyond the marketing of the product, what do you make of the availability of medical treatments for sexual dysfunction? Are they to be championed for expanding choices that individuals are free to accept or reject? Are they to be regarded with skepticism for contributing to the medicalization of sexuality, or for the financial gains of pharmaceutical companies?

Susman refers to potential interest in Intrinsa among younger women who experience low sex drive, although there is no data to support its effectiveness in younger women. What other suggestions would you make to a friend who has a low sex drive? Why might women be unconcerned about low sexual desire, as Susman suggests?

Juster, Schubach, and Taylor state that young people are "coming to sexual maturity full of fears and confusion and misunderstandings," receiving misinformation—or no information—about sexual pleasure and satisfaction for both partners. Do you agree or disagree? How would you recommend that young people learn about sexual pleasure? Juster et al also contend that too much emphasis is placed on vaginal intercourse as the "ultimate sexual goal," and that this may also contribute to lower levels of sexual satisfaction in women. Some sex educators teach about "outercourse" (non-penetrative sexual behaviors) as a way for couples to enjoy pleasurable—and safer—sexual activities that are more mutually satisfying without the performance pressures that are sometimes associated with vaginal intercourse. What do you think of outercourse as a sexual expression for adults? For young people?

The Sexuality Information and Education Council of the United States (SIECUS) published *New Expectations: Sexuality Education for Mid and Later Life,* a sexuality education resource designed to address the changing sexual experiences and needs of adults. Learning about sexuality and developing positive feelings about sexuality may go a long way toward helping adults avoid or overcome sexual difficulties without medication. How would you feel about a loved one participating in a sex ed class for older adults? Would you consider participating in such a class as an older adult?

Suggested Readings

Associated Press, "F.D.A. Panel Says Sex Patch Needs More Testing," *New York Times* (December 2, 2004).

J.R. Berman and J. Bassuk, "Physiology and Pathophysiology of Female Sexual Function and Dysfunction," *World Journal of Urology* (vol. 20, no. 2, 2002).

L. Berman, "Not In the Mood? Now There's a Patch," accessed at www.bermancenter.com (October 29, 2004).

L. Berman, "Women's Sexual Health Deserves Equal Attention," *USA Today* (November 22, 2004).

P. Brick, "Outercourse Is In" *Teaching Safer Sex* (Planned Parenthood of Greater Northern New Jersey, 1998).

P. Brick and J. Lunquist, *New Expectations: Sexuality Education in Mid and Later Life* (SIECUS, 2003).

E. Kaschak and L. Tiefer, *A New View of Women's Sexual Problems* (Haworth Press, 2002).

M. Kaufman, "Safety Tests Urged for Libido Patch," *Washington Post* (December 3, 2004).

J. Lite, "Stuck on the Love Patch," *New York Daily News* (October 2, 2004).

C. Peale, "P&G Poised to Move on Intrinsa," *The Cincinnati Enquirer* (November 28, 2004).

C. Shultz, "Let Us Women Patch It Together," *Cleveland Plain Dealer* (November 8, 2004).

K.E. Walsh and J.R. Berman, "Sexual Dysfunction in the Older Woman: An Overview of the Current Understanding and Management," *Drugs & Aging* (vol. 21, no. 10, 2004, pp. 655–675).

Internet References . . .

The Abstinence Clearinghouse

The Abstinence Clearinghouse is a national, nonprofit organization that promotes the practice of sexual abstinence through the distribution of educational materials and by providing speakers on the topic.

www.abstinence.net

The Alan Guttmacher Institute

The Alan Guttmacher Institute The Alan Guttmacher Institute is a nonprofit organization focused on sexual and reproductive health research, policy analysis, and public education.

http://www.guttmacher.org

Go Ask Alice!

Go Ask Alice is the health question-and-answer Internet service produced by Columbia University's Health Promotion program. The service works to provide readers with reliable, accessible information about various aspects of health, including sexuality, sexual health, and relationships.

www.goaskalice.columbia.edu

Planned Parenthood Federation of America

Planned Parenthood Federation of America, Inc., is the world's largest and most trusted voluntary reproductive health care organization, and provider of sexuality education.

www.plannedparenthood.org

The American Journal of Sexuality Education

The *American Journal of Sexuality Education* is a peer-reviewed journal that provides sexuality educators and trainers at all skill levels with current research about sexuality education, sample lesson plans, scholarly commentary, educational program reports, and media reviews.

http://ajse.haworthpress.com

Sexuality Information and Education Council of the United States

Sexuality Information and Education Council of the United States (SIECUS) advocates for the right of all people to accurate information, comprehensive education about sexuality, and sexual health services, and has served as a national voice for sexuality education for more than 40 years.

www.siecus.org

Sex and Schools

*M*any *debates involving sexuality are centered around the sexual information that young people are exposed to in the academic environment. This section examines four contemporary issues involving students and schools. Working backwards chronologically, we examine the college student, and the "sexual health" of college campuses as measured in a report by Trojan Brand condoms; high school students, and whether sexuality education should include the teaching of sexual abstinence; whether or not preteens should get a vaccination to prevent one of the most prolific—and cancer-causing—viruses, the human papillomavirus before they start middle school; and whether or not students, starting in the youngest grades, are exposed to teacher gender biases.*

- Does the Availability of "Sexual Health Services" Make Some College Campuses Healthier than Others?

- Should Sex Ed Teach about Abstinence?

- Should Children Have an HPV Vaccination before They Enroll in School?

- Do Schools Perpetuate a Gender Bias?

ISSUE 6

Does the Availability of "Sexual Health Services" Make Some College Campuses Healthier than Others?

YES: David M. Hall, from "The Positive Impact of Sexual Health Services on College Campuses," An Original Essay Written for This Volume (2007)

NO: Jens Alan Dana, from "A Different Sort of Measure," An Original Essay Written for This Volume (2006)

ISSUE SUMMARY

YES: David M. Hall, a graduate professor of human sexuality at Widener University, outlines and comments favorably on the "Sexual Health Report Card," a ranking of 100 universities in the United States by Trojan Condoms. Dr. Hall describes the various sexual health indicators for college campuses, as measured by the report, and argues for better sexuality education programs.

NO: Jens Alan Dana, a student and school newspaper editor at Brigham Young University, which was ranked lowest in the Trojan survey, argues that the rankings were unscientific, and based on a subjective set of criteria that were self-serving to Trojan's interests in marketing condoms.

Have you ever considered what makes a college campus "sexually healthy"? College students are used to being graded all the time in the courses they take. A report card filled with "A's" naturally signifies excellence; one with "F's" is failing, with many possibilities in between. In 2006, the makers of Trojan brand condoms gave a report card to 100 college campuses, grading them in terms of their sexual health, as measured by seven categories:

1. **Web site**—Does the school offer a helpful and informative sexual information Web site? Consider, for example the "Go Ask Alice!" Web site operated by New York's Columbia University, which was not evaluated in this study.

2. **Condoms**—Does the school offer condoms (at the health center, or elsewhere), with directions to help its students avoid sexually transmitted infections and unwanted pregnancy?
3. **Contraception**—Are other methods of contraception available on campus, including emergency contraception? Is information about the benefits and drawbacks of different types of contraception provided?
4. **HIV & STD Testing**—Are HIV and other tests for sexually transmitted infections available on campus? Are they free? Are results timely?
5. **Sexual Assault Counseling**—Are sexual assault counseling services available on campus? Is there a hotline or Web site for students who have been sexually assaulted?
6. **Advice Column**—Does the student newspaper feature a forum that addresses sexual issues?
7. **Counseling Services/Other Outreach**—Does the college offer other services, such as peer counseling, campus events, or other outreach?

Based on these criteria, at least one college was graded in each of the 50 states. Yale finished #1, the only college with straight A's. But Ivy League status was not a clear indicator of sexual health as Trojan measured it: Dartmouth finished #63 and Harvard and Brown finished #43 and #44. The results were also not regional: The top five were from all parts of the country, from the East Coast to the West Coast, and middle America too!

There were some commonalities in the lower ranking schools. Ranked #99 was the Catholic institution Notre Dame, and at #100 was Brigham Young University, run by the Church of Latter Day Saints. Christian leaders cried "Foul!" saying that the Trojan standards were not fair indicators of "sexual health" to campuses that championed Christian values of sexual abstinence before marriage. Christian minister Albert Mohler declared that schools who scored well on the Trojan report card actually abdicated their "in loco parentis" responsibility to guide the morality of their students.

In the following essays, David M. Hall, a professor who teaches a graduate course on the history and ethics of human sexuality, outlines and comments on the importance of the findings of the Trojan Sexual Health Report Card, and advocates for sexuality education. Jens Alan Dana, an editor for *The Daily Universe*, the student newspaper of Brigham Young University, responds that the rankings were unscientific, and based on a subjective set of criteria that were self-serving to Trojan's interests in marketing condoms.

YES

David M. Hall

The Positive Impact
of Sexual Health Services
on College Campuses

Sexual Health of Teenagers and Young Adults

The average age of first sexual intercourse is 17.4 for girls and 16.9 for boys. Among high school students, 17 percent of males and 12 percent of females have already had four or more sexual partners. Those ages 18–24 are more likely to choose the birth control pill over a condom as their primary method of contraception (Kaiser Family Foundation, 2006). By the age of 21, almost 20 percent of Americans require treatment for a sexually transmitted infection (STI) (Van Vranken, 2004). The majority of teens and college students are sexually active. While this is true in every region of America, the quality of sexuality information and resources varies significantly from one school to another.

It is clear that too many teens and college students are making sexual decisions that can have an adverse impact on their future. Considering this fact, colleges and universities have a responsibility to help their students make sexual decisions consistent with their goals. Trojan condoms generated significant attention for venturing into this debate with a study of their own, ranking the sexual health on 100 college campuses. The results of this research were published in newspapers and blogs across America. Due to Trojan's support for safer sex information and resources, those opposed to providing students with scientifically accurate sexuality information were quick to criticize this study.

The Trojan National Survey of Sexual Health on College Campuses

Trojan condoms, the popular condom manufacturer, ranked 100 universities for their effectiveness in fostering healthy sexuality on college campuses. These rankings were of schools across America that are both large in population and familiar to the general public. Trojan stated that these results represented 23 percent of U.S. undergraduate students at four-year colleges (Bruno, 2006).

Trojan gave each of the 100 schools a grade point average (GPA) and rank based on the following seven categories:

1. **A college or university website that offers sexuality information and advice.** Specific criteria included whether the website is easy to find, easy to navigate, informative (e.g., hours, location, services, costs, departments, testing, assault reporting, and counseling), offers online advice, provides STD/STI information and treatment, and provides email communication with staff.
2. **The availability of condoms and safer sex information and advice.** Specific criteria included whether condoms are available from the college health center, the cost of condoms, and providing instructions and cautions for condom use.
3. **The availability of contraception and safer sex information and advice.** Specific criteria included discussions of benefits and drawbacks of contraception, the availability of emergency contraception, and health notices and updates.
4. **On-campus testing for HIV and other STDs.** Specific criteria included the type of testing, timeliness of the results, the cost of testing, and whether this is provided on or off-site.
5. **Counseling and services for survivors of sexual assault.** Specific criteria included a separate sexual assault website, sexual assault services, counseling, and a 24-hour hotline.
6. **A school newspaper or web-based column featuring advice regarding sexuality issues or relationships.** Specific criteria included a feature in the student newspaper or an online forum, addressing issues from the student body, and providing links to national columns such as "Go Ask Alice."
7. **Education through campus community outreach such as counseling services, peer counseling, campus events, and other programs.** Specific criteria included peer counseling programs, specialized counseling programs, campus education programs, special events, and guest speakers.

Based on an examination of these criteria, Trojan revealed the top ten schools of the 100 surveyed for having policies that promote positive sexual health on campus: (1) Yale University, 4.0 GPA; (2) University of Iowa, 3.6 GPA; (3) University of Michigan-Ann Arbor, 3.6 GPA; (4) Stanford University, 3.6 GPA; (5) Oregon State University, 3.4 GPA; (6) Princeton University, 3.4 GPA; (7) University of New Hampshire, 3.4 GPA; (8) Duke University, 3.4 GPA; (9) Ohio State University, 3.3 GPA; and (10) University of Illinois at Urbana-Champaign, 3.1 GPA.

The schools that scored at the bottom of the Trojan study are (90) Minnesota State University–Mankato, 0.9 GPA; (91) University of Nevada–Reno, 0.9 GPA; (92) University of Wyoming, 0.9 GPA; (93) University of Louisville, 0.7 GPA; (94) Texas Tech, 0.7 GPA; (95) Clemson University, 0.6 GPA; (96) University of Memphis, 0.3 GPA; (97) Oklahoma State University, 0.1 GPA;

(98) University of Utah, 0.1 GPA; (99) University of Notre Dame, 0.0 GPA; and (100) Brigham Young University (0.0 GPA).

According to a Trojan's press release announcing the study results, Vice President of Marketing Jim Daniels provided the following rationale for programs that provide for the sexual health of college students: "We live in a country with the highest rates of new STIs and unintended pregnancies of any Western nation, and we applaud those schools that provide fact-based, accurate and comprehensive information about sexual health to all students. While we understand there are a variety of reasons some schools do not provide these resources to students, we feel that comprehensive education and access to information is the best way to ensure people make smart decisions about protection should they choose to be sexually active" (Bruno, 2006).

Daniels continued by explaining the implications of this research and recommended action: "We know that 18 to 24-year-olds use condoms only for one in four sex acts, and we believe that it is important for those who choose to be sexually active and are at risk for STIs to understand the risks, and use a condom for every sex act. With this survey, we hope to shine a light on the need for greater discussion about these issues, which can help lead to lower rates of infection and unintended pregnancies" (Bruno, 2006).

The survey reveals valuable data for constructing a sexually healthy undergraduate campus. The Trojan study found that of the schools they examined, 93 percent offered some type of student testing of HIV and STI but only 24 percent offered this testing for free. Only 32 percent of schools had any sort of sex column available online or through the college newspaper. Only 24 percent of the colleges and universities surveyed provided free condoms for students (Bruno, 2006). The survey demonstrated that too few schools are acknowledging and supporting the sexual health needs of their students.

Discussion

Of course critics of this research stress the flaws of this study, and some of their criticisms are valid. First, it is in Trojan's economic best interest to encourage the use of condoms. A corporation certainly would not release a scientific study unless it strengthened the argument for the consumption of their product. Second, there are other criteria that could be useful for a thorough examination of the sexual health of a campus. For example, an examination of required course content related to sexuality information would have been preferable to gathering information about student programs with optional and haphazard attendance.

While this research has its flaws—and though critics are adamant about stressing the study's flaws—it is critical to note that all studies have flaws. Of course weaknesses in the research should be acknowledged by anyone examining the results. Furthermore, it is difficult to rank in a hierarchy the sexual health of 100 colleges.

However, the flaws of this study are secondary concerns from the stand-point of examining sexual health on college campuses. The criteria examined in the Trojan study merits consideration about the sexual health of a school community. The seven criteria from this study, though imperfect, if imple-mented properly can foster sexual literacy and improved sexual decision making consistent with one's future goals.

The criterion of this research is in stark contrast to the hundreds of mil-lions of taxpayer dollars being spent on abstinence-only education. Studies have demonstrated that teens who pledge abstinence fail to see that translate into lower rates of contracting STIs (Bruckner and Bearman, 2005). Further-more, Marty Klein (2006) illustrated that abstinence-only education disadvan-tages teens and young adults because it is preparing millions of youths for what they will not experience: abstinence until marriage.

It is the well intentioned but misguided supporters of abstinence-only education who are leading critics of Trojan's research. A closer examination of the seven criteria of the Trojan study is merited considering the reactionary criticism of this study.

First, evaluating a school's website is a valuable and necessary inclusion when rating the sexual health of a school. College students obtain a wide variety of information online. Scientifically accurate sexuality information available via a website is significantly less threatening for many students when compared with asking questions in person. Unfortunately, the average web surfer may be unaware of which websites offer credible and scientifically accurate information. A school-based website addresses this problem. Any college or university that offers this information to their students can disseminate quality sexuality information at the student's convenience.

Second, access to condoms and scientifically accurate information about condoms is critical. As noted earlier, young people prefer using the birth con-trol pill over condoms (Kaiser Family Foundation, 2006). While the birth con-trol pill provides significant protection from pregnancy, it fails to protect students from contracting HIV and other STIs. Disseminating condoms and scientifically accurate information allows sexually active students the oppor-tunity to minimize their chances of contracting HIV and other STIs. Further-more, free condoms ensure that students obtain the safer sex protection that they need regardless of their socioeconomic status.

Third, information about other forms of contraception allows sexually active heterosexual students to dramatically reduce their chances of an unin-tended pregnancy. A reduction in unintended pregnancies leads to a subse-quent reduction in abortions. Contraception allows students to maximize their birth control options in the event that they choose to be sexually active. Free access to contraception ensures that students obtain the necessary pregnancy reduction methods regardless of their socioeconomic status.

Fourth, HIV and STI testing are critical to avoid students further spread-ing these viruses and infections. Those who are sexually active and at-risk should get tested so that they can take the necessary steps to protect others with which they might otherwise be sexually active. If these tests are free and guarantee confidentiality or anonymity, students will be further encouraged to obtain regular tests.

Fifth, students who are survivors of sexual assault have a variety of needs that a college or university has the responsibility to provide. They have emotional needs that are critical to address through counseling due to the pain and humiliation of their experience. They may need emergency contraception in the event that the victim is a woman who has been vaginally raped by a man. They may want to get tested for a STI. If they have reason to believe that the rapist is HIV positive, they may want to take post exposure prophylaxis for one month to reduce by 79 percent their chance of contracting HIV (New Mexico AIDS Education and Training Center, 2006).

Sixth, it is disheartening to learn that only one-third of schools had any type of sex advice column. Peer education about abstinence, contraception, HIV, sexual transmitted infections, sexual assault, dating violence, lesbian and gay issues, transgender issues, and other human sexuality topics can be extraordinarily influential. Peers have a unique level of credibility in educating about these sensitive issues. The anonymity of a website and newspaper column allows students to explore these issues without having to ask potentially embarrassing questions.

Seventh, counseling and education programs are critical in helping students make informed sexual decisions. While website and newspaper information are valuable tools for raising awareness, effective sexuality education must also work to change behavior. In effective sexuality education, cognitive, affective, and behavioral learning domains are addressed (Hedgepeth and Helmich, 1996). Campus programs can be particularly effective in addressing the behavioral learning domain. Seminars, workshops, and other campus events can help students develop the skills to make decisions in the best interest of their sexual health.

The Trojan study might have been further enhanced by examining what qualities are found in effective sexuality education programs. Simply meeting Trojan's criteria does not mean that the education is effectively impacting sexual decision making and behavior. According to the National Campaign to Prevent Teen Pregnancy (2003), effective sexuality education programs . . .

1. **Have a specific, narrow focus on behavioral goals.** For example, spend significant time on goals such as delaying sexual intercourse or using condoms.
2. **Are based on theoretical approaches that have been effective in influencing other risky health-related behavior.** This can be evidenced by including the reasoned action theory, cognitive behavior theory, and planned behavior theory. These theories are used to identify the risks and the reasons for behavioral change.
3. **Provide clear messages about sex and protection against STDs or pregnancy.** For example, consistently convincing students that not having sex or using condoms is the best thing to do.
4. **Provide basic, not detailed, information.** An example of this can be emphasizing the basic facts that young people need to avoid unprotected sex rather than details about all forms of contraception.

5. **Address peer pressure.** An effective strategy is to discuss beliefs and misperceptions of sex and sexual pressure.
6. **Teach communication skills.** For example, providing information about and practicing the skills of communication, such as negotiation and refusal, are critical in effective sexuality education.
7. **Include activities that are interactive.** Such methodologies include games, simulations, small group discussions, role-playing, and written exercises that will personalize the experience for participants.
8. **Reflect the age, sexual experience, and culture of the young people in the program.** For college age students, programs should emphasize avoiding unprotected sex, stressing abstinence, and the cultural norms experienced by students who are having sex.
9. **Last longer than several hours.** Programs that last longer than 14 hours are shown to have the greatest impact on sexual behavior.
10. **Carefully select leaders and train them.** Those who provide trainings should have been trained from six hours to three days in content information and teaching strategies.

A challenge in implementing these programs on college campuses are that they are achieved most easily with a captive audience in a curriculum-based setting. However, colleges should work to implement high-yield strategies for effective sexuality education as much as possible as they are research-based solutions that will foster healthier sexual activity. Clearly, significant challenges and roadblocks exist in finding ways to provide the depth of experiences that impact sexual decision making and behavior.

Regardless of the imperfections of the Trojan study, the company has triggered a valuable debate on college and university campuses about the best way to disseminate information and resources to promote the sexual health of their student body. At its core, this study is urging colleges and universities to maximize access to sexuality information and resources. Students would be well-advised to closely examine the study and question their own institution on ways in which the sexual well-being of their student body can be best supported. Combining Trojan's areas of examination with the National Campaign to Prevent Teen Pregnancy's ten qualities for effective sexuality education will enhance the sexual health of college students.

References

Bruckner, H., & Bearman, P. (2005). After the promise: The STD consequences of adolescent virginity pledges. *Journal of Adolescent Health, 36*, 271–278.

Bruno, M. (2006, September 19). New survey points to disparity of access to information about sexual health on college campuses nationwide: Yale tops list as most sexually healthy on Trojan Sexual Health Report Card. Edelman.

Hedgepeth, E. and Helmich, J. (1996). *Teaching about sexuality and HIV: Principles and methods for effective education.* New York: New York University Press.

Kaiser Family Foundation (2006, September). Sexual health statistics for teenagers and young adults in the United States. . . .

Klein, M. (2006). *America's war on sex: The attack on law, lust and liberty.* Westport, CT: Praeger.

National Campaign to Prevent Teen Pregnancy (2003, September). Science says: Characteristics of effective curriculum-based programs.

New Mexico AIDS Education and Training Center (2006, August 11). Fact sheet 156: Treatment after exposure to HIV. . . .

Van Vranken, M. (2004, November). About sexually transmitted diseases (STDs). . . .

NO

A Different Sort of Measure

Fishermen and marketing agents have more in common than you'd imagine. Among other things, they both have the same objective—to get attention. Even as a fisherman knows he needs to draw a fish to his bait to have a successful day, a marketing director knows he needs to get his company's logo in the public spotlight to keep afloat. It doesn't matter how much money the fisherman spent on his equipment or how much money fueled the marketing director's ad campaign. At the end of the day, if the fisherman's cooler is empty or if the marketing director's promotion doesn't attract anyone's attention, they've both failed.

A lousy fisherman will just skewer a worm with a hook and cast it out into the middle of the lake, hoping a fish will notice it. In much the same way, a mediocre marketing director will buy advertising space in a newspaper, commercial time on a television channel or a billboard on a freeway, and hope that draws attention to his company. On the other hand, an expert fisherman will know his prey. He will bait his hook with a mayfly—the most beautiful of all aquatic insects, and he won't just stand on the lakeshore, waiting for the fish to come to his bait; he will cast it where he knows the fish will find it. In the same way, an expert marketing director won't flippantly spend his company's money on methods that may or may not attract attention. He will entice the public's attention with bait that is too irresistible to pass up.

Marketing directors work with a different sort of bait, of course. Instead of a lure fashioned to look like a tasty bug, they often use news releases—concisely written documents intended to "tip off" the media about something newsworthy the company is doing. Instead of a plump rainbow trout, the marketing director is fishing for the media's attention. He knows that if he can produce a news release that catches the media's interest, he will catch the public's attention. His company will score free an article in the local newspaper and perhaps a 45-second feature on the local evening news. If the marketing director did his job right, he'll be able to catch multiple media outlets with the same news release, just like his fisherman colleague catches many fish with the same bait. Even as fishermen have their tall tales and legends, future marketing prodigies will spin folklore about the Trojan Sexual Health Report—the news release that hooked a thousand newspapers.

It's important to understand the genesis of this whole chain of events was a simple news release. It's the reason the tidal wave of hastily written, anonymous blogs swept through the Internet, one of which sarcastically stated, "[Brigham Young University's] sex education policy: don't talk about it and they won't do it." It's why idealistic, ill-informed freshman rifled off letters to BYU's campus newspaper, *The Daily Universe*, decrying "backward and utterly irresponsible university policies." It's what prompted news reporters around the country to shower a BYU spokeswoman's office with phone calls, demanding an explanation, and a good sound bite, for the so-called lack of on-campus sexual health services. Before all of this happened, there was a 12-page news release that Trojan, the condom manufacturer, disseminated to the media.

I first learned of the Trojan study when I unfolded a copy of Utah's *Desert Morning News* and a bolded, triple-stack, front-page headline jumped off the page at me 3-dimensional style, screaming, "Does BYU deserve F or A for sex health?" I reread the headline to make sure I understood it correctly, and then I laughed so hard the muscles on the back of my head cramped up. What's so funny is BYU is one of the largest, privately owned, religious universities in the nation that requires each of its students to adhere to a strict code of sexual abstinence while they are registered students. This policy of abstinence is an extension of the teachings of the university's owner and operator—The Church of Jesus Christ of Latter-day Saints. While this policy appears restrictive, and downright cruel, I should stress that each student who enrolls voluntarily commits to this standard. The majority of BYU students come from homes where we were taught sexual relations should be reserved until marriage. We are fully aware of the campus' abstinence policy before we come here; in fact, many of us came here because of it. My freshman year of college, I studied at a community college in Wyoming, and, by the end of the year, I was weary of ending dates by explaining that I wasn't turning down their advances because I didn't think they were attractive. When I came to BYU, it was refreshing to be among peers that shared my value; it was also great to no longer be known as "the guy that hasn't been laid yet" (it's amazing how quickly college gossip spreads, isn't it?).

While I'm not delusional enough to believe an abstinence-only policy means the BYU campus' collective sexual health is without blemish, I've always been confident enough that we have a clean bill of health, compared to other universities. Yet, Trojan challenged that belief by awarding our school seven straight goose eggs, which results in a solid 0.0 sexual health GPA and a 100th-place ranking—a place BYU is not used to being at when it comes to university rankings. After I finished the Desert Morning News article, I noticed the other local newspapers in Utah County also ran front-page stories based on the study. Later that day, I checked the Internet to see what other news organizations were covering the health report. A google search for "Trojan Sexual Health Report" revealed more than 300,000 results. I found many college newspaper articles based on the report, but I was also amazed to see a large number of stories written by professional newspapers. On the blogosphere, the valiant bloggers were already dissecting the contents of several news articles based on the news release. One anonymous blogger said he hoped the ranking would awaken the university to the irresponsible nature of its policies regarding the treatment of sexual health topics on campus. He warned, "This stick-your-head-in-the-sand approach is going to come back to bite you in the butt." Again, the back of my head started to cramp. Once I'd rubbed the laugh-induced cramp out of my neck, I decided the serious tone of the blog posts and the news articles warranted an inspection of the actual health report. After all, I am a journalist. Besides, I might have laughed too quickly. I tracked down a copy and reviewed the Trojan Sexual Health Report. For a moment, I was a fish, swimming through a cloudy lake. I spotted a flash of light. I swam up to it and circled it a few times. The scent emanating from the object nearly overpowered me, and I almost bit down on it. I almost swallowed the health report, hook, line and sinker. But then, I saw the hook.

From the various blogs on the Internet, as well as several letters to the editor, it seems people think the last-place finish meant BYU is a festering, decadent cesspool, a veritable cornucopia of every possible STD known to man. I must admit I too was misled by the perceived aura of credibility the newspaper articles radiated. The articles based on the study touted some very serious national statistics about the rate of STDs and a very credible company compiled the ranking system for Trojan. But after seeing the source of all this discussion, I realize Trojan Sexual Health Report is simply a news release camouflaged as a credible sexual health report. It is a manifestation of the differing philosophies that BYU and Trojan brand condoms have when it comes to promoting sexual health. Moreover, the "health report" contains serious flaws in research methods and data analysis that undermine its conclusions.

Trojan's marketing director cleverly labeled the document a health report, but it is a news release in every sense of the word—and a good one, too. Whatever Trojan is paying their marketing staff isn't enough because this team clearly demonstrated an uncanny ability to bait the media. Upon first glance, the news release seems credible. It's a list comprising 100 different universities and colleges across the U.S., ranked according to their level of sexual health. According to the news release's methodology, Sperling's Best Places— an agency that specializes in data analysis—appraised each school based on several different criteria, including:

- The availability of sex health information on a university's Web site.
- The availability of condoms and contraception on campus.
- Provision of HIV and STD testing at student health centers.
- Sexual assault counseling and services.
- Whether or not the university newspaper publishes a sex advice columnist or not.
- The proliferation of sex discussions on campus.

The criteria seem fairly reasonable, but bear in mind who's sponsoring and contracting the health report—Trojan. If the underlying message of the news release were boiled down to its most basic substance, it would be "Supply more condoms to university students and the national rate of STDs and unwanted pregnancies will decrease." The news release even included a plug for Trojan brand condoms, "America's No. 1 condom." What more can be expected? Trojan is a commercial business that profits from the sale of condoms. It's similar to a news release *The Daily Universe* received December

2005 from The Princeton Review and Wrigley. The Princeton review cited high numbers of stressed college students during final examinations and recommended chewing gum to abate the problem. Surprise, surprise, they said chewing gum reduces stress. I don't contest Trojan's right to distribute material promoting their products, but to do so under the guise of intellectual or academic qualifications is dishonest, to say the least. In fact, for Trojan to be ranking universities based on availability of condoms is like putting the rooster in charge of guarding the henhouse, as one of my professors phrased it. If the ranking were a genuine research project, it would be heavily challenged and picked apart under peer review. The fact that a company that has a demonstrated interest in the report's conclusions sired this study undermines it credibility because it neglects to include other solutions to help reduce the national rate of STDs.

It is a disappointment, but not a surprise, that the Trojan news release didn't list abstinence as a solution to the STD pandemic. It's not in their business' interests to promote alternatives that would compromise their sales promotion. Besides, since they ranked both BYU and Notre Dame at the bottom of the report card, they appear to believe abstinence-only policies must be at the root of the spike of STD rates. It's not an argument I'm unfamiliar with. Critics often assume the abstinence-only policy is a shabby attempt to address the spread of STDs and unwanted pregnancies without broaching the subject of sex. Teaching abstinence only worsens the problem, they claim, because it propagates ignorance about sexual health. Proponents of abstinence, they dispute, brainwash people to believe sex is "dirty," something to fear, something to sweep under the rug. Some critics punctuate their point by simplifying an abstinence talk into a satirical scenario:

"Son . . . uh, what do you know about abstinence?"
"Doesn't it mean don't have sex?"
"That's right. I'm glad we had this talk."

I concede critics' claims are not always untrue. In fact, I know several people who have grown up with a meager knowledge regarding sexual health because their parents were too reticent to talk about sex. The seven straight Fs the Trojan Health Report Card awarded BYU assume we, the college students, are a generation of young adults raised in a bubble, a throng of individuals who are void of any knowledge regarding sexual health. But, in Sperling's haste to assess our school, they failed to accurately depict the sexual health education we receive at BYU.

The news release's ranking system is severely flawed because Sperling representatives didn't contact a single administrator or student at BYU while they graded the university's sexual health services. They just surfed the BYU Web site to see what they could find on the issue. It's true the university's Web site doesn't dedicate a whole section to matters pertaining to sexual health, but that does not mean services aren't available on campus. The Women's Services and Resources Center frequently sponsors classes on healthy relationships, pornography addiction and seminars aimed to educate women on what to do if they are sexually assaulted. In addition, if Sperling researchers would have gone beyond the skim-only method, they would have discovered BYU's student health center does provide prescriptions for contraceptives and tests for HIV and STDs. These blunders and misrepresentations of fact show exactly how lackadaisically Sperling approached this study, but it also undercuts the study's authoritative statement that BYU students know little or nothing about sex.

We believe the subject of sex is a discussion that is too important to be left to a student to study on his or her own. Just because BYU students agree to practice strict abstinence doesn't mean we don't talk about sex or know nothing about it. I've enrolled in general requirement classes where we've discussed sexually transmitted diseases. I've sat through lectures where we've unabashedly discussed sexual intercourse. I know what a diaphragm is, and I know what a condom is. BYU students aren't as clueless as the 0.0 GPA implies. We understand the severity of becoming infected with a sexually transmitted disease. But more important than this, the religious climate of our school allows our discussions to transcend the mere physical consequences of sex. In an environment nurtured by understanding, we learn that the sexual relationship is one that encompasses a person's emotional and—dare I say it?—spiritual being. Contrary to critics' assumption, we don't think sex is filthy; we don't fear it; we don't sweep it under the rug. We believe that sex is the ultimate expression of love that should be reserved for one's spouse. Are our reasons primarily a matter of morality? Yes. But as time passes, our reasons are also becoming highly pragmatic as well. The policy of abstinence reaffirms our values, but it is also our way to curb the spread of STDs and unplanned pregnancies. According to Trojan's methodology, we are sexually unhealthy, but a less-subjective, more factual measure of sexual health proves otherwise.

If Trojan is correct in its assumptions, a school that ranks lower on its sexual health report should be more prone to a higher incidence of STDs and unwanted pregnancies. This trend should be manifest in credible, published statistics. Although it's difficult to procure numbers for the rate of STDs at BYU, we can examine the statistics of the Utah County Health Office, where the BYU Student Health Center, and a dozen other health centers, report their statistics annually. According to the Health Center, Utah County reported 94 people in 100,000 suffered from chlamydia in 2005, which is nearly a fourth of the national average. Health officials concede they saw a 50 percent increase in the number of chlamydia cases treated, but they attribute this increase to more efficient and acceptable testing methods, rather than a sudden outbreak. In addition to this low rate, the Utah Department of Health Web site stated Utah ranked 43rd with a gonorrhea rate of 28.8 cases per 100,000 people, compared with 113.5 cases per 100,000 nationwide. Also, the state of Utah ranked 37th for syphilis rates of .32 per 100,000. If Trojan factored these statistics into its ranking system, BYU would not have faired so poorly. Instead, Trojan opted not to include such statistics and chose rather to conduct biased research that would support their preconceived notions that those colleges with a higher visibility of sexual health services will naturally have a cleaner bill of health. But we cannot be naïve enough to believe throwing condoms at the problem, and drilling young people over and over again on the dangers of unprotected sex, will effectually solve the problem.

I don't discredit Trojan's intentions for drafting the news release. STD prevention is a serious issue we need to address. As Trojan stated, 65 million Americans suffer from an STD and, by the end of the year, another 19 million more will be infected. This pernicious plague not only causes untold physical and emotional suffering to those infected individuals, it also costs millions of dollars to treat annually. Trojan's intent to generate much-needed discussion is well placed. They are to be applauded for devising a marketing ploy that attracted so much attention and generated so much public discussion. But they demonstrated inadequate research methods and exercised preferential treatment, endorsing a course of action that favors their commercial interests. In determining which schools were sexually healthier than other schools based on subjective measures, rather than hard statistics, their findings inaccurately reflected BYU students as an uneducated horde whose "antiquated standard" of abstinence is counterproductive because it propagates ignorance about sexual health. But we believe our commitment to abstinence doesn't inhibit our knowledge about sexual health; it enables us to discuss sex from a physical, emotional and spiritual perspective. A long time ago, abstinence was purely a matter of morality and tradition. But the sexual revolution mitigated the social mores concerning abstinence and downplayed the special nature of the sexual relationship. Sex became as casual as a handshake, and, as a consequence, the spread of STDs has become just as casual. Attempts to counter the tide of STDs have improved over the years, but for all the technological advances, there is still no prophylactic as effective as abstinence. Trojan probably thought if they included this in their news release, it would compromise the strength of their assertion. Unfortunately, they didn't realize shabby research methods and prejudiced conclusions already weakened their assertion.

POSTSCRIPT

Does the Availability of "Sexual Health Services" Make Some College Campuses Healthier than Others?

It might be interesting to investigate how "sexually healthy" your college campus is, based on the criteria set forth in the Trojan report. (Take a look at the full list of rankings on the pages that follow.) If your university was ranked, do you agree with the report's assessment of your school? If your school was not ranked, how do you think it would fare? What is your university Web site like? Can you get accurate sexual information? The report mentioned Columbia University's Web site "Go Ask Alice!" as a model (see www.alice.columbia.edu). How would you rate this Web site? How about your school newspaper—is there a regular column for sexual advice or information?

How available are condoms or other contraceptives? Emergency contraception? If a student is worried about HIV or other sexually transmitted infections, can she or he get tested easily on campus? Is rape crisis counseling available? What types of counseling services are available? Does your college offer a "Sex Week" like Yale's or peer-counseling programs like those offered at many other universities?

Are these appropriate indicators of "sexual health"? What other indicators of sexual health would you identify? For students studying at religious institutions that might prohibit such sexual services, or require sexual abstinence of their students, what criteria do you think would be appropriate to measure sexual health? Should there be separate measurements based on the ideologies fostered by different school cultures?

Dr. Hall commented on studies of teens who pledge abstinence. This research examined high school-aged teens who make virginity pledges, and found that 88 percent of these teens fail to keep their pledge. Those who are more successful tend to delay sexual intercourse for about 18 months. Research on colleges that ask students to make an abstinence pledge in accordance with their policies has not yet been compiled. Do you think young adults would be more successful with abstinence pledges in college, or less successful? Why? Would your expectation be any different if the student were entering a university such as Brigham Young, where the student knows the school's expectations regarding student sexuality? Should a university offer preventative sexual health services, and treatment services for college students who change their decisions and decide to have sexual intercourse?

What do you think of Trojan issuing the report? Is it all about marketing hype (i.e., to sell more condoms), as Jens Alan Dana charges, and does that diminish the credibility or significance of the report's findings? Finally, what did you think of Dr. Hall's advocacy for sexuality education at the collegiate level? How does his description of effective sexuality education programs compare with the sex ed courses that you might have had at your university or high school?

Suggested Readings

M. Bruno, "New Survey Points to Disparity of Access to Information about Sexual Health on College Campuses Nationwide: Yale Tops List as Most Sexually Healthy on Trojan Sexual Health Report Card," *Edelman* (September 2006)

N. Doyle, "Auburn Ranks Low in Sexual Health Survey," *The Auburn Plainsman* (September 26, 2006).

S. Duin, "Orange and Black, Their Condoms Wave," *The Oregonian* (September 28, 2006).

C. Macbeth, "University Earns a Clean Bill of Health," *Yale Daily News* (September 26, 2006).

A. Mohler, "The Corruption of the University," www.albertmohler.com (September 2006).

S. Rosenbloom, "Here's Your Syllabus, and Your Condom," *New York Times* (September 24, 2006).

M. Slevin, "Monitoring Sex at C.U.," *The Cornell Daily Sun* (October 11, 2006).

C. Zach, "CSU Ranks 23rd in Sex Knowledge," *The Rocky Mountain Collegian* (October 30, 2006).

Table

Trojan Sexual Health Report Card Results

Complete Rankings

Rank	School	Score	Web site	Con-dom avail.	Contra-ception	HIV & STI testing	Sexual assault services	Advice column, Q&As	Lecture, outreach programs
1	Yale University	4.0	A	A	A	A	A	A	A
2	University of Iowa	3.6	A	A	A	A	B	A	C
3	University of Michigan–Ann Arbor	3.6	A	A	A	A	B	C	A
4	Stanford University	3.6	A	A	A	A	A	D	A
5	Oregon State University	3.4	B	A	A	C	A	A	B
6	Princeton University	3.4	A	A	A	C	A	C	A

Complete Rankings

Rank	School	Score	Web site	Con-dom avail.	Contra-ception	HIV & STI testing	Sexual assault services	Advice column, Q&As	Lecture, outreach programs
7	University of New Hampshire	3.4	A	A	A	C	A	C	A
8	Duke University	3.4	A	A	A	A	A	F	A
9	Ohio State University	3.3	A	C	A	A	B	C	A
10	University of Illinois at Urbana–Champaign	3.1	A	A	A	A	B	F	B
11	University of South Carolina–Columbia	3.0	B	A	A	A	B	F	B
12	New York University	3.0	A	A	A	C	B	F	A
13	Rutgers University–New Brunswick	2.9	B	F	A	B	A	A	C
14	University of North Carolina at Chapel Hill	2.7	B	F	A	C	B	B	A
15	Pennsylvania State University	2.7	B	F	A	A	C	B	B
16	George Washington University	2.7	A	F	A	C	C	A	B
17	University of Arizona	2.7	A	F	C	C	A	A	B
18	Johns Hopkins University	2.7	B	A	A	A	C	F	C
19	University of Nevada–Las Vegas	2.7	C	A	C	A	B	F	A
20	Syracuse University	2.7	A	F	A	A	B	D	B
21	University of Wisconsin–Madison	2.7	A	A	A	A	C	F	D
22	University of Rhode Island	2.6	B	A	C	C	C	C	B
23	Colorado State University	2.6	A	F	C	C	B	A	B
24	University of Alaska Anchorage	2.6	B	F	A	A	B	C	C
25	University of Georgia	2.6	A	F	A	C	C	A	C
26	University of Nebraska at Lincoln	2.6	B	F	A	A	B	F	A

Continued

Rank	School	Score	Web site	Con-dom avail.	Contra-ception	HIV & STI testing	Sexual assault services	Advice column, Q&As	Lecture, outreach programs
27	University of Cincinnati	2.4	B	A	D	C	C	C	B
28	University of Kentucky	2.4	B	A	C	C	B	F	B
29	University of Southern California	2.4	B	F	A	C	B	C	B
30	Louisiana State University A&M	2.4	B	F	C	C	B	A	B
31	University of Southern Mississippi	2.4	C	F	A	C	B	B	B
32	University of Colorado at Boulder	2.4	C	F	A	A	C	C	B
33	University of Vermont	2.4	B	F	A	F	B	A	B
34	Michigan State University	2.4	B	F	A	A	C	F	A
35	Montana State University-Bozeman	2.3	A	F	C	C	B	C	B
36	University of Oklahoma Norman Campus	2.3	B	F	A	C	C	B	C
37	North Carolina State University at Raleigh	2.3	A	F	A	C	C	C	C
38	Washington University in St. Louis	2.3	B	F	A	C	A	F	B
39	Texas A&M University	2.3	D	A	A	A	B	F	F
40	University of California–Berkeley	2.1	A	F	C	C	B	C	C
41	University of Virginia	2.1	B	F	B	B	C	B	D
42	University of Missouri–Columbia	2.1	B	A	D	D	B	F	B
43	Harvard University	2.1	B	F	A	C	B	F	B
44	Brown University	2.1	B	F	A	A	C	F	C
45	University of Hawaii at Manoa	2.1	C	F	A	A	B	F	C
46	Virginia Polytechnic	2.1	C	F	A	A	B	F	C
47	New Mexico State University	2.1	F	A	A	B	C	F	C

Rank	School	Score	Web site	Con-dom avail.	Contra-ception	HIV & STI testing	Sexual assault services	Advice column, Q&As	Lecture, outreach programs
48	Boise State University	2.0	B	F	C	C	B	C	C
49	University of Florida	2.0	C	F	A	D	C	C	B
50	University of Connecticut	2.0	D	A	A	C	C	F	D
51	Georgia State University	2.0	D	A	A	C	D	F	C
52	SUNY at Buffalo	2.0	C	F	A	A	C	F	C
53	The University of Texas–Austin	2.0	B	F	C	A	A	D	F
54	University of Minnesota–Twin Cities	2.0	B	F	F	A	B	F	A
55	University of Miami	1.9	C	F	A	C	C	C	D
56	Indiana University–Bloomington	1.9	B	F	A	C	D	C	D
57	University of Washington–Seattle Campus	1.9	C	F	A	B	C	D	D
58	Howard University	1.9	B	F	C	C	B	F	B
59	Purdue University	1.9	C	F	A	C	B	F	C
60	Kansas State University	1.9	B	F	A	C	B	F	D
61	University of Maryland–College Park	1.7	C	F	A	C	C	F	C
62	Washington State University	1.7	B	F	D	B	B	F	C
63	Dartmouth College	1.7	C	F	A	C	B	F	D
64	Auburn University	1.7	C	F	A	C	B	F	D
65	University of Pittsburgh	1.6	C	F	C	C	C	D	C
66	George Mason University	1.6	C	F	C	A	D	F	C
67	West Virginia University	1.6	D	F	A	C	B	F	D

Continued

Complete Rankings

Rank	School	Score	Web site	Con-dom avail.	Contra-ception	HIV & STI testing	Sexual assault services	Advice column, Q&As	Lecture, outreach programs
68	University of California–Los Angeles	1.4	C	F	C	B	C	F	D
69	Iowa State University	1.4	D	F	C	A	D	F	C
70	Arizona State University–Tempe Campus	1.4	D	F	A	C	C	F	D
71	The University of Alabama	1.3	D	F	C	D	D	C	C
72	University of Massachusetts–Amherst	1.3	D	F	C	C	C	F	C
73	Boston University	1.3	D	F	C	C	C	F	C
74	Mississippi State University	1.3	D	F	D	D	B	F	B
75	University of Delaware	1.3	C	F	A	D	D	F	D
76	University of Arkansas	1.3	D	F	A	C	D	F	D
77	University of Oregon	1.3	D	F	A	C	D	F	D
78	Texas Christian	1.1	C	F	C	D	D	F	C
79	University of Kansas	1.1	C	F	C	C	D	F	D
80	Georgetown University	1.1	D	C	C	C	D	F	F
81	University of Mississippi	1.1	D	F	C	C	C	F	D
82	South Dakota State University	1.1	D	F	D	B	C	F	D
83	Florida State University	1.1	C	F	C	C	C	F	F
84	Marquette University	1.1	D	F	F	C	B	F	C
85	University of North Dakota	1.1	D	F	F	A	F	D	C
86	University of New Mexico	1.0	C	F	D	C	D	F	D

Rank	School	Score	Web site	Con-dom avail.	Contra-ception	HIV & STI testing	Sexual assault services	Advice column, Q&As	Lecture, outreach programs
87	Temple University	1.0	D	F	C	D	C	F	D
88	The University of Tennessee	1.0	D	F	D	B	D	F	D
89	University of Maine	0.9	D	F	C	D	D	F	D
90	Minnesota State University–Mankato	0.9	D	F	D	C	D	F	D
91	University of Nevada–Reno	0.9	D	F	D	C	D	F	D
92	University of Wyoming	0.9	D	F	D	B	F	F	D
93	University of Louisville	0.7	D	F	F	C	D	F	D
94	Texas Tech	0.7	D	F	F	F	C	F	C
95	Clemson University	0.6	D	F	D	F	D	F	D
96	University of Memphis	0.3	D	F	F	F	F	D	F
97	Oklahoma State University	0.1	F	F	F	F	D	F	F
98	University of Utah	0.1	F	F	F	F	F	F	D
99	University of Notre Dame	0.0	F	F	F	F	F	F	F
100	Brigham Young University	0.0	F	F	F	F	F	F	F

Table

Trojan Sexual Health Report Card Fact Sheet

Key Study Findings

- This study represents 23 percent of total college students in the US and is representative of the college population
- 93 percent of schools surveyed offer some type of STD testing to students—with 24 percent offering free testing on campus
- Only 32 percent of schools have a sex advice column online or in the school paper
- With the exception of Oregon State University which received a B, all schools in the top ten received an A in the website category

Continued

- 76 percent of schools surveyed do not provide free condoms to students
- Regional breakdown of schools: 29 schools from the West, 27 schools from the South, 25 schools from the Northeast and 19 schools from the Midwest

1. Yale University
2. University of Iowa
3. University of Michigan–Ann Arbor
4. Stanford University
5. Oregon State University

6. Princeton University
7. University of New Hampshire
8. Duke University
9. Ohio State University
10. University of Illinois at Urbana–Champaign

11. University of South Carolina–Columbia
12. New York University
13. Rutgers University–New Brunswick
14. University of North Carolina at Chapel Hill
15. Pennsylvania State University

16. George Washington University
17. University of Arizona
18. Johns Hopkins University
19. University of Nevada–Las Vegas
20. Syracuse University

21. University of Wisconsin–Madison
22. University of Rhode Island
23. Colorado State University
24. University of Alaska Anchorage
25. University of Georgia

26. University of Nebraska at Lincoln
27. University of Cincinnati
28. University of Kentucky
29. University of Southern California
30. Louisiana State University A&M

31. University of Southern Mississippi
32. University of Colorado at Boulder
33. University of Vermont
34. Michigan State University
35. Montana State University–Bozeman

36. University of Oklahoma Norman Campus
37. North Carolina State University at Raleigh
38. Washington University in St. Louis
39. Texas A&M University
40. University of California–Berkeley

41. University of Virginia
42. University of Missouri–Columbia
43. Harvard University
44. Brown University
45. University of Hawaii at Manoa

46. Virginia Polytechnic
47. New Mexico State University
48. Boise State University
49. University of Florida
50. University of Connecticut

51. Georgia State University
52. SUNY at Buffalo
53. The University of Texas-Austin
54. University of Minnesota-Twin Cities
55. University of Miami

56. Indiana University–Bloomington
57. University of Washington–Seattle Campus
58. Howard University
59. Purdue University
60. Kansas State University

61. University of Maryland–College Park
62. Washington State University
63. Dartmouth College
64. Auburn University
65. University of Pittsburgh

66. George Mason University
67. West Virginia University
68. University of California-Los Angeles
69. Iowa State University
70. Arizona State University–Tempe Campus

71. The University of Alabama
72. University of Massachusetts–Amherst
73. Boston University
74. Mississippi State University
75. University of Delaware
76. University of Arkansas
77. University of Oregon
78. Texas Christian
79. University of Kansas
80. Georgetown University
81. University of Mississippi
82. South Dakota State University
83. Florida State University
84. Marquette University
85. University of North Dakota
86. University of New Mexico
87. Temple University
88. The University of Tennessee
89. University of Maine
90. Minnesota State University–Mankato
91. University of Nevada–Reno
92. University of Wyoming
93. University of Louisville
94. Texas Tech
95. Clemson University
96. University of Memphis
97. Oklahoma State University
98. University of Utah
99. University of Notre Dame
100. Brigham Young University

From press release by Trojan Brand Condoms, September 2006. Copyright © 2006 by Edelman. Reprinted by permission.

ISSUE 7

Should Sex Ed Teach about Abstinence?

YES: William J. Taverner, from "Reclaiming Abstinence in Comprehensive Sex Education," *Contemporary Sexuality* (2007)

NO: Maureen Kelly, from "The Semantics of Sex Ed: Or, Shooting Ourselves in the Foot as We Slowly Walk Backwards," *Educator's Update* (2005)

ISSUE SUMMARY

YES: William J. Taverner, sexuality educator and editor of *Taking Sides,* argues that sexuality education should teach about abstinence, and introduces a new model to replace problematic abstinence education models of the past.

NO: Sexuality educator Maureen Kelly argues that the framing of abstinence by conservatives has essentially made the term politically volatile, and that the one-size-fits-all definition has rendered the term useless to educators.

Should sex education teach students about abstinence? It sounds like a fairly straightforward question. Many who favor an abstinence-only approach to sex education might say, "Yes! Abstinence is the only 100% effective method for preventing pregnancy and the transmission of sexually transmitted infections (STIs). It should be the only thing we teach our students!" Others, who favor a comprehensive approach, might say, "Well, abstinence is an important concept, and we should include it in the discussion, as well as addressing other contraceptive methods and ways to prevent STIs." Some may say, "Since so many young people are already having sexual intercourse, why bother teaching abstinence?" Still others may say, "Wait—what exactly do you mean by abstinence?"

Surprising as it may sound, the definition of abstinence isn't as clear cut as one might think. And who holds the power to define the term at a particular point in time greatly adds to the confusion—and acceptance—of that definition. The strict, eight-point definition of abstinence education that *both*

Taverner and Kelly reject says that federally funded abstinence-only-until marriage education must:

1. Have as its exclusive purpose the teaching of the social, physiological, and health gains to be realized from abstaining from sexual activity;
2. Teach that abstinence from sexual activity outside of marriage is the expected standard for all school-age children;
3. Teach that abstinence from sexual activity is the only certain way to avoid out-of-wedlock pregnancy, sexually transmitted diseases, and other associated health problems;
4. Teach that a mutually faithful monogamous relationship in the context of marriage is the expected standard of human sexual activity;
5. Teach that sexual activity outside of the context of marriage may have harmful psychological and physical effects;
6. Teach that bearing children out-of-wedlock is likely to have harmful consequences for the child, the child's parents, and society;
7. Teach young people how to reject sexual advances and how alcohol and drug use increases vulnerability to sexual advances; and
8. Teach the importance of attaining self-sufficiency before engaging in sexual activity.

Sex educators often feel constrained by definitions and regulations handed down by agencies or governments. In some cases, they work within the system, following guidelines and adhering to definitions they may or may not agree with, but feel compelled to uphold. Others find creative ways to challenge definitions and expectations while still working within the specified framework. Some may disagree so strongly with the definitions that they reject them outright and actively seek systematic change. These are not uncommon occurrences in the paths of social movements. Which tactic is more effective is generally a matter of debate among academics, activists, and historians.

In the following essays, William J. Taverner, the director of the Center for Family Life Education, outlines a new framework for teaching about abstinence as a vital component of sexuality education. Maureen Kelly, vice president for education and training for Planned Parenthood of the Southern Finger Lakes, maintains that the framing of abstinence by conservatives has essentially made the term politically volatile, and that the one-size-fits-all definition has rendered the term useless to educators.

YES

William J. Taverner

Reclaiming Abstinence in Comprehensive Sex Education

Two e-mails I received came from separate ends of the ideological universe, as it relates to the abstinence-only-until-marriage verses comprehensive sex education culture wars, but both had a similarly hostile tone. The subject of this electronic wrath was the new theoretical and pedagogical concepts introduced in a sex education manual I coauthored with Sue Montfort, *Making Sense of Abstinence: Lessons for Comprehensive Sex Education* (Taverner & Montfort, 2005).

The first e-mail followed a very short editorial in the *Wall Street Journal* that commented on one of the themes of the manual—that it was necessary to discuss with youth the way they *define* abstinence, so as to better help them be successful with this decision. The e-mail began as follows:

> *Dear Mr. Taverner:*
> *Abstinence means NO SEX. Only a pointy head liberal could think there was some other definition, and it is pointy headed liberals that give liberalism a bad name. It takes the cake that you would . . . write some papers on trying to define abstinence. I have done that in four words above.*

More later on this writer's comments about defining abstinence—and on my seemingly pointy head, too! The more recent e-mail followed the announcement of the annual sex ed conference of The Center for Family Life Education (CFLE) that went to thousands of sex educators by e-mail. Themed on the manual, the announcement was titled "The Abstinence Experience: Teaching about Abstinence in the Context of Comprehensive Sex Education." The conference featured sex education leaders from prominent organizations—Answer (Formerly the Network for Family Life Education), the California Family Health Council, Montclair State University, the Sexuality Information and Education Council of the United States (SIECUS), and trainers from the CFLE. This e-mail read, simply:

> *Please REMOVE my email address from this mailing list. I am 100% against ABSTINENCE!*

This is not the first time someone has asked to be taken off the e-mail list. People ask to be unsubscribed when they are no longer working in the field of sex education, or when they only do so peripherally, or when their inboxes are generally too clogged. Usually the request to unsubscribe is polite. But beyond the rude tone of this request, the last sentence stopped me in my tracks:

I am 100% against ABSTINENCE!

The capitalized ABSTINENCE was the writer's doing, not mine. Did I read this right? Or did he mean he was against abstinence *education?* Maybe he meant *abstinence-only-until-marriage-education?* But I *did* read it correctly; in fact, I cut and pasted the writer's remarks to this article! He was against *ABSTINENCE.* How could that be? If a person chooses to abstain from sexual intercourse, or any other sexual behaviors, or drugs, alcohol, chocolate, or whatever, how could *anyone* be against that? And yet this is a common theme I have experienced since we wrote *Making Sense of Abstinence.* It seems some comprehensive sex educators and advocates are *turned off* by the word "abstinence." The atmosphere among some might best be described as anti-abstinence. The anecdotal evidence:

- Upon reviewing the final manuscript for our new abstinence manual, one well-respected reviewer asked not to be identified in the acknowledgments. She explained that while she thought the manual was great, she also thought it would be a bad career move to become too closely associated with the "world of abstinence."
- One prominent sex education leader urged us to reconsider the title of both our manual and our conference. He did not think we should be promoting abstinence, instead favoring the term "delaying intercourse." (Imagine a title such as *Making Sense of Delaying Intercourse*— what could more clearly illustrate the disconnect between adults and teens who *never* think of themselves as "delaying intercourse," but who *do* sometimes choose abstinence?)
- A CFLE educator having a casual conversation with a colleague asked if that colleague would be coming to our annual conference. The colleague said he had not yet received our flyer. The CFLE educator was surprised, since we had sent the flyers out over a month ago, and this individual had been on our mailing list for many years. Upon hearing the title of the conference, he replied, "That was *you?* I threw that out when I saw the word 'abstinence'!"

What was going on here? Sue Montfort and I spent a year and a half writing *Making Sense of Abstinence.* It was nominated for four sex ed awards, to date, winning two. It had been showcased by SIECUS at a Congressional Briefing in Washington, D.C. And yet while most colleagues were embracing this new model for abstinence education, some were clearly shunning the idea of *any* abstinence education.

My first real understanding of the distaste some sexologists have for the word "abstinence" came to light as I proudly stood by my "Making Sense of Abstinence" poster session at a conference of the American Association of Sexuality Educators, Counselors, and Therapists (AASECT). As colleagues walked by the four-panel poster that my intern, Laura Minnichelli, had created, many veered off their paths suddenly, as if the word "abstinence," would jump off the poster and bite them. Some looked briefly at the poster and gave a look of disgust, perhaps wondering how an "abstinence" poster infiltrated a sexology conference. Those who stopped to ask about it seemed puzzled initially. They saw the poster's worksheets on masturbation, outercourse, the lack of efficacy of virginity pledge programs, and they gradually came to recognize that this was a *different* type of abstinence program. As these thoughtful individuals left, they offered words of thanks and encouragement that there was *finally* a sex ed program out that there was reframing abstinence education.

There is no doubt that any self-respecting sex educator has good reason to be skeptical of a new abstinence manual. I can understand and even appreciate the sideways looks that sexologists give after ten years of federal funding for abstinence-only-until-marriage programs, and 25 years since the first "chastity education" federal funds were issued. Over $1 billion has produced curricula that are directive, simplistic and insulting to teens—programs that want to tell teens *what to think,* not how to *think for themselves.*

Abstinence-only-until-marriage programs virtually ignore the nearly 50% of teens who *are* having intercourse (Centers for Disease Control, 2006). They tell these teens to get with the program, but have no advice, otherwise, for teens that *don't* get with the program. At worst, they give misleading or inaccurate information about condom and contraceptive efficacy. These programs ignore lesbian and gay teens (and their families) who are told to abstain until marriage, but who don't have a legal right to marry, except those who are residents of Massachusetts. These programs produce virginity pledge programs, where 88% of teens who pledge virginity fail to keep that pledge, and are one-third less likely to use condoms at first intercourse (Brückner & Bearman, 2005).

There are many reasons to bemoan the current state of abstinence education, as it has been done so poorly. Just read Congressman Henry Waxman's report (U.S. House of Representatives, 2004). Perhaps consider the wisdom of Dr. Michael Carrera, who reminds us that expecting outcomes when we tell kids to "just say no," is no different than expecting a person's clinical depression to be treated by saying, "Have a nice day!" Or teacher/columnist Deborah Roffman, who compares abstinence-only education to the sex-hungry media: both, Roffman explains, tell teens exactly what to do. The media scream, "Always say yes," abstinence-only programs admonish, "Just say no," but *neither* encourage teens to *think* for themselves. That is, of course, the whole point of learning.

Certainly there are many reasons that justify the collective distaste for the current abstinence education paradigm among sex educators. The state of abstinence-only education is just awful, from the moralizing, shame and fear-based tactics to the sideshow industry that markets abstinence slogans on bill-boards, t-shirts, mugs, and even chewing gum. ("Abstinence gum—for *chewzing* an abstinent lifestyle.")

But all complaints about abstinence-only-until-marriage education aside, what is wrong with educating about the *choice* of abstinence? Doesn't the polling research say that American parents want their children to learn about abstinence? When comprehensive sex educators trumpet the latest polling data from groups like the Kaiser Family Foundation that says parents support comprehensive sex education, how do we miss the fact that the same polling data reveals parental desire for their kids to learn about abstinence? What are we doing about this, and how can we react to the word "abstinence" so negatively when we are supposedly teaching it as a *part* of comprehensive sex education?

A New Model

The pedagogical concepts introduced in *Making Sense of Abstinence* make it unlike any abstinence education manual produced to date. There are four key themes that are woven throughout the manual's sixteen lessons: (1) abstinence education needs to help young people *define* abstinence in ways that help them understand and apply their decisions in real life; (2) abstinence education needs to include decision-making, skills-building opportunities; (3) abstinence education is not just talking about which behaviors to *avoid*, but also the behaviors that are *permitted* in a person's decision; (4) abstinence education needs to help young people protect their sexual health, and transition safely when they decide to no longer abstain.

Defining Abstinence

Remember the guy who called me a "pointy headed liberal"? Define abstinence? Well, DUH! Abstinence means "no sex," right? Next time you are with a group of professionals, or a group of students, ask them to take out their cell phones and call three people. Have their friends, colleagues, coworkers, children, parents, etc. define the terms "sex" and "abstinence." You will be amazed, as I always am, with the discordant results you get. Do the definitions address only vaginal intercourse? Oral or anal intercourse? Other touching behaviors? Masturbation? What reasons or motivations emerge? Religious? Parental? Pregnancy prevention? Prevention of sexually transmitted infections? Assessing one's readiness? Marriage? Protecting one's mental health? When one person defines "sex," as "a loving, intimate, physical, connection between two people," does that mean that kissing is sex? And, thus, abstinence is no kissing? When one says, simply, that "abstinence means no sex," does this mean one must also avoid the aforementioned feelings of intimacy and love?

If this seems like a trivial exercise, consider the following definitions of abstinence printed or posted by a variety of health-promoting organizations:

> *"Abstinence is . . . not having sex with a partner. This will keep the sperm from joining the egg."* . . .

> *"Abstinence is . . . no intercourse. Not even any semen on the vulva. Pretty straight-forward."* (Kinsey Institute's Sexuality Information Service for Students)

Hmmm. So abstinence means no *vaginal* intercourse. But wait . . .

> *"For protection against infection . . . abstinence means avoiding vaginal, anal, and oral-genital intercourse, or participating in any other activity in which body fluids are exchanged."* . . .

So, the motivation here is avoiding infections that may be transmitted via body fluid exchange. This could include oral, anal, or vaginal intercourse. It also seems to refer tacitly to another fluid through which HIV could be transmitted: breast milk. So, does one practice abstinence by not breastfeeding her child? From the *Dictionary of Sexology* (Francoeur, 1997):

"A definition of abstinence may include not engaging in masturbation."

and

"The practices of tantric yoga recommend short periods of abstinence to concentrate one's sexual energy and prepare for more intense responses when sexual intercourse is resumed."

Ah, so abstinence is periodic, for the purpose of making sex *better!* How about some input from abstinence-only programs:

"Abstinence is . . . voluntarily refraining from all sexual relationships before marriage in order to uplift your own self-worth and provide the freedom to build character, develop career potentials and practice true love." (As cited by Kempner, 2001)

Abstinence for career potential? Never came up in my job interviews, but who knows today? Back to reality, Thoraya Obaid, executive director of the United Nations Populations Fund, reminds us that abstinence is not always a choice:

"Abstinence . . . is meaningless to women who are coerced into sex."

As I collected all these definitions, I was surprised when glossaries on websites for lesbian, gay, bisexual, and transgender teens repeatedly came up empty on definitions for abstinence. I asked my friend and colleague, Lis Maurer, about this. Lis is the director of Ithaca College's Center for LGBT Education and Outreach Services, and she explained:

I remember a high school class where we were taught about abstinence. Afterward, several of us non-straight students got together and reacted. Some said, "OK—we're totally in the clear!" Others said, "No, we were ignored—they really don't know we exist!" and yet others were just completely confused, as if the lecture was in some other language.

Finally, . . . sums up all this confusion quite nicely:

"Abstinence is . . . avoiding sex. Sex, of course, means different things to different people."

Indeed. What might abstinence mean to a teen?

"I'm proud that my boyfriend and I have decided to be abstinent. We have oral sex, but definitely not real sex, you know?

The importance of helping teens define abstinence cannot be under-scored enough. A recent evaluation of one abstinence-only program found that teens developed more positive attitudes toward abstinence following the program. That seems like good news, but the study went on to explain that "abstinence" meant "abstaining from sexual intercourse," which meant, "the male's penis is in the female's vagina. Some slang names for sexual intercourse are 'having sex,' 'making love,' or 'going all the way.'" (Laflin, et al, 2005). So while these teens were developing their positive feelings toward abstinence, they were learning nothing about how abstinence might *also* mean avoiding other sexual behaviors, including anal and oral intercourse that could trans-mit a sexually transmitted infection. The teen cited said earlier could easily have been a participant in this abstinence-only education program.

The evidence is clear that teens need opportunities to discuss what absti-nence means to them. They need worksheets, activities, and discussion oppor-tunities to reflect on their reasons for choosing abstinence, and specifically what behaviors they will avoid while abstaining. If they ultimately decide *not* to avoid oral sex, anal sex, etc., then they need further information about pro-tection from sexually transmitted infections.

Decision-Making, Skills-Building Lessons

Maybe you've seen a billboard sign that says, "VIRGIN: Teach Your Kid It's Not a Dirty Word!" Or maybe you're familiar with the slogan, "Quit your urgin', be a virgin!" One of the abstinence slogans that always gets a chuckle is "Good cow-girls keep their calves together." The list goes on and on, and many of them are cute, catchy, and memorable. But none of them speak to the complex decision-making skills that really need to be developed in young people to help them make decisions that are meaningful and responsible in their lives.

Young people need opportunities to develop concrete steps for "using" abstinence effectively. Abstinence is not just a state of being; it is a method to be *used*. This is an important distinction. The former implies passivity; i.e., no need to think about anything when abstinence is the foregone conclusion. The latter encourages young people to think about *how* they are going to be effective with their decisions, to develop the skills to be successful with their decisions, and to re-evaluate their decisions as need be.

Abstinence skills include learning to plan for sexual abstinence, and prac-ticing assertive communication, so that one can better stand up for one's deci-sions. It involves learning about sexual response, so that one can understand and manage their sexual feelings in ways that are consistent with their values and decisions. It involves negotiation and enforcing boundaries with one's partner. It involves so much more than "Just say no!" or other simplistic, "educational" approaches that are far more directive than they are educational.

A relatively new model, supported by the federal government seeks to improve upon abstinence-only programs by teaching an "ABC" model. ABC stands for "Abstinence," "Be faithful," and "Use Condoms," and unfortunately it is not much more comprehensive than its abstinence-only cousin. The United States exported its ABC's to Uganda for the purposes of HIV prevention. The hier-archical ABC approach stresses Abstinence first; while Be faithful reserved for those who can't seem to practice Abstinence; and Condoms are reserved strictly for the sex workers.

A closer look at this new sloganistic approach exposes a model that is devoid of critical thinking and skills building. For example, what if a person is using "B" but their partner isn't. That person is likely to learn about three new letters, "S," "T," and "D." Further, what if a person ditches "A," in favor of "B" without using C? Does anyone in these programs ever mention the possibility of an unplanned or unwanted "P"? Simplistic models like this continue to reveal the importance of helping young people think through their abstinence decisions and become effective abstinence users.

It's Not Just What You Avoid . . .

Why is it that we are not talking about masturbation when we are teaching about abstinence? Twelve years ago a U.S. surgeon general was fired for suggesting this might be a good idea. Masturbation is one of the safest sexual behaviors around, perhaps the safest. There is no risk of getting pregnant, no risk of getting a sexually transmitted infection, no risk of getting *anything*, except pleasure. As Woody Allen said, "Don't knock masturbation. It's having sex with someone you love!"

So why does masturbation have such a stigma in America. I have a clue that maybe it has something to do with the things that have been written about it. Sylvester Graham, a New York preacher, wrote in 1834 that a masturbator grows up:

> "with a body full of disease, and with a mind in ruins, the loathsome habit still tyrannizing over him, with the inexorable imperiousness of a fiend of darkness." (Graham, 1834)

And, in 1892, a prominent nutritionist, John Harvey Kellogg, wrote this:

> "As a sin against nature, [masturbation] has no parallel except in sodomy. The habit is by no means confined to boys; girls also indulge in it, though it is to be hoped, to a less fearful extent than boys, at least in this country. Of all the vices to which human beings are addicted, no other so rapidly undermines the constitution, and so certainly makes a complete wreck of an individual as this, especially when the habit is begun at an early age. It wastes the most precious part of the blood, uses up the vital forces, and finally leaves the poor victim a most utterly ruined and loathsome object.
> Suspicious signs are: bashfulness, unnatural boldness, round shoulders and a stooping position, lack of development of the breasts in females, eating chalk, acne, and the use of tobacco." (Kellogg, 1892)

No wonder the anxiety! It didn't matter that neither statement was true. People still flocked to buy the recommended antidotes, Sylvester's Graham crackers and Kellogg's Corn Flakes, both of which were supposed to suppress the urge to masturbate (and neither of which contained sugar or cinnamon in those days!).

More than a century later, our American culture still retains myths and misinformation. Perhaps if we can make young people feel a little less anxious about a behavior in which so many already engage, we can help them recognize masturbation as an important, safe *alternative* to intercourse.

Abstinence education needs to discuss other safe sexual behaviors, including outercourse, that get young people thinking about non-genital activities that are safe, and will keep them free of sexually transmitted infections and pregnancy. These behaviors—masturbation and outercourse—have inexplicably been omitted from abstinence-only curricula. It is as if we really think that if we don't mention these topics, teens won't think of it either! Have we really become that disconnected with our nation's youth? We really need to examine *why* information about masturbation and outercourse is omitted in abstinence education. Is it to keep information about sexual pleasure from young people? What gives educators the right to withhold *any* information from young people, especially information that might help keep them safe, while feeling positively about themselves?

Susie Wilson, who ran the Network for Family Life Education (now Answer), gave a review of *Making Sense of Abstinence,* and she put it better than I could have:

> "[Students] will learn that there is a long continuum of behaviors between "saying no" and "doing it" that will keep them safe, not sorry. Educators will feel more secure about teaching tough topics such as oral sex, masturbation and outercourse, when they see they are allied with discussion about personal values, decision-making and communication."

This is exactly what we are trying to do with our our model for abstinence education.

Help Young People Protect Themselves If/When Their Decisions Change

A final, critical part of abstinence education is the need to help young people protect themselves if and when their abstinence decisions change. It is no longer enough for us to bury our heads in the sand and just hope that teens remain abstinent through high school, college, and into young adulthood (or up until age 29, as the new federal abstinence-only guidelines suggest). We need to equip them with the skills to make that transition safely.

One way is to help them identify signs of *"sexual readiness"*. Students might read stories about other teens who are making sexual decisions, and assess and discuss how ready (or not) these teens are against any number of sexual readiness checklists. Consider these two teen quotes:

> "At times I get all hot with my partner and I feel like I really want to have sex. At other times, I know that I shouldn't have sex until I am ready. The problem is that sometimes I feel like I am ready and other times I feel like I am not ready. What should I do?"

and

> "I've been going out with this guy—he's 18. Everything was romantic at first, but now he's gotten real pushy. Last time we were alone, he gave me a

beer. I didn't feel like drinking, but he kept pushing it on me, so I drank it just to shut him up. Now he's pushing the sex thing on me. It's like we don't talk about anything but sex. I know he's tired of waiting for me, but I think things are getting out of hand, and I'm not sure I'm ready."

Both teens deserve much more than a catchy slogan. They need tools and discussion to help them identify how one knows when one is ready, and how to identify coercion in a relationship, and how to leave coercive relationships. We need to help young people actively think of their decisions in their sexual lives. Sexual intercourse is not something that people are just supposed to stumble into, without thinking of their decisions and their potential consequences. By contrast, the current culture of abstinence-only education supports teens making virginity pledges, which simply do not work. 88% of teens who make such a pledge break it! (Brückner & Bearman, 2005). And those teens are less likely to use protection, because they've never learned about condoms or contraceptives, or they've been taught only about failure rates.

In training teachers, I often say that "Sex education *today* is not necessarily for *tonight*." This is very applicable when it comes to abstinence education. We need to think about sex education in the context of a lifetime of sexual decision making, and abstinence as a conscious decision that is one's right to assert at anytime in their life. At the same time, we need to help teens gain knowledge and develop skills to protect their sexual health if and when they decide to no longer abstain, whether it is tonight, or in college, or when they celebrate a commitment ceremony, or after they walk down the aisle.

Young people need more from sex education. They need education that includes the *choice* to abstain. They need accurate information, not evasive, undefined terms, or misleading, or false information. Young people need and deserve respect, not to be subjected to scare tactics. They need to develop skills to be successful with abstinence; not to hear catchy slogans. They need to be met where they are, and recognized for their ability to make responsible decisions about their sexual lives. They need abstinence education, but they deserve better than what they've been getting so far.

References

Brückner, H. & Bearman, P. (2005). "After the promise: the STD consequences of adolescent virginity pledges," *Journal of Adolescent Health,* No. 36: 271–278.

Centers for Disease Control and Prevention. (2006). *Youth risk behavior surveillance—United States, 2005.* Atlanta, GA: Centers for Disease Control.

Francoeur, R.T. (1997). *The Complete Dictionary of Sexology,* New York: Continuum.

Graham, S. (1834). *A Lecture to Young Men on Chastity.* Boston, MA: Pierce.

Kellogg, J.H. (1892). *Plain Facts for Old and Young.* Burlington, IA: I.F. Segner.

Kempner, M.E. (2001). *Toward a Sexually Healthy America: Abstinence-Only-Until-Marriage Programs that Try to Keep Our Youth 'Scared Chaste.'* New York: Sexuality Information & Education Council of the United States.

Laflin, M.T., Sommers, J.M., & Chibucos, T.R., "Initial Findings in a Longitudinal Study of the Effectiveness of the *Sex Can Wait* Sexual Abstinence Curriculum for Grades 5–8," *American Journal of Sexuality Education,* 1(1):103–118.

Taverner, B. & Montfort, S. (2005). *Making Sense of Abstinence: Lessons for Compre-hensive Sex Education.* Morristown, NJ: The Center for Family Life Education, Planned Parenthood of Greater Northern New Jersey.

U.S. House of Representatives, Committee on Government Reform (2004). *The Content of Federally Funded Abstinence-Only Education Programs*, prepared for Rep. Henry A. Waxman. Washington, DC: The House, December 2004.

Maureen Kelly  **NO**

The Semantics of Sex Ed: Or, Shooting Ourselves in the Foot as We Walk Slowly Backwards

Should Sex Ed Teach about Abstinence?

No. And when I say no, I need to add two important caveats. First, I need to add quotation marks around the word "abstinence" because my answer pertains to the word "abstinence" not the life-affirming concept of personal choice and sexual decision-making across a vast span of sexual possibilities (more coarsely and simplistically placed on a continuum from not-doing to doing "it," whatever "it" may be). Second, when I refer to "abstinence" I am specifically referring to the strict eight-point definition of what "abstinence education" must include which is laid out in the 1996 federal Welfare Reform Law's abstinence-only-until-marriage provision. One highlight on the list of target groups for abstinence-only-until-marriage programs is all unmarried people under the age of thirty. Federally funded abstinence education for unmarried thirty year olds? Just say no.

Why do I take such issue with a word? In the dozen-plus years that I have worked as a professional sex educator I have watched secrets and lies take a growing hold on sex ed policies and programs. The highjacking of the word "abstinence" and the claiming of the moral high ground by opponents to sex ed is a striking example.

It's almost a cliché how the whole sex ed vs. abstinence ed debate has unraveled. It's just one more intentionally crafted pro vs. anti political dichotomy that infiltrates citizen's daily lives and choices. And one of the more cunning aspects of the "abstinence" conversation in America is that the Friday-night-wrestling-smack-down nature of the debate does not acknowledge that, once again, a political debate completely misses the obvious and neglects to uncover the fact that the extreme permutations of the political concept of "abstinence" as applied to health information content and funding, is a failure. Seek out the data! Read the reports! What did Waxman say? Look to Western Europe for innovative and effective roadmaps! But please, don't succumb to fear and politics and allow "abstinence" to be the only right, moral, good choice to make or lesson to teach; take a risk. Stir the pot.

We need to elevate this debate but I believe to do that we have to abandon the word "abstinence." However, when the pot is stirred, fear takes hold and people seem to freak out a bit.

When chatting about plans for an upcoming educational presentation, one teacher actually said "I didn't want a controversy, so I invited the abstinence people in." There's just so much wrong with this! First, I am amazed that a certified teacher does not find the contrary controversial! Isn't it far more controversial to deny information to youth, mislead kids about health facts, and to hold all youth to a singular heterosexual standard? And the sneaky underlying assumption is also flawed. To assume that good sex educators do not talk about sexual decision-making (of which NOT doing "it" is always an option!) is just wrong. Talking about personal sexual choices and teaching tips and tools for making effective and responsible and safe sexual decisions—yes *and no* decisions—are cornerstones of good sex ed. Again, it's dirty politics that tarnish this conversation, that make us focus our energy and worry on words and perceptions and fear of controversy or repercussions, not on young people. They are the ones losing!

The problem here is language. Semantics. Let's look at *abstinence*. Now, as a concept, abstinence is without moral judgment, without coercion and does not withhold information. Abstinence is simply about *not doing something*. People abstain from a lot of things. Certain foods, voting, paying taxes, alcohol; the scope of *abstinence* as a concept is deep and broad and has a rich social, religious, and political history filled with social protest and acts of resistance. The "abstinence" vis-à-vis sex ed discussion certainly has all that too!

As you may notice, I've been pissed off about this word for a while now. My anger bubbles up from a place of disbelief about how some people can't see the truth. I am incensed when I see people who, once exposed to the truth, whatever that truth may be—the war, gay marriage, taxes, sex ed—don't act in accordance with that truth but rather, stick fiercely to their strongly held beliefs even when they are in direct conflict with the facts.

I am also deeply troubled by the reality that many of us—sex ed advocates and educators—have gotten sucked into the defensive, no-win abstinence debate. We have science, data, a majority of parents, common sense and all of Western Europe on our side in support of smart and sane sex ed but we are losing. We are losing because we are hemorrhaging from our defensive wounds.

And, thanks to George Lakoff (UC Berkeley linguistics professor and Rockridge Institute Fellow) I have shifted from a full pissed off boil to a smarter, more informed and productive simmer. Here's why: I've been mad at the wrong things. I have been mad at issues and people, not frameworks. Although I flirt with stepping above the fray and getting glimpses of why people act (and vote) the way they do, I haven't quite grasped the depth and breadth of the real battle being waged. What has facilitated this transformation are insights from Mr. Lakoff's 2004 book *Don't Think of an Elephant: Know Your Values and Frame the Debate—The Essential Guide for Progressives* combined with reactions and reflections about how the brilliance of framing—and reframing—can help us win the sex ed war.

First and foremost, we must begin by understanding the power of mental structures—the power of *frames*. Frames are the ties that bind; they are the unconscious connectors that define our actions, reactions, perceptions and worldview. Frames are about way more than just the words; ideas are the foundation for the frame and the words are the messengers that deliver the ideas. And simply enough, in order to change the world, we must understand and acknowledge the power of these frames—as words *and* ideas—and then go about the vital business of changing them; *reframing is social change.*

> Reframing is changing the way the public sees the world. It is changing what counts as common sense. Because language activates frames, new language is required for new frames. Thinking differently requires speaking differently.[1]

The progressive movement as a whole, and we, as sex ed advocates and educators, are caught in a defensive cycle marked by reaction to words and ideas and philosophies that do not represent our view, our thinking and what we know to be true and right. As we do this we are unwittingly giving credibility to a frame that we do not believe.

Our opponents brilliantly crafted a powerful frame around "abstinence" that conjures a happy, ideal fairyland where kids are safe and protected from the mean, scary and unpredictable world. Who the heck wouldn't want that? I *love* the idea of protecting the young people I care about from bad things; it's a natural urge. So, when I say "no, I am against abstinence" (as a political and social means of control and a troubling marriage of church and state) I am in essence rejecting their frame yet still defining myself through their frame. That's where it gets really confusing! By being opposed to their idea but using their words, I end up standing for nothing.

Because, when I say "I am against abstinence," I am in effect saying, "I want kids to be unsafe, unprotected and get exposed to mean, scary and unpredictable things" (because that's what happens when you make your argument based on your opposition's language rather than your own inspiration). And none of us want that! We are caught in a defensive loop trying to explain that, yes, we believe in abstinence (safe, happy protected kids) but we want abstinence-plus or abstinence-based education (if they do end up having sex, they should have access to information and supplies that protect them); this approach is totally wrong. We are, by default, accepting our opponents' framework while trying to add our own footnote. And we have forgotten that most people don't read footnotes.[2]

One particularly troubling outcome of our tacit acceptance of our opponent's framing of abstinence is that we can easily be dismissed as confused and inconsistent (if we are for abstinence, as their frame defines it, how in the world can we be for birth control education for youth as well?). We seem to forget that "abstinence" as used by our opponents is not at all akin to the actual definition of the word, but rather it evokes a feeling, a philosophy and an idea—a frame—that is diametrically opposed to our view. The simple act of using the word "abstinence"—*no mater how we might mean it*—activates their frame, not ours. We are shooting ourselves in the foot as we walk slowly backwards.

> This gives us a basic principle of framing, for when you are arguing against the other side; do not use their language. Their language picks out a frame—and it won't be the frame you want.[3]
>
> Framing is about getting language that fits your worldview. It is not just language. The ideas are primary—and the language carries those ideas, evokes those ideas.[4]

Another problem; our in-fighting divides us and keeps us vulnerable. Why are some of us taking abstinence money and others lobbying their States to give it all back to the Feds? Why do some of us want to feverishly reclaim the language of "abstinence" while others want to totally eradicate it from our parlance? We have to ask these questions, talk about them and commit to finding and applying a common approach. We must get beyond the "my way is the right way" division of our field. We are stuck and until we step above this soul sucking and divisive in-fighting to discover and capitalize on the unity of our movement, our fight will remain amongst ourselves and do little to change the world. As all this swirls around us, we are rendering our own work less and less effective, articulate and strong because *we are fighting among ourselves in service of their vision, not ours.* We must stop our own in-fighting, stop fighting their war for them, stop using the word "abstinence" and take a bold and brave step right off the battlefield and say, why the heck are we fighting here any way? It's a bad war, not based on truth and it's not good for our country or our kids, period.

So, what should we do about this? We need to intentionally and thoughtfully become the object-center of our debate; we need to reframe our arguments for and definitions of sex ed in reference to *our* values, vision and morality; not in reference to our opponents'. We must remember that when we attack our opponents' stance by disagreeing with it but building on it rather than offering a viable alternative, we fail to move our agenda forward. *Our agenda?* Yes! Our Agenda. We do have one and we need to talk about it more.

And to do that, we have to take one more step inside Lakoff's world. We need to understand the dynamic of the strict father vs. nuturant parent paradigm. It is this paradigm that exposes the stark differences of vision and value between our opponents and us. It is precisely why, when I listen to the rhetoric of our opponents, I cringe. Why? I don't subscribe to the Strict Father frame. I'm more of a nurturant chick. At my core, I don't buy into the Father Knows Best, teach kids what to think not how to think, pick-yourself-up-by-your-bootstraps, stop your crying or I'll give you something to cry about, one nation under god, don't have sex until you're married paradigm. Conversely, I'm more of a fan of empathy and nurturance, open, two-way communication, honesty, choice, trust, integrity, opportunity and freedom.

To be effective in re-framing our version of what sex ed should be, we must understand that we cannot simply borrow from the strict father foundation of the abstinence-only-until-marriage frame, but rather, we must create and propose new and radical ideas that evoke a distinct and powerful frame that encompasses the spirit of nurturance. By nature, that cannot be a frame based on an abstinence-plus message, in fact, to be most effective, it will be an antithetical concept compared to the spirit of current abstinence messages touted by the strict father moralists.

Our version of sex ed is about asking, choosing, discussing, considering, exploring, learning, and offering open, honest access to information and exposure to diverse options. Now, that's a real alternative to the abstinence-only-until-marriage model! Maybe ours is called the teach-me-trust-me-and mentor-me model? Or maybe the Freedom, Opportunity and Awareness Act of 2007? To be successful in reframing our work, we must understand that the battle for sex ed is a sub-battle that shares values and vision with the progressive movement as a whole. And, as we get better at gathering around our common goals—and investing less in the self-defeating, chase your own tail, me-first conundrum that is identity politics—we will triumph. Our ideas resonate with people; we simply need to find the words that resonate as much as our ideas.

But fear sells. So, we need to tell the truth and bust the myth that "abstinence will save the world" because it's just not true. The fear is real and visceral for those who worry that if we talk to kids about sex they will transmogrify into sex crazed, insatiable fiends without remorse, protection or forethought (sounds more like a member of congress than a teen who got honest and complete sex ed). The great irony is, that despite their hearts being in the right place (*we all want our kids to be OK, safe and smart!*) they have it all wrong. The fact is, the more we talk about sex in age appropriate, frank, honest, accurate ways, the *safer our kids are.* Yes, despite the fears and worries of well meaning people *when we don't give our kids sex ed, we end up with much bigger problems than when we do.* Just look at our teen pregnancy, STD and abortion rates for that evidence!

And then, take a look at western Europe as an example of what could be. Young people in Germany, the Netherlands and France are given a lot of education and access to information about s-e-x. But here's the kicker—these European kids that are getting all this sex ed early and often, they are having less sex, with fewer partners, at a later age than their US peers, with less negative outcomes, fewer abortions, fewer teen births, and fewer STDs.[5] No kidding. It seems that the more we take the shame and taboo-filled mystique from sex and help it assume a normal, natural, spoken about and human part of our lives, the better off we all are.

So what do I propose as alternatives to abstinence-only-until-marriage programming for our kids? Simple: teach the facts, tell the truth, and include everyone. We need to work side by side to remove the shame and secrecy that shrouds our conversation and education about sex. It's the shame and secrecy that truly put our kids at risk, not sex ed.

I would like to eradicate the use of the word "abstinence" while explicitly and frequently teaching about the concept of choice vis-à-vis sex. Teach about when or whether to have sex. Teach about sexual choices and safety and responsibly. Teach about saying yes and teach about saying no. Just TEACH!

The complexities of sex, relationships and communication require depth and
• breadth in teaching style; not a one-size-fits-all-just-say-no approach.
    We have to talk about it and prepare for it, because sex is a part of life.

Notes

1. Page xi, *Don't Think of an Elephant! Know Your Values and Frame the Debate: The Essential Guide for Progressives,* George Lakoff, Chelsea Green Publishing, 2004
2. Just checking. . .
3. page 3, op cit
4. page 4, ibid
5. Advocates for Youth, . . ."European Approaches to Adolescent Sexual Behavior & Responsibility," 1999.

POSTSCRIPT

Should Sex Ed Teach about Abstinence?

Academics, educators, and activists may often agree on a desired outcome, but may strongly disagree on the best approach to meet that end. In her essay, Maureen Kelly argues that sex educators' use of the "frame" of abstinence only helps to serve a conservative agenda that promotes abstinence as the *only* acceptable means of contraception and STI prevention. She challenges the way in which abstinence was defined by the federal government and rejects the use of the term. Taverner embraces the term while working to challenge its definition from within the existing structure. Is Taverner shooting himself, and the movement for comprehensive sex education, in the foot, as Kelly suggests, by using the terminology of a system he seeks to question? Should Kelly and other sex educators reclaim the language of abstinence as part of comprehensive sex education, as Taverner suggests?

Should sex educators challenge preconceived notions of topics like abstinence while working within federal guidelines for abstinence-only education? What might be the benefits of such an approach? What might be the consequences? How can an educator challenge students to think about the definition(s) of abstinence and apply the possible meanings to their own decisions? In his essay, Taverner mentions a colleague proposing "delayed intercourse" as an alternative term to abstinence. Do you think Kelly would accept this term?

A new bill is being considered by Congress that would allow federal funding for more comprehensive approaches to sexuality education that *both* Taverner and Kelly might champion. This bill would require programs to:

1. Be age-appropriate and medically accurate;
2. Not teach or promote religion;
3. Teach that abstinence is the only sure way to avoid pregnancy or sexually transmitted diseases;
4. Stress the value of abstinence while not ignoring those young people who have had or are having sexual intercourse;
5. Provide information about the health benefits and side effects of all contraceptives and barrier methods as a means to prevent pregnancy;
6. Provide information about the health benefits and side effects of all contraceptives and barrier methods as a means to reduce the risk of contracting sexually transmitted diseases, including HIV/AIDS;
7. Encourage family communication about sexuality between parent and child;
8. Teach young people the skills to make responsible decisions about sexuality, including how to avoid unwanted verbal, physical, and

sexual advances and how not to make unwanted verbal, physical, and sexual advances; and

9. Teach young people how alcohol and drug use can affect responsible decision making.

How does this approach differ from the current federal guidelines listed in the introduction to this issue? In what ways are they similar? Which approach would you want for your children? Which of these items do you agree with? Disagree with? What do you think of the government saying that sexual behaviors should happen only within the context of marriage? Or claiming that people will suffer harmful psychological effects if they have sexual behaviors outside of marriage? Furthermore, how does a gay or lesbian person handle the message "abstinence until marriage" in a country that, except for Massachusetts, makes same-sex marriages illegal?

Think back to your own sexuality education in high school. Did it include learning about condoms, contraception, and other aspects of human sexuality? Was abstinence taught? And if so, was it within the framework of the federal guidelines described by Kelly, or was it more comprehensive, as Taverner describes? If you had to give your high school sex education a grade, what would it be?

Suggested Readings

Advocates for Youth and Sexuality Education Council of the United States, *Toward a Healthy America: Roadblocks Imposed by the Federal Government's Abstinence-Only-Until-Marriage Education Program* (2001).

J. Blake, *Words Can Work: When Talking to Kids about Sexual Health* (Blake Works, 2004).

Brückner, H. & Bearman, P. "After the Promise: The STD Consequences of Adolescent Virginity Pledges," *Journal of Adolescent Health,* no. 36, pp. 271–278 (2005).

Kempner, M.E. *Toward a Sexually Healthy America: Abstinence-Only-Until-Marriage Programs that Try to Keep Our Youth 'Scared Chaste'* (New York: Sexuality Information & Education Council of the United States, 2001).

D. Satcher. *The Surgeon General's Call to Action to Promote Sexual Health and Responsible Sexual Behavior* (Washington, D.C.: United States Department of Health and Human Services, 2001).

Taverner, B. & Montfort, S. *Making Sense of Abstinence: Lessons for Comprehensive Sex Education* (Morristown, NJ: The Center for Family Life Education, Planned Parenthood of Greater Northern New Jersey, 2005).

U.S. House of Representatives, Committee on Government Reform. *The Content of Federally Funded Abstinence-Only Education Programs,* prepared for Rep. Henry A. Waxman (Washington, DC: The House, December 2004).

ISSUE 8

Should Children Have an HPV Vaccination before They Enroll in School?

YES: Cynthia Dailard, from "The Public Health Promise and Potential Pitfalls of the World's First Cervical Cancer Vaccine," *The Guttmacher Report on Public Policy* (Winter 2006)

NO: Roni Rabin, from "A New Vaccine for Girls, but Should It Be Compulsory?" *New York Times* (July 18, 2006)

ISSUE SUMMARY

YES: Cynthia Dailard, a senior public policy associate for the Alan Guttmacher Institute, outlines the potential for a new vaccination to prevent the spread of the human papillomavirus (HPV), a sexually transmitted infection that causes genital warts and most cases of cervical cancer. Dailard explains and summarizes the views of experts who believe that widespread vaccinations of preadolescent girls will dramatically reduce the incidence of HPV in the United States and abroad, especially in developing nations.

NO: *New York Times* columnist Roni Rabin acknowledges the potential for the HPV vaccination, but contends that cervical cancer can be staved off more economically by encouraging girls and women to have routine Pap smears.

What is HPV? Many people who know about sexually transmitted infections (STI), like genital herpes, gonorrhea, and HIV, seem to be surprisingly unfamiliar with the term human papillomavirus (HPV). Yet HPV is one of the most common STIs in the United States! The acronym HPV includes more than 100 strains of viruses, about 30 of which can infect the genital area. The Centers for Disease Control (CDC) estimates that 20 million Americans are currently infected with HPV, and that 6.2 million Americans are newly infected every year. The CDC further estimates that at least *half* of people who have intercourse will acquire HPV at some point in their lives, and that at least 80 percent of women will have acquired genital HPV infection by age 50. Some

HPV infections can cause cervical cancer. Strains of HPV can sometimes cause genital warts. Genital or anal cancers caused by HPV are possible, but rare.

In June 2006, the United States Food and Drug Administration (FDA) approved a new cervical cancer vaccine called Gardasil. The decision was met with an enthusiastic response from health care providers around the world. The vaccine works by protecting against two strands of the HPV that are responsible for over 70 percent of all cervical cancers. In order to be most effective, women need to be vaccinated before they begin having sexual intercourse.

The introduction of the vaccine was not without controversy. Many public health officials were quick to praise the vaccine and encourage its use. Some even called for the mandatory vaccination of elementary school girls. Other groups voiced strong objections to the vaccine and mandatory vaccinations. Bridget Maher, spokesperson for the Family Research Council (FRC), a conservative Christian group, was quoted in *New Scientist,* and other sources, as saying, "Giving the HPV vaccine to young women could be potentially harmful, because they may see it as a license to engage in premarital sex." The FRC and other abstinence-until-marriage-promoting organizations stressed that sexual abstinence was the only effective way to prevent HPV and all other sexually transmitted infections.

The Religious Right's initial focus on the potential sexual "promiscuity" that vaccines might bring eventually yielded, as conservatives reframed the debate to be about the impact of *mandatory* vaccinations. They warned that compulsory vaccinations violated "parents' rights" to make decisions for their children, and explained that young people who did not have sex before marriage need not worry about HPV or any other infections.

Vaccine proponents countered that vaccinating girls against HPV would not make them more likely to engage in unprotected intercourse, and that parents should be sure to discuss the risks of contracting other STIs with their children as part of a continuing dialogue about healthy sexuality.

Other angles of debate formed, with some commentators simply distrustful of vaccines, despite evidence and reassurance from the CDC that the "risks of serious disease from not vaccinating are far greater than the risks of serious reaction to a vaccination." And still others argued that maybe they needn't be mandatory because routine Pap smears already do a good job at detecting cancerous cells.

In the following essays, Cynthia Dailard, a senior public policy associate for the Alan Guttmacher Institute, presents the case for early vaccination, while acknowledging concerns that some may have. *New York Times* columnist Roni Rabin argues that mandatory vaccination against HPV is unnecessary, especially when considering cervical cancer is generally detected and treated early through the practice of regular Pap smears.

YES

Cynthia Dailard

The Public Health Promise and Potential Pitfalls of the World's First Cervical Cancer Vaccine

After a decade in development, a cervical cancer vaccine appears poised to become available to American women later this year. Given the vaccine's demonstrated high level of effectiveness in preventing transmission of the two strains of human papillomavirus (HPV) responsible for most cases of cervical cancer, researchers believe that widespread vaccination has the potential to reduce cervical cancer deaths around the world by as much as two-thirds. The vaccine, therefore, holds the promise of being an enormous public health advance, both for women in the United States and for women in developing countries, who disproportionately bear the global burden of cervical cancer.

Because HPV is sexually transmitted, experts say the vaccine needs to be administered to as many young adolescent females as possible prior to sexual activity to achieve maximum effectiveness. Adolescents, however, are typically considered to be a difficult population to reach through immunization programs. For the HPV vaccine, moreover, the politics of teen sex are likely to exacerbate many of the practical challenges involved in achieving high vaccination rates—practical challenges that are magnified exponentially in developing countries, where the vaccine is needed most.

What the Science Says

Virtually all cases of cervical cancer are linked to HPV, an extremely common sexually transmitted infection (STI) that is typically asymptomatic and harmless; most people never know they are infected, and most infections typically resolve on their own. The infection is so common, in fact, that it is considered virtually a "marker" for sexual activity; according to a 1997 *American Journal of Medicine* article, nearly three in four Americans between the ages of 15 and 49 have been infected with HPV at some point in their life.

Of the 30 known types of HPV that are sexually transmitted, more than 13 types have the potential to lead to cervical cancer; two of these types, HPV 16 and 18, are associated with 70% of all cases of cervical cancer. In the United States, notwithstanding the prevalence of HPV infection, cervical cancer is

Dailard C, The public health promise and potential pitfalls of the world's first cervical cancer vaccine, *Guttmacher Policy Review*, 2006, 9(1):6–9. Reprinted by permission.

relatively rare. This is largely due to the widespread availability of Pap tests, which can detect cervical cancer in its earliest and most treatable stages, as well as precancerous changes of the cervix, which can be treated before cervical cancer sets in. Nonetheless, the American Cancer Society estimates that in 2006, almost 10,000 cases of invasive cervical cancer will occur in American women, resulting in 3,700 deaths. More than half of all U.S. women diagnosed with cervical cancer have not had a Pap test in the last three years. These women are disproportionately low-income women and women of color who lack access to basic health services.

In resource-poor developing countries, the incidence of cervical cancer is much higher, and the disease is far more lethal. Of the 225,000 annual deaths from cervical cancer globally, 80–85% occur to women in developing countries. Most of these deaths occur in Sub-Saharan Africa, South Asia and Latin America—where the public health infrastructure is extremely poor and basic preventive health services such as Pap smears are largely unavailable. Because women in these regions typically do not receive care until their disease is well advanced, it is usually fatal (related article, August 2003, page 4).

A cervical cancer vaccine would therefore represent an enormous step forward for women's health. There are actually two currently under development. Merck & Company filed an application for approval of its vaccine, Gardasil, with the federal Food and Drug Administration (FDA) in December; it expects an expedited decision—which is reserved for medications that treat unmet medical needs—from the agency in June. It has also submitted applications to regulatory agencies in Europe, Australia, Mexico, Brazil, Argentina, Taiwan and Singapore. GlaxoSmithKline will be seeking regulatory approval of its vaccine, Cervarix, in Europe in March 2006 and at the end of the year in the United States. Both vaccines target HPV 16 and 18, although Merck's vaccine also offers protection against two types of HPV that cause almost all cases of genital warts. A consortium of agencies funded by the Bill & Melinda Gates Foundation, and which includes Harvard University, the International Agency for Research on Cancer, PATH and the World Health Organization, is laying the groundwork for implementation of the vaccine in the developing world, expecting that it may be licensed in selected developing countries as early as 2007.

Targeting Teens

To become widely available in the United States, a vaccine must win the endorsement of the Advisory Committee on Immunization Practices (ACIP) in addition to FDA approval. Organized by the federal Centers for Disease Control and Prevention (CDC), ACIP is a 15-member panel authorized under federal law to recommend who should receive a vaccination, when and how often they should receive it, and the appropriate dosage. In deciding whether to recommend a vaccine, the committee must weigh a host of factors, including efficacy, benefits and risks, and cost-effectiveness. It also determines whether the vaccine should be available through the federal Vaccines for Children Program, which provides free vaccines to doctors serving eligible low-income children. Although ACIP's recommendations are not binding, they are followed closely by physicians and medical professional organizations, and ACIP's endorsement determines with virtual certainty whether a vaccine becomes the standard of care in this country. ACIP recommendations are also widely relied upon by insurers for setting reimbursement policy and by states for public funding purposes.

Perhaps the single most important decision for ACIP will be the optimal age for administering an HPV vaccine. While the typical American female has intercourse for the first time at age 17, 13% do so prior to age 15, according to the 2002 National Survey of Family Growth. Because HPV infection is so widespread, most cases of HPV are acquired soon after women become sexually active, with the peak incidence currently occurring at age 19. Merck's trials, moreover, found that the vaccine produced a stronger immunological response in adolescents aged 10–15 than in women aged 16–23. For these reasons, both Merck and GlaxoSmithKline are recommending that all girls receive their vaccines when they are 10–12 years old.

There are other practical reasons for targeting this age-group. In order to address the historical lack of emphasis on adolescent immunization, ACIP, the American Academy of Pediatrics, the American Association of Family Physicians and the American Medical Association in 1996 jointly identified ages 11–12 as the optimal time for adolescent immunizations. Currently, the federal Childhood and Adolescent Immunization Schedule recommends that every 11–12-year-old receive two vaccines (a new vaccine for bacterial meningitis and a combined booster for tetanus, diphtheria and whooping cough); it also recommends that they be assessed for "catch-up" shots at that time.

If the vaccine is recommended for preadolescent girls, acceptability among pediatricians and parents will be key to its success. Survey results released in October by researchers from the CDC and the University of California found that most pediatricians would be willing to administer the vaccine to their patients. And, several surveys of parents published in 2005 in the *Journal of Adolescent Health* and elsewhere suggest that parental acceptance of the vaccine will in fact be high. Many of those surveyed who initially expressed reservations about the vaccine changed their minds when educated about HPV and cervical cancer, suggesting the importance of counseling and education targeting parents during an adolescent health visit.

Finally, each state decides for itself whether a particular vaccine will be required in order for children to enroll in school, and they typically rely on ACIP recommendations in making this determination. According to a 2005 report on adolescent vaccination by the National Foundation for Infectious Diseases (NFID), school-based immunization requirements are by far the most effective means to ensure rapid and widespread use of childhood or adolescent vaccines. Adolescents are typically a hard-to-reach population for vaccine programs, and adding a vaccine to the list of those required for school enrollment boosts vaccination rates considerably—and far more effectively than guidelines recommending the vaccine for certain age-groups or high-risk populations. NFID also notes that timing an adolescent vaccination to middle school entry (ages 11–12) is important given that dropout rates begin to climb at age 13. Along these lines, younger dropouts are at particularly high risk of early sexual activity and poor sexual and reproductive health outcomes, suggesting an even greater imperative for a school-based requirement targeting 11–12-year-olds.

The Politics of Teen Sex

No sooner had Merck publicly announced the results of its long-term clinical trials in October 2005 than conservative activists began suggesting that inoculating young adolescents against HPV would encourage teenage sexual promiscuity. The heads of various "family values" groups publicly declared that they would not vaccinate their own children. Vaccination "sends the wrong message," asserted Tony Perkins of the Family Research Council (FRC). "Our concern is that this vaccine will be marketed to a segment of the population that should be getting a message about abstinence." This shot across the bow signaled that the cervical cancer vaccine could become the next battlefront in the social conservatives' crusade to advance an abstinence-only-unless-married agenda, and that leading activists would be working to ensure that it would meet the same regulatory fate as efforts to bring emergency contraception over the counter.

Yet, these same groups now appear to be softening their stance. A statement on the FRC website now says that "media reports suggesting that the Family Research Council opposes all development or distribution of such vaccines are false" and that it "welcomes the news that vaccines are in development." At the same time, the statement warns, "we will seek to ensure that there is full disclosure to the public of what these vaccines can and cannot achieve, their efficacy, and their risks (including side effects) and benefits. We believe that adults must be provided with sufficient information to make an informed, free choice whether to vaccinate either themselves or their children for HPV."

Whether the new FRC statement heralds a genuine change in posture on the part of social conservatives remains to be seen. A more likely scenario, perhaps, is that leaders of that movement have made a tactical decision not to oppose federal approval of the cervical cancer vaccine outright but, rather, to hold their fire for 50 state battles over whether the vaccine will be mandatory for middle and high school students. The public health ramifications of such a decision could still be significant. Because universal uptake of the vaccine will have the most impact on cervical cancer rates, efforts designed to prevent mandatory vaccination programs in the name of "parental control" may ultimately hinder the eradication of cervical cancer in the United States.

Beyond Politics

Beyond these political challenges, the impending roll-out of a cervical cancer vaccine raises some very serious practical challenges, as well as a range of longer-term scientific, logistical and policy questions that must be confronted over time (see box). One immediate challenge, for example, is successfully providing the vaccine's three required doses over a six-month period to adolescents, who, unlike infants and toddlers, do not typically make frequent, successive visits to a doctor's office or health care clinic. Moreover, the three-shot regimen is likely to be relatively expensive—somewhere in the vicinity of $100–150 per shot, according to newspaper reports. And since ongoing clinical trials to date have only demonstrated the vaccine's effectiveness for four years, it may be that booster shots will be needed—either later in adolescence or during adulthood.

If anything, the challenges in developing countries are more acute, and overcoming them may be far more difficult. These include raising awareness of the need for a vaccine where knowledge of HPV is very low; ensuring acceptability among parents, providers and policymakers in cultural and political contexts that are particularly sensitive to teenage sexuality; delivering a series of three injections to a population that often has minimal contact with health care facilities or providers; and ensuring that the vaccines are affordable in extremely-low-resource settings. While some global health experts, as in the United States, note the appeal of school-based vaccination programs as a means for reaching large numbers of adolescents, sizeable proportions particularly of female adolescents in many developing countries do not enroll in school or leave school prior to the recommended age of vaccination.

Despite these considerable challenges, one thing is certain: widespread vaccination against HPV in order to prevent cervical cancer would bring an enormous payoff to women, both in the United States and abroad. It can only be hoped that the politics will not be allowed to sabotage the promise first.

KEY SCIENTIFIC, LOGISTICAL AND POLICY QUESTIONS ABOUT THE CERVICAL CANCER VACCINE

- Should older women who are already sexually active receive "catch-up" vaccines at the start of any vaccination effort?
- Should males be vaccinated, both to prevent HPV transmission to women and to protect against HPV-related genital and anal cancers, as well as genital warts, in men?
- Could a therapeutic vaccine be developed to help those who are already infected with HPV or have a persistent infection?
- Could a vaccine be developed that targets additional cancer-causing types of HPV?
- Could the HPV vaccine be combined with other vaccinations for ease of administration, and would that help to institutionalize the adolescent health visit?
- Will uptake of the vaccine prompt professional medical organizations and public health entities to change their recommendations for Pap smears, and what might longer recommended intervals between Pap smears mean for women's health and health care-seeking behavior?
- Will the uninsured, the underinsured and those who rely on public programs for their care be able to access this relatively expensive vaccine, or will the vaccine simply widen the cervical cancer disparities that already exist?

Roni Rabin  **NO**

A New Vaccine for Girls, but Should It Be Compulsory?

Around the time report cards came home this spring, federal health officials approved another new vaccine to add to the ever-growing list of recommended childhood shots—this one for girls and women only, from 9 to 26, to protect them from genital warts and cervical cancer.

One of my own daughters, who just turned 9, would be a candidate for this vaccine, so I've been mulling this over. A shot that protects against cancer sounds like a great idea, at first. States may choose to make it mandatory, though the cost for them to do so would be prohibitive.

But let's think carefully before requiring young girls to get this vaccine, which protects against a sexually transmitted virus, in order to go to school. This isn't polio or measles, diseases that are easily transmitted through casual contact. Infection with this virus requires intimate contact, of the kind that doesn't occur in classrooms.

Besides, we already know how to prevent cervical cancer in this country, and we've done a darn good job of it. In the war against cancer, the battle against cervical cancer has been a success story.

Why, then, did federal health officials recommend the inoculation of about 30 million American girls and young women against the human papillomavirus, a sexually transmitted disease that in rare cases leads to cervical cancer?

Vaccine supporters say that some 3,700 American women die of cervical cancer each year, and close to 10,000 cases are diagnosed. Cervical cancer has a relatively high survival rate, but every death is tragic and treatment can rob women of their fertility.

Still, you have to see the numbers in context. Cervical cancer deaths have been dropping consistently in the United States—and have been for decades.

Cervical cancer has gone from being one of the top killers of American women to not even being on the top 10 list. This year cervical cancer will represent just 1 percent of the 679,510 new cancer cases and 1 percent of the 273,560 anticipated cancer deaths among American women. By contrast, some 40,970 women will die of breast cancer and 72,130 will die of lung cancer.

According to the American Cancer Society Web site, "Between 1955 and 1992, the number of cervical cancer deaths in the United States dropped by 74 percent." Think about it: 74 percent.

The number of cases diagnosed each year and the number of deaths per year have continued to drop, even though the population is growing.

From 1997 to 2003, the number of cervical cancers in the United States dropped by 4.5 percent each year, while the number of deaths dropped by 3.8 percent each year, according to a government Web site that tracks cancer trends, called SEER or Surveillance, Epidemiology and End Results. . . . This, while many other cancers are on the rise.

If current trends continue, by the time my 9-year-old daughter is 48, the median age when cervical cancer is diagnosed, there will be only a few thousand cases of the cancer in women, and about 1,000 deaths or fewer each year, even without the vaccine.

The secret weapon? Not so secret. It's the Pap smear. A simple, quick, relatively noninvasive test that's part and parcel of routine preventive health care for women. It provides early warnings of cellular changes in the cervix that are precursors for cancer and can be treated.

An American Cancer Society spokeswoman said that most American women who get cervical cancer these days are women who either had never had a Pap smear or had not followed the follow-up and frequency guidelines. So perhaps we could redirect the public money that would be spent on this vaccine—one of the most expensive ever, priced at $360 for the series of three shots—to make sure all women in the United States get preventive health care.

Because even if you have the new vaccine, which protects against only some of the viral strains that may bring on cervical cancer, you still need to continue getting Pap smears.

To be clear, I'm talking only about American women. Sadly, hundreds of thousands of women worldwide die of cervical cancer each year because they don't have access to Pap smears and the follow-up care required. For them, and for American women at high risk, the vaccine should be an option.

Black, Hispanic and some foreign-born women are at higher risk, though rates have dropped precipitously among blacks. Certain behavior—smoking, eating poorly, having multiple sexual partners and long-term use of the pill, for example—are also associated with an increased risk. But most people infected with the human papillomavirus clear it on their own.

Vaccine supporters, including the American Cancer Society, say the immunization will reduce abnormal Pap test results, and the stress, discomfort and cost of follow-up procedures and painful treatments. That's a strong argument for the vaccine.

But vaccines carry risks. In recent years, children have been bombarded with new immunizations, and we still don't know the full long-term implications. One vaccine, RotaShield, was removed from the market in 1999, just a year after being approved for infants.

Merck has tested the cervical cancer vaccine in clinical trials of more than 20,000 women (about half of them got the shot). The health of the subjects was followed for about three and a half years on average. But fewer than

1,200 girls under 16 got the shots, among them only about 100 9-year-olds, Merck officials said, and the younger girls have been followed for only 18 months.

Public health officials want to vaccinate girls early, before they become sexually active, even though it is not known how long the immunity will last.

But girls can also protect themselves from the human papillomavirus by using condoms; a recent study found that condoms cut infections by more than half. Condoms also protect against a far more insidious sexually transmitted virus, H.I.V.

So yes, by all means, let's keep stamping out cervical cancer. Let's make sure women and girls get Pap smears.

POSTSCRIPT

Should Children Have an HPV Vaccination before They Enroll in School?

Many sexually transmitted infections (STI) are treatable and curable. Trichomoniasis, for example, afflicts more than 7 million Americans every year, but these cases can be treated and cured. The same is true for chlamydia (nearly 3 million new cases annually), gonorrhea (700,000 new cases annually), and other infections that are *bacterial* or *parasitic*.

As noted in the Introduction, HPV is one of the most common STIs. It is a *viral* infection, which, like herpes and HIV, cannot be cured. However, most people who acquire HPV will eventually clear the infection on their own. When there are manifestations of HPV, such as genital warts, they can be treated and removed, though reoccurrence is possible.

The Centers for Disease Control says that most of the 20 million Americans who currently have HPV don't even know they are infected. The virus lives in the skin, or in the mucous membranes, usually causing no symptoms. The asymptomatic nature of HPV may aid its spread. Given the potential harm that HPV can do, from genital warts to cancer, what is the best public health solution? What are the benefits of vaccinating young girls against HPV before they enroll in school? Should these vaccinations be mandatory? When do you think the appropriate age for this vaccine should be? Are routine Pap smears enough, as Rabin suggests?

Might vaccinating at an early age make teen girls more likely to have unprotected intercourse, as the Family Research Council suggested? What do you think of the argument that teens who are sexually abstinent have no need for the vaccination? What if they change their decisions and decide to have intercourse sooner than they had planned (or sooner than their parents had wished)? If they do wait to have intercourse until adulthood, what if their partner did not wait, and was exposed to HPV? Also, studies show that one in six women will be the victim of sexual assault, and that 44 percent of victims are under the age of 18. Should teens be vaccinated to prevent infection caused by rape or a sexual assault?

And finally, what about the boys? The current vaccine is available for girls, but what about the exposure of males to HPV. Should the vaccination be available to young males to help further stave off the spread of this virus, and its impact on everyone?

Suggested Readings

J. Cornblatt, "HPV Vaccine Is the Hot Shot on Campus." *Newsweek* (Sept. 25, 2006).

J. T. Cox, "Epidemiology and natural history of HPV." *Journal of Family Practice,* 55(11), Nov. 2006.

A. F. Dempsey, et al., "Factors that Are Associated with Parental Acceptance of Human Papillomavirus Vaccines: A Randomized Intervention Study of Written Information about HPV (Human Papillomavirus)" *Pediatrics* 117(5), May 2006.

Editorial, "Should HPV Vaccines Be Mandatory for All Adolescents?" *The Lancet,* Oct 7, 2006: p1212(1).

S. London, "Frequent Male Condom Use Decreases Women's Risk of HPV Infection," *International Family Planning Perspectives,* 32(3), Sept. 2006.

M. C. Mahoney, "Protecting Our Patients from HPV and HPV-Related Diseases: The Role of Vaccines." *Journal of Family Practice,* 55(11), Nov. 2006.

L. E. Manhart et. al, "Human Papillomavirus Infection among Sexually Active Young Women in the United States: Implications for Developing a Vaccination Strategy." *Sexually Transmitted Diseases,* 33(8), Aug. 2006.

P. Sprigg, "Pro-Family, Pro-Vaccine—But Keep It Voluntary," *Washington Post* (July 15, 2006).

ISSUE 9

Do Schools Perpetuate
a Gender Bias?

YES: Janice Weinman, from "Girls Still Face Barriers in Schools That Prevent Them From Reaching Their Full Potential," *Insight on the News* (December 14, 1998)

NO: Judith Kleinfeld, from "In Fact, the Public Schools Are Biased Against Boys, Particularly Minority Males," *Insight on the News* (December 14, 1998)

ISSUE SUMMARY

YES: Janice Weinman, executive director of the American Association of University Women (AAUW), states that, while there has been some progress since the AAUW published its study entitled *How Schools Shortchange Girls* in 1991, its 1998 review of 1,000 research studies entitled *Gender Gaps: Where Schools Still Fail Our Children* found that girls still face a gender gap in math, science, and computer science.

NO: Psychologist and author Judith Kleinfeld argues that despite appearances, girls still have an advantage over boys in terms of their future plans, teachers' expectations, and everyday school experiences. Furthermore, minority males in particular are at a disadvantage educationally.

In every country there are more male architects than female architects. Why is this so? Why do females outnumber males in other careers? Are these gender differences due to teachers paying more attention to male students than to female students, taking more questions from males than females, and/or guiding males into certain courses and academic tracks and females into less challenging ones? Do female teachers favor female students over male students? Do male teachers tend not to refer male students for counseling or remedial courses when they really need this extra help? Are the gender differences we see in post-school career paths due to a social bias?

In 1970 women accounted for only 8 percent of all medical degrees, 5 percent of law degrees, and 1 percent of dental degrees. In 1990, women earned 36 percent of medical degrees, 40 percent of law degrees, and 32 percent of dental degrees. In 1999 more women than men attended college. The women also earned higher grades and graduated more often.

In an article entitled "Sex Differences in the Brain," *Scientific American* (September 1992), Doreen Kimura, a professor of psychology and neural research, probes beneath the surface of possible gender biases in American schools. She describes a wide range of differences in the way males and females learn and states that these differences are a reflection of differing hormonal influences on fetal brain development. Kimura maintains that this helps to explain differences in occupational interests and overall capabilities between the sexes.

On the other hand, social psychologist Carol Tavris concludes in *The Mismeasure of Women* (Peter Smith Publishers, 1998), that scientific efforts conducted over the past century have yielded enough conflicting views and distorted findings to invalidate the idea that gender differences are rooted in the brain. She maintains that although biology is not irrelevant to human behavior, it is not fully responsible. The notion of gender difference, in her opinion, has consistently been used to define women as fundamentally different from and inferior to men in body, psyche, and brain.

The question of whether women and men are essentially similar or different is often drowned in emotional responses, unspoken assumptions, and activist politics. This sometimes results in patriarchal biases that dogmatically stress gender differences as justification for "natural gender roles" and can lead to sex discrimination. But similar emotional responses, unspoken assumptions, and activist politics are just as likely to result in a different bias that dogmatically maintains that the only significant difference between men and women is in their sexual anatomy.

For 3,000 years many Western thinkers have viewed human development as the result to two separate, parallel, noninteracting influences. *Nature*—genes and hormones—was believed to be dominant before birth and irrelevant after birth. *Nurture*—the learning and social environment—was believed to be irrelevant during the nine months of pregnancy, but would dominate after birth.

As you read these two selections, see if you can detect any traces or undercurrents of the *Nature vs. Nurture* debate. If you find these undercurrents, do they influence your own appraisal of the arguments presented?

In the following selections, Janice Weinman cites an AAUW report in order to support her conviction that both the quantity and quality of education for females falls short of that for males. Judith Kleinfeld counters that males, particularly minority males, are at a disadvantage when it comes to educational opportunities. She asserts that the AAUW report is merely "junk science."

YES

Janice Weinman

Girls Still Face Barriers in Schools That Prevent Them From Reaching Their Full Potential

The American Association of University Women, or AAUW, has been a non-profit, nonpartisan advocate for equal opportunities for women and girls for more than a century. Specifically, we work to improve education for girls.

The need for this is clear. AAUW's 1992 report, *How Schools Shortchange Girls*, reviewed more than 1,300 studies and documented disturbing evidence that girls receive an inequitable education, both in quality and quantity, in America's classrooms. In particular, we found girls faced a gender gap in math and science.

In October, the AAUW Educational Foundation released *Gender Gaps: Where Schools Still Fail Our Children*. Synthesizing 1,000 research studies, *Gender Gaps* measures schools' progress in providing a fair and equitable education since 1992. While girls have improved in some areas, such as math and science, they face an alarming new gap in technology that threatens to make women bystanders in the 21st-century economy.

Gender Gaps found that girls make up only a small percentage of students in computer-science classes. While boys are more likely to enroll in advanced computer-applications and graphics courses, girls take data-entry and clerical classes, the 1990s version of typing. Boys enter the classroom with more prior experience with computers and other technology than girls. Girls consistently rate themselves significantly lower than boys on computer ability, and boys exhibit higher self-confidence and a more positive attitude about computers than do girls.

Critics such as Professor Judith Kleinfeld have questioned why research should focus on the educational experiences of girls. They contend that girls are in fact doing quite well in school. The attention AAUW brings to girls and gender equity, they argue, leads to the neglect of boys.

AAUW believes that all students deserve a good education. To make sure that all students are performing to high academic standards, educators must address the learning needs of different groups of students—boys and girls, African-Americans and Hispanics, rich and poor. AAUW agrees that boys, like girls, face academic challenges. In fact, *Gender Gaps* clearly highlights the fact that boys still lag behind in communications skills. These gaps must be addressed by schools so that all children, boys and girls, have equal opportunity to develop to their full potential.

AAUW's work to eliminate gender bias in the classroom and address gender gaps in education benefits both boys and girls. Rather than pit one group against another, we believe this is a win-win scenario for all students. However, since Kleinfeld does make some specific charges against AAUW's research, allow me to address her claims.

First, Kleinfeld's report—commissioned by the conservative Women's Freedom Network—uses 1998 figures, which show girls improving in math and science, to critique our 1992 finding that there was a gender gap in math and science. That's like using today's lower crime rates to say a 6-year-old study on increasing crime rates created a false alarm. AAUW recognizes and applauds the gains girls have made during the last six years. In fact, *Gender Gaps* documents the improvements girls have made in math and science since AAUW brought national attention to the problem in 1992.

Even if you look at the most recent data, the way Kleinfeld does, there still are significant gender differences in schools that must be addressed, including grades and test scores, health and development risks and career development.

As both *How Schools Shortchange Girls* and *Gender Gaps* reported, girls earn better grades than boys. Despite this fact, boys continue to score higher than girls on high-stakes tests—the Preliminary Scholastic Assessment Tests, or PSAT, the Scholastic Assessment Tests, or SAT, the American College Test, or ACT—that determine college admissions and scholarship opportunities. Boys score higher on both the math and verbal sections on these exams, with the gender gaps being the widest for high-scoring students.

As both *Gender Gaps* and Kleinfeld point out, girls' enrollment in advanced placement, or AP, or honors courses is comparable to those of boys, except in AP physics and AP computer science. In fact, more girls take AP English, foreign language and biology. However, girls do not score as well as boys on the AP exams that can earn college credit, even in subjects such as English where girls earn top grades.

Girls' academic success also is affected by the tough issues facing students—pregnancy, violence and harassment—that rarely are discussed in school. AAUW believes that schools can play a key role in developing healthy and well-balanced students.

Although Kleinfeld tries to discredit AAUW's work by pointing to the large number of boys in special education, our 1992 report paid careful attention to the fact that boys outnumbered girls in these programs by startling percentages. It also cited studies on learning disabilities and attention-deficit disorders that indicated that they occurred almost equally in boys and girls.

Girls continue to be more vulnerable to some risks than boys. As *Gender Gaps* reports, one in five girls has been sexually or physically abused, one in four shows signs of depression and one in four doesn't get health care when she needs it. Schools limit gender equity when they fail to confront or discuss risk factors for students.

AAUW also is well-known for our research on self-esteem. In 1991, AAUW commissioned the first national scientific survey on self-esteem, *Short-changing Girls, Shortchanging America*. This survey was stratified by region, included an unprecedented number of children (3,000 children ages 9 to 15), and rigorously was reviewed by a team of academic advisers. The 1991 survey offered solid evidence of differences in self-esteem between girls and boys.

Although girls who were surveyed for *Shortchanging Girls, Shortchanging America* self-reported that teachers called on and gave more attention to girls, their self-esteem nevertheless declined. Despite girls' perceptions, the 1992 report, which looked at many other studies in addition to the AAUW survey, found that girls received significantly less attention than boys in the classroom. Contrary to what Kleinfeld asserts, neither AAUW's 1991 survey nor 1992 report drew a causal relationship between self-esteem and academic achievement. AAUW's research on self-esteem looked at multiple patterns across multiple indicators—including general self-esteem, family importance, academic self-esteem, isolation, voice, acceptance, friends and attention in classrooms—and used multiple methodologies. The repeated conclusion our research revealed is that girls face a dramatic drop in self-esteem as they get older that has devastating consequences on their aspirations and their futures. Kleinfeld's work looks at only two questions from our survey to draw her own conclusions.

Beyond K–12 public schools, Kleinfeld looks at college degrees to declare that women have achieved parity in the professional world. Although more women than men enter college, entry into higher education doesn't guarantee equitable conditions. That's why AAUW has worked to include key provisions in the reauthorization of the Higher Education Act to make sure women's needs are addressed on campus. For example, although women are three times as likely as men to be single parents while in college, campus-based child care still is hard to find and afford.

And women still are underrepresented in nontraditional fields such as math and science that lead to greater earning power upon graduation. There are disparities at the undergraduate, master's and doctorate levels in these fields, which have a profound effect on careers.

You only need to look outside of the classroom and into the boardroom to see that women are still a long way from equality. Women earn only 76 cents for every dollar that a man earns. In 1995, women represented 70 per cent of all adults with incomes below the poverty level, and two out of three minimum-wage earners are women. Out of the entire Fortune 500, there are only two female CEOs and a total of seven in the Fortune 1,000. And women only make up 11 percent of Congress.

No one wins in Kleinfeld's who's-worse-off debate. AAUW's work to eliminate gender bias in the classroom and address gender gaps in education benefits both boys and girls. Our research has resonated with parents, teachers and policymakers who have used our research as a catalyst for positive change in their public schools. Our 1,500 branches across the country conduct programs to empower and encourage young girls. Our fellowships help women succeed in school and advance into fields that historically have been off limits.

AAUW believes that all students deserve a good education and the opportunity to develop to their full potential. And we know from experience that we can help girls close the gender gap—we've seen them improve in math and science. Now we must do the same for technology to make sure all students have the technological skills to compete in the 21st century.

Judith Kleinfeld  **NO**

In Fact, the Public Schools Are Biased Against Boys, Particularly Minority Males

T hink back to your own school days. Who got into more trouble in school—the boys or the girls? Who got the best grades—the boys or the girls? Who was the valedictorian in your high school—a boy or a girl?

Yes, school is just the same as you remember it.

Feminist-advocacy groups such as the American Association of University Women, or AAUW, have promoted a big lie: the idea that schools shortchange girls. The AAUW studies are advocacy research—junk science. In fact, their latest study is going to give me lots of examples for my research-methods class on how to lie with statistics. It's all there—graphs drawn to make a little gap look like a big one, percentages calculated with the wrong numerical base to show that girls score lower than boys on advanced placement, or AP, tests in English when the girls actually score higher. Such a gold mine of tricks!

Why the deception? The short answer is money. The long answer is money and career advancement. The idea that females are victims garners millions of dollars in federal and foundation funding for feminist-advocacy groups to launch special programs for girls. This idea also helps well-educated women gain special preferences in their battle for elite jobs at the top.

Who are the real victims? The losers are the students the schools really do shortchange—mostly minority males. Women's-advocacy groups have hijacked the moral capital of the civil-rights movement to promote the special interests of well-off, well-connected women. Along the way they have scared many parents, who are worrying about their daughters in the schools when they should be worrying about their sons.

When I told my own university students that the AAUW had just discovered a new gender gap—a computer gap—a great groan arose from the class. Puzzled and surprised, I asked each student how he or she used computers. Are women really going to be bystanders in the technological 21st century, as the AAUW would have us believe?

The students' answers laid bare the fallacy in the AAUW's latest headline-grabber. The women in the class, no less than the men, could use spreadsheets, databases and word-processing programs. The women could search the Internet. The women learned the computer programs they needed to use.

So what's all the hysteria about the computer gap? If you read the 1998 AAUW report, you will be in for a surprise. All this uproar comes down to a difference of 5 percent in the proportion of male high-school students (30 per cent) compared to female high-school students (25 percent) who sign up for computer-science courses. These are the kinds of courses that teach computer-programming skills for students interested in computer-science careers.

Males indeed are more likely than females to choose computer science as a career. So what? Women aren't as interested as men in turning into Dilberts-in-a-cubicle. According to a report on women in mathematics and science from the National Center for Education Statistics, twice as many female college students (20 percent) compared to male college students (less than 10 per cent) now seek prestigious professional careers.

The truth is that males and females have somewhat different interests and somewhat different areas of intellectual strength and weakness, and these differences show up in schools. Here are the facts:

Grades: Females are ahead.   If the schools were biased against girls, such bias should be easy to detect. After all, the schools give clear and measurable rewards: grades, class rank and honors. These rewards are valuable in getting into an elite college or getting a good job.

Every study, even the AAUW's own 1998 report, concedes that girls consistently earn higher grades than boys throughout their schooling. Girls get higher class rank and more academic honors in every field except mathematics and science (I'll discuss this difference later). Girls, not boys, are more apt to be chosen for gifted and talented programs, the gateway into a far higher-quality education. Girls drop out of school less often than boys and less often repeat a grade. Wherever the schools hand out the prizes, girls get more than their share.

Standardized achievement tests: Females do better in some subjects; males do better in others.   Even though girls get better grades, the schools still might be shortchanging girls if they actually aren't learning as much as boys. Grades, after all, have a lot to do with whether students are willing to play along with the school's demands for neatness and conformity.

On standardized tests, females surpass males by a mile on tests of writing ability. Females also surpass males in reading achievement and in study skills. Males surpass females on tests of science, mathematics and a few areas of social studies.

The gender gap in mathematics and science is closing, as the AAUW 1998 report admits. The gender-equity police take credit for it, but the real cause is higher graduation requirements in high school. Girls now take just as many high-school science and mathematics courses as boys do, with the exception of a small difference in physics.

In a nutshell, boys end up with lower grades than girls even in subjects where standardized tests show boys know more. So against which sex are schools biased?

High-stakes tests: What's really going on. The AAUW makes much of the fact that males surpass females on high-stakes tests, such as the Scholastic Assessment Tests, or SAT. Here's what they don't tell you. More than 75,500 additional females take the SAT than males, and these "additional" females are less likely to have taken rigorous academic courses than other students, points out a 1998 College Board study on sex and the SAT.

Here is the way the trick works. Let's say you are comparing the top-10 male basketball players with the top 10 female players in the same high school. Assume that the males and the females have the same shooting ability. But then add to the female group five girls who try hard but aren't as good. Of course, the female shooting average will be lower than the males'.

The AAUW pulls a similar trick in comparing scores on AP tests, tough tests taken by the most advanced high-school students. The AAUW report admits that girls take AP tests in greater number than boys but pulls a fast one by saying that these girls earn lower scores even in areas of historic strength, such as English.

Take a look at the actual facts in the federal report, *The Condition of Education 1998*. Almost twice as many girls as boys took the AP English test. Among the girls, 46 per 1,000 12th-graders got a score of 3 or higher, qualifying them for college credit. Among the boys, 27 per 1,000 12th-graders got such a high score. What's the truth? Girls earn far higher scores than boys on the AP English test, the opposite of what the AAUW claims.

Males fall at the extremes—flaming failures and academic stars. More boys do show up at the top in fields such as mathematics and science. But then more boys also show up at the bottom. Boys are twice as likely to be placed in special-education classes for the learning-disabled. Boys outnumber girls by 4-1 in neurological impairments such as autism or dyslexia.

This has less to do with bias than with biology. On many human characteristics, including intellectual abilities, males are just more variable than females. More males show up at the high end of the bell curve and more males show up at the low end of the bell curve. From the standpoint of natural selection, males are the more expendable sex. Nature takes more chances with males, producing more oddities of every kind, whether genius or insanity.

Women's advocacy groups push programs to equalize male and females in mathematics and science. Social engineering cannot make real differences go away, nor should it.

College success: Females now surpass males. Many people don't realize that women have become the majority of college students. In 1996, women earned 55 percent of bachelor's degrees and 55 percent of all master's degrees, and African-American females are much further ahead.

Insofar as self-esteem is concerned, both girls and boys have rather high opinions of themselves. The best research, now accepted even by feminist-advocacy groups, shows no difference between teenage boys and girls in self-esteem. The latest AAUW report on gender gaps is strangely silent about the self-esteem gap they trumpeted a few years ago.

NO / Judith Kleinfeld

On the issue of whether girls get less class participation than boys, it is clear that teachers do not silence girls. Everyone agrees that teachers give boys more attention of the negative, disciplinary kind. Who gets more academic attention? This research is a confusing mess, with no clear patterns.

So, who are the public schools biased against? The right answer is boys. Many studies show that American schools, far from shortchanging girls, are biased against boys. In fact, the AAUW found the same thing but buried these results in unpublished tables. I had to badger the AAUW office for weeks to get a 1990 Greenberg-Lake survey and pay close to $100 for the photocopying. But you can see that the AAUW had good reason to hide these findings. According to the AAUW's hidden study, both boys and girls agree, sometimes by overwhelming margins, that teachers think girls are smarter, compliment girls more often and like to be around girls more.

The media doesn't often report studies which contradict the feminist party line. A good example is the 1997 report on gender issues published by the Met-Life Foundation, an organization with no political ax to grind. This study concludes:

1. Contrary to the commonly held view that boys are at an advantage over girls in school, girls appear to have an advantage over boys in terms of their future plans, teachers' expectations, everyday experiences at schools and interactions in the classroom;
2. Minority girls hold the most optimistic views of the future and are the group most likely to focus on education goals;
3. Minority boys are the most likely to feel discouraged about the future and the least interested in getting a good education; and
4. Teachers nationwide view girls as higher achievers and more likely to succeed than boys.

If anyone needs help in school, it is minority boys. They are the victims of the AAUW's junk science.

POSTSCRIPT

Do Schools Perpetuate a Gender Bias?

Jerome Kagan, a major researcher in the development of personality, asserts that many prefer to downplay nature and emphasize nurture when discussing the origin of psychological differences in males and females. This tendency, he says, owes much to the prevailing commitment Americans have to egalitarianism. If differences between individuals, between the genders, or between gender orientations are innate and biologically based, there is little that can be done about them. If, however, differences are due to inequities in the social environment, there may be a lot that can be done to reduce or eliminate these differences. But there is a third option. This option has three essential components. First is the belief that male and female brains and personalities are gender differentiated by hormones and genes as a fetus is developing in the womb and after birth. Second is the observation that parents, teachers, and society engage in biased gender scripting. Third is the conclusion that innate biological differences in the brain interact with gender-biased scripting at critical periods throughout our lives.

Alice Rossi, in her 1983 Presidential Address to the American Sociological Association, pointed out that attempts to explain human behavior and therapies that seek to change behavior "carry a high risk of eventual irrelevance [if they] neglect the fundamental biological and neural differences between the sexes [and] the mounting evidence of sexual dimorphism from the biological and neural sciences." Although Rossi seems to favor the belief that male and female brains are wired differently, she offers an important distinction. She carefully states that gender "diversity is a biological fact, while [gender] equality is a political, ethical, and social precept."

If the biological and neuropsychological evidence supports the existence of significant differences in male and female brains, then we have to be careful to view these differences as part of human diversity and not in terms of superior versus inferior or good versus bad. Human diversity does not necessarily deny or obstruct human equality, because human equality is a political, moral, and social issue. Too often human diversity is used to support the superiority of one group over another group.

On the other hand, educators of all grades may need to carefully examine the ways in which boys and girls are treated differently in their classrooms. Some researchers have observed a tendency for educators of preschool students to compliment boys on their *performance* (e.g., "Billy, you're such a good runner!") and girls on their *appearance* (e.g., "Karen, you look so pretty today!"). Furthermore, when an educator gives a simple instruction like, "I need a few strong boys to help me move some chairs," she or he may be completely unaware that the directions exclude girls from the possibility of helping. Educators who begin to recognize that the key skill needed for such an activity is *strength* and not *being a boy* will help their students make empowering strides toward life's opportunities.

Suggested Readings

N. Angier, "How Biology Affects Behavior and Vice Versa," *The New York Times* (May 30, 1995).

A. Fausto-Sterling, *Myths of Gender: Biological Theories About Women and Men,* 2d ed. (Basic Books, 1992).

C. Gorman, "Sizing Up the Sexes," *Time* (January 20, 1992).

D. Kimura, "Sex Differences in the Brain," *Scientific American* (September 1992).

R. Pool, *Eve's Rib: Searching for the Biological Roots of Sex Differences* (Crown Publishers, 1994).

C. Tavris, *The Mismeasure of Woman: Why Women Are Not the Better Sex, the Inferior Sex, or the Opposite Sex* (Simon & Schuster, 1992).

L. Wright, "Double Mystery," *The New Yorker* (August 7, 1995).

Internet References . . .

Emergency Contraception Web Site

Operated by the Office of Population Research at Princeton University and the Association of Reproductive Health Professionals, this Web site provides accurate information about emergency contraception derived from the medical literature and a directory of local clinicians willing to provide emergency contraceptives.

http://www.not-2-late.com

Food and Drug Administration (FDA)

The FDA is a government body overseen by the U.S. Department of Health and Human Services. Among its many responsibilities is to promote and protect public health by helping safe and effective products reach the market in a timely way.

http://www.fda.gov

RESOLVE: The National Infertility Association

RESOLVE: The National Infertility Association provides education, advocacy, and support related to infertility.

http://www.resolve.org

Stem Cell Information

This Web site, operated by the National Institutes of Health, provides basic information on stem cells and links describing the status of research and federal policy.

http://stemcells.nih/gov

Reproductive Technology

*S*ome *of the most contentious modern debates involve reproduction: Should abortion be legal and accessible? Should abortion be restricted at some stages of embryonic or fetal development? Should parents be encouraged to space the births of their children? Is the use of contraception a moral decision for people who do not wish to become parents? Should schools teach about contraception? Should people avoid sex that does not result in the possibility of pregnancy? If so, does this include sex between two males or two females? Does it mean all oral, anal, or touching sex is illicit? Does it mean no sex should take place when a woman is beyond menopause, or if one or both partners are disabled?*

In this section, we examine three contemporary issues that involve emerging reproductive technology: techniques that would enable parents-to-be to select the gender of their children; access to emergency contraception that prevents pregnancy before implantation of a fertilized egg; and the role of discarded, frozen embryos, created by in vitro fertilization, in preventing diseases.

- Should Parents Be Allowed to Select the Sex of Their Baby?

- Should Emergency Contraception Be Available over the Counter?

- Should Federal Funding of Stem Cell Research Be Restricted?

ISSUE 10

Should Parents Be Allowed to Select the Sex of Their Baby?

YES: John A. Robertson, from "Extending Preimplantation Genetic Diagnosis: Medical and Non-medical Uses," *Journal of Medical Ethics* (vol. 29, 2003)

NO: Marcy Darnovsky, from "Revisiting Sex Selection: The Growing Popularity of New Sex Selection Methods Revives an Old Debate," http://www.gene-watch.org/genewatch/articles/17-1darnovsky.html (January–February 2004)

ISSUE SUMMARY

YES: Law professor John A. Robertson argues that preimplantation genetic diagnosis (PGD), a new technique that allows parents-to-be to determine the gender of their embryo before implantation in the uterus, should be permissible. Robertson argues that it is not sexist to want a baby of a particular gender, and that the practice should not be restricted.

NO: Marcy Darnovsky, associate director of the Center for Genetics and Society, argues that by allowing PGD for sex selection, governments are starting down a slippery slope that could create an era of consumer eugenics.

The practice of selecting the sex of a child is nothing new. Historically, couples who wanted a child of a specific gender might abandon an unwanted child of the other gender in the wilderness, leave the baby on the doorstep of a church or orphanage, or kill the unwanted baby. Although these practices still continue in some societies today, sex selection has also changed in significant ways. The development of ultrasound technology, for example, allows expecting parents to determine the gender of the baby before it is born, and some couples might consider abortion if the child is not the desired sex. Parents might feel additional pressure to make this decision in countries like China, which has a "one child" policy, whereby additional children receive no governmental support—a critical consideration in a communist nation that also places higher value on male infants than females.

For many Americans, the idea of sex selection by abandonment, abortion, or infanticide would be considered unethical, if not appalling. But in other areas of the world, the practice is carried out routinely to help parents meet strong cultural preferences to produce a male child. Such actions are based in the entrenched sexism of these male-dominated societies.

A seemingly more ethical technique that sorted sperm before conception has offered about a 50–85 percent effectiveness rate at predetermining sex for the past 30 years. More recently a new development in medical technology known as preimplantation genetic diagnosis (PGD), previously used to screen embryos for markers that may signal diseases like cystic fibrosis, now allows people using in vitro fertilization to select the sex of an embryo, with 99.9 percent accuracy, before it is implanted in the uterus. To many satisfied customers, this has provided the opportunity to "balance" a family, by adding a child of the other sex or evening out the number of male and female children. In some cases, first-time parents simply desire a child of one sex or the other.

While the use of PGD for medical reasons, such as screening for Down syndrome, in an embryo are generally seen as acceptable, there is less consensus concerning its use for nonmedical reasons, including sex selection. Is wanting to choose the sex of your child sexist? Does it reflect or perpetuate a gender bias in society? If selecting the sex of your unborn child is possible and legal, what about predetermination of other characteristics, such as eye color? Height? Musical ability? Sexual orientation?

In the following selections, John A. Robertson, professor at the University of Texas School of Law, argues that using PGD for sex selection in certain instances is not inherently sexist, and that it—and perhaps other nonmedical types of PGD should not be regulated based on the fear of what could possibly happen at some future time. Marcy Darnovsky, associate director of the Center for Genetics and Society, argues that by allowing PGD for sex selection, governments are starting down a slippery slope that could create an era of consumer eugenics.

YES

Extending Preimplantation Genetic Diagnosis: Medical and Non-Medical Uses

PGD and Its Prevalence

PGD has been available since 1990 for testing of aneuploidy in low prognosis in vitro fertilisation (IVF) patients, and for single gene and X linked diseases in at risk couples. One cell (blastomere) is removed from a cleaving embryo and tested for the genetic or chromosomal condition of concern. Some programmes analyse polar bodies extruded from oocytes during meiosis, rather than blastomeres.[1] Cells are then either karyotyped to identify chromosomal abnormalities, or analysed for single gene mutations and linked markers.

Physicians have performed more than 3000 clinical cycles of PGD since 1990, with more than 700 children born as a result. The overall pregnancy rate of 24% is comparable to assisted reproductive practices which do not involve embryo or polar body biopsy.[1] Four centres (Chicago, Livingston (New Jersey), Bologna, and Brussels) accounted for nearly all the reported cases. More than 40 centres worldwide offer the procedure, however, including other centres in the United States and Europe, four centres in London and centres in the eastern Mediterranean, Southeast Asia, and Australia.

More than two thirds of PGD has occurred to screen out embryos with chromosomal abnormalities in older IVF patients and in patients with a history of miscarriage. About 1000 cycles have involved single gene mutational analysis.[1] Mutational analysis requires additional skills beyond karyotyping for aneuploidies, including the ability to conduct the multiplex polymerase chain reaction (PCR) of the gene of interest and related markers.

Several new indications for PGD single gene mutational analysis have recently been reported. New uses include PGD to detect mutations for susceptibility to cancer and for late onset disorders such as Alzheimer's disease.[2, 3] In addition, parents with children needing hematopoietic stem cell transplants have used PGD to ensure that their next child is free of disease and a good tissue match for an existing child.[4] Some persons are also requesting PGD for gender selection for both first and later born children, and others have speculated that selection of embryos for a variety of non-medical traits is likely in the future.

From *Journal of Medical Ethics*, vol. 29, 2003, pp. 213(4). Copyright © 2003 by BMJ Publishing Group. Reprinted by permission.

PGD is ethically controversial because it involves the screening and likely destruction of embryos, and the selection of offspring on the basis of expected traits. While persons holding right to life views will probably object to PGD for any reason, those who view the early embryo as too rudimentary in development to have rights or interests see no principled objection to all PGD. They may disagree, however, over whether particular reasons for PGD show sufficient respect for embryos and potential offspring to justify intentional creation and selection of embryos. Donation of unwanted embryos to infertile couples reduces this problem somewhat, but there are too few such couples to accept all unwanted embryos, and in any event, the issue of selecting offspring traits remains.

Although ethical commentary frequently mentions PGD as a harbinger of a reproductive future of widespread genetic selection and alteration of prospective offspring, its actual impact is likely to be quite limited.[5, 6] Even with increasing use the penetrance of PGD into reproductive practice is likely to remain a very small percentage of the 150 000 plus cycles of IVF performed annually throughout the world. Screening for susceptibility and late onset diseases is limited by the few diseases for which single gene predispositions are known. Relatively few parents will face the need to conceive another child to provide an existing child with matched stem cells. Nor are non-medical uses of PGD, other than for gender, likely to be practically feasible for at least a decade or more. Despite the limited reach of PGD, the ethical, legal, and policy issues that new uses raise, deserve attention.

New Medical Uses

New uses of PGD may be grouped into medical and non-medical categories. New medical uses include not only screening for rare Mendelian diseases, but also for susceptibility conditions, late onset diseases, and HLA matching for existing children.

Embryo screening for susceptibility and late onset conditions are logical extensions of screening for serious Mendelian diseases. For example, using PGD to screen out embryos carrying the p53 or BRCA1&2 mutations prevent the birth of children who would face a greatly increased lifetime risk of cancer, and hence require close monitoring, prophylactic surgery, or other preventive measures. PGD for highly penetrant adult disorders such as Alzheimer's or Huntington's disease prevents the birth of a child who will be healthy for many years, but who in her late 30s or early 40s will experience the onset of progressive neurological disease leading to an early death.

Although these indications do not involve diseases that manifest themselves in infancy or childhood, the conditions in question lead to substantial health problems for offspring in their thirties or forties.[7] Avoiding the birth of children with those conditions thus reflects the desire of parents to have offspring with good prospects for an average life span. If PGD is accepted to exclude offspring with early onset genetic diseases, it should be accepted for later onset conditions as well.

PGD for adult onset disorders does mean that a healthy child might then be born to a person with those conditions who is likely to die or become incompetent while the child is dependent on her.[8] But that risk has been tolerated in other cases of assisted reproduction, such as intrauterine insemination with sperm of a man who is HIV positive, IVF for women with cystic fibrosis, and use of gametes stored prior to cancer therapy. As long as competent caregivers will be available for the child, the likely death or disability of a parent does not justify condemning or stopping this use, anymore than that reproduction by men going off to war should be discouraged.

A third new medical indication—HLA matching to an existing child—enables a couple to have their next child serve as a matched hematopoietic stem cell donor for an existing sick child. It may also ensure that the new child does not also suffer from that same disease. The availability of PGD, however, should not hinge on that fact, as the Human Fertilisation and Embryology Authority, in the UK, now requires.[9] A couple that would coitally conceive a child to be a tissue donor should be free to use PGD to make sure that that child will be a suitable match, regardless of whether that child is also at risk for genetic disease. Parents who choose PGD for this purpose are likely to value the new child for its own sake, and not only for the stem cells that it will make available. They do not use the new child as a "mere means" simply because they have selected HLA matched embryos for transfer.[10, 11]

Non-Medical Uses of PGD

More ethically troubling has been the prospect of using PGD to screen embryos for genes that do not relate to the health of resulting children or others in the family. Many popular accounts of PGD assume that it will eventually be used to select for such non-medical traits as intelligence, height, sexual orientation, beauty, hair and eye colour, memory, and other factors.[5, 6] Because the genetic basis of those traits is unknown, and in any case is likely to involve many different genes, they may not be subject to easy mutational analysis, as Mendelian disease or susceptibility conditions are. Aside from gender, which is identifiable through karyotyping, it is unrealistic to think that non-medical screening for other traits, with the possible exception of perfect pitch, will occur anytime soon.

Still, it is useful to consider the methodology that ethical assessment of non-medical uses of PGD, if available, should follow. The relevant questions would be whether the proposed use serves valid reproductive or rearing interests; whether those interests are sufficient to justify creating and destroying embryos; whether selecting for a trait will harm resulting children; whether it will stigmatise existing persons, and whether it will create other social harms.

To analyse how these factors interact, I discuss PGD for sex selection and for children with perfect pitch. Similar issues would arise with PGD for sexual orientation, for hair and eye color, and for intelligence, size, and memory.

PGD for Gender Selection

The use of medical technology to select the sex of offspring is highly controversial because of the bias against females which it usually reflects or expresses, and the resulting social disruptions which it might cause. PGD for gender selection faces the additional problem of appearing to be a relatively weak reason for creating and selecting embryos for discard or transfer.

The greatest social effects of gender selection arise when the gender of the first child is chosen. Selection for first children will overwhelmingly favour males, particularly if one child per family population policies apply. If carried out on a large scale, it could lead to great disparities in the sex ratio of the population, as has occurred in China and India through the use of ultrasound screening and abortion.[12, 13] PGD, however, is too expensive and inaccessible to be used on a wide scale for sex selection purposes. Allowing it to be used for the first child is only marginally likely to contribute to societal sex ratio imbalances. But its use is likely to reflect cultural notions of male privilege and may reinforce entrenched sexism toward women.

The use of PGD to choose a gender opposite to that of an existing child or children is much less susceptible to a charge of sexism. Here a couple seeks variety or "balance" in the gender of offspring because of the different rearing experiences that come with rearing children of different genders. Psychologists now recognise many biologically based differences between male and female children, including different patterns of aggression, learning, and spatial recognition, as well as hormonal differences.[14, 15] It may not be sexist in itself to wish to have a child or children of each gender, particularly if one has two or more children of the same gender.

Some feminists, however, would argue that any attention to the gender of offspring is inherently sexist, particularly when social attitudes and expectations play such an important role in constructing sex role expectations and behaviours.[16] Other feminists find the choice of a child with a gender different from existing children to be morally defensible as long as "the intention and consequences of the practice are not sexist", which is plausibly the case when gender variety in children is sought.[17] Desiring the different rearing experiences with boys and girls does not mean that the parents, who have already had children of one gender, are sexists or likely to value unfairly one or the other gender.[18]

Based on this analysis the case is weak for allowing PGD for the first child, but may be acceptable for gender variety in a family. With regard to the first child, facilitating preferences for male firstborns carries a high risk of promoting sexist social mores. It may also strike many persons as too trivial a concern to meet shared notions of the special respect due preimplantation embryos. A proponent of gender selection, however, might argue that cultural preferences for firstborn males should be tolerated, unless a clearer case of harm has been shown. If PGD is not permitted, pregnancy and abortion might occur instead.

The case for PGD for gender variety is stronger because the risk of sexism is lessened. A couple would be selecting the gender of a second or subsequent children for variety in rearing experiences, and not out of a belief that one gender is privileged over another. Gender selection in that case would occur without running the risks of fostering sexism and hurting women.[18]

The question still arises whether the desire for gender variety in children, even if not sexist, is a strong enough reason to justify creating and discarding embryos. The answer depends on how strong an interest that is. No one has yet marshalled the evidence showing that the need or desire for gender variety in children is substantial and important, or whether many parents would refrain from having another child if PGD for gender variety were not possible. More evidence of the strength and prevalence of this need would help in reaching a conclusion. If that case is made, then PGD for gender variety might be acceptable as well.[19]

The ethics committee of the American Society of Reproductive Medicine (ASRM) has struggled with these issues in a series of recent opinions. It initially addressed the issue of PGD for gender selection generally, and found that it "should be discouraged" for couples not going through IVF, and "not encouraged" for couples who were, but made no distinction between PGD for gender selection of first and later children.[20] Subsequently, it found that pre-conception gender selection would be acceptable for purposes of gender variety but not for the first child.[18]

Perceiving these two positions to be inconsistent, a doctor who wanted to offer PGD for gender selection inquired of the ethics committee why pre-conception methods for gender variety, which lacked 100% certainty, were acceptable but PGD, which guaranteed that certainty, was not. Focusing only on the sexism and gender discrimination issue, the chair of the ethics committee, in a widely publicised letter, found that PGD for gender balancing would be acceptable.[21] When the full committee reconsidered the matter, it concluded that it had not yet received enough evidence that the need for gender variety was so important in families that it justified creating and discarding embryos for that purpose.[19] In the future if such evidence was forthcoming then PGD for gender variety might also be acceptable.

What might constitute such evidence? One source would be families with two or more children of one gender who very much would like to have another child but only if they could be sure that it would be a child of the gender opposite of existing children. Given the legitimacy of wanting to raise children of both genders, reasonable persons might find that this need outweighs the symbolic costs of creating and discarding embryos for that purpose.

Another instance would be a case in which a couple has had a girl, but now wants a boy in order to meet cultural norms of having a male heir or a male to perform funeral rituals or play other cultural roles. An IVF programme in India is now providing PGD to select male offspring as the second child of couples who have already had a daughter.[22] Because of the importance of a male heir in India, those couples might well consider having an abortion if pregnant with a female fetus (even though illegal in India for that purpose). In that setting PGD for gender selection for gender variety appears to be justified.

PGD for Perfect Pitch

Perfect or "absolute" pitch is the ability to identify and recall musical notes from memory.[23] Although not all great or successful musicians have perfect pitch, a large number of them do. Experts disagree over whether perfect pitch is solely inborn or may also be developed by early training, though most agree that a person either has it or does not. It also runs in families, apparently in an autosomal dominant pattern.[23] The gene or genes coding for this capacity have not, however, been mapped, much less sequenced. Because genes for perfect pitch may also relate to the genetic basis for language or other cognitive abilities, research to find that gene may be forthcoming.

Once the gene for perfect pitch or its linked markers are identified, it would be feasible to screen embryos for those alleles, and transfer only those embryos that test positive. The prevalence of those genes is quite low (perhaps three in 100) in the population, but high in certain families.[23] Thus only persons from those families who have a strong interest in the musical ability of their children would be potential candidates for PGD for perfect pitch. Many of them are likely to take their chances with coital conception and exposure of the child to music at an early age. Some couples, however, may be willing to undergo IVF and PGD to ensure musical ability in their child. Should their request be accepted or denied?

As noted, the answer to this question depends on the importance of the reproductive choice being asserted, the burdens of the selection procedure, its impact on offspring, and its implications for deselected groups and society generally. The strongest case for the parents is if they persuasively asserted that they would not reproduce unless they could select that trait, and they have a plausible explanation for that position. Although the preference might appear odd to some, it might also be quite understandable in highly musical families, particularly ones in which some members already have perfect pitch. Parents clearly have the right to instill or develop a child's musical ability after birth. They might reasonably argue that they should have that right before birth as well.

If so, then creating and discarding embryos for this purpose should also be acceptable. If embryos are too rudimentary in development to have inherent rights or interests, then no moral duty is violated by creating and destroying them.[24] Some persons might think that doing so for trivial or unimportant reasons debases the inherent dignity of all human life, but having a child with perfect pitch will not seem trivial to parents seeking this technique. Ultimately, the judgment of triviality or importance of the choice within a broad spectrum rests with the couple. If they have a strong enough preference to seek PGD for this purpose and that preference rationally relates to understandable reproductive goals, then they have demonstrated its great importance to them. Only in cases unsupported by a reasonable explanation of the need—for example, perhaps creating embryos to pick eye or hair colour, should a person's individual assessment of the importance of creating embryos be condemned or rejected.

A third relevant factor is whether musical trait selection is consistent with respect for the resulting child. Parents who are willing to undergo the costs and burdens of IVF and PGD to have a child with perfect pitch may be so overly invested in the child having a musical career that they will prevent it from developing its own personality and identity. Parents, however, are free to instill and develop musical ability once the child is born, just as they are entitled to instill particular religious views. It is difficult to say that they cross an impermissible moral line of risk to the welfare of their prospective child in screening embryos for this purpose. Parents are still obligated to provide their child with the basic education and care necessary for any life plan. Wanting a child to have perfect pitch is not inconsistent with parents also wanting their child to be well rounded and equipped for life in other contexts.

A fourth factor, impact on deselected groups, is much less likely to be an issue in the case of perfect pitch because there is no stigma or negative association tied to persons without that trait. Persons without perfect pitch suffer no stigma or opprobrium by the couple's choice or public acceptance of it, as is arguably the case with embryo selection on grounds of gender, sexual orientation, intelligence, strength, size, or other traits. Nor is PGD for perfect pitch likely to perpetuate unfair class advantages, as selection for intelligence, strength, size, or beauty might.

A final factor is the larger societal impact of permitting embryo screening for a non-medical condition such as perfect pitch. A valid concern is that such a practice might then legitimise embryo screening for other traits as well, thus moving us toward a future in which children are primarily valued according to the attractiveness of their expected characteristics. But that threat is too hypothetical to justify limiting what are otherwise valid exercises of parental choice. It is highly unlikely that many traits would be controlled by genes that could be easily tested in embryos. Gender is determined by the chromosome, and the gene for pefect pitch, if ever found, would be a rare exception to the multifactorial complexity of such traits. Screening embryos for perfect pitch, if otherwise acceptable, should not be stopped simply because of speculation about what might be possible several decades from now.

PGD for Other Non-Medical Traits

The discussion of PGD for perfect pitch illustrates the issues that would arise if single gene analysis became possible for other traits, such as sexual orientation, hair or eye colour, or height, intelligence, size, strength, and memory. In each case the ethical assessment depends on an evaluation of the importance of the choice to the parents and whether that choice plausibly falls within societal understandings of parental needs and choice in reproducing and raising children. If so, it should usually be a sufficient reason to create and screen embryos. The effect on resulting offspring would also be of key moral importance. Whether selection carries a public or social message about the worth of existing groups should also be addressed.

Applying this methodology might show that some instances of non-medical selection are justified, as we have seen with embryo selection for gender variety and perhaps for having a child with perfect pitch. The acceptability of PGD to select other non-medical traits will depend on a careful analysis of the relevant ethical factors, and social acceptance of much greater parental rights to control the genes of offspring than now exists.

Conclusion

Although new indications are emerging for PGD, it is likely to remain a small part of reproductive practice for some time to come. Most new indications serve legitimate medical purposes, such as screening for single gene mutations for late onset disorders or susceptibility to cancer. There is also ethical support for using PGD to assure that a child is an HLA match with an existing child.

More controversial is the use of PGD to select gender or other non-medical traits. As with medical uses, the acceptability of non-medical screening will depend upon the interests served and the effects of using PGD for those purposes. Speculations about potential future non-medical uses should not restrict new uses of PGD which are otherwise ethically acceptable.

References

1. International Working Group on Preimplantation Genetics. Preimplantation genetic diagnosis: experience of 3000 clinical cycles. Report of the 11th annual meeting, May 15, 2001. *Reprod Biomedicine Online* 2001;3:49–53.

2. Verlinsky Y, Rechitsky S, Verlinsky O, et al. Preimplantation diagnosis of P53 tumor suppressor gene mutations. *Reprod Biomedicine Online* 2001;2:102–5.

3. Verlinsky Y, Rechitsky S, Schoolcraft W, et al. Preimplantation diagnosis for fanconi anemia combined with HLA matching. *JAMA* 2001;285:3130–3.

4. Verlinsky Y, Rechitsky S, Verlinsky O, et al. Preimplantation diagnosis for early-onset alzheimer's disease caused by V717L mutation. *JAMA* 2002;283:1018–21.

5. Fukuyama F. *Our postmodern future: consequences of the biotechnology revolution.* New York: Farrar, Strauss, & Giroux, 2002.

6. Stock G. *Redesigning humans: our inevitable genetic future.* New York: Houghton Mifflin, 2002.

7. Simpson JL. Celebrating preimplantation genetic diagnosis of p53 mutations in Li-Fraumeni syndrome. *Reprod Biomedicine Online* 2001;3: 2–3.

8. Towner D, Loewy RS. Ethics of preimplantation diagnosis for a woman destined to develop early-onset alzheimer disease. *JAMA* 2002;283:1038–40.

9. Human Fertilisation and Embryology Authority. Opinion of the ethics committee. Ethical issues in the creation and selection of preimplantation embryos to produce tissue donors. London: HFEA, 2001 Nov 22.

10. Pennings G, Schots S, Liebaers I. Ethical considerations on preimplantation genetic diagnosis for HLA typing to match a future child as a donor of haematopoietic stem cells to a sibling. *Hum Reprod* 2002;17:534–8.

11. Robertson JA, Kahn J, Wagner J. Conception to obtain hematopoietic stem cells. *Hastings Cent Rep* 2002;32:34–40.

12. Sen A. More than 100 million women are missing. *New York Review of Books* 1990;37:61–8.

13. Eckholm E. Desire for sons drives use of prenatal scans in China. *The New York Times* 2002 Jun 21: A3.

14. Jaccoby EE, Jacklin CN. *The psychology of sex differences.* Palo Alto: Stanford University Press, 1974.

15. Robertson JA. Preconception gender selection. *Am J Bioeth* 2001;1:2–9.

16. Grubb A, Walsh P. Gender-vending II. *Dispatches* 1994;1:1–3.

17. Mahowald MB. *Genes, women, equality.* New York: Oxford University Press, 2000: 121.

18. American Society of Reproductive Medicine, Ethics Committee. Preconception gender selection for nonmedical reasons. *Fertil Steril* 2001;75:861–4.

19. Robertson JA. Sex selection for gender variety by preimplantation genetic diagnosis. *Fert Steril* 2002;78:463.

20. American Society of Reproductive Medicine, Ethics Committee. Sex selection and preimplantation genetic diagnosis. *Fertil Steril* 1999;72:595–8.

21. Kolata G. Society approves embryo selection. *The New York Times* 2001 Sept 26: A14.

22. Malpani A, Malpani A, Modi D. Preimplantation sex selection for family balancing in India. *Hum Reprod* 2002;17:11–12.

23. Blakeslee S. Perfect pitch: the key may lie in the genes. *The New York Times* 1990 Nov 30: 1.

24. American Society of Reproductive Medicine, Ethics Committee. Ethical considerations of assisted reproductive technologies. *Fertil Steril* 1994;62(suppl):32–7S.

Marcy Darnovsky  **NO**

Revisiting Sex Selection:
The Growing Popularity of
New Sex Selection Methods
Revives an Old Debate

In the United States and a few other prosperous, technologically advanced nations, methods of sex selection that are less intrusive or more reliable than older practices are now coming into use. Unlike prenatal testing, these procedures generally are applied either before an embryo is implanted in a woman's body, or before an egg is fertilized. They do not require aborting a fetus of the "wrong" sex.

These pre-pregnancy sex selection methods are being rapidly commercialized—not, as before, with medical claims, but as a means of satisfying parental desires. For the assisted reproduction industry, social sex selection may be a business path toward a vastly expanded market. People who have no infertility or medical problems, but who can afford expensive out-of-pocket procedures, are an enticing new target.

For the first time, some fertility clinics are openly advertising sex selection for social reasons. Several times each month, for example, the *New York Times'* Sunday Styles section carries an ad from the Virginia-based Genetics & IVF (in-vitro fertilization) Institute, touting its patented sperm sorting method. Beside a smiling baby, its boldface headline asks, "Do You Want To Choose the Gender Of Your Next Baby?"

Recent trends in consumer culture may warm prospective parents to such offers. We have become increasingly accepting of—if not enthusiastic about—"enhancements" of appearance (think face-lifts, collagen and Botox injections, and surgery to reshape women's feet for stiletto heels) and adjustments of behavior (anti-depressants, Viagra, and the like). These drugs and procedures were initially developed for therapeutic uses, but are now being marketed and normalized in disturbing ways. When considering questions of right and wrong, of liberty and justice, it is well to remember that the state is not the only coercive force we encounter.

This constellation of technological, economic, cultural, and ideological developments has revived the issue of sex selection, relatively dormant for more than a decade. The concerns that have always accompanied sex selection debates are being reassessed and updated. These include the prospect that selection could reinforce misogyny, sexism, and gender stereotypes; undermine the well-being of children by treating them as commodities and subjecting them to excessive parental expectations or disappointment; skew sex ratios in local populations; further the commercialization of reproduction; and open the door to a high-tech consumer eugenics.

Sex Selection Debates in the United States

Sex selection is not a new issue for U.S. feminists. In the 1980s and early 1990s, it was widely discussed and debated, especially by feminist bioethicists. This was the period when choosing a boy or girl was accomplished by undergoing prenatal diagnostic tests to determine the sex of a fetus, and then terminating the pregnancy if the fetus was of the undesired sex.

Ultrasound scanning and amniocentesis, which had been developed during the 1970s to detect, and usually to abort, fetuses with Down's syndrome and other conditions, were on their way to becoming routine in wealthier parts of the world. Soon they were also being openly promoted as tools for enabling sex-selective abortions in South and East Asian countries where the cultural preference for sons is pervasive. Opposition in these countries, especially strong in India, mounted in the early 1980s and remains vibrant today.

Throughout the 1980s and early 1990s, feminists and others in the U.S. who addressed the issue of sex selection were—almost universally—deeply uneasy about it. Not all opposed it equally, but none were enthusiastic or even supportive.

Some, like Helen Bequaert Holmes, pointed out that the deliberate selection of the traits of future generations is a form of eugenics.[1] Many deplored the practice as a symptom of a sexist society, in effect if not always in intent. In a book-length treatment of these concerns, published in 1985, philosopher Mary Anne Warren asked whether the practice should be considered an aspect of what she dubbed 'gendercide'—"no less a moral atrocity than genocide"—and published an entire book on the topic in 1985.[2]

But there was also broad consensus among feminists that any effort to limit sex-selective abortions, especially in the U.S., would threaten reproductive rights. Warren, despite her misgivings, argued that choosing the sex of one's child was sexist only if its intent or consequence was discrimination against women. She concluded that "there is great danger that the legal prohibition of sex selection would endanger other aspects of women's reproductive freedom," and considered even moral suasion against the practice to be unwarranted and counterproductive.

By the mid-1990s, the discussion had reached an impasse. No one liked sex selection, but few were willing to actively oppose it. Sex selection largely faded as an issue of concern for U.S. feminists, especially outside the circles of an increasingly professionalized bioethics discourse.

Separating Sex Selection from Abortion Politics

The new technologies of sex selection (and, perhaps, their potential profits) have prompted some bioethicists to argue in favor of allowing parents to choose their offspring's sex. As in past debates on other assisted reproductive procedures, they frame their advocacy in terms of "choice," "liberty," and "rights." John Robertson, a lawyer and bioethicist close to the fertility industry, is one of the leading proponents of this approach. In a lead article of the Winter 2001 issue of *American Journal of Bioethics*, Robertson wrote, "The risk that exercising rights of procreative liberty would hurt offspring or women— or contribute to sexism generally—is too speculative and uncertain to justify infringement of those rights."[3]

Robertson's claims are based on a world view that gives great weight to individual preferences and liberties, and little to social justice and the common good. As political scientist Diane Paul writes in a commentary on Robertson's recent defense of "preconception gender selection," "If you begin with libertarian premises, you will inevitably end up having to accept uses of reprogenetic technology that are even more worrisome" than sex selection.[4]

Definitions of procreative liberty like Robertson's are expansive—indeed, they often seem limitless. They are incapable, for example, of making a distinction between terminating an unwanted pregnancy—that is, deciding whether and when to bear children—and selecting the qualities and traits of a future child. However, sex selection and abortion are different matters, especially when a pregnancy is not involved.

Since new sex selection technologies are used before pregnancy, political discussions and policy initiatives which address them need not directly affect women's rights or access to abortion. In fact, many countries already prohibit "non-medical" sex selection, with no adverse impact on the availability or legality of abortion. One such nation is the United Kingdom, where, in November, 2003, after a comprehensive reconsideration of the issue, their Human Fertilization and Embryology Authority recommended that sex selection for social reasons continue to be prohibited, and that the Authority's purview be expanded to include regulation of sperm sorting technologies as well as other sex selection procedures. Even in the United States, where abortion rights are imminently threatened, the emergence of pre-pregnancy technologies should make it far easier than before, when sex determination meant selective abortion, to consider sex selection apart from abortion politics.

Eugenics: Is the Slope Becoming More Slippery?

When Mary Anne Warren considered sex selection in 1985, she summarily dismissed concerns of its contribution to a new eugenics as "implausible" on the grounds that "[t]here is at present no highly powerful interest group which is committed to the development and use of immoral forms of human genetic engineering."[5]

However, less than two decades later, a disturbing number of highly powerful figures are in fact committed to the development and use of a form of human genetic engineering that huge majorities here and abroad consider immoral—inheritable genetic modification, or manipulating the genes passed on to our children. These scientists, bioethicists, biotech entrepreneurs, and libertarians are actively advocating a new market-based, high-tech eugenics.

Princeton University molecular biologist Lee Silver, for example, positively anticipates the emergence of genetic castes and human sub-species. "[T]he GenRich class and the Natural class will become . . . entirely separate species," he writes, "with no ability to cross-breed, and with as much romantic interest in each other as a current human would have for a chimpanzee."[6] Nobel laureate James Watson promotes redesigning the genes of our children with statements such as, "People say it would be terrible if we made all girls pretty. I think it would be great."[7]

Silver's and Watson's remarks (and all too many similar ones) refer to technologies that are being used routinely in lab animals, but have not been applied to human beings. However, pre-implantation genetic diagnosis (PGD), the most common new sex selection method, is very much related to these technologies. It was introduced in 1990 as a way to identify and discard embryos affected by serious genetic conditions, and thus prevent the birth of children with particular traits. Though PGD is touted as a medical tool, disability advocates have pointed out that many people who have the conditions it targets live full and satisfying lives. PGD, they say, is already a eugenic technology.

In recent years, PGD has begun to be used to screen for more and more genetic attributes—late-onset conditions, tissue types suitable for matching those of a future child's sick sibling, and sex. Advocacy of even greater permissiveness in the use of PGD is beginning to pepper the professional literature. Bioethicist Edgar Dahl recently published an essay arguing that if a "safe and reliable genetic test" for sexual orientation were to become available, "parents should clearly be allowed" to use it, as long as they are permitted to select for homosexual as well as heterosexual children.[8] Bioethicist Julian Savulescu even baits disability advocates with the argument that we "should allow people deliberately to create disabled children."[9]

Concern about consumer eugenics and the commodification of children looms large for critics of social sex selection. As part of a recent campaign aimed at the Human Fertilization and Embryology Authority, the UK-based bioethics group Human Genetics Alert writes, "If we allow sex selection it will be impossible to oppose 'choice' of any other characteristics, such as appearance, height, intelligence, et cetera. The door to 'designer babies' will not have been opened a crack—it will have been thrown wide open."[10]

Another British NGO, Gene Watch UK [*no relation to* GeneWatch *magazine—ed.*] puts it this way: Allowing sex selection "would represent a significant shift towards treating children as commodities and [subjecting] the selection of a child's genetic make-up . . . to parental choice, exercised through paying a commercial company to provide this 'service'."[11]

Some researchers, bioethicists, and fertility practitioners have publicly opposed such uses of PGD, and expressed alarm at what the new push for social sex selection seems to portend. In September, 2001, Robertson, then acting chair

If wishes, choices, and preferences are to be appropriately balanced with social justice and the common good, they cannot be unthinkingly transformed into protected liberties, much less codified rights. Isolated from social consequences, both wishes and liberties are at best naïve.

Notes

1. Humber and Almeder, eds. "Sex Preselection: Eugenics for Everyone?" *Biomedical Ethics Reviews*, 1985

2. Mary Ann Warren. *Gendercide: The Implications of Sex Selection*. Rowman & Littlefield, 1985

3. John A. Robertson. "Preconception Gender Selection," *American Journal of Bioethics,* Winter 2001

4. Dian Paul. "Where Libertarian Premises Lead," *American Journal of Bioethics,* Winter 2001

5. Mary Ann Warren. *Gendercide: The Implications of Sex Selection*. Rowman & Littlefield, 1985

6. Lee Silver. *Remaking Eden*. Avon, 1997

7. Shaoni Bhattacharya. "Stupidity should be cured, says DNA discoverer," *New Scientist*, February 28, 2003 . . .

8. Edgar Dahl. "Ethical Issues in New Uses of Preimplantation Genetic Diagnosis," *Human Reproduction*, Vol. 18 No. 7

9. Julian Savunescu, from the title of a November 25, 2003 presentation in London. . . .

10. "The Case Against Sex Selection," December 2002 . . .

11. "GeneWatch UK Submission to the HFEA Consultation on Sex Selection," January 2003

12. Gina Kolata. "Fertility Ethics Authority Approves Sex Selection," *The New York Times*, September 28, 2001

13. Margaret Talbot. "Jack or Jill? The era of consumer-driven eugenics has begun," *The Atlantic Monthly*, March 2002

14. Meredith Wadman. "So You Want A Girl?," *Fortune*, February 2001

15. Susan Sachs. "Clinics' Pitch to Indian Émigrés," *New York Times*, August 15, 2001

16. Lisa Belkin. "Getting the Girl," *The New York Times Magazine*, July 25, 1999

17. "Choosing Your Baby's Gender," . . . November 7, 2002

18. Belkin.

19. Dorothy Roberts, *Killing the Black Body: Race, Reproduction, and the Meaning of Liberty*, New York: Vintage Books, 1997, p. 286

POSTSCRIPT

Should Parents Be Allowed to Select the Sex of Their Baby?

Imagine yourself in the position of being able to choose the sex of your future children. What would be the benefits of having a daughter as opposed to a son, or vice versa? How much of these benefits rest on your expectations of your future child's personality? Are these traits inherently tied to their sex or gender?

Now imagine the way your future child looks. How tall is s/he? What color eyes does s/he have? Hair color? Is your child athletic? Artistic? Intelligent? In the near future, it may be possible to make your "dream family" come true, for around $18,000 per child. If you had the economic means, would you? Why or why not?

Is there something about yourself that you consider unique? Is it a physical ability or talent, or even a physical feature that sets you apart from the crowd? Did it come from your mother or father—or is it distinctive from all of your family members? Now imagine that your parents told you that they wanted you to have this feature so bad that they "selected" it while you were still an embryo. Would you feel any less unique? What if they simply said they wanted you to be a certain sex? Would that change the way you feel about yourself? Would you feel different about a friend whose athletic talent was thanks in part to their parents' design, rather than nature's (though both would require discipline and hard work to cultivate)?

Do you consider it acceptable to use PGD (or other prenatal techniques) to predetermine the characteristics of your baby? Is it acceptable to screen for hereditary debilitating conditions and diseases? What did you make of Darnovsky claim that allowing PGD for sex selection could pave the way for "designer babies"?

Robertson challenged the "slippery slope" argument by stating "Speculations about potential future non-medical uses should not restrict new uses of PGD which are otherwise ethically acceptable." Do you agree? Is genetic sex selection medically ethical? Is preferring a child of one sex inherently sexist? If genetic markers are found for musical ability, intelligence, sexual orientation, or any other trait, will companies begin to offer the selection or deselection of these traits to potential parents and customers? Should these types of procedures be regulated or restricted even if they do not yet exist?

Suggested Readings

A. R. Fahrenkrog. "A Comparison of International Regulation of Preimplantation Genetic Diagnosis and a Regulatory Suggestion for the

United States," *Transnational Law & Contemporary Problems* 15(2), Spring 2006.

M. Healy, "Fertility's New Frontier," *Los Angeles Times* (July 21, 2003).

S. Matthew Liao, "The Ethics of Using Genetic Engineering for Sex Selection," *Journal of Medical Ethics*, 31(2), Feb. 2005.

B. Trivedi, "Boy or Girl? Embryo Tests Give Parents the Choice," *New Scientist*, Sept. 30, 2006.

ISSUE 11

Should Emergency Contraception Be Available over the Counter?

YES: Jane E. Brody, from "The Politics of Emergency Contraception," *New York Times Magazine* (August 24, 2004)

NO: United States Food and Drug Administration, from "FDA's Decision Regarding Plan B: Questions and Answers," www.fda.gov/cder/drug/infopage/planB/planBQandA.htm

ISSUE SUMMARY

YES: *New York Times* columnist Jane E. Brody believes that politics, not science, drove the FDA's decision not to allow emergency contraception to be made available over the counter.

NO: The Food and Drug and Drug Administration, responsible for regulating all drugs dispensed in the United States, says that its decision was not political, and that it would reconsider its decision if presented with evidence that girls under age 16 could take it safely without parental supervision.

What is emergency contraception? In the past, it was nicknamed "the morning after pill," indicating that it is a method of postcoital contraception—that is, it can be taken *after* unprotected vaginal intercourse to prevent pregnancy. The term "emergency contraception" (or e.c.) is more accurate because it can be taken not just the "morning after," but also *several* mornings after, up to 120 hours (or 5 days) after unprotected intercourse. However, it is *most* effective when begun sooner. If a woman begins taking emergency contraception within one day after unprotected intercourse, she reduces her risk of pregnancy by 95 percent; within three days, pregnancy risk is reduced by 75 percent; and so on.

Emergency contraception is sometimes confused with the "abortion pill," more commonly known as RU-486, mifepristone, or medical abortion. The abortion pill is quite different from e.c. Whereas the abortion pill will induce a nonsurgical abortion when taken up to seven weeks after a pregnancy begins, emergency contraception is taken to *prevent* a pregnancy before it begins. Using a high dose of hormones found in the contraceptive pill, it works in multiple ways—(a) it stops a woman from ovulating (or releasing an egg), so that the egg does not become fertilized; (b) if ovulation has occurred, it may prevent the egg and sperm from joining; and (c) if fertilization does occur, it may prevent the fertilized egg from implanting in the wall of the uterus so that a pregnancy cannot begin. If a fertilized egg has already implanted, emergency contraception does not work.

In the spring of 2004, the United States Food and Drug Administration (FDA), the government body that regulates the dispensing of all medications, rejected a proposal to make one type of emergency contraception known as "Plan B" available over the counter. This decision surprised many, as the FDA rejected the recommendations and conclusions of its own advisory panel. Some speculated that President George W. Bush's religiously conservative administration was behind the decision. Conservatives generally reject the clinical definition of pregnancy, claiming that life begins when an egg is fertilized, not when the egg implants, as medical organizations and textbooks say. They also believe that increased accessibility of emergency contraception will lead to increased sexual promiscuity.

After the 2004 decision, women who were in need of emergency contraception were left with the same limited options as before. They could get a prescription from their doctor or from a family planning center like Planned Parenthood. However, many women's health care providers and activists again expressed concern that the requirement to visit a doctor or clinic in order to get a prescription for e.c. created a barrier to young women seeking services. It was believed that some women may delay this important decision if they are uncomfortable telling a doctor about their sexual behavior, or may feel embarrassed visiting a family planning center. This may be especially true when a woman is seeking emergency contraception because of a rape or sexual assault.

In the following selections, columnist Jane E. Brody claims that the FDA's decision was politically motivated, while the FDA defends and explains its decision.

YES

Jane E. Brody

The Politics of Emergency Contraception

"Emergency Contraception: Politics Trumps Science at the F.D.A." That is the title of an editorial by Dr. David A. Grimes in the August issue of *Obstetrics & Gynecology,* the journal of the American College of Obstetricians and Gynecologists.

Dr. Grimes is hardly the only one distressed by the Food and Drug Administration's decision in May to refuse to grant over-the-counter access to the morning-after emergency contraceptive known as Plan B. Six months earlier, the agency's advisory committees voted 23 to 4 in favor of removing the requirement that a woman first obtain a prescription from a doctor before she can buy this product. In nearly all cases, the agency abides by the votes of its advisory panels. But not this time. And the reason, Dr. Grimes and other medical leaders have said, is that the agency's "decision-making process is being influenced by political considerations."

The politics in this case involve, indirectly, the Bush administration's advocacy of "abstinence only" to prevent pregnancy in unwed teenagers and, more directly, its objection to abortion, which emergency contraception is not. And Dr. Grimes points out that the rate of unplanned pregnancies in this country "is unparalleled among industrialized nations," and that "each year, nearly 2 percent of all women of reproductive age have an induced abortion."

Women at risk of an unwanted pregnancy deserve to know the reasons that so many leading scientists and organizations have endorsed over-the-counter status for emergency contraception and the reasons that others have objected.

The Need for Intervention

Plan B is a progesterone-based after-the-fact contraceptive meant to be taken as soon as possible after a sexual encounter that places a woman at risk of pregnancy. It is supposed to be used within 72 hours after unprotected intercourse, but it is most effective when taken sooner, within 12 to 24 hours.

There are two other options that can be used when a woman needs post-coital contraception: a drug called Preven that is in effect a high-dose birth control pill, and insertion of a copper IUD, both of which also require a doctor's intervention.

There are many reasons a woman may need postcoital contraception. Condoms can break, diaphragms and cervical caps can become dislodged, IUDs can be expelled unknowingly and birth control pills forgotten. In addition, some women, particularly teenagers, fail to anticipate a sexual encounter or may need to feel "swept away" and are thus unprepared to protect themselves against an unwanted pregnancy. And then there is rape resulting in pregnancy.

As Dr. Fatim H. Lakha and colleagues noted in the July issue of *Women's Health in Primary Care,* "Unprotected sexual intercourse is a fact of life." When that happens, they said, "unintended pregnancy can be prevented" by the use of emergency contraception.

The Objections

Some opponents of emergency contraception confuse it with abortion. But an abortion can occur only after a pregnancy has been established. The National Institutes of Health and the obstetricians group define pregnancy as beginning with the implantation of a fertilized egg in the uterus. Emergency contraception, on the other hand, has no effect once a fertilized egg implants in the womb. It cannot dislodge an established pregnancy or harm a developing embryo. Nor does it appear to work by destroying a fertilized egg or preventing implantation, which would negate the concerns of those who consider fertilization, not implantation, the start of pregnancy.

The mechanism of action of Plan B and Preven is not definitively known, but the evidence indicates that they delay or inhibit ovulation and make the cervical mucus inhospitable to sperm. A woman need not be ovulating at the time of intercourse to become pregnant. Sperm can live for several days in a woman's genital tract waiting for an egg to fertilize. Another objection to emergency contraception is the fear that its ready availability would encourage teenage sexual encounters or foster careless sex among couples who might otherwise have used ordinary contraception. To date, controlled studies have found no evidence that women would neglect to use precoital contraception in favor of an emergency contraceptive, especially since the former is a more reliable way to prevent an unwanted pregnancy.

Nor is there evidence that teenagers would be encouraged to engage in risky sexual behavior. "This is analogous to suggesting that a fire extinguisher beneath the kitchen sink makes one a risky cook," Dr. Grimes wrote.

In fact, one study published this year in *The Journal of Pediatric and Adolescent Gynecology* found no increase in unprotected intercourse when young sexually active teenage girls were given easy access to emergency contraception through an advance prescription. A third objection is that without a doctor to explain the proper use of emergency contraception, women, and especially teenagers, would fail to use it properly. Again, studies have shown that women who were able to self-administer emergency contraception did so correctly and at the proper time and suffered no adverse effects.

An Interim Solution

Any delay in reaching a doctor, getting a prescription for emergency contraception and finding a pharmacy that stocks the drug can render it ineffective. Without any intervention, the average woman's chance of becoming pregnant after one act of unprotected intercourse is 8 percent. When Plan B is used within 24 hours of unprotected intercourse, the pregnancy rate is about four-tenths of 1 percent, or 4 per 1,000, rising to 2.7 percent when treatment begins 48 to 72 hours after. Proper use of emergency contraception, on average, reduces the risk of pregnancy by about 85 percent, and more if the treatment is used within 12 hours. Side effects with Plan B are minor—nausea in about 15 percent of cases, vomiting in 1 percent and a delay in the next menstrual period in 5 percent.

Side effect rates are higher with Preven, which includes an estrogen component as well as a progesterone.

Unless the F.D.A. allows Plan B to be sold without a prescription, advocates for easy access to the drug advise women to get a prescription from their doctors and fill it well before they need it. Unfortunately, few teenagers would be likely to take such a step, unless they are already receiving regular gynecological care. In addition, the added cost of a medical visit can make access to Plan B prohibitive for many women, especially teenagers.

Six states, including California and Washington, have laws that allow a woman to buy emergency contraception from a pharmacist without a prescription. Other states might consider following suit. Still, education must coincide with access. Even in California, only 29 percent of the women most at risk of an unintended pregnancy were aware of emergency contraception, according to a new study in *The American Journal of Obstetrics and Gynecology*.

Finally, every woman must realize that emergency contraception is a backup, not a substitute for more reliable precoital contraception. Emergency contraception is not as effective in preventing pregnancy as, say, oral contraceptives, implants or the copper IUD. And if, after using emergency contraception, a woman fails to menstruate within three or four weeks, she is advised to take a pregnancy test, which is included in the emergency contraceptive packet.

United States Food and Drug Administration

 **NO**

FDA's Decision Regarding Plan B: Questions and Answers

1. What is emergency contraception?

Emergency contraception is a method of preventing pregnancy to be used after a contraceptive fails or after unprotected sex. It is not for routine use. Drugs used for this purpose are called emergency contraceptive pills, post-coital pills, or morning after pills. Emergency contraceptives contain the hormones estrogen and progestin (levonorgestrel), either separately or in combination. FDA has approved two products for prescription use for emergency contraception—Preven (approved in 1998) and Plan B (approved in 1999).

2. What is Plan B?

Plan B is emergency contraception, a backup method to birth control. It is in the form of two levonorgestrel pills (0.75 mg in each pill) that are taken by mouth after unprotected sex. Levonorgestrel is a synthetic hormone used in birth control pills for over 35 years. Plan B can reduce a woman's risk of pregnancy when taken as directed if she has had unprotected sex. Plan B contains only progestin, levonorgestrel, a synthetic hormone used in birth control pills for over 35 years. It is currently available only by prescription.

3. How does Plan B work?

Plan B works like other birth control pills to prevent pregnancy. Plan B acts primarily by stopping the release of an egg from the ovary (ovulation). It may prevent the union of sperm and egg (fertilization). If fertilization does occur, Plan B may prevent a fertilized egg from attaching to the womb (implantation). If a fertilized egg is implanted prior to taking Plan B, Plan B will not work.

4. What steps did FDA take in considering switching Plan B from prescription to nonprescription (over-the-counter (OTC)) status?

FDA received an application to switch Plan B from prescription to nonprescription status. FDA staff reviewed the scientific data contained in the

From the United States Food and Drug Administration, 2004. www.fda.gov/cder/drug/omfopage/planB/planBQand A.htm application which included among other data, an actual use study and a label comprehension study.

On December 16, 2003, we held a public advisory committee meeting with a panel of medical and scientific experts from outside the federal government. The members of the Nonprescription Drugs Advisory Committee and the Advisory Committee for Reproductive Health, met jointly to consider the safety and effectiveness data of nonprescription use of Plan B. Although the joint committee recommended to FDA that this product be sold without a prescription, some members of the committee, including the Chair, raised questions concerning whether the actual use data were generalizable to the overall population of nonprescription users, chiefly because of inadequate sampling of younger age groups.

Following the advisory committee meeting, FDA requested additional information from the sponsor pertaining to adolescent use. The sponsor submitted this additional information to FDA in support of their pending application to change Plan B from a prescription to an over-the-counter product. This additional information was extensive enough to qualify as a major amendment to the NDA. Under the terms of the Prescription Drug User Fee Act (PDUFA) performance goals, major amendments such as this may trigger a 90-day extension of the original PDUFA deadline.

Now FDA has completed its review of the supplemental application and concluded that the application could not be approved at this time because 1) adequate data were not provided to support a conclusion that young adolescent women can safely use Plan B for emergency contraception without the professional supervision of a licensed practitioner and 2) a proposal from the sponsor to change the requested indication to allow for marketing of Plan B as a prescription-only product for women under 16 years of age and a nonprescription product for women 16 years and older was incomplete and inadequate for a full review. Therefore, FDA concluded that the application was not approvable.

5. Why didn't FDA follow the recommendation of the Advisory Committees?

The recommendations of FDA advisory committees are advisory in nature and the Agency is not bound to follow their recommendations. FDA makes a decision on whether a product should be approved after evaluating all data and considering the recommendations of the advisory committee.

6. Why did FDA issue a Not Approvable letter?

The agency issued a Not Approvable letter because the supplemental application did not meet the criteria for approval in that it did not demonstrate that Plan B could be used safely by young adolescent women for emergency contraception without the professional supervision of a licensed practitioner. The issuance of a Not Approvable letter does not mean that a supplemental application cannot be approved. The Not Approvable letter describes what the applicant would need to do to obtain approval for the supplemental application. In this case, the applicant would have to either provide additional data demonstrating that Plan B can be used safely by women under 16 years of age without the professional supervision of a practitioner licensed by law to administer the drug or provide additional support for the revised indication to allow for marketing Plan B as prescription-only for women under the age of 16 and as nonprescription for women 16 years of age and older.

> 7. *Was there a difference of opinion within the Center for Drug Evaluation and Research (CDER) regarding the final decision?*

Yes, there was a difference of opinion within CDER. The scientific interchange of ideas is widely encouraged during the review process to ensure a thorough vetting of the issues. However, ultimately, a final decision must be made based on the evaluation of the data, taking into account all of the views expressed.

> 8. *Is this FDA's final decision regarding the availability of Plan B for OTC use?*

No. The Not Approvable letter to the sponsor outlines what the sponsor must do to obtain approval of the supplemental application.

Wide availability of safe and effective contraceptives is important to public health. We look forward to working with the sponsor if they decide to pursue making this product available without a prescription.

> 9. *Oral contraceptives have been used for four decades, and this product has been approved and used safely since 1999. How could FDA turn it down?*

Oral contraceptives as a class of drugs are only available by prescription. This product has been used safely by prescription only and for the reasons already stated, it is not being made available for OTC use at this time.

> 10. *The sponsor has talked about making the product over-the-counter for young women over a certain age and behind-the-counter for younger girls. Is there evidence to support such a scheme? Does FDA have the authority to carry it out?*

The sponsor has submitted a plan and the FDA is examining its regulatory authority to approve a product marketed in this manner.

> 11. *Did the FDA bow to political pressure in making this decision?*

No. This decision was made within the Center for Drug Evaluation and Research.

> 12. *Dr. Steven Galson signed the letter FDA sent to the sponsor. Does Dr. Galson usually sign such letters? Why did Dr. Galson sign the letter?*

No, Dr. Galson does not usually sign regulatory action letters. However, his opinion of the adequacy of the data in young adolescents differed from that of the review staff. He believes that additional data are needed and for that reason he made the decision to take final action within the Office of the Center Director.

POSTSCRIPT

Should Emergency Contraception Be Available over the Counter?

The *New England Journal of Medicine* immediately criticized the FDA's decision, saying, "The data overwhelmingly demonstrate that emergency contraception is safe and effective when available without a prescription." Forty-one members of Congress also asked the FDA to reconsider its decision. Two members, a Republican and a Democrat, Louise M. Slaughter (D-NY) and Christopher Shays (R-CT), called for an investigation of the FDA's decision-making process, and for the resignation of FDA officials responsible for the decision.

In making its decision, the FDA underscored its concern that emergency contraception first be proven safe for adolescent women under age 16. This is not a typical standard for determining the over-the-counter status of other medications. Normally, when considering whether or not a drug is safe, the FDA examines its toxicity, side effects, how it makes its way through a person's system, and whether or not it is addictive. The FDA's response makes reference to Dr. Steven Galson, the acting director of the FDA's Center for Drug Evaluation and Research. At a teleconference, Mr. Galson added that he worried about young women having access to emergency contraception, saying it might make them more likely to have sex without a condom.

A 2004 study by the Alan Guttmacher Institute disproved this assertion, finding that teens who were provided with *advance* doses of emergency contraception did not have more unprotected intercourse. Moreover, these teens were significantly more likely to use emergency contraception sooner, when necessary, than those who had to rely on a provider to dispense it.

Health professionals recognized the need to make emergency contraception easily accessible. Several high-ranking FDA officials, including the director of the Office of Women's Health resigned in protest over the decision. Over the next two-and-a-half years, institutional and grassroots campaigns lobbied officials and continued to press for over-the-counter availability of emergency contraception. In August of 2006, the Food and Drug Administration granted approval for the over-the-counter sale of emergency contraception for women 18 and over.

About 42 million American women, or seven in 10 women of reproductive age (15 to 45) are sexually active and do not want to become pregnant. Yet about half of America's annual 6.3 million pregnancies are accidental. Researchers believe that widespread use and availability of emergency contraception could prevent an estimated 1.7 million unintended pregnancies and 800,000 abortions every year.

What is your opinion? What are the benefits (or barriers) to having a doctor examine a patient before dispensing emergency contraception? The

FDA's recent decision still requires women under the age of 18 to obtain a prescription before they can access the drug. Do you think there should be age restrictions on access to emergency contraception?

Suggested Readings

H. Boonstra, "FDA Rejects Expert Panel Recommendation, Blocks OTC Switch for Plan B Emergency Contraception," *The Guttmacher Report on Public Policy,* vol. 7, no. 2, June 2004.

H. Boonstra, "Emergency Contraception: Steps Being Taken to Improve Access," *The Guttmacher Report on Public Policy,* vol. 5, no. 5, December 2002.

H. Boonstra, "Emergency Contraception: The Need to Increase Public Awareness," *The Guttmacher Report on Public Policy,* vol. 5, no. 4, October 2002.

P. Brick and B. Taverner, "The Importance of Timing: Knowing the Difference Between Emergency Contraception and Mifepristone," in *Educating about Abortion.* Morristown, NJ: Planned Parenthood of Greater Northern NJ, 2001.

P. Brick and B. Taverner, "Emergency Contraception: For Emergency Use Only!" in *Positive Images: Teaching Abstinence, Contraception, and Sexual Health.* Morristown, NJ: Planned Parenthood of Greater Northern NJ, 2001.

J. M. Drazen, M. F. Greene, and A. J. J. Wood, "The FDA, Politics, and Plan B," *The New England Journal of Medicine,* April 8, 2004.

R. MacLean, "Teenagers Given Advance Emergency Contraception Still Use Pill and Condoms," *Perspectives on Sexual and Reproductive Health,* vol. 36, no. 3, May/June 2004.

R. G. Sawyer and E. Thompson, "Knowledge and Attitudes about Emergency Contraception in University Students," *College Student Journal,* vol. 37, issue: 4, 2003.

ISSUE 12

Should Federal Funding of Stem Cell Research Be Restricted?

YES: George W. Bush, from "Remarks by the President on Stem Cell Research" (August 9, 2001)

NO: Douglas F. Munch, from "Why Expanded Stem Cell Research and Less Federal Government Interference Are Needed in the U.S.," An Original Essay Written for This Volume (2002)

ISSUE SUMMARY

YES: President George W. Bush explains his decision to permit limited federal funding of embryonic stem cell research for the purpose of seeking treatments for serious diseases.

NO: Douglas F. Munch, a management consultant to the pharmaceutical and biotechnology industries, criticizes President Bush's decision for not fully reflecting the will of the people and for being too restrictive to have any meaningful impact on medical science and the lives of people affected by serious diseases.

For decades Americans have debated the subject of abortion, largely with respect to the question, "When does life begin?" In 2001 this debate took a sharp turn toward arguing the ethics of studying embryonic stem cells for their potential usefulness in treating serious and chronic diseases, like Parkinson's, Alzheimer's, and juvenile diabetes. Embryonic stem cells are derived from human embryos and have the capacity to become any type of human cell. This capacity is a characteristic not shared by fetal tissue or adult stem cells. It is believed that the manipulation and replication of embryonic stem cells can ultimately lead to therapies that could be used to treat diseases that afflict millions.

So, how does this relate to the abortion debate and the question of when life begins? Some opponents of stem cell research believe that a human being is created the moment that sperm and egg meet and cells begin dividing. To these opponents, the scientific use of an embryo's stem cells, which would lead to the embryo's destruction, is no different than killing a human being. Supporters of embryonic stem cell research believe that these embryos, formed a few days after conception and slated for inevitable destruction anyway, are not to be afforded protection at the expense of people with terminal illnesses who could be treated. It is important to note that there are many other subjective opinions about when human life begins, reflecting various individual or religious beliefs.

The surplus of embryos in question is the product of in vitro fertilization, a reproductive process commonly used by infertile couples. In this process, ova (eggs) are fertilized with sperm outside the uterus. The resulting embryo is then implanted inside the uterus. It is a common practice to form several embryos during the in vitro fertilization process, with each serving as "backup" in the event that the preceding implantation fails. Subsequently, most unused embryos are stored indefinitely in a frozen state. Few are intentionally destroyed, and even fewer are donated for medical research.

On August 9, 2001, President George W. Bush informed the nation of his decision to permit limited federal funding of embryonic stem cell research. His decision would permit research on 64 stem cell lines already in existence. Some praised the decision as a fair and reasonable compromise; others feared the limits would prevent any meaningful impact on the lives of millions of people with serious diseases; still others criticized the decision as incongruent with the president's pro-life position. The decision created an atypical rift among "pro-life" individuals and groups. Some, like Pope John Paul II and the National Conference of Catholic Bishops, criticized the decision, while others, like conservative members of Congress (Orrin Hatch, Trent Lott) and the National Right to Life Organization, expressed support for the decision.

A few Hollywood celebrities drew public attention to the subject and lobbied in favor of embryonic stem cell research. Actor Christopher Reeve, who was paralyzed in a horse-riding accident, became a public face of the pro-stem cell research argument. Following Bush's decision, he expressed concern that "[T]his political compromise may seriously hinder progress toward finding treatments and cures for a wide variety of diseases and disorders that affect 100 million Americans." Reeves passed away in October 2004, sparking a resurgence in the stem cell debate less than a month before the November presidential election. Actress Mary Tyler Moore, who has battled juvenile diabetes for 30 years, and actor Michael J. Fox, who has Parkinson's disease, were also vocal supporters of federal research funding. Moore voiced her support for the president's decision, while Fox was skeptical about the limitations. Nancy Reagan, whose husband, former-president Ronald Reagan, died after battling Alzheimer's disease for many years, has expressed support for stem cell research while staunchly opposing abortion. The former first lady's public stance illuminates the conflict expressed by many conservatives. The issue was again brought to the nation's attention during the mid-term elections of 2006. Many candidates touted their support or opposition for stem cell research and, again, celebrities campaigned heavily on opposing sides of the debate.

In the following selections, Bush explains his decision to authorize limited federal funding of embryonic stem cell research and describes the ethical arguments he considered in making his decision. Douglas F. Munch comments that Bush's decision does not represent the public interest and falls far too short to enable scientists to develop cures for debilitating and terminal diseases.

YES

George W. Bush

Remarks by the President on Stem Cell Research

THE PRESIDENT: Good evening. I appreciate you giving me a few minutes of your time tonight so I can discuss with you a complex and difficult issue, an issue that is one of the most profound of our time.

The issue of research involving stem cells derived from human embryos is increasingly the subject of a national debate and dinner table discussions. The issue is confronted every day in laboratories as scientists ponder the ethical ramifications of their work. It is agonized over by parents and many couples as they try to have children, or to save children already born.

The issue is debated within the church, with people of different faiths, even many of the same faith coming to different conclusions. Many people are finding that the more they know about stem cell research, the less certain they are about the right ethical and moral conclusions.

My administration must decide whether to allow federal funds, your tax dollars, to be used for scientific research on stem cells derived from human embryos. A large number of these embryos already exist. They are the product of a process called in vitro fertilization, which helps so many couples conceive children. When doctors match sperm and egg to create life outside the womb, they usually produce more embryos than are planted in the mother. Once a couple successfully has children, or if they are unsuccessful, the additional embryos remain frozen in laboratories.

Some will not survive during long storage; others are destroyed. A number have been donated to science and used to create privately funded stem cell lines. And a few have been implanted in an adoptive mother and born, and are today healthy children.

Based on preliminary work that has been privately funded, scientists believe further research using stem cells offers great promise that could help improve the lives of those who suffer from many terrible diseases—from juvenile diabetes to Alzheimer's, from Parkinson's to spinal cord injuries. And while scientists admit they are not yet certain, they believe stem cells derived from embryos have unique potential.

You should also know that stem cells can be derived from sources other than embryos—from adult cells, from umbilical cords that are discarded after babies are born, from human placenta. And many scientists feel research on these type of stem cells is also promising. Many patients suffering from a

From George W. Bush, Remarks by the President on Stem Cell Research (August 9, 2001).

range of diseases are already being helped with treatments developed from adult stem cells.

However, most scientists, at least today, believe that research on embryonic stem cells offer the most promise because these cells have the potential to develop in all of the tissues in the body.

Scientists further believe that rapid progress in this research will come only with federal funds. Federal dollars help attract the best and brightest scientists. They ensure new discoveries are widely shared at the largest number of research facilities and that the research is directed toward the greatest public good.

The United States has a long and proud record of leading the world toward advances in science and medicine that improve human life. And the United States has a long and proud record of upholding the highest standards of ethics as we expand the limits of science and knowledge. Research on embryonic stem cells raises profound ethical questions, because extracting the stem cell destroys the embryo, and thus destroys its potential for life. Like a snowflake, each of these embryos is unique, with the unique genetic potential of an individual human being.

As I thought through this issue, I kept returning to two fundamental questions: First, are these frozen embryos human life, and therefore, something precious to be protected? And second, if they're going to be destroyed anyway, shouldn't they be used for a greater good, for research that has the potential to save and improve other lives?

I've asked those questions and others of scientists, scholars, bioethicists, religious leaders, doctors, researchers, members of Congress, my Cabinet, and my friends. I have read heartfelt letters from many Americans. I have given this issue a great deal of thought, prayer and considerable reflection. And I have found widespread disagreement.

On the first issue, are these embryos human life—well, one researcher told me he believes this five-day-old cluster of cells is not an embryo, not yet an individual, but a pre-embryo. He argued that it has the potential for life, but it is not a life because it cannot develop on its own.

An ethicist dismissed that as a callous attempt at rationalization. Make no mistake, he told me, that cluster of cells is the same way you and I, and all the rest of us, started our lives. One goes with a heavy heart if we use these, he said, because we are dealing with the seeds of the next generation.

And to the other crucial question, if these are going to be destroyed anyway, why not use them for good purpose—I also found different answers. Many argue these embryos are byproducts of a process that helps create life, and we should allow couples to donate them to science so they can be used for good purpose instead of wasting their potential. Others will argue there's no such thing as excess life, and the fact that a living being is going to die does not justify experimenting on it or exploiting it as a natural resource.

At its core, this issue forces us to confront fundamental questions about the beginnings of life and the ends of science. It lies at a difficult moral intersection, juxtaposing the need to protect life in all its phases with the prospect of saving and improving life in all its stages.

As the discoveries of modern science create tremendous hope, they also lay vast ethical mine fields. As the genius of science extends the horizons of what we can do, we increasingly confront complex questions about what we should do. We have arrived at that brave new world that seemed so distant in 1932, when Aldous Huxley wrote about human beings created in test tubes in what he called a "hatchery."

In recent weeks, we learned that scientists have created human embryos in test tubes solely to experiment on them. This is deeply troubling, and a warning sign that should prompt all of us to think through these issues very carefully.

Embryonic stem cell research is at the leading edge of a series of moral hazards. The initial stem cell researcher was at first reluctant to begin his research, fearing it might be used for human cloning. Scientists have already cloned a sheep. Researchers are telling us the next step could be to clone human beings to create individual designer stem cells, essentially to grow another you, to be available in case you need another heart or lung or liver.

I strongly oppose human cloning, as do most Americans. We recoil at the idea of growing human beings for spare body parts, or creating life for our convenience. And while we must devote enormous energy to conquering disease, it is equally important that we pay attention to the moral concerns raised by the new frontier of human embryo stem cell research. Even the most noble ends do not justify any means.

My position on these issues is shaped by deeply held beliefs. I'm a strong supporter of science and technology, and believe they have the potential for incredible good—to improve lives, to save life, to conquer disease. Research offers hope that millions of our loved ones may be cured of a disease and rid of their suffering. I have friends whose children suffer from juvenile diabetes. Nancy Reagan has written me about President Reagan's struggle with Alzheimer's. My own family has confronted the tragedy of childhood leukemia. And, like all Americans, I have great hope for cures.

I also believe human life is a sacred gift from our Creator. I worry about a culture that devalues life, and believe as your President I have an important obligation to foster and encourage respect for life in America and throughout the world. And while we're all hopeful about the potential of this research, no one can be certain that the science will live up to the hope it has generated.

Eight years ago, scientists believed fetal tissue research offered great hope for cures and treatments—yet, the progress to date has not lived up to its initial expectations. Embryonic stem cell research offers both great promise and great peril. So I have decided we must proceed with great care.

As a result of private research, more than 60 genetically diverse stem cell lines already exist. They were created from embryos that have already been destroyed, and they have the ability to regenerate themselves indefinitely, creating ongoing opportunities for research. I have concluded that we should allow federal funds to be used for research on these existing stem cell lines, where the life and death decision has already been made.

Leading scientists tell me research on these 60 lines has great promise that could lead to breakthrough therapies and cures. This allows us to explore the promise and potential of stem cell research without crossing a fundamental moral line, by providing taxpayer funding that would sanction or encourage further destruction of human embryos that have at least the potential for life.

I also believe that great scientific progress can be made through aggressive federal funding of research on umbilical cord placenta, adult and animal stem cells which do not involve the same moral dilemma. This year, your government will spend $250 million on this important research.

I will also name a President's council to monitor stem cell research, to recommend appropriate guidelines and regulations, and to consider all of the medical and ethical ramifications of biomedical innovation. This council will consist of leading scientists, doctors, ethicists, lawyers, theologians and others, and will be chaired by Dr. Leon Kass, a leading biomedical ethicist from the University of Chicago.

This council will keep us apprised of new developments and give our nation a forum to continue to discuss and evaluate these important issues. As we go forward, I hope we will always be guided by both intellect and heart, by both our capabilities and our conscience.

I have made this decision with great care, and I pray it is the right one.

Thank you for listening. Good night, and God bless America.

Douglas F. Munch  **NO**

Why Expanded Stem Cell Research and Less Federal Government Interference Are Needed in the U.S.

On August 9, 2001, President George W. Bush presented his remarks on stem cell research to the American Public. The President cleverly rode the political fence on his decision to allow stem cell research, but only utilizing those 64 stem cell lines already in existence worldwide. Unfortunately, the President's decision does not go far enough in supporting this important research and that in time, perhaps sooner then he expects, the issue will have to be revisited.

The potential of stem cell research will be realized through the invention of new therapies for currently incurable diseases. Diabetes, heart disease, cancer, Alzheimer's disease, Parkinson's disease, multiple sclerosis and ALS [Lou Gehrig's disease] are some of the diseases expected to benefit from the development of knowledge about stem cells. But that is not all. Stem cell research may open the doors to understanding how genes control cell differentiation. It can also give us much improved insight into new drug development and toxicity to human cells as well as organ transplant rejection.

Why is public funding of this research such a contentious decision? The government sits squarely in the middle of the controversy surrounding the subject. On one side is the vast landscape of government funded research, with medical scientists requesting increased access to embryonic stem cells accompanied by substantially increased funding and support from the National Institutes for Health (NIH) and other government sources. On the other side is an equally vast landscape of public opinion that is divided on highly emotional moral and ethical grounds. This question is further complicated by the President's own conservative theological views and his pronounced political support from the conservative Christian right opposing this research. Since public sentiment drives most political positions in our current age of opinion polls, the arbitrator of public money, largely the political party in power, feels obligated to find its own balance between public funding for public good and defining that good. As a result, while the President's remarks cover the waterfront of stem cell research science and ethics, his decision does not go far enough.

As I view this debate, there are very different points of view coming into play across the nation. There is a definite complex of opposing theological perspectives, coupled with medical/scientific, ethical, and economic points of view.

Theological Perspectives

At the core, the theological debate revolves around the issue of when human life begins. Theologians testifying before the National Bioethics Advisory Commission indicated that religious tradition offers no support to the idea that the fertilized egg goes through some earlier human stage before acquiring the moral status of a person. A commonly expressed conservative position states that human life begins at the moment of conception when the sperm and egg cell are united since the fertilized egg has the potential to become a human being. Other positions vary widely. Some hold that human life begins upon implantation of the egg in the uterus. Historical Catholic teaching and a current Jewish position state that human life begins with quickening (when a pregnant woman can feel fetal movements some time in the fourth month of pregnancy).

Few denominations have taken an official position on the appropriateness of stem cell research. Most church leaders of various denominations appear to be undecided about the matter but some are leaning toward supporting the research. In 1997 the United Church of Christ's General Synod approved serious research on "human pre-embryos through the 14th day of fetal development."

The Episcopal, Evangelical Lutheran, and United Methodist churches have declined to take a position on the matter until . . . their national meetings convene. Other religions are similarly noncommittal. As an example, the Unitarian Universalist Association seems to favor the funding of stem cell work within its pro-science and pro-research tradition, but has reportedly not taken an official position. The Church of Jesus Christ of Latter Day Saints (Mormon Church) similarly is noncommittal on the matter stating that it "merits cautious scrutiny." Reformed Jews, Presbyterian Church USA, and the United Church of Christ seem to be generally favoring the research, although their official positions are not developed and there seem to be many nuances to consider.

Judaism discourages interfering with nature's plan for no good reason, but even Conservative Jews may favor stem cell research. Rabbi Elliott Dorff, Vice Chairman of the Conservative Movement's Committee on Law and Standards, indicated that "the research can serve a common good, combating disease."

There is no Islamic official position in the United States, but Moslem teaching holds that life does not begin until the fertilized egg is attached to the uterine wall, a position which would allow research on embryonic stem cells.

The President's personal and political position appears to be largely influenced by his close relationship with the Christian Conservative Right. Strong opposition to stem cell research has been voiced from both the Roman

Catholic Church and the Christian Conservative Right. In a recent visit to the Vatican, the Pope told President Bush that "stem cell research devalues and violates human life." However, these views, and the President's decision, may not be reflected by the general public.

Public Opinion

Recent polls indicate that there is wide support among Americans for stem cell research in contrast to the largely undecided official position of religious authorities. As individuals learn more about the promise of this research and the scientific and ethical implications, the polls show that public opinion favors stem cell research. In an NBC news poll on July 12, 2001, fully 70 percent of Roman Catholics support stem cell research versus 69 percent of the overall U.S. population. Among Catholics, only 22 percent oppose the research versus 23 percent of the overall population. In a June 2001 poll in Utah, the overall population was 62 percent in favor of stem cell research and 27 percent against. Of individuals identifying themselves as "very conservative" 47 percent favored the research while only 35 percent opposed.

The point is that there are many independent views about the humanity of a fertilized egg. Human beings are unable to resolve this fundamental issue on any grounds, scientific or theological, leaving the matter to individual conscience. It is therefore not up to the government to impose an ethical or moral standard about this research. That decision should be up to the individual scientist with funding awarded based on merit for creative scientific thinking that enhances human understanding about these cells, their function and usefulness.

The human race has become cocreators of our world with God. Observation of modern man's impact on our society makes this obvious. Scientists have prevented extinction of animal species, produced transgenic animals used for medical research, genetically modified cell lines for the production of medicine, invented and implemented in-vitro fertilization (IVF), prepared gene replacement therapies to treat disease, and introduced new genes into food products to improve yield and reduce susceptibility to disease. Whether one likes it or not, we humans are already using our gift of free will, intelligence and creativity to alter this world and change the natural course of evolution. The die is cast. It will continue to be our responsibility to use our creative powers and scientific knowledge for ethical and moral purpose from which all people benefit. As cocreators, stem cell research will be no different.

Scientific and Medical Grounds

The President's remarks about the scientific and medical benefit are very favorable toward stem cell research. So favorable that it seems his conclusion to limit the stem cell lines to those existing as of August 9, 2001, is inconsistent with his preamble. But, there are also important issues that the President underplayed in his address.

Human stem cell research is a relatively new medical field. It was only in 1981 that British scientists created the first animal stem cell line from mouse embryos. In 1996 Congress banned the use of federal funding for research where human embryos would be destroyed in the process. Hence, private funding from Geron Corporation enabled scientists at the Wisconsin Alumni Research Foundation (WARF) to develop and patent a method to separate stem cells from the blastocyst in 1998. As of August 9, 2001, there were 64 separate lines of human stem cells available worldwide. Sweden has 24 lines, the U.S. has 20, India has 10, Australia has 6, and Israel has 4. Only these lines are eligible for research funded by the federal government. This by itself is potentially problematic.

Among these 64 lines of stem cells that are approved for funding, many are derived from frozen embryos that are known to be much less robust, reportedly having only 1 chance in 100 of developing to the blastocyst stage (a colony of about 200 undifferentiated stem cells). It is still unknown how many of these lines will be satisfactory for research purposes. Research quality stem cells must have normal chromosomes and genes. They must be able to reproduce without limit and they must be capable of differentiation into all other human cells. While scientists anticipate that these cells will reproduce indefinitely, this is an assumption that may not work out in the future. We cannot know how many of these approved cell lines will develop into useful research material or if they will provide adequate quantities of material to meet research standards and demand.

While stem cells may be obtained from adult tissues (i.e. fat, bone marrow, or brain) and other fetal cell lines (umbilical or placenta), these cells may have started down a differentiation pathway and therefore have more limited research potential. Experts recognize that stem cells from the blastocyst stage of the embryo are ideal because they are completely undifferentiated and have the potential to become any of the approximately 260 cell lines in the human body. Today, medical scientists have only limited knowledge about the theoretical and practical issues necessary to derive therapeutic benefit from the science, although the theoretical potential is great. Additionally, today's stem cells are being grown in a mouse cell culture to trick the stem cells to differentiate, which also limits the research and therapeutic potential due to the potential contamination of the human cells. Much work remains to be done and will be done. If not in the U.S., then the work will be engaged by scientists in other countries where fewer barriers are imposed.

Ethical Issues

The President's remarks appropriately address the possibility of misuse of stem cell research potentially leading to the serious abuse of human reproductive cloning which is properly banned in most countries. However, all technologies have potential for misuse by unscrupulous individuals inclined to manipulate the system for their own ill-gotten gain.

The President appropriately states that the U.S. has a "long and proud record of upholding the highest standards of ethics." We have achieved this record through exercise of individual conscience superimposed over a sound foundation of knowledge, ethics, and through peer pressure from other scientists, not through government imposed legislation. There are already safeguards in the research funding system to protect against such activity—specifically, the long established peer review system awards research grants to worthy (and ethical) projects. Investigational review boards (IRB) protect patients against potentially harmful or immoral clinical research. The system works and the government should not meddle with it or use it as an excuse to install barriers or artificially limit funding for this important work.

In-vitro fertilization (IVF) procedures have produced a large number of unused frozen embryos, as the President correctly pointed out in his remarks. Again, his comments do not adequately address the issues. Unused embryos may remain frozen for many years as they are rarely adopted, donated, or destroyed when they are unwanted. We know that extra embryos are a consequence of IVF.

People choosing to avail themselves of this procedure should be required to undertake the moral and ethical responsibility of determining the disposition of their unused cells as part of their overall decision making and medical informed consent process. I believe that this decision should be required at the time people choose IVF to achieve pregnancy. Otherwise, unused embryos are likely to remain frozen as a burden to society. I would suggest that the options include donation of the embryos for stem cell research purposes. This decision is a personal one, and should be driven by individual conscience. After all, when faced with the tragic death of a child, many parents now take comfort in donating some of the child's tissues to help others as transplants. Should not the same opportunity to benefit others be available to IVF "parents"? If morality is the issue, then where is the morality in abandoning human embryos in a frozen and indeterminate state, leaving them as someone else's problem or to deteriorate in the freezer?

Economic Issues

Several economic factors may also be considered. U.S. Government-funded research has been the most important incubator for new ideas in the world. This support has historically been provided without prior assessment of economic potential. Industries have been started as a result and perhaps hundreds of biotech and health care companies owe their existence to government funded research programs. Inadequate support of stem cell research will unwittingly block the creation of entrepreneurial companies focused on the developing new therapies based on knowledge discovered with federal grant support.

U.S. companies, developing state-of-the-art commercial products for health care, make a substantial contribution to our economy and to maintaining our worldwide superiority in medicine and therapeutics. Supporting basic research at the federal level forms the groundwork for establishing important intellectual property positions for American entrepreneurs and corporations. Placing hurdles in the way of U.S. scientists will move discovery to other nations where there are fewer or no impediments to this research. On August 28th, 2001, the *Washington Post* reported an Indian stem cell scientist to say that the Bush policy "creates a windfall for researchers in such countries as India that do not face such constraints." Another reports that Bush's announcement has opened up a "new pot of gold" for science and business outside the U.S.

By putting political barriers in front of scientists who develop new treatments for disease, we are not only impeding economic and medical progress in the U.S. but also risk losing our leading scientists. Dr. Roger Pedersen, a prominent scientist from the University of California, San Francisco, has announced that he is leaving the U.S. to work in England where research restrictions are not as burdensome. Others will also leave if government restrictions get in the way of science.

Concluding Remarks

Like the President, I have come to express my position on these sensitive matters regarding stem cell research after much thought and personal deliberation. I believe that the views I have presented here support the sanctity of human life. They also allow our American culture to prevail where strong social and ethical values are the underpinnings of the exercise of our gift of free will. Our democratic system enables this to occur. Our federal government should not legislate against its own system by seeking to establish and impose state ethics on our free society.

POSTSCRIPT

Should Federal Funding of Stem Cell Research Be Restricted?

The question of whether or not embryonic stem cell research should be restricted may come down to fundamental beliefs about the origin of human life. Does life begin at the moment of conception, as many "pro-life" individuals contend? If so, what is to be done with excess embryos already created in the in vitro fertilization process but not destined for implantation? "Pro-choice" individuals may have an easier time with this question, as they reject the belief that a fertilized egg is a human being. The opportunity to improve the lives of people with severe illnesses may be seen as no match to the comparative value of a cluster of cells that is not destined for pregnancy.

In his speech, the president raised the issue of human cloning. His statement, "[T]he next step could be to clone human beings to create individual designer stem cells, essentially to grow another you to be available in case you need another heart or lung or liver," requires some clarification. Scientists who have expressed an intention to clone humans are relying on adult stem cells to create a whole cloned human person. Adult cells would be taken from an adult, their DNA injected into a human ovum, and that ovum implanted into a woman's uterus to create a cloned person. Most scientists dismiss this as both unethical and nearly impossible. However, substituting one's DNA for the DNA in embryonic stem cells to create specialized (and perfectly genetically matched cells) is possible. Interestingly, this issue played a role in a November 2006 voter referendum in Missouri. On the ballot was the Stem Cells Research and Cures Initiative, which would allow any stem cell research deemed legal by the federal government to be legal in Missouri. Opponents of the measure ran a multi-media assault on the measure, claiming that the measure would lead towards legalization of cloning, despite the fact that language in the measure that would specifically ban human cloning. The measure passed by a narrow margin.

How do you assess the president's compromise? Did it go far enough or does it fall short of being useful for those afflicted with incurable illnesses? What ethical considerations would guide you in deciding this matter?

Suggested Readings

"Stem Cell Disappointment," *Arizona Daily Star* (August 12, 2001).

"Stem Cells: Not Far Enough," *The Providence Journal* (August 12, 2001).

S. Begley, "Cellular Divide," *Newsweek* (July 9, 2001).

S. Begley, "Did the President Go Far Enough?" *Newsweek* (August 20, 2001).

A. Breznican, "Celebs Supporting Stem Cell Research," *Associated Press* (August 9, 2001).

T. Lindberg, "The Politics of Stem Cell Research: President Bush Got the Headlines He Wanted," *The Washington Times* (August 14, 2001).

The White House, "Fact Sheet: Embryonic Stem Cell Research," available at http://www.whitehouse.gov (August 9, 2001).

K. L. Woodward, "A Question of Life or Death: Untangling the Knottiest of Ethical Dilemmas," *Newsweek* (July 9, 2001).

Internet References . . .

Alliance for Marriage

Alliance for Marriage is a nonprofit research and education organization dedicated to promoting marriage and addressing the epidemic of fatherless families in the United States. It educates the public, the media, elected officials, and civil society leaders on the benefits of marriage for children, adults, and society.

http://www.allianceformarriage.org

Alternatives to Marriage Project

The Alternatives to Marriage Project advocates for equality and fairness for unmarried people, including people who choose not to marry, cannot marry, or live together before marriage.

http://www.unmarried.org

American Civil Liberties Union (ACLU)

The ACLU works to defend and preserve the individual rights and liberties guaranteed to every person in this country by the Constitution and laws of the United States.

http://www.aclu.org

Electronic Frontier Foundation

The Electronic Frontier Foundation works to educate the press, policymakers, and the general public about civil liberties issues related to technology.

http://www.eff.org.

Federal Communications Commission (FCC)

The FCC is a United States government agency charged with regulating interstate and international communications by radio, television, wire, satellite, and cable.

http://www.fcc.gov

Human Rights Campaign

The Human Rights Campaign is America's largest gay and lesbian organization. It seeks to increase public understanding through innovative education and communication strategies.

http://www.hrc.org

Rape, Abuse, & Incest National Network (RAINN)

RAINN is the nation's largest anti-sexual assault organization. It operates the National Sexual Assault Hotline at 1-800-656-HOPE and carries out programs to prevent sexual assault, help victims, and ensure that rapists are brought to justice.

http://www.rainn.org/

UNIT 4

Sex and Society

*C*ompeting *philosophical forces drive concerns about human sexuality on a societal level. Some are primarily focused on the well-being
of individuals (or groups of individuals) and their right to individual
expression versus their protection from harm; others are mainly
concerned with either maintaining or questioning established social
norms; still others are engaged by the extent to which the law should
impose on a citizen's privacy. This section examines six such questions
that affect our social understanding of sexuality.*

- Should Same-Sex Marriage Be Legal?

- Should Society Support Cohabitation before Marriage?

- Is Pedophilia Always Harmful?

- Should Female Circumcision Be Banned?

- Should the FCC Restrict Broadcast "Indecency"?

- Should Sexual Content on the Internet Be Restricted?

ISSUE 13

Should Same-Sex Marriage Be Legal?

YES: Human Rights Campaign, from *Answers to Questions about Marriage Equality* (Human Rights Campaign, 2004)

NO: John Cornyn, from "In Defense of Marriage," *National Review* (July 2004)

ISSUE SUMMARY

YES: The Human Rights Campaign (HRC), America's largest gay and lesbian organization, explains why same-sex couples should be afforded the same legal right to marry as heterosexual couples.

NO: John Cornyn, United States senator from Texas, says a constitutional amendment is needed to define marriage as permissible only between a man and a woman. Senator Cornyn contends that the traditional institution of marriage needs to be protected from activist courts that would seek to redefine it.

On May 17, 2004, Massachusetts became the first state in the United States to grant marriage licenses to same-sex couples. The state acted under the direction of its supreme court, which had found that withholding marriage licenses from lesbian and gay couples violated the state constitution. More than 600 same-sex couples applied for marriage licenses that first day alone. The first same-sex couple to be issued marriage licenses was Marcia Kadish and Tanya McClosky. That couple had waited over 18 years for the day to arrive. Since then, over 3,000 same-sex marriages have been performed in Massachusetts.

After the Massachusetts ruling, gay and lesbian couples across the country sought marriage licenses from their municipalities. Many were denied, while others found loopholes in laws that allowed them to file for licenses. In Oregon, for example, the law stated that marriage is a "civil contract entered into in person by males at least 17 years of age and females at least 17 years of age." Since the law did not state that males had to marry females, gay and lesbian marriages were never technically against the law. Marriage licenses were also issued in counties in California, New Jersey, New York, and Washington. In San Francisco, Mayor Gavin Newsom challenged state law and allowed city officials to wed same-sex couples. For the time being, the gay and lesbian marriages and marriage licenses in all states other than Massachusetts were ruled illegal and invalid.

The court ruling that paved the way for same-sex marriage in Massachusetts opened a firestorm of controversy. Supporters heralded the decision as a step towards equality for all Americans. Opponents of gay and lesbian nuptials spoke out against the redefinition and destruction of traditional marriage. President Bush endorsed a constitutional amendment that would define marriage as being between a man and a woman saying that "the sacred institution of marriage should not be redefined by a few activist judges."

Several years earlier, President Clinton signed the Defense of Marriage Act (DOMA), which said that states were not required to recognize same-sex marriages performed in other states. Nevertheless, supporters of the constitutional amendment believe DOMA is not enough to keep courts from redefining traditional marriage. Gay rights supporters oppose the amendment, which they feel unjustly writes discrimination into the Constitution. Even many conservatives oppose the amendment because they believe it to be too strong of a federal intrusion into the rights of states. The issue was pressed to the forefront of the 2004 elections when questions concerning gay and lesbian marriage were asked in the vice presidential and presidential debates. On election day that year, eleven states (including Oregon) voted on measures that would define marriage in their state as being between a man and a woman, thus banning same-sex marriage in those states. All eleven of those measures passed.

In the mid-term elections of 2006, seven states followed suit, but Arizona became the first state in which voters rejected an all-out ban. The 2006 elections came shortly on the heels of a New Jersey Supreme Court ruling that the state must offer the same benefits and responsibilities that married couples hold to same-sex couples, either in the form of marriage or a "parallel statutory structure" such as civil unions. At the present time, the state legislature has 180 days from the day of the ruling to decide whether to offer marriage or something akin to civil unions.

In the following essays, the Human Rights Campaign (HRC) answers common questions about same-sex marriage and the law, religion, and family. HRC also reviews the benefits that same-sex marriages could potentially have for gay and lesbian couples and society. Senator John Cornyn argues that the traditional definition of marriage is threatened by activist judges who seek to redefine the most fundamental union the world has ever known. Cornyn states that protecting marriage is about ensuring that relationships consisting of husband and wife will remain the "gold standard" for raising children.

YES

Human Rights Campaign

Answers to Questions About Marriage Equality

10 Facts

1. Same-sex couples live in 99.3 percent of all counties nationwide.
2. There are an estimated 3.1 million people living together in same-sex relationships in the United States.
3. Fifteen percent of these same-sex couples live in rural settings.
4. One out of three lesbian couples is raising children. One out of five gay male couples is raising children.
5. Between 1 million and 9 million children are being raised by gay, lesbian and bisexual parents in the United States today.
6. At least one same-sex couple is raising children in 96 percent of all counties nationwide.
7. The highest percentages of same-sex couples raising children live in the South.
8. Nearly one in four same-sex couples includes a partner 55 years old or older, and nearly one in five same-sex couples is composed of two people 55 or older.
9. More than one in 10 same-sex couples include a partner 65 years old or older, and nearly one in 10 same-sex couples is composed of two people 65 or older.
10. The states with the highest numbers of same-sex senior couples are also the most popular for heterosexual senior couples: California, New York and Florida.

Why Same-Sex Couples Want to Marry

Many same-sex couples want the right to legally marry because they are in love—either they just met the love of their lives, or more likely, they have spent the last 10, 20 or 50 years with that person—and they want to honor their

---

These facts are based on analyses of the 2000 Census conducted by the Urban Institute and the Human Rights Campaign. The estimated number of people in same-sex relationships has been adjusted by 62 percent to compensate for the widely-reported undercount in the Census. . . .

From *Answers to Questions About Marriage Equality*, 2004. Copyright © 2004 by Human Rights Campaign. Reprinted by permission.

relationship in the greatest way our society has to offer, by making a public commitment to stand together in good times and bad, through all the joys and challenges family life brings.

Many parents want the right to marry because they know it offers children a vital safety net and guarantees protections that unmarried parents cannot provide.

And still other people—both gay and straight—are fighting for the right of same-sex couples to marry because they recognize that it is simply not fair to deny some families the protections all other families are eligible to enjoy.

Currently in the United States, same-sex couples in long-term, committed relationships pay higher taxes and are denied basic protections and rights granted to married heterosexual couples. Among them:

- **Hospital visitation.** Married couples have the automatic right to visit each other in the hospital and make medical decisions. Same-sex couples can be denied the right to visit a sick or injured loved one in the hospital.
- **Social Security benefits.** Married people receive Social Security payments upon the death of a spouse. Despite paying payroll taxes, gay and lesbian partners receive no Social Security survivor benefits—resulting in an average annual income loss of $5,528 upon the death of a partner.
- **Immigration.** Americans in binational relationships are not permitted to petition for their same-sex partners to immigrate. As a result, they are often forced to separate or move to another country.
- **Health insurance.** Many public and private employers provide medical coverage to the spouses of their employees, but most employers do not provide coverage to the life partners of gay and lesbian employees. Gay employees who do receive health coverage for their partners must pay federal income taxes on the value of the insurance.
- **Estate taxes.** A married person automatically inherits all the property of his or her deceased spouse without paying estate taxes. A gay or lesbian taxpayer is forced to pay estate taxes on property inherited from a deceased partner.
- **Retirement savings.** While a married person can roll a deceased spouse's 401(k) funds into an IRA without paying taxes, a gay or lesbian American who inherits a 401(k) can end up paying up to 70 percent of it in taxes and penalties.
- **Family leave.** Married workers are legally entitled to unpaid leave from their jobs to care for an ill spouse. Gay and lesbian workers are not entitled to family leave to care for their partners.
- **Nursing homes.** Married couples have a legal right to live together in nursing homes. Because they are not legal spouses, elderly gay or lesbian couples do not have the right to spend their last days living together in nursing homes.
- **Home protection.** Laws protect married seniors from being forced to sell their homes to pay high nursing home bills; gay and lesbian seniors have no such protection.

- **Pensions.** After the death of a worker, most pension plans pay survivor benefits only to a legal spouse of the participant. Gay and lesbian partners are excluded from such pension benefits.

Why Civil Unions Aren't Enough

Comparing marriage to civil unions is a bit like comparing diamonds to rhinestones. One is, quite simply, the real deal; the other is not. Consider:

- Couples eligible to marry may have their marriage performed in any state and have it recognized in every other state in the nation and every country in the world.
- Couples who are joined in a civil union in Vermont (the only state that offers civil unions) have no guarantee that its protections will even travel with them to neighboring New York or New Hampshire—let alone California or any other state.

Moreover, even couples who have a civil union and remain in Vermont receive only second-class protections in comparison to their married friends and neighbors. While they receive state-level protections, they do not receive any of the *more than 1,100 federal benefits and protections of marriage.*

In short, civil unions are not separate but equal—they are separate *and* unequal. And our society has tried separate before. It just doesn't work.

Marriage:	Civil unions:
• State grants marriage licenses to couples.	• State would grant civil union licenses to couples.
• Couples receive legal protections and rights under state and federal law.	• Couples receive legal protections and rights under state law only.
• Couples are recognized as being married by the federal government and all state governments.	• Civil unions are not recognized by other states or the federal government.
• Religious institutions are not required to perform marriage ceremonies.	• Religious institutions are not required to perform civil union ceremonies.

"I Believe God Meant Marriage for Men and Women. How Can I Support Marriage for Same-Sex Couples?"

Many people who believe in God—and fairness and justice for all—ask this question. They feel a tension between religious beliefs and democratic values that has been experienced in many different ways throughout our nation's history. That is why the framers of our Constitution established the principle of separation of church and state. That principle applies no less to the marriage issue than it does to any other.

Indeed, the answer to the apparent dilemma between religious beliefs and support for equal protections for all families lies in recognizing that marriage has a significant religious meaning for many people, but that it is also a legal contract. And it is strictly the legal—not the religious—dimension of marriage that is being debated now.

Granting marriage rights to same-sex couples would *not* require Christianity, Judaism, Islam or any other religion to perform these marriages. It would not require religious institutions to permit these ceremonies to be held on their grounds. It would not even require that religious communities discuss the issue. People of faith would remain free to make their own judgments about what makes a marriage in the eyes of God—just as they are today.

Consider, for example, the difference in how the Catholic Church and the U.S. government view couples who have divorced and remarried. Because church tenets do not sanction divorce, the second marriage is not valid in the church's view. The government, however, recognizes the marriage by extending to the remarried couple the same rights and protections as those granted to every other married couple in America. In this situation—as would be the case in marriage for same-sex couples—the church remains free to establish its own teachings on the religious dimension of marriage while the government upholds equality under law.

It should also be noted that there are a growing number of religious communities that have decided to bless same-sex unions. Among them are Reform Judaism, the Unitarian Universalist Association and the Metropolitan Community Church. The Presbyterian Church (USA) also allows ceremonies to be performed, although they are not considered the same as marriage. The Episcopal Church and United Church of Christ allow individual churches to set their own policies on same-sex unions.

"This Is Different from Interracial Marriage. Sexual Orientation Is a Choice"

> *"We cannot keep turning our backs on gay and lesbian Americans. I have fought too hard and too long against discrimination based on race and color not to stand up against discrimination based on sexual orientation. I've heard the reasons for opposing civil marriage for same-sex couples. Cut through the distractions, and they stink of the same fear, hatred, and intolerance I have known in racism and in bigotry."*
>
> — Rep. John Lewis, D-Ga., a leader of the black civil rights movement, writing in *The Boston Globe,* Nov. 25, 2003

Decades of research all point to the fact that sexual orientation is not a choice, and that a person's sexual orientation cannot be changed. Who one is drawn to is a fundamental aspect of who we are.

In this way, the struggle for marriage equality for same-sex couples is just as basic as the fight for interracial marriage was. It recognizes that Americans should not be coerced into false and unhappy marriages but should be free to marry the person they love—thereby building marriage on a true and stable foundation.

"Won't This Create a Free-for-All and Make the Whole Idea of Marriage Meaningless?"

Many people share this concern because opponents of gay and lesbian people have used this argument as a scare tactic. But it is not true. Granting same-sex couples the right to marry would in no way change the number of people who could enter into a marriage (or eliminate restrictions on the age or familial relationships of those who may marry). Marriage would continue to recognize the highest possible commitment that can be made between two adults, plain and simple.

Organizations That Support Same-Sex Parenting

American Academy of Pediatrics

American Academy of Family Physicians

Child Welfare League of America

National Association of Social Workers

North American Council on Adoptable Children

American Bar Association

American Psychological Association

American Psychiatric Association

American Psychoanalytic Association

"I Strongly Believe Children Need a Mother and a Father"

Many of us grew up believing that everyone needs a mother and father, regardless of whether we ourselves happened to have two parents, or two *good* parents.

But as families have grown more diverse in recent decades, and researchers have studied how these different family relationships affect children, it has become clear that the *quality* of a family's relationship is more important than the particular *structure* of families that exist today. In other words, the qualities that help children grow into good and responsible adults—learning how to learn, to have compassion for others, to contribute to society and be respectful of others and their differences—do not depend on the sexual orientation of their parents but on their parents' ability to provide a loving, stable and happy home, something no class of Americans has an exclusive hold on.

That is why research studies have consistently shown that children raised by gay and lesbian parents do just as well on all conventional measures of child development, such as academic achievement, psychological well-being and social abilities, as children raised by heterosexual parents.

That is also why the nation's leading child welfare organizations, including the American Academy of Pediatrics, the American Academy of Family Physicians and others, have issued statements that dismiss assertions that only heterosexual couples can be good parents—and declare that the focus should now be on providing greater protections for the 1 million to 9 million children being raised by gay and lesbian parents in the United States today.

"What Would Be Wrong with a Constitutional Amendment to Define Marriage as a Union of a Man and Woman?"

In more than 200 years of American history, the U.S. Constitution has been amended only 17 times since the Bill of Rights—and in each instance (except for Prohibition, which was repealed), it was to extend rights and liberties to the American people, not restrict them. For example, our Constitution was amended to end our nation's tragic history of slavery. It was also amended to guarantee people of color, young people and women the right to vote.

The amendment currently under consideration (called the Federal Marriage Amendment) would be the only one that would single out one class of Americans for discrimination by ensuring that same-sex couples would not be granted the equal protections that marriage brings to American families.

Moreover, the amendment could go even further by stripping same-sex couples of some of the more limited protections they now have, such as access to health insurance for domestic partners and their children.

Neither enshrining discrimination in our Constitution nor stripping millions of families of basic protections would serve our nation's best interest. The Constitution is supposed to protect and ensure equal treatment for *all* people. It should not be used to single out a group of people for different treatment.

TEXT OF PROPOSED FEDERAL MARRIAGE AMENDMENT

"Marriage in the United States shall consist only of the union of a man and a woman.

Neither this [C]onstitution [n]or the constitution of any state, nor state or federal law, shall be construed to require that marital status or the legal incidents thereof be conferred upon unmarried couples or groups."

— H.J. Resolution 56, introduced by Rep. Marilyn Musgrave, R-Colo., in May 2003. It has more than 100 co-sponsors. A similar bill was introduced in the U.S. Senate in November 2003. In February 2004, President Bush said that he would support a constitutional amendment to define marriage as between only a man and a woman.

"How Could Marriage for Same-Sex Couples Possibly Be Good for the American Family—or Our Country?"

"We shouldn't just allow gay marriage. We should insist on gay marriage. We should regard it as scandalous that two people could claim to love each other and not want to sanctify their love with marriage and fidelity."

— Conservative Columnist David Brooks, writing in
The New York Times, Nov. 22, 2003.

The prospect of a significant change in our laws and customs has often caused people to worry more about dire consequences that could result than about the potential positive outcomes. In fact, precisely the same anxiety arose when some people fought to overturn the laws prohibiting marriage between people of different races in the 1950s and 1960s. (One Virginia judge even declared that "God intended to separate the races.")

But in reality, opening marriage to couples who are so willing to fight for it could only strengthen the institution for all. It would open the doors to more supporters, not opponents. And it would help keep the age-old institution alive.

As history has repeatedly proven, institutions that fail to take account of the changing needs of the population are those that grow weak; those that recognize and accommodate changing needs grow strong. For example, the U.S. military, like American colleges and universities, grew stronger after permitting African Americans and women to join its ranks.

Similarly, granting same-sex couples the right to marry would strengthen the institution of marriage by allowing it to better meet the needs of the true diversity of family structures in America today.

"Can't Same-Sex Couples Go to a Lawyer to Secure All the Rights They Need?"

Not by a long shot. When a gay or lesbian person gets seriously ill, there is no legal document that can make their partner eligible to take leave from work under the federal Family and Medical Leave Act to provide care—because that law applies only to married couples.

When gay or lesbian people grow old and in need of nursing home care, there is no legal document that can give them the right to Medicaid coverage without potentially causing their partner to be forced from their home—because the federal Medicaid law only permits married spouses to keep their home without becoming ineligible for benefits.

And when a gay or lesbian person dies, there is no legal document that can extend Social Security survivor benefits or the right to inherit a retirement plan without severe tax burdens that stem from being "unmarried" in the eyes of the law.

These are only a few examples of the critical protections that are granted through more than 1,100 federal laws that protect only married couples. In the absence of the right to marry, same-sex couples can only put in place a handful of the most basic arrangements, such as naming each other in a will or a power of attorney. And even these documents remain vulnerable to challenges in court by disgruntled family members.

"Won't This Cost Taxpayers too Much Money?"

No, it wouldn't necessarily cost much at all. In fact, treating same-sex couples as families under law could even save taxpayers money because marriage would require them to assume legal responsibility for their joint living expenses and reduce their dependence on public assistance programs, such as Medicaid, Temporary Assistance to Needy Families, Supplemental Security Income disability payments and food stamps.

Put another way, the money it would cost to extend benefits to same-sex couples could be outweighed by the money that would be saved as these families rely more fully on each other instead of state or federal government assistance.

For example, two studies conducted in 2003 by professors at the University of Massachusetts, Amherst, and the University of California, Los Angeles, found that extending domestic partner benefits to same-sex couples in California and New Jersey would save taxpayers millions of dollars a year.

Specifically, the studies projected that the California state budget would save an estimated $8.1 million to $10.6 million each year by enacting the most comprehensive domestic partner law in the nation. In New Jersey, which passed a new domestic partner law in 2004, the savings were projected to be even higher—more than $61 million each year.

(Sources: "Equal Rights, Fiscal Responsibility: The Impact of A.B. 205 on California's Budget," by M. V. Lee Badgett, Ph.D., IGLSS, Department of Economics, University of Massachusetts, and R. Bradley Sears, J.D., Williams Project, UCLA School of Law, University of California, Los Angeles, May 2003, and "Supporting Families, Saving Funds: A Fiscal Analysis of New Jersey's Domestic Partnership Act," by Badgett and Sears with Suzanne Goldberg, J.D., Rutgers School of Law-Newark, December 2003.)

"Where Can Same-Sex Couples Marry Today?"

In 2001, the Netherlands became the first country to extend marriage rights to same-sex couples. Belgium passed a similar law two years later. The laws in both of these countries, however, have strict citizenship or residency requirements that do not permit American couples to take advantage of the protections provided.

In June 2003, Ontario became the first Canadian province to grant marriage to same-sex couples, and in July 2003, British Columbia followed suit—becoming the first places that American same-sex couples could go to get married.

In November 2003, the Massachusetts Supreme Judicial Court recognized the right of same-sex couples to marry—giving the state six months to begin issuing marriage licenses to same-sex couples. It began issuing licenses May 17, 2004.

In February 2004, the city of San Francisco began issuing marriage licenses to same-sex couples after the mayor declared that the state constitution forbade him to discriminate. The issue is being addressed by California courts, and a number of other cities have either taken or are considering taking steps in the same direction.

Follow the latest developments in California, Oregon, New Jersey, New Mexico, New York and in other communities across the country on the HRC Marriage Center. . . .

Other nations have also taken steps toward extending equal protections to all couples, though the protections they provide are more limited than marriage. Canada, Denmark, Finland, France, Germany, Iceland, Norway, Portugal and Sweden all have nationwide laws that grant same-sex partners a range of important rights, protections and obligations.

For example, in France, registered same-sex (and opposite-sex) couples can be joined in a civil "solidarity pact" that grants them the right to file joint tax returns, extend social security coverage to each other and receive the same health, employment and welfare benefits as legal spouses. It also commits the couple to assume responsibility for household debts.

Other countries, including Switzerland, Scotland and the Czech Republic, also have considered legislation that would legally recognize same-sex unions.

"What Protections Other Than Marriage Are Available to Same-Sex Couples?"

At the federal level, there are no protections at all available to same-sex couples. In fact, a federal law called the "Defense of Marriage Act" says that the federal government will discriminate against same-sex couples who marry by refusing to recognize their marriages or providing them with the federal protections of marriage. Some members of Congress are trying to go even further by attempting to pass a Federal Marriage Amendment that would write discrimination against same-sex couples into the U.S. Constitution.

At the state level, only Vermont offers civil unions, which provide important state benefits but no federal protections, such as Social Security survivor benefits. There is also no guarantee that civil unions will be recognized outside Vermont. Thirty-nine states also have "defense of marriage" laws explicitly prohibiting the recognition of marriages between same-sex partners.

Domestic partner laws have been enacted in California, Connecticut, New Jersey, Hawaii and the District of Columbia. The benefits conferred by these laws vary; some offer access to family health insurance, others confer co-parenting rights. These benefits are limited to residents of the state. A family that moves out of these states immediately loses the protections.

10 Things You Can Do

Every Family Deserves Equal Protections.
How Can I Help?

1. Urge your members of Congress to oppose the Federal Marriage Amendment, or any constitutional amendment to ban marriage for same-sex couples. Make a personal visit if you can. HRC's field team can help you. Or fax a message through HRC's Action Network. . . .

2. Sign the Million for Marriage petition . . . and ask 10 friends and family to do the same.

3. Talk to your friends and family members about the importance of marriage for same-sex couples and their children. Recent polls of the GLBT community show that many people have not yet talked to parents, siblings or other family members about the discrimination they face. Nothing moves the hearts and minds of potential straight allies more than hearing the stories of someone they know who is gay, lesbian, bisexual or transgender. For more information, download "Talking about Marriage Equality" from HRC's Online Action Center.

4. Write a letter to the editor of your local newspaper saying why you support marriage for same-sex couples and why a constitutional amendment against it is a bad idea.

5. Next time you hear someone say marriage is only meant for heterosexual couples, speak up. If you hear this on a radio program, call in. If you hear it on television, call or send an e-mail. If it comes up in conversation, set the record straight.

6. Host a house party to educate your friends and family about marriage equality. Invite a diverse group and inspire them to write letters to Congress and your state government at your house party. . . .

7. Meet with clergy and other opinion leaders in your community and ask them to join you in speaking out in support of marriage equality and against the Federal Marriage Amendment. Let HRC know the results. . . .

8. Share your story about why marriage equality matters to you and send it to HRC's family project. . . . Personal stories are what move hearts and minds.

9. Become a member of HRC and support our work on behalf of marriage equality. . . .

10. Register to vote and support fair-minded candidates. . . .

Additional National Resources

Human Rights Campaign . . .

HRC is the nation's largest national organization working to advance equality based on sexual orientation and gender expression and identity to ensure that gay, lesbian, bisexual and transgender Americans can be open, honest and safe at home, at work and in their communities. Of particular interest to people following the marriage issue:

The Human Rights Campaign Foundation's FamilyNet

Project . . . offers the most comprehensive resources about GLBT families, covering marriage, parenting, aging and more. HRC's Action Center. . ., offers important updates about what's happening in legislatures nationwide and the latest online grassroots advocacy tools.

Other important resources include:

American Civil Liberties Union . . .

ACLU works in courts, legislatures and communities throughout the country to defend and preserve the individual rights and liberties guaranteed by the Constitution and laws of the United States.

Freedom to Marry Collaborative . . .

A gay and non-gay partnership working to win marriage equality.

Children of Lesbians and Gays Everywhere (COLAGE) . . .

Fosters the growth of daughters and sons of GLBT parents by providing education, support and community, advocating for their rights and rights of their families.

Dignity USA . . .

Works for respect and justice for all GLBT persons in the Catholic Church and the world through education, advocacy and support.

Family Pride Coalition . . .

A national education and civil rights organization that advances the well-being of GLBT parents and their families through mutual support, community collaboration and public understanding.

Federation of Statewide LGBT Advocacy Organizations . . .

The GLBT advocacy network of state/territory organizations committed to working with each other and with national and local groups to strengthen statewide advocacy organizing and secure full civil rights in every U.S. state and territory.

Gay & Lesbian Advocates & Defenders . . .

The GLBT legal organization that successfully brought the case that led to the civil union law in Vermont and the recognition of marriage equality in Massachusetts.

Gay & Lesbian Victory Fund . . .

Committed to increasing the number of openly gay and lesbian public officials at federal, state and local levels of government.

Lambda Legal . . .

A national legal group committed to achieving full recognition of the civil rights of, and combating the discrimination against, the GLBT community and people with HIV/AIDS, through impact litigation, education and public policy work.

Log Cabin Republicans . . .

Operates within the Republican Party for the equal rights of all Americans, including gay men and women, according to the principles of limited government, individual liberty, individual responsibility, free markets and a strong national defense.

Marriage Equality USA . . .

Works to secure the freedom and the right of same-sex couples to engage in civil marriage through a program of education, media campaigns and community partnerships.

National Center for Lesbian Rights . . .

A national legal resource center devoted to advancing the rights and safety of lesbians and their families through a program of litigation, public policy advocacy, free legal advice and counseling and public education.

National Black Justice Coalition . . .

An ad hoc coalition of black GLBT leaders who have come together to fight against discrimination in our communities, to build black support for marriage equality and to educate the community on the dangers of the proposal to amend the U.S. Constitution to discriminate against GLBT people.

National Gay & Lesbian Task Force . . .

Dedicated to building a national civil rights movement of GLBT people through the empowerment and training of state and local leaders, and research and development of national policy.

National Latina/o Lesbian, Gay, Bisexual & Transgender Organization (LLEGÓ) . . .

Develops solutions to social, health and political disparities that exist due to discrimination based on ethnicity, sexual orientation and gender identity affecting the lives and well-being of Latina/o GLBT people and their families.

Parents, Families & Friends of Lesbians & Gays (PFLAG) . . .

Promotes the health and well-being of GLBT people, their families and friends, through support, education and advocacy with the intention of ending discrimination and securing equal civil rights.

Soulforce . . .

An interfaith movement committed to ending spiritual violence perpetuated by religious policies and teachings against GLBT people through the application of the principles of non-violence.

Universal Fellowship of Metropolitan Community Churches . . .

A worldwide fellowship of Christian churches with a special outreach to the world's GLBT communities.

John Cornyn  **NO**

In Defense of Marriage: The Amendment That Will Protect a Fundamental Institution

In 1996, three fourths of the House and Senate joined President Bill Clinton in a strong bipartisan effort to defend the traditional institution of marriage, by enacting the federal Defense of Marriage Act (DOMA). That act defined, as a matter of federal law, the institution of marriage as the union of one man and one woman—reflecting the views of the vast majority of Americans across the country. Today, as it debates a constitutional amendment to defend marriage, the Senate will revisit precisely the same question: Should the institution of marriage continue to be defined as the union of one man and one woman— as it has been defined for thousands of years?

Since the 1996 vote, two things have changed. First, activist courts have so dramatically altered the meaning of the Constitution, that traditional marriage laws are now under serious threat of being invalidated by judicial fiat nationwide—indeed, the process has already begun in numerous states across the country. Second, the broad bipartisan consensus behind marriage that was exhibited in 1996 has begun to fracture. Some who supported DOMA just a few years ago are, for partisan reasons, unwilling to defend marriage today. Although the defense of marriage should continue to be a bipartisan endeavor—and kept out of the hands of activist lawyers and judges—there is no question that both the legal and the political landscapes have changed dramatically in recent years.

Commitment to Marriage

One thing has never changed, however: Throughout our nation's history, across diverse cultures, communities, and political affiliations, Americans of all stripes have remained committed to the traditional institution of marriage. Most Americans strongly and instinctively support the following two fundamental propositions: Every human being is worthy of respect, and the traditional institution of marriage is worthy of protection. In communities across America, adults form caring relationships of all kinds, while children are raised through the heroic efforts of parents of all kinds—including single parents, foster parents, and adoptive parents. We admire, honor, and respect those relationships and those efforts.

At the same time, most Americans believe that children are best raised by their mother and father. Mankind has known no stronger human bond than that between a child and the two adults who have brought that child into the world together. For that reason, family and marriage experts have referred to the traditional institution of marriage as the "gold standard" for raising children. Social science simply confirms common sense. Social science also confirms that, when society stops privileging the traditional institution of marriage (as we have witnessed in a few European nations in recent years), the gold standard is diluted, and the ideal for raising children is threatened.

There are a number of important issues facing our nation—and the raising and nurturing of our next generation is one of them. Nearly 120 years ago, in the case of *Murphy* v. *Ramsey*, the U.S. Supreme Court unanimously concluded that "no legislation can be supposed more wholesome and necessary in the founding of a free, self-governing commonwealth" than "the idea of the family, as consisting in and springing from *the union for life of one man and one woman in the holy estate of matrimony*" (emphasis added). That union is "the sure foundation of all that is stable and noble in our civilization; the best guaranty of that reverent morality which is the source of all beneficent progress in social and political improvement." Moreover, that same Court unanimously praised efforts to shield the traditional institution of marriage from the winds of political change, by upholding a law "which endeavors to withdraw all political influence from those who are practically hostile to its attainment."

False Arguments

Today, however, the consensus behind marriage appears to be unraveling. Of course, those who no longer support traditional marriage laws do not say so outright. Instead, they resort to legalistic and procedural arguments for opposing a marriage amendment. They hope to confuse the issue in the minds of well-meaning Americans and to distract them from the importance of defending marriage, by unleashing a barrage of false arguments.

For example:

- *Why do we need a federal constitutional amendment, when we already have DOMA?*

The need for a federal constitutional amendment is simple: The traditional institution of marriage is under constitutional attack. It is now a national problem that requires a national solution. Legal experts and constitutional scholars across the political spectrum recognize and predict that the *only way* to preserve the status quo—the *only way* to preserve the traditional institution of marriage—is a constitutional amendment.

Immediately after the U.S. Supreme Court announced its decision in *Lawrence* v. *Texas* in June 2003, legal experts and commentators predicted that, under *Lawrence*, courts would begin to strike down traditional marriage laws around the country.

In *Lawrence*, the Court explicitly and unequivocally listed "marriage" as one of the "constitutional" rights that, absent a constitutional amendment, must be granted to same-sex couples and opposite-sex couples alike. Specifically, the Court stated that "our laws and tradition afford constitutional protection to personal decisions relating to *marriage*, procreation, contraception, family relationships, child rearing, and education. . . . Persons in a homosexual relationship may seek autonomy for these purposes, just as heterosexual persons do" (emphasis added). The *Lawrence* majority thus adopted the view endorsed decades ago by one of its members—Justice Ruth Bader Ginsburg. While serving as general counsel of the American Civil Liberties Union, she wrote that traditional marriage laws, such as anti-bigamy laws, are unconstitutional and must be struck down by courts.

It does not take a Supreme Court expert to understand the meaning of these words. And Supreme Court experts agree in any event. Legal scholars are a notoriously argumentative bunch. So it is particularly remarkable that the nation's most recognized constitutional experts—including several liberal legal scholars, like Laurence Tribe, Cass Sunstein, Erwin Chemerinsky, and William Eskridge—are in remarkable harmony on this issue. They predict that, like it or not, DOMA or other traditional marriage laws across the country will be struck down as unconstitutional by courts across the country.

Indeed, the process of invalidating and eradicating traditional marriage laws nationwide has already begun. Most notably, four justices of the Massachusetts Supreme Judicial Court invalidated that state's marriage law in its *Goodridge* decision issued last November, which it reaffirmed in February.

Those decisions were breathtaking, not just in their ultimate conclusion, but in their rhetoric as well. The court concluded that the "deep-seated religious, moral, and ethical convictions" that underlie traditional marriage are "no rational reason" for the institution's continued existence. It argued that traditional marriage is a "stain" on our laws that must be "eradicated." It contended that traditional marriage is "rooted in persistent prejudices" and "invidious discrimination," rather than in the best interest of children. Amazingly, it even suggested abolishing the institution of marriage outright, stating that "if the Legislature were to jettison the term 'marriage' altogether, it might well be rational and permissible." And for good measure, the court went out of its way to characterize DOMA itself as unconstitutionally discriminatory.

Without a federal constitutional amendment, activist courts, and judges will only continue striking down traditional marriage laws across the country—including DOMA itself. Lawsuits challenging traditional marriage laws are now pending in courtrooms across America—including four lawsuits in federal court.

In 2000, Nebraska voters ratified a state constitutional amendment protecting marriage in that state. Yet that state constitutional amendment has been challenged in federal district court as violating federal constitutional law. As Nebraska's attorney general, Jon Bruning, testified last March, the state expects the federal district judge to strike down its constitutional amendment.

A federal lawsuit has also been filed in Florida to strike down DOMA as unconstitutional under *Lawrence*. Lawyers are similarly claiming that DOMA is unconstitutional in a pending federal bankruptcy case in Washington state. And in Utah, lawyers have filed suit arguing that traditional marriage laws, such as that state's anti-polygamy law, must be struck down under *Lawrence*. And that just covers lawsuits in federal court—in addition, dozens of suits have been filed in state courts around the country.

A representative of the Lambda Legal organization—a champion of the ongoing nationwide litigation campaign to abolish traditional marriage laws across the country—recently stated: "We won't stop until we have [same-sex] marriage nationwide." This nationwide litigation campaign also enjoys the tacit, if not explicit, support of leading Democrats—including Sens. John Kerry and Ted Kennedy, Rep. Jerrold Nadler, and former presidential candidates Howard Dean and Carol Moseley Braun. All of them have attacked DOMA as unconstitutional, and thus presumably *want* DOMA to be invalidated by the courts—and without a constitutional amendment, their wishes may very well come true. The only way to stop the lawsuits, and to ensure the protection of marriage, is a constitutional amendment.

- *Why do we need an amendment now?*

Last September, the Senate subcommittee on the Constitution, Civil Rights and Property Rights examined the threat posed to the traditional institution of marriage by the *Lawrence* decision.

Detractors of the hearing scoffed that the threat was a pure fabrication, motivated by partisan politics. But then, just two months later, the Massachusetts *Goodridge* decision, relying specifically on *Lawrence*, struck down that state's traditional marriage law—precisely as predicted at the hearing.

Detractors then scoffed that the *Goodridge* decision would not stick. They argued that the state's own constitutional amendment process would be sufficient to control their courts. But then, the Massachusetts court reaffirmed its decision in February. The court even refused to bend after the Massachusetts legislature formally approved a state constitutional amendment—an amendment that can only take effect, if ever, no earlier than 2006.

Detractors then scoffed that DOMA had not been challenged, so there was no reason to take constitutional action at the federal level. But then, lawyers began to challenge DOMA. Cases are now pending in federal courts in Florida and Washington. Additional challenges are, of course, inevitable.

The truth is that, for these detractors, there will never be a good time to protect the traditional institution of marriage—because they don't want to protect the traditional institution of marriage. The constitutional amendment to protect marriage is not a "preemptive strike" on the Constitution, as detractors allege—it's a precautionary solution. Parents take responsible precautions to protect their children. Spouses take responsible precautions to protect their marriage. Likewise, government has the responsibility to take precautions to protect the institution of marriage.

- *Why can't the states handle this? After all, isn't marriage traditionally a state issue?*

This argument borders on the fraudulent. There is nothing that a state can do to fully protect itself against federal courts hostile to its laws except a federal constitutional amendment. Nebraska has already done everything it can, on its own, to defend marriage—up to and including a state constitutional amendment. Yet its amendment has already been challenged in federal court, where it is expected to be struck down. As state and local officials across the country have repeatedly urged, when it comes to defending marriage, the real threat to states' rights is judicial activism—not Congress, and certainly not the democratic process.

Moreover, the Constitution cannot be amended without the consent of three-fourths of the state legislatures. States can protect marriage against judicial activism—but only if Congress provides them the opportunity to consider a federal constitutional amendment protecting marriage.

- *Isn't our Constitution too sacred for such a political issue as defending marriage?*

No one is suggesting that the Constitution should be amended lightly. But the defense of marriage should not be ridiculed as a political issue. Nor should we disparage the most democratic process established under our Constitution by our Founding Fathers.

Our Founding Fathers specifically insisted on including an amendment process in the Constitution, because they humbly believed that no man-made document could ever be perfect. The constitutional amendment process was deliberatively considered and wisely crafted, and we have no reason to fear it.

We have amended the Constitution no fewer than 27 times—most recently in 1992 to regulate Congressional pay increases. The sky will not fall if Americans exercise their democratic rights to amend it again. Surely, the protection of marriage is at least as important to our nation as the regulation of Congressional pay, the specific manner in which we coin our money, or the countless other matters that can be found in our nation's charter.

Moreover, there is a robust tradition of constitutional amendments to reverse constitutional decisions by the courts with which the American people disagree—including the 11th, 14th, 16th, 19th, 24th, and 26th Amendments.

Opponents of the marriage amendment apparently have no objection to the courts amending the Constitution. Yet the power to amend the Constitution belongs to the American people, through the democratic process—not the courts. The courts alter the Constitution—under the guise of interpretation— far more often than the people have. Because of *Lawrence*, it is inevitable that the Constitution will be amended on the issue of marriage—the only question is how, and by whom. Legal scholars across the political spectrum agree that a constitutional amendment by the people is the only way to fully protect marriage against the courts.

- *Why would we ever want to write discrimination into the Constitution? Why would we ever want to roll back the Bill of Rights?*

This argument is offensive, pernicious—and revealing.

Marriage is not about discrimination—it is about children. It is offensive to characterize the vast majorities of Americans who support traditional marriage—individuals like Reverend Ray Hammond of the Bethel African Methodist Episcopal Church in Boston, Reverend Richard Richardson of the St. Paul African Methodist Episcopal Church in Boston, and Pastor Daniel de Leon, Sr., of Alianza de Ministerios Evangélicos Nacionales (AMEN) and Templo Calvario in Santa Ana, California—as bigots. It is offensive to characterize the laws, precedents, and customs of all fifty states as discriminatory. And it is offensive to slander the 85 senators who voted for DOMA as hateful.

Moreover, it is *precisely because* some activists believe that traditional marriage is about discrimination, and not about children, that they believe that all traditional marriage laws are unconstitutional and therefore must be abolished by the courts. These activists leave the American people with no middle ground. They accuse others of writing discrimination into the Constitution—yet they are the ones writing the American people out of our constitutional democracy.

Just last week, representatives of Sens. John Kerry and John Edwards said that the marriage amendment would "roll back rights." If you believe that traditional marriage is only about discrimination and about violating the rights of adults—as Sens. Kerry and Edwards apparently believe—then you have no choice but to oppose all traditional marriage laws. Any other position is incoherent at best—and deceptive at worst.

Marriage Protection

So the issue has been joined—precisely as it was in 1996. Despite typical Washington Beltway tricks to overcomplicate and confuse matters, the question remains a simple one: Should marriage, defined as the union of one man and one woman, be protected against judicial activism and the will of legal and political elites? If you believe that the answer is yes—as vast majorities of Americans do—then you have no legal option but to support a federal constitutional amendment protecting marriage.

The American people believe that every human being deserves respect, and the traditional institution of marriage deserves protection. As members of Congress continue to debate this issue, we should also remember what else the American people deserve: honesty.

The Honorable John Cornyn is a United States senator from Texas and chairman of the Senate Judiciary subcommittee on the Constitution, Civil Rights and Property Rights. He is a former state-supreme-court justice and state attorney general. Since September 2003, he has chaired three hearings to examine the legal threat to the traditional institution of marriage.

POSTSCRIPT

Should Same-Sex Marriage Be Legal?

While the United States considers a constitutional amendment that would prohibit same-sex marriage, several countries around the world have given legal status to same-sex couples, including Denmark, France, Germany, the Netherlands, Sweden, Iceland, Belgium, Norway, and South Africa. In 2003 Canada removed language from its laws that confined marriage to a man and a woman.

In the United States, attitudes remain divided. According to a Gallup poll conducted in May 2006, 58 percent of Americans believed that same-sex marriages should not be recognized. An even 50 percent of those polled supported a constitutional amendment that would define marriage as being between a man and a woman.

Support is stronger for civil unions—a concept intended as a legal equivalent to marriage, in all but name. A 2004 poll showed that 54 percent of Americans support civil unions. One state, Vermont, has enacted legislation permitting civil unions, permitting spousal rights to same-sex couples within that state only. The New Jersey State Supreme Court recently decided that the state must offer equal rights to gay and lesbian partnerships, but fell short of endorsing gay marriage or civil unions. It is up to the state legislature to decide if New Jersey will become the second state to legalize gay marriage or the second state with legalized civil unions. Other states—including California, Hawaii, and Maine—have laws that provide spousal-like rights to unmarried couples. Some regard civil unions as an acceptable compromise to this divisive debate, but others regard such arrangements with memories of the "separate but equal" days of segregation.

Opponents of same-sex marriage frequently rely on biblical references to condemn the practice. They cite passages that describe marriage as between man and woman (1 Cor 7:2), and others that denounce homosexuality in general (Lev 18:22; Cor 6:9; 1 Tim 1:9–11). Yet, if the Bible is to be relied upon for enacting marital legislation, other biblical passages may give legislators pause, such as those that endorse polygamy (Gen 29:17–28; 2 Sam 3:2–5) and a man's right to have concubines (2 Sam 5:13; 1 Kings 11:3; 2 Chron 11:21), or those that prohibit divorce (Deut 22:19; Mark 10:9) or mandate female virginity in order for a marriage to be valid (if a wife is not a virgin, she can be executed, the Bible says) (Deut 22:13–21).

Biblical references and implications notwithstanding, the Human Rights Campaign says that fully recognized same-sex marriages are essential to ensuring the same legal protections and benefits that are available to heterosexual married couples. Do you agree? Do you believe civil unions are a just substitution? Why or why not?

Cornyn argues that while the efforts of single, foster, and adoptive parents are heroic, the relationship between a child and its biological mother and father are the "gold standard." Do you believe that single-parent families, adoptive families, and gay and lesbian families cause that gold standard to be "diluted," as Cornyn states?

How do you view the argument to amend the U.S. Constitution? What potential benefits or difficulties do you foresee resulting from this action? Finally, what do you believe is the *purpose* of marriage? Is marriage primarily about love? Rights? Children and family? Monogamy? Other considerations? Do you regard it as primarily a religious institution or a legal institution? Is there any *single, predominant* purpose of marriage, or are there many purposes worthy of consideration?

Suggested Readings

R. H. Bork, "Stop Courts From Imposing Gay Marriage," *Wall Street Journal* (August 7, 2001).

M. Bronski, "Over the Rainbow," *Boston Phoenix* (August 1–August 7, 2003).

S. Feldhan and D. Glass, "Why is Reality TV Marriage OK When Gay Marriage is Not?" *Atlanta Journal-Constitution* (December 2003).

R. Goldstein, "The Radical Case for Gay Marriage: Why Progressives Must Join this Fight," *The Village Voice* (September 3–9, 2003).

J. Jacoby, "The Timeless Meaning of Marriage," *Boston Globe* (November 2003).

B. Knickerbocker, "A Drubbing for Same Sex Marriage," *Christian Science Monitor* (November 2004).

K. Mantilla, "Gay Marriage: Destroying the Family to Save the Children," *Off Our Backs,* vol. 34, no. 5–6, p. 22 (May–June 2004).

J. Rauch, "Leave Gay Marriage to the States," *The Wall Street Journal* (July 27, 2001).

ISSUE 14

Should Society Support Cohabitation Before Marriage?

YES: Dorian Solot and Marshall Miller, from *Unmarried to Each Other: The Essential Guide to Living Together as an Unmarried Couple* (Marlowe & Company, 2002)

NO: David Popenoe and Barbara Dafoe Whitehead, from *Should We Live Together? What Young Adults Need to Know About Cohabitation Before Marriage: A Comprehensive Review of Research* (The National Marriage Project, 2001)

ISSUE SUMMARY

YES: Dorian Solot and Marshall Miller, founders of the Alternatives to Marriage Project (www.unmarried.org), describe some of the challenges faced by people who choose to live together without marrying, and offer practical advice for couples who face discrimination.

NO: David Popenoe and Barbara Dafoe Whitehead, directors of the National Marriage Project (marriage.rutgers.edu), contend that living together before marriage is not a good way to prepare for marriage or avoid divorce. They maintain that cohabitation weakens the institution of marriage and poses serious risks for women and children.

What do Americans think of sexual relationships and living together before marriage? Attitudes have changed dramatically during the past generation. In a 1969 Gallup poll of American adults, two-thirds said it was morally wrong for a man and a woman to have sexual relations before marriage. A more recent (2001) poll revealed that only 38 percent of American adults share this opinion today. These two surveys focus on the sexual behavior of young people before marriage. When the question is broadened to examine how today's Americans feel about couples "living together," or cohabiting, 52 percent approve.

In practice, more than one-half of Americans live together before marrying. Many cohabiting couples will live together for a relatively short period of time, with most couples either breaking up or marrying within about

1½ years, though couples with children are more likely to stay together. In addition, the 2000 U.S. Census indicates that there are almost 4 million opposite-sex, unmarried households in the United States. (These households include both couples who have been married previously and those who have never been married.) Forty-one percent of these households have at least one child under the age of 18.

Like their married counterparts, infidelity is not common among the majority of cohabiting couples, though rates are slightly different. According to the U.S. chapter of the *International Encyclopedia of Sexuality* (Continuum, 2004), about 94 percent of married persons had sex only with their spouse during the last year, compared with 75 percent of cohabiting persons.

Despite the growing acceptance of cohabitation, couples who live together without marrying often face pressure from family and loved ones to "tie the knot." For some, marriage may be in their future plans; others may be perfectly happy with their decision not to marry; still other couples may be legally restricted from marrying—as of 2004, only Massachusetts permits same-sex couples to legally marry. Recognizing the pressures and discrimination some cohabiting couples may face, the Alternatives to Marriage Project advocates for the "equality and fairness for unmarried people, including people who choose not to marry, cannot marry, or live together before marriage."

The first essay that follows is from a chapter of *Unmarried to Each Other: The Essential Guide to Living Together as an Unmarried Couple,* a guide written by the organization's cofounders, Dorian Solot and Marshall Miller.

On the other side of the debate is the National Marriage Project, which expresses concern about the growing trend toward greater acceptance of cohabitation. The National Marriage Project provides "research and analysis on the state of marriage in America and to educate the public on the social, economic and cultural conditions affecting marital success and child well-being." The second essay, written by the National Project's co-directors, David Popenoe and Barbara Dafoe Whitehead, provides commentary and analysis of existing literature on cohabitation. It warns young people, especially young women, of the dangers of cohabitation to them and their children.

YES

YES ↙

**Dorian Solot and
Marshall Miller**

When Others Disagree: Surviving Pressure and Discrimination

We wish living together were easy. We wish all parents welcomed the news of their child's cohabitation with cries of, "How wonderful, darling! I'll bring over a lasagna so you won't have to worry about dinner while you unpack." We wish friends threw celebratory bashes, ministers blessed the new level of love and commitment, wise neighbors shared their insights about getting through hard times, and landlords cheerfully added another name to the lease.

Unfortunately, that's not the world in which we live. While an unmarried couple moving to the block generally isn't worthy of backyard gossip anymore, it's not unusual for partners to run into snags along the way. For gay, lesbian, bisexual, and transgender (GLBT) people, homophobia is often a bigger problem than marital status discrimination, though the two are closely linked. This chapter offers insights on some common challenges from the outside, and suggests practical ways to deal with those who predict catastrophe for your relationship, those who nudge you down the aisle, and those who discriminate against you. Although we can't guarantee the naysayers will help load furniture into your U-Haul for the big move, if you're lucky they might give you a friendly wave as you pull away.

Pressure Not To Live Together

There's no question acceptance of cohabitation has come a long way quickly. In a span of a few decades the act of sharing a home without sharing a marriage license has been transformed from scandalous to normal. Today it's something most people do before they marry. But despite how common it's become, living together still draws frowns, wrinkled brows, and even outright condemnation from some people. Nicole describes her parents as "rigid Catholics" and says they frequently tell her she's "living in sin." Her father warns her of eternal damnation, saying, "Your life on earth is so short, but eternity is so long."

> *Every holiday it's a nightmare filled with anxiety when we have to get together with my family, because my mother makes it so uncomfortable for the two of us. Even though we've been together for nine years, and I don't rely on her financially or anything, she makes it very, very uncomfortable. About six*

From the book UNMARRIED TO EACH OTHER: THE ESSENTIAL GUIDE TO LIVING TOGETHER AS AN UNMARRIED COUPLE. Copyright © 2002 by Dorian Solot and Marshall Miller. Appears by permission of the publisher Marlowe & Co., A division of Avalon Publishing Group. Notes omitted.

223

months ago it all came to a head. She said that I wasn't welcome at her house, so I don't go to her house anymore except at holidays.

This intense disapproval isn't because cohabiting partners store their toothbrushes so close together, or because people believe that seeing your sweetheart's morning bedhead should be an experience only for married spouses. The real reason why there's opposition to unmarried people living together is this: cohabitors have sex. Of course, *lots* of unmarried people have sex, whether they live with their lovers or not. At least 70 percent of first-time brides and 83 percent of first-time grooms are not virgins on their wedding day—the percentages are even higher for younger generations—revealing exactly how much unmarried lovemaking is going on. Much of that sex involves far less love and commitment than is present in many cohabiting relationships. But the nose-wrinklers care about sex between cohabitors because there's no attempt to hide it, no polite, "We were just sitting here in the back room having a conversation. Really!" When romantically-involved unmarried people live together, everyone assumes they're having sex, and critics say they're flaunting it. That's where the arguments begin. . . .

MOM ALWAYS KNOWS

Have you heard the joke about the cohabiting guy whose mother came to dinner? His mom had long been suspicious of the relationship between her son, John, and his roommate, Julie. When they had her over for dinner one night, John read his mother's mind, and volunteered, "I know what you must be thinking, Mom, but I assure you, Julie and I are just roommates."

About a week later, Julie came to John and said, "Ever since your mother came to dinner, I haven't been able to find the beautiful silver gravy ladle. You don't suppose she took it, do you?" John said, "Well, I doubt it, but I'll write her a letter just to be sure." So he sat down and wrote a letter:

"Dear Mother, I'm not saying you did take a gravy ladle from my house, and I'm not saying you did not take a gravy ladle from my house, but the fact remains that one has been missing ever since you were here for dinner. Love, John."

Several days later, John received a letter from his mother:

"Dear Son, I'm not saying that you do sleep with Julie, and I'm not saying that you do not sleep with Julie, but the fact remains that if she were sleeping in her own bed, she would have found the gravy ladle by now. Love, Mother."

The Arguments

Whether you're already living together or just talking about it, odds are you've crossed paths with some of the common arguments against cohabitation. Maybe your relatives are the number one anti-cohabiting campaigners in your life, or perhaps you've encountered a sermon in church or read some disturbing statistics about living together in the newspaper. Whatever the source, almost every line of argument fits into one of these categories: Living in Sin Arguments, Pseudo-Scientific Arguments, or Mars and Venus Arguments. Each one emphasizes a different concern and warrants a different response. Below are explanations about the problems with each kind of argument, and tips for how to respond.

Living In Sin Arguments: The Moral View Against Cohabitation

These are the classic arguments, the meat and potatoes, of why you shouldn't live with your partner. You've probably heard, "Cohabitors are living in sin. It's wrong," or "The Bible says you shouldn't cohabit," or "People who shack up are undermining family values." Those are just the polite versions. At their most hostile, these sometimes bring dire warnings of hellfire and eternal doom.

Words like these can be deeply hurtful, particularly when respected people of faith aim them at people of their own religion. Some cohabitors feel forced to choose between their faith and their relationship, even when the relationship is a good one. Anita says:

> I have been in so much turmoil about my perplexing situation. I am forty-nine-years-old and engaged to a wonderful man, but because of my past divorce I will lose all my medical benefits if I marry. I love this man with all my heart. I want to marry by my Christian beliefs, but I have a heart problem and limited funds, so I cannot afford to lose my health insurance. We live together, and we are happy. But I am so torn. I pray all the time for God to love me and not scorn me for what I am doing. I would love to have His blessing upon us without the legal marriage, and to know that we will still go to heaven.

Jacquie says that the Bible's messages are the only things that trouble her about being in an unmarried relationship.

> According to the scriptures, I'm in trouble. The book of Deuteronomy says that my former husband is my husband until the day they throw dirt on me. In the church's eyes, we are wrong. In the African-American community, that is one of the biggest things that we struggle with.

Fortunately, there are many religious and ethical people who disagree with this moralistic view against cohabitation, and believe in supporting healthy, loving relationships regardless of marital status.

How To Respond to Living in Sin Arguments

Understand the Bible in today's context. You might be surprised to realize that despite claims like, "Cohabitation is entirely contrary to God's law," there's nothing in the Judeo-Christian Bible that explicitly says cohabitation is wrong. In fact, the Bible includes teachings about holy unmarried relationships that are valid alternatives to marriage, and poems in the Song of Songs that celebrate an unmarried relationship. Rabbi Arthur Waskow says of these, "I believe that the Song of Songs is our best guide from the ancient tradition as to how sexuality could express the joyful and pleasurable celebration of God."

While parts of the Bible do address "fornication," or sex between unmarried people, many religious leaders and scholars believe that some Biblical teachings are no longer applicable to today's world. Of the many mores mentioned and permitted in the Bible, most faith traditions—liberal, mainstream, fundamentalist, and evangelical alike—now condemn behaviors such as polygamy, slavery, and the treatment of women as property. Reverend Jim Maynard of American Baptists Concerned says, "Most hold that the Bible is inspired by God but written in the words of humans. It contains human perspectives and prejudice that reflect that time and place in which it was written. What is normal for one day and time is not always applicable to others." While the Bible can provide inspiration and guidance, many clergy agree that one need not interpret it literally to remain true to one's faith. It's the relationship between the two spouses (even legally unmarried ones) and God that ultimately matters, not the opinion of the minister or the cranky lady in the front pew.

Many Christian leaders have called for the church to stay focused on Jesus's message of love. For instance, in 2000 Dr. William Walsh, the Bishop of Killaloe in Ireland, publicly apologized for the Catholic Church's attitude towards cohabiting couples and said, "Christ did not condemn those who failed to meet the ideals of the church . . . We must not condemn. We must not question the nature of that love that may not meet with our ideals. We must celebrate family, and all that is possible in family; the love between married spouses and between parents and children; the love of the unmarried mother and unmarried father and their children, and the struggle that being an unmarried mother and father can be in our society."

Help others respect your decision.   If the person who accuses you of "living in sin" is close to home—a parent or relative, member of your faith community, or someone else with whom you'll have an ongoing relationship—you can work to help him better understand and respect your decision to live together. It helps to know exactly what concerns him. If the values underlying your relationship are his primary care, he may soften if he realizes you share his values of commitment, honesty, love, and integrity. It might help him to understand what your relationship means to you, how your shared values are central to your love, and why you aren't or can't be married. Witnessing you put these values into practice over a period of years can be the most powerful way to earn the respect of these doubters. Few would remain judgmental of Anita, the woman above with a heart problem, if they understood her situation and saw the Christian values woven into her daily life.

Other objectors' opposition to living together stems from a deeply held moral or religious belief that opposes all unmarried sex and rigidly upholds heterosexual marriage as the only acceptable form of family. A friendly conversation is unlikely to transform one of these types into someone who supports your relationship. It might be possible, though, to come to respect each other's points of view, mutually understand that you've made different choices, and agree to disagree. Marshall experienced this "hate the sin, love the sinner" approach firsthand:

> *Before his death at age ninety-one, my grandfather regularly attended Sunday services at his southern Virginia Baptist retirement home. One of his preacher's favorite pastimes was rallying against those who "live in sin." Although our living together had never seemed to concern my grandfather before he moved to the retirement home, over time this preacher's message caused him to decide that he no longer wanted to see or talk to Dorian and me because of the sin he felt we were committing. His silent treatment lasted for months, and while it hurt us, we were fortunate to have support from the rest of my family. After lots of conversations with my parents, he eventually came around, reaching out to us with the compromise, "I don't hate you, I just hate what you're doing." We were glad to have several months of positive re-connections before he passed away.*

It's not easy, and sometimes not even possible, to reach this point with every family member. But it can be worth trying.

Live the kind of "family values" that matter.   Pundits and politicians who lament "declining family values" are usually talking about a narrow view of family. In the real world, family ties aren't based on whether you're legally married, have children, or are heterosexual. Unmarried partners can be a family unit, and part of each other's extended families. Connect with each other's extended families by going to visit them (especially for important occasions like reunions, graduations, performances, and significant birthdays and anniversaries), spending holidays together, planning opportunities for each other's relatives to meet each other, signing greeting cards together, staying connected by phone and email, and finding common interests or hobbies to explore with "in-laws" (some unmarried people jokingly call theirs "out-laws"). Joan said this kind of positive family relationship earned her and her male partner, Fran, a respectful tolerator, if not a supporter:

> *Fran's dad is eighty-four and very opinionated. He's been a deacon in the Catholic Church. Considering how conventional and traditional his views are, it's amazed both of us that he has accepted me and accepted our relationship as well as he has. It's really been a pleasure. I think it's because he kind of likes me, and I like him. He's also very close to Fran, and I think it's really important to him to maintain Fran's love and goodwill and the closeness that they have. I think he would like it if Fran got married, but he doesn't make an issue of it.*

The more your relationship fits into your family's culture, the easier it becomes for people to choose to forget about how you are different. Finding ways for each other's relatives to meet and connect is one of the most powerful ways we've found to strengthen ties. Dorian describes one method we've used:

> *Marshall and I each have sisters who are much younger than we are. When we were in college they'd sometimes visit us, so we decided to create an annual "Sister Convergence" weekend. Starting when the girls were six, seven, and eight, they'd come every spring with teddy bears and sleeping bags in tow, eat*

piles of peanut butter and jelly sandwiches, teach us the sing-song hand-clapping games they'd learned on the playground, make embroidery-thread friendship bracelets they'd sell to our housemates, and surprise us with stealth tickling attacks. The hiding of the peanut butter jar's top became part of the annual tradition; back home they'd talk to us on the phone, giggling with glee when they heard we'd finally discovered where they stowed it behind a sofa cushion or deep in a sock drawer. They grew up knowing each other and looking forward to their weekends together. Even though they're not related, I think they feel like each other's extended families.

Create your own family.   Unfortunately, being connecting to extended family isn't an option for everyone. Many who have been rejected from or need to separate themselves from their family of origin find tremendous strength by forming an intentional family. These kinds of families can include your partner, close friends, or other people who play a significant role in your life. You might choose to share holidays or important events with them, and see them as a place to turn for support during difficult times.

Find a supportive faith community.   If you're a religious person, you may not have to settle for a faith community that condemns your relationship. You can tell a lot about a given church's stance on diverse families by looking at its approach to gay and lesbian issues. Some denominations and many individual churches, synagogues, and clergy have affirmed their support for GLBT people, and these are more likely to welcome all kinds of "non-traditional" relationships. Unitarian Universalists, Quakers, Reform and Reconstructionist Jews, and the United Church of Christ are particularly known for welcoming all people, regardless of their sexual orientation or marital status. . . .

Pseudo-Scientific Arguments: The "Scientific" View Against Cohabitation

In the 1980s and 1990s, when arguments based on morality ceased to pack the punch they once did, anti-cohabitation campaigners donned crisp white lab coats, re-tooling their messages for today's science-trusting public. The new arguments sound like, "Living together before marriage increases the risk of divorce," "Cohabitors are less committed to each other than married couples," and "Cohabiting couples experience more domestic violence than married ones." Gwen heard them from her mother:

I received a major backlash from both my parents in response to my choice to live with my boyfriend. My mother actually called and lectured to me extensively for forty minutes about the various kinds of research to substantiate her opinion that cohabiting relationships are very unhealthy.

Arguments like these can be confusing, since to many couples it makes intuitive sense to live together before tying the knot. The reality is, many of the statistics batted around in the media don't tell the whole story. It's not a coincidence the general public is becoming familiar with these semi-truths—some political groups have made them a central part of their anti-cohabitation campaigns.

Yet most of the facts about cohabitation that are published in respected research journals and presented at academic conferences draw quite different conclusions.

How to Understand the Truth Behind Pseudo-Scientific Arguments

Understand the difference between "the average cohabitor" and your life. You are not necessarily "average." With eleven million cohabitors in this country, it is nearly impossible to draw any meaningful conclusions about what we all have in common. Yet pseudo-scientific arguments do just that.

People live with a partner for incredibly varied reasons—if cohabitors were paint colors, we'd be a veritable rainbow. For sake of explanation, imagine that one kind of cohabitor, couples who live together as a step between dating and marriage, are red paint. Senior citizens who live together so they don't lose their pensions will be yellow paint, and unmarried couples of several decades' duration with no plans to marry are green. Low-income couples who would like to marry but want to be sure their future spouse can help them escape poverty are blue.

Anytime a researcher comes up with an average about cohabitors, she takes all the red, yellow, green, blue, and a bunch of other colors for all the other cohabitors, stirs them together, and come up with a oh-so-serious, scientifically accurate shade of—you guessed it—brown. As everyone focuses on this average number that's been produced—the muddy brown color—they forget that this average is utterly meaningless when it comes to understanding the red cohabitors, the yellow ones, or any of the others.

Cohabiting types that exist in large numbers affect the color of the whole pool when it's averaged. So since poor people, whom we colored blue, cohabit at higher rates than middle or upper-class ones, the average brown color will always have a blue tint. That means that certain characteristics about poor people, like the fact that they tend to have more health problems and higher rates of depression will make the average for *all* cohabitors look more depressed and unhealthy. But those tendencies aren't necessarily true for other cohabitors in the pool. Average cohabiting couples who plan to marry or are considering marriage have characteristics very similar to married people. Green cohabitors in very long-term relationships are statistically a small splash—their characteristics hardly show up in the average at all.

In short, because of the way some groups pull the average up or down, statistics about cohabitation often lead to distorted conclusions. Poor people who cohabit in large numbers make the average cohabitor income look low, but if you're making a good salary, that doesn't affect you. There are higher levels of alcoholism in the cohabitor population because people are less likely to marry partners with alcohol problems, but that doesn't mean that living together will drive you to drink. The quality of your relationship—not any statistical average—determines whether your union will be strong.

Realize there is no evidence that cohabitation causes divorce. It's true research finds that on average, cohabitors who later marry have a higher divorce rate than those who marry without living together first. But it's a misrepresentation to say that cohabitation *causes* divorce. Here's why. This research compares two groups of people, those who live together before they marry and those who don't. But people aren't randomly assigned to these different groups—they choose to live together or not because they're different kinds of people. Those who don't live together before marriage are a minority today, and they tend to be more conservative, with stronger religious beliefs and stronger opposition to divorce. Given this, it's no surprise that this group doesn't consider divorce an acceptable option. The difference between the two groups' divorce rates is likely attributable to the types of people in each group, not because the cohabitation ruins their relationships. As Sociologist Judith Seltzer writes, "Claims that individuals who cohabit before marriage hurt their chances of a good marriage pay too little attention to this evidence."

Given that many couples cohabit to test their compatibility before making a lifetime commitment to marriage, could cohabitation actually result in *lower* divorce rates? It's possible. The divorce rate has been falling slightly since its peak two decades ago. During that same time period, the cohabitation rate has skyrocketed. There's no way to know for certain how the changes in divorce and cohabitation affect each other—just because two things happen at the same time (correlation) doesn't prove that one caused the other (causation). Since some cohabitors live together to try out a relationship but then ultimately break up, it's likely these people successfully avoided a marriage that would have ended in divorce. Chances are good the divorce rate would be higher if not for cohabitation.

Cohabitation opponents make a lot of noise about divorce statistics because divorce is such a common fear. When you look at all the facts, whether you divorce ultimately may not have much to do with whether you live together. If you never marry, you don't need to worry about divorce, though the end of a long-term relationship has the same emotional impact. Chapter 4 is about what you can do to keep your relationship strong.

Know that commitment and marriage are not the same thing.   As with most stereotypes, there's a grain of truth to the claim that cohabitors are less committed than married spouses. Dating couples are usually less committed than married ones, too. Since most people move through the stages from dating to living together to marriage, you'd expect average commitment levels to follow the same trends—lowest among dating couples, highest among married ones—and they do.

Of course there are some cohabitors who have no commitment to each other, just as there are married couples who aren't very committed and soon got divorced. Other cohabitors' levels of commitment easily match the most loving, stable married pairs. Some have plans to marry and just haven't done so yet, while others stay together for decades without a marriage license. In all murkiness of averages, there's no way to distinguish the couple who's owned a home together for thirty years from one who moved in together last week when one partner got evicted. Sure, scientists can come up with an average number to indicate commitment among cohabitors. But it won't tell you anything about your own relationship.

It's worth pondering how those scientists even come up with a number that equals commitment. It's a slippery concept to pin down using a survey—imagine trying to compare your commitment to your relationship to your friend's commitment to his using a numerical scale. One oft-cited study of cohabitors and married couples found a difference of 1.3 points on a twenty point scale of "commitment," and a finding that small isn't unusual. So the pundits are telling the truth when they say cohabitors on average aren't as committed as married people—but it sure isn't the whole truth.

The best way to win the argument over commitment is to prove your relationship can stand the test of time. As the years tick by and you weather some tough times, outsiders will realize you're in it for the long haul. Calling yours a "committed relationship" or describing yourselves as "life partners" if that describes you can help people understand.

Understand the "accumulation factor." Cohabitation opponents exaggerate every negative research conclusion about the subject while ignoring research that finds cohabitors are just like everyone else. One of the most alarming claims might be that cohabiting women are at higher risk of domestic violence than married ones. What's actually going on? First of all, there isn't much of a difference between married and cohabiting women on this characteristic. One British study that's often cited found that 2 percent of married women had experienced domestic assault in the previous year, compared with 3 percent of cohabiting women. Nonetheless, since any amount of domestic violence is unacceptable, even a 1 percent difference could be cause for concern.

A more recent study explores why that difference exists. It finds that if you track a group of new cohabitors over time, the ones with less violent relationships are more likely to marry. No surprise there. The couples still in the cohabitor pool after the non-violent couples marry—the ones who "accumulate"—are probably using excellent judgement by deciding not to make a lifetime commitment to a dangerous partner. But they affect the average for the whole pool, and make it look as if cohabitors have more abusive relationships. It's likely that a similar process clouds a great deal of the research that compares married to unmarried people.

Marriage isn't a shield that can protect anyone from abuse, and cohabitation isn't automatically a battleground. A non-violent partner is unlikely to turn aggressive because you've cohabited too long. An abusive partner is unlikely to be transformed if you get married, and in fact, marrying could put you at greater risk. Marital status is a poor way to predict whether any particular relationship will be safe.

Mars and Venus Arguments: The Gendered View Against Cohabitation

Mars and Venus Arguments assume that all men (from Mars) are looking for sex without responsibility, while all women (from Venus) are looking for husbands and babies soon after. Mars and Venus are believed to be in their own orbits, at risk for major problems when they interact or live together. Women are most often the targets of these kinds of arguments, but men aren't immune. Perhaps you've heard, "In cohabitation, men get to have sex without making a commitment," "Women are the ones who get hurt by living together," or, "He won't buy the cow if you give away the milk for free."

It's certainly possible to run into these kinds of problems if you and your partner haven't talked about what living together means to you. If one of you thinks it's a new level of commitment while the other thinks it's a way to split the rent check, you're headed for trouble. If one partner thinks you're practically engaged while the other sees the setup as a roommate "with benefits," there's conflict ahead. But if you're on the same page because you've had a few of those capital letter Relationship Talks, you're unlikely to be taken by surprise, whatever your gender. Don't be surprised if Mars is the one dreaming of hearth and home, while Venus is hesitant to get tied down—gender roles aren't what they used to be. Sebastian gets a kick out of reminding people of this:

> My friends and acquaintances will say to me, "Oh, how long have you guys been together?" I'll say, "Almost eight years." They're in shock, and of course the next question is, "Why don't you get married?," as if they're asking, what's wrong with you? And of course they immediately assume that Janna wants to get married and I don't, because I want to go sow my wild oats, afraid of commitment, guy problem, or whatever. It's actually kind of fun to pop their bubble, to explain the decision that we've made together. I enjoy seeing them try to take that in.

Despite all the stereotypes, many more women have serious hesitations about marrying than men. Among hundreds of long-term male-female unmarried couples we've talked to, it's nearly always the woman who feels strongly about not marrying. Women's preferences about marriage generally seem to "trump" their male partners, perhaps because they tend to have stronger feelings on the issue—if a woman wants to marry, she'll keep looking until she finds a man who consents, and Stacey is a typical example:

> I've been with my partner for fifteen years and we've lived together ever since my pregnancy and the birth of our daughter, who is now ten. My father always wanted to know why we didn't get married. He pestered me about it, refusing to accept that I didn't wish to be married—after all, he thought, all women want to get married. One day he finally asked my partner straight out why he didn't marry me. When my partner said he was more than willing to get married, but that I was the one refusing, I think my father just gave up.

How To Respond to Mars and Venus Arguments
Point out that it's a lot easier to have sex without commitment if you're not living together. If you're feeling bold, try, "We were making love long before we made the commitment to move in together." People who truly want sex without commitment don't cohabit—they just find a casual relationship or one-night-stand. By comparison, most partners who move in together are already in an intimate, sexual relationship and want to *increase* their level of connection and commitment. We don't know anyone who decided to cohabit because they wanted sex without commitment. As Mark told us, "My girlfriend and I intend

to marry but do not want to rush into it before we are truly ready. We decided to live together because we were spending all our time together, anyway—why rent two apartments when we could rent one? We saw living together as a commitment to each other."

Point out that humans are not cattle.   "Mom, I'm not a cow," ought to suffice. Many younger women have never even heard the warning that if they "give away the milk for free," their partner "won't buy the cow." The adage used to refer to women who "gave away" sex without holding out for marriage. The theory was that if the man could get sex without paying the price (marriage), he would never feel the need to say "I do." Women of older generations were probably surprised to read the recent discussion about the saying on the Alternatives to Marriage Project's online list:

> *Someone mentioned the old adage about the cow and men getting free milk. What is this supposed to mean? Isn't the woman getting "free milk," as well? After all, women do enjoy sex, too.*

> —Jessica

> *I've been saying that to my boyfriend for about fifteen years. I also told him that if he wanted to get married, he shouldn't have moved in with me. When I saw the phrase, I thought the woman was getting the free milk.*

> —Tori

Most women today recognize themselves as sexual beings with their own desires, who choose sexual relationships or not based on their own situation and values. It doesn't make sense to men today, either. More than eight in ten first-time grooms has had sex before he marries, yet there men stand at the altar, undeterred by all that "free milk."

Gendered double standards still exist. Women are still expected to guard sex, are labeled "sluts" if they're perceived to be having too much sex, and are targeted for warnings about "ruining their reputations." Men, on the other hand, are told they need to guard their money. Guys hear that if they're not careful, while he's busy enjoying sex with his live-in lover, she will max out his credit cards and expect a stream of expensive gifts until she finds the next guy to run off with. The best way to prevent being taken advantage of is to understand your partner thoroughly—whatever your gender or what you want to protect. Know whether each of you is responsible with money, what sex means to each partner, and what your expectations are about commitment and monogamy. If you're clear about what living together means for you, it'll be much easier to calm the fears provoked by Mars and Venus alarmists. . . .

David Popenoe and
Barbara Dafoe Whitehead

 **NO**

Should We Live Together? What Young Adults Need to Know about Cohabitation Before Marriage: A Comprehensive Review of Recent Research

Executive Summary

Cohabitation is replacing marriage as the first living together experience for young men and women. When blushing brides walk down the aisle at the beginning of the new millennium, well over half have already lived together with a boyfriend.

For today's young adults, the first generation to come of age during the divorce revolution, living together seems like a good way to achieve some of the benefits of marriage and avoid the risk of divorce. Couples who live together can share expenses and learn more about each other. They can find out if their partner has what it takes to be married. If things don't work out, breaking up is easy to do. Cohabiting couples do not have to seek legal or religious permission to dissolve their union.

Not surprisingly, young adults favor cohabitation. According to surveys, most young people say it is a good idea to live with a person before marrying.

But a careful review of the available social science evidence suggests that living together is not a good way to prepare for marriage or to avoid divorce. What's more, it shows that the rise in cohabitation is not a positive family trend. Cohabiting unions tend to weaken the institution of marriage and pose special risks for women and children. Specifically, the research indicates that:

- Living together before marriage increases the risk of breaking up after marriage.
- Living together outside of marriage increases the risk of domestic violence for women, and the risk of physical and sexual abuse for children.

- Unmarried couples have lower levels of happiness and wellbeing than married couples.

Because this generation of young adults is so keenly aware of the fragility of marriage, it is especially important for them to know what contributes to marital success and what may threaten it. Yet many young people do not know the basic facts about cohabitation and its risks. Nor are parents, teachers, clergy and others who instruct the young in matters of sex, love and marriage well acquainted with the social science evidence. Therefore, one purpose of this paper is to report on the available research.

At the same time, we recognize the larger social and cultural trends that make cohabiting relationships attractive to many young adults today. Unmarried cohabitation is not likely to go away. Given this reality, the second purpose of this paper is to guide thinking on the question: "should we live together?" We offer four principles that may help. These principles may not be the last words on the subject but they are consistent with the available evidence and may help never-married young adults avoid painful losses in their love lives and achieve satisfying and long-lasting relationships and marriage.

1. **Consider not living together at all before marriage.** Cohabitation appears not to be helpful and may be harmful as a try-out for marriage. There is no evidence that if you decide to cohabit before marriage you will have a stronger marriage than those who don't live together, and some evidence to suggest that if you live together before marriage, you are more likely to break up after marriage. Cohabitation is probably least harmful (though not necessarily helpful) when it is prenuptial—when both partners are definitely planning to marry, have formally announced their engagement and have picked a wedding date.
2. **Do not make a habit of cohabiting.** Be aware of the dangers of multiple living together experiences, both for your own sense of wellbeing and for your chances of establishing a strong lifelong partnership. Contrary to popular wisdom, you do not learn to have better relationships from multiple failed cohabiting relationships. In fact, multiple cohabiting is a strong predictor of the failure of future relationships.
3. **Limit cohabitation to the shortest possible period of time.** The longer you live together with a partner, the more likely it is that the low-commitment ethic of cohabitation will take hold, the opposite of what is required for a successful marriage.
4. **Do not cohabit if children are involved.** Children need and should have parents who are committed to staying together over the long term. Cohabiting parents break up at a much higher rate than married parents and the effects of breakup can be devastating and often long lasting. Moreover, children living in cohabiting unions with stepfathers or mother's boyfriends are at higher risk of sexual abuse and physical violence, including lethal violence, than are children living with married biological parents.

Should We Live Together? What Young Adults Need to Know about Cohabitation Before Marriage: A Comprehensive Review of Recent Research

Living together before marriage is one of America's most significant and unexpected family trends. By simple definition, living together—or unmarried cohabitation—is the status of couples who are sexual partners, not married to each other, and sharing a household. By 2000, the total number of unmarried couples in America was almost four and three-quarters million, up from less than half a million in 1960.[1] It is estimated that about a quarter of unmarried women between the ages of 25 and 39 are currently living with a partner and about half have lived at some time with an unmarried partner (the data are typically reported for women but not for men). Over half of all first marriages are now preceded by cohabitation, compared to virtually none earlier in the century.[2]

What makes cohabitation so significant is not only its prevalence but also its widespread popular acceptance. In recent representative national surveys nearly 66% of high school senior boys and 61% of the girls indicated that they "agreed" or "mostly agreed" with the statement "it is usually a good idea for a couple to live together before getting married in order to find out whether they really get along." And three quarters of the students stated that "a man and a woman who live together without being married" are either "experimenting with a worthwhile alternative lifestyle" or "doing their own thing and not affecting anyone else."[3]

Unlike divorce or unwed childbearing, the trend toward cohabitation has inspired virtually no public comment or criticism. It is hard to believe that across America, only thirty years ago, living together for unmarried, heterosexual couples was against the law.[4] And it was considered immoral—living in sin—or at the very least highly improper. Women who provided sexual and housekeeping services to a man without the benefits of marriage were regarded as fools at best and morally loose at worst. A double standard existed, but cohabiting men were certainly not regarded with approbation.

Today, the old view of cohabitation seems yet another example of the repressive Victorian norms. The new view is that cohabitation represents a more progressive approach to intimate relationships. How much healthier women are to be free of social pressure to marry and stigma when they don't. How much better off people are today to be able to exercise choice in their sexual and domestic arrangements. How much better off marriage can be, and how many divorces can be avoided, when sexual relationships start with a trial period.

Surprisingly, much of the accumulating social science research suggests otherwise. What most cohabiting couples don't know, and what in fact few people know, are the conclusions of many recent studies on unmarried cohabitation and its implications for young people and for society. Living together before marriage may seem like a harmless or even a progressive family trend until one takes a careful look at the evidence.

How Living Together Before Marriage May Contribute to Marital Failure

The vast majority of young people today want to marry and have children. And many if not most see cohabitation as a way to test marital compatibility and improve the chances of long-lasting marriage. Their reasoning is as follows: Given the high levels of divorce, why be in a hurry to marry? Why not test marital compatibility by sharing a bed and a bathroom for a year or even longer? If it doesn't work out, one can simply move out. According to this reasoning, cohabitation weeds out unsuitable partners through a process of natural de-selection. Over time, perhaps after several living-together relationships, a person will eventually find a marriageable mate.

The social science evidence challenges the popular idea that cohabiting ensures greater marital compatibility and thereby promotes stronger and more enduring marriages. Cohabitation does not reduce the likelihood of eventual divorce; in fact, it is associated with a higher divorce risk. Although the association was stronger a decade or two ago and has diminished in the younger generations, virtually all research on the topic has determined that the chances of divorce ending a marriage preceded by cohabitation are significantly greater than for a marriage not preceded by cohabitation. A 1992 study of 3,300 cases, for example, based on the 1987 National Survey of Families and Households, found that in their marriages prior cohabitors "are estimated to have a hazard of dissolution that is about 46% higher than for noncohabitors." The authors of this study concluded, after reviewing all previous studies, that the enhanced risk of marital disruption following cohabitation "is beginning to take on the status of an empirical generalization."[5]

More in question within the research community is why the striking statistical association between cohabitation and divorce should exist. Perhaps the most obvious explanation is that those people willing to cohabit are more unconventional than others and less committed to the institution of marriage. These are the same people, then, who more easily will leave a marriage if it becomes troublesome. By this explanation, cohabitation doesn't cause divorce but is merely associated with it because the same types of people are involved in both phenomena.

There is substantial empirical support for this position. Yet, in most studies, even when this "selection effect" is carefully controlled statistically, a negative effect of cohabitation on later marriage stability still remains. And no positive contribution of cohabitation to marriage has ever been found.[6]

The reasons for a negative "cohabitation effect" are not fully understood. One may be that while marriages are held together largely by a strong ethic of commitment, cohabiting relationships by their very nature tend to undercut this ethic. Although cohabiting relationships are like marriages in many ways—shared dwelling, economic union (at least in part), sexual intimacy, often even children—they typically differ in the levels of commitment and autonomy involved. According to recent studies, cohabitants tend not to be as committed as married couples in their dedication to the continuation of the relationship and reluctance to terminate it, and they are more oriented toward their own personal autonomy.[7] It is reasonable to speculate, based on these studies, that once this low-commitment, high-autonomy pattern of relating is learned, it becomes hard to unlearn. One study found, for example, that "living with a romantic partner prior to marriage was associated with more negative and less positive problem solving support and behavior during marriage." A reason for this, the authors suggest, is that because long-term commitment is less certain in cohabitation, "there may be less motivation for cohabiting partners to develop their conflict resolution and support skills."[8]

The results of several studies suggest that cohabitation may change partners' attitudes toward the institution of marriage, contributing to either making marriage less likely, or if marriage takes place, less successful. A 1997 longitudinal study conducted by demographers at Pennsylvania State University concluded, for example, "cohabitation increased young people's acceptance of divorce, but other independent living experiences did not." And "the more months of exposure to cohabitation that young people experienced, the less enthusiastic they were toward marriage and childbearing."[9]

Particularly problematic is serial cohabitation. One study determined that the effect of cohabitation on later marital instability is found only when one or both partners had previously cohabited with someone other than their spouse.[10] A reason for this could be that the experience of dissolving one cohabiting relationship generates a greater willingness to dissolve later relationships. People's tolerance for unhappiness is diminished, and they will scrap a marriage that might otherwise be salvaged. This may be similar to the attitudinal effects of divorce; going through a divorce makes one more tolerant of divorce.

If the conclusions of these studies hold up under further investigation, they may contain the answer to the question of why premarital cohabitation should effect the stability of a later marriage. The act of cohabitation generates changes in people's attitudes toward marriage that make the stability of marriage less likely. Society wide, therefore, the growth of cohabitation will tend to further weaken marriage as an institution.

An important caveat must be inserted here. There is a growing understanding among researchers that different types and life-patterns of cohabitation must be distinguished clearly from each other. Cohabitation that is an immediate prelude to marriage, or prenuptial cohabitation—both partners plan to marry each other in the near future—is different from other forms. There is some evidence to support the proposition that living together for a short period of time with the person one intends to marry has no adverse effects on the subsequent marriage. Cohabitation in this case appears to be very similar to marriage; it merely takes place during the engagement period.[11] This proposition would appear to be less true, however, when one or both of the partners has had prior experience with cohabitation, or brings children into the relationship.

Cohabitation as an Alternative to Marriage

According to the latest information available, 46% of all cohabitations in a given year can be classified as precursors to marriage.[12] Most of the remainder

Percentage of High School Seniors Who "Agreed" or "Mostly Agreed" with the Statement That "It Is Usually a Good Idea for a Couple to Live Together before Getting Married in Order to Find Out Whether They Really Get Along," by Period, United States

	Boys	Girls
1976–1980	44.9	32.3
1981–1985	47.4	36.5
1986–1990	57.8	45.2
1991–1995	60.5	51.3
1996–2000	66.0	61.3

Source: *Monitoring the Future 2000*, and earlier surveys conducted by the Survey Research Center at the University of Michigan

can be considered some form of alternative to marriage, including trial marriages, and their number is increasing. This should be of great national concern, not only for what the growth of cohabitation is doing to the institution of marriage but for what it is doing, or not doing, for the participants involved. In general, cohabiting relationships tend in many ways to be less satisfactory than marriage relationships.

Except perhaps for the short term prenuptial type of cohabitation, and probably also for the post-marriage cohabiting relationships of seniors and retired people who typically cohabit rather than marry for economic reasons,[13] cohabitation and marriage relationships are qualitatively different. Cohabiting couples report lower levels of happiness, lower levels of sexual exclusivity and sexual satisfaction, and poorer relationships with their parents.[14] One reason is that, as several sociologists not surprisingly concluded after a careful analysis, in unmarried cohabitation "levels of certainty about the relationship are lower than in marriage."[15]

It is easy to understand, therefore, why cohabiting is inherently much less stable than marriage and why, especially in view of the fact that it is easier to terminate, the break-up rate of cohabitors is far higher than for married partners. After 5 to 7 years, 39% of all cohabiting couples have broken their relationship, 40% have married (although the marriage might not have lasted), and only 21% are still cohabiting.[16]

Still not fully known by the public at large is the fact that married couples have substantial benefits over the unmarried in labor force productivity, physical and mental health, general happiness, and longevity.[17] There is evidence that these benefits are diluted for couples who are not married but merely cohabiting.[18] Among the probable reasons for the benefits of marriage, as summarized by University of Chicago demographer Linda Waite,[19] are:

- *The long-term contract implicit in marriage.* This facilitates emotional investment in the relationship, including the close monitoring of each other's behavior. The longer time horizon also makes specialization more likely; working as a couple, individuals can develop those skills in which they excel, leaving others to their partner.

- *The greater sharing of economic and social resources by married couples.* In addition to economies of scale, this enables couples to act as a small insurance pool against life uncertainties, reducing each person's need to protect themselves from unexpected events.
- *The better connection of married couples to the larger community.* This includes other individuals and groups (such as in-laws) as well as social institutions such as churches and synagogues. These can be important sources of social and emotional support and material benefits.

In addition to missing out on many of the benefits of marriage, cohabitors may face more serious difficulties. Annual rates of depression among cohabiting couples are more than three times what they are among married couples.[20] And women in cohabiting relationships are more likely than married women to suffer physical and sexual abuse. Some research has shown that aggression is at least twice as common among cohabitors as it is among married partners.[21] Two studies, one in Canada and the other in the United States, found that women in cohabiting relationships are about nine times more likely to be killed by their partner than are women in marital relationships.[22]

Again, the selection factor is undoubtedly strong in findings such as these. But the most careful statistical probing suggests that selection is not the only factor at work; the intrinsic nature of the cohabiting relationship also plays a role. As one scholar summed up the relevant research, "regardless of methodology. . . .cohabitors engage in more violence than spouses."[23]

Why Cohabitation Is Harmful for Children

Of all the types of cohabitation, those involving children is by far the most problematic. In 2000, 41% of all unmarried-couple households included a child under eighteen, up from only 21% in 1987.[24] For unmarried couples in the 25–34 age group the percentage with children is higher still, approaching half of all such households.[25] By one recent estimate nearly half of all children today will spend some time in a cohabiting family before age 16.[26]

One of the greatest problems for children living with a cohabiting couple is the high risk that the couple will break up.[27] Fully three quarters of children born to cohabiting parents will see their parents split up before they reach age sixteen, whereas only about a third of children born to married parents face a similar fate. One reason is that marriage rates for cohabiting couples have been plummeting. In the last decade, the proportion of cohabiting mothers who go on to eventually marry the child's father declined from 57% to 44%.[28]

Parental break up, as is now widely known, almost always entails a myriad of personal and social difficulties for children, some of which can be long lasting. For the children of a cohabiting couple these may come on top of a plethora of already existing problems. Several studies have found that children currently living with a mother and her unmarried partner have significantly more behavior problems and lower academic performance than children in intact families.[29]

It is important to note that the great majority of children in unmarried-couple households were born not in the present union but in a previous union of one of the adult partners, usually the mother.[30] This means that they are living with an unmarried "stepfather" or mother's boyfriend, with whom the economic and social relationships are often tenuous. For example, unlike children in stepfamilies, these children have few legal claims to child support or other sources of family income should the couple separate.

Child abuse has become a major national problem and has increased dramatically in recent years, by more than 10% a year according to one estimate.[31] In the opinion of most researchers, this increase is related strongly to changing family forms. Surprisingly, the available American data do not enable us to distinguish the abuse that takes place in married-couple households from that in cohabiting-couple households. We do have abuse-prevalence studies that look at stepparent families (both married and unmarried) and mother's boyfriends (both cohabiting and dating). Both show far higher levels of child abuse than is found in intact families.[32] In general, the evidence suggests that the most unsafe of all family environments for children is that in which the mother is living with someone other than the child's biological father. This is the environment for the majority of children in cohabiting couple households.[33]

Part of the differences indicated above are due to differing income levels of the families involved. But this points up one of the other problems of cohabiting couples—their lower incomes. It is well known that children of single parents fare poorly economically when compared to the children of married parents. Not so well known is that cohabiting couples are economically more like single parents than like married couples. While the 1996 poverty rate for children living in married couple households was about 6%, it was 31% for children living in cohabiting households, much closer to the rate of 45% for children living in families headed by single mothers.[34]

One of the most important social science findings of recent years is that marriage is a wealth enhancing institution. According to one study, childrearing, cohabiting couples have only about two-thirds of the income of married couples with children, mainly due to the fact that the average income of male cohabiting partners is only about half that of male married partners.[35] The selection effect is surely at work here, with less well-off men and their partners choosing cohabitation over marriage. But it also is the case that men when they marry, especially those who then go on to have children, tend to become more responsible and productive.[36] They earn more than their unmarried counterparts. An additional factor not to be overlooked is the private transfer of wealth among extended family members, which is considerably lower for cohabiting couples than for married couples.[37] It is clear that family members are more willing to transfer wealth to "in-laws" than to mere boyfriends or girlfriends.

Who Cohabits and Why

Why has unmarried cohabitation become such a widespread practice through-out the modern world in such a short period of time? Demographic factors are surely involved. Puberty begins at an earlier age, as does the onset of sexual activity, and marriages take place at older ages mainly because of the longer time period spent getting educated and establishing careers. Thus there is an extended period of sexually active singlehood before first marriage. Also, our sustained material affluence enables many young people to live on their own for an extended time, apart from their parents. During those years of young adulthood, nonmarital cohabitation can be a cost-saver, a source of companionship, and an assurance of relatively safe sexual practice. For some, cohabitation is a prelude to marriage, for some, an alternative to it, and for yet others, simply an alternative to living alone.[38]

More broadly, the rise of cohabitation in the advanced nations has been attributed to the sexual revolution, which has virtually revoked the stigma against cohabitation.[39] In the past thirty years, with the advent of effective contraceptive technologies and widespread sexual permissiveness promoted by advertising and the organized entertainment industry, premarital sex has become widely accepted. In large segments of the population cohabitation no longer is associated with sin or social impropriety or pathology, nor are cohabiting couples subject to much, if any, disapproval.

Another important reason for cohabitation's growth is that the institu-tion of marriage has changed dramatically, leading to an erosion of confi-dence in its stability. From a tradition strongly buttressed by economics, religion, and the law, marriage has become a more personalized relationship, what one wag has referred to as a mere "notarized date." People used to marry not just for love but also for family and economic considerations, and if love died during the course of a marriage, this was not considered sufficient reason to break up an established union. A divorce was legally difficult if not impo-ssible to get, and people who divorced faced enormous social stigma.

In today's marriages love is all, and it is a love tied to self-fulfillment. Divorce is available to everyone, with little stigma attached. If either love or a sense of self-fulfillment disappear, the marriage is considered to be over and divorce is the logical outcome.

Fully aware of this new fragility of marriage, people are taking caution-ary actions. The attitude is either try it out first and make sure that it will work, or try to minimize the damage of breakup by settling for a weaker form of union, one that avoids a marriage license and, if need be, an eventual divorce.

The growth of cohabitation is also associated with the rise of feminism. Traditional marriage, both in law and in practice, typically involved male leadership. For some women, cohabitation seemingly avoids the legacy of patriarchy and at the same time provides more personal autonomy and equal-ity in the relationship. Moreover, women's shift into the labor force and their growing economic independence make marriage less necessary and, for some, less desirable.

Underlying all of these trends is the broad cultural shift from a more religious society where marriage was considered the bedrock of civilization and people were imbued with a strong sense of social conformity and tradition, to a more secular society focused on individual autonomy and self invention. This cultural rejection of traditional institutional and moral authority, evident in all of the advanced, Western societies, often has had "freedom of choice" as its theme and the acceptance of "alternative lifestyles" as its message.

In general, cohabitation is a phenomenon that began among the young in the lower classes and then moved up to the middle classes.[40] Cohabitation in America—especially cohabitation as an alternative to marriage—is more common among Blacks, Puerto Ricans, and disadvantaged white women.[41] One reason for this is that male income and employment are lower among minorities and the lower classes, and male economic status remains an important determinant as to whether or not a man feels ready to marry, and a woman wants to marry him.[42] Cohabitation is also more common among those who are less religious than their peers. Indeed, some evidence suggests that the act of cohabitation actually diminishes religious participation, whereas marriage tends to increase it.[43]

People who cohabit are much more likely to come from broken homes. Among young adults, those who experienced parental divorce, fatherlessness, or high levels of marital discord during childhood are more likely to form cohabiting unions than children who grew up in families with married parents who got along. They are also more likely to enter living-together relationships at younger ages.[44] For young people who have already suffered the losses associated with parental divorce, cohabitation may provide an early escape from family turmoil, although unfortunately it increases the likelihood of new losses and turmoil. For these people, cohabitation often recapitulates the childhood experience of coming together and splitting apart with the additional possibility of more violent conflict. Finally, cohabitation is a much more likely experience for those who themselves have been divorced.

Conclusion

Despite its widespread acceptance by the young, the remarkable growth of unmarried cohabitation in recent years does not appear to be in children's or the society's best interest. The evidence suggests that it has weakened marriage and the intact, two-parent family and thereby damaged our social well-being, especially that of women and children. We can not go back in history, but it seems time to establish some guidelines for the practice of cohabitation and to seriously question the further institutionalization of this new family form.

In place of institutionalizing cohabitation, in our opinion, we should be trying to revitalize marriage—not along classic male-dominant lines but along modern egalitarian lines. Particularly helpful in this regard would be educating young people about marriage from the early school years onward, getting them to make the wisest choices in their lifetime mates, and stressing the importance of long-term commitment to marriages. Such an educational venture could build on the fact that a huge majority of our nation's young people still express the strong desire to be in a long-term monogamous marriage.

These ideas are offered to the American public and especially to society's leaders in the spirit of generating a discussion. Our conclusions are tentative, and certainly not the last word on the subject. There is an obvious need for more research on cohabitation, and the findings of new research, of course, could alter our thinking. What is most important now, in our view, is a national debate on a topic that heretofore has been overlooked. Indeed, few issues seem more critical for the future of marriage and for generations to come.

Notes

1. U. S. Census Bureau. *Statistical Abstract of the United States: 2000* (Washington, DC: GPO, 2001): 52.

2. Larry Bumpass and Hsien-Hen Lu. "Trends in Cohabitation and Implications for Children's Family Contexts in the U.S.," *Population Studies* 54 (2000) 29–41. The most likely to cohabit are people aged 20 to 24.

3. J. G. Bachman, L. D. Johnston and P. M. O'Malley, *Monitoring the Future: Questionnaire Responses from the Nation's High School Seniors, 2000.* (Ann Arbor, MI: Institute for Social Research, University of Michigan: 2001).

4. The state statutes prohibiting "adultery" and "fornication," which included cohabitation, were not often enforced.

5. Alfred DeMaris and K. Vaninadha Rao, "Premarital Cohabitation and Subsequent Marital Stability in the United States: A Reassessment," *Journal of Marriage and the Family* 54 (1992): 178–190. A Canadian study found that premarital cohabitation may double the risk of subsequent marital disruption. Zheng Wu, *Cohabitation* (New York: Oxford University Press, 2000), 149.

6. The relationship between cohabitation and marital instability is discussed in the following articles: Alfred DeMaris and William MacDonald, "Premarital Cohabitation and Marital Instability: A Test of the Unconventional Hypothesis." *Journal of Marriage and the Family* 55 (1993): 399–407; William J. Axinn and Arland Thornton, "The Relationship Between Cohabitation and Divorce: Selectivity or Causal Influence," *Demography* 29-3 (1992): 357–374; Robert Schoen "First Unions and the Stability of First Marriages," *Journal of Marriage and the Family* 54 (1992): 281–284; Elizabeth Thomson and Ugo Colella, "Cohabitation and Marital Stability: Quality or Commitment?" *Journal of Marriage and the Family* 54-9 (1992): 259–267; Lee A. Lillard, Michael J. Brien, and Linda J. Waite, "Premarital Cohabitation and Subsequent Marital Dissolution: A Matter of Self-Selection?" *Demography,* 32-3 (1995): 437–457; David R. Hall and John Z. Zhao, "Cohabitation and Divorce in Canada: Testing the Selectivity Hypothesis," *Journal of Marriage and the Family* 57 (1995): 421–427; Marin Clarkberg, Ross M. Stolzenberg, and Linda Waite, "Attitudes, Values, and Entrance into Cohabitational versus Marital Unions," *Social Forces* 74-2 (1995): 609–634; Stephen L. Nock, "Spouse Preferences of Never-Married, Divorced, and Cohabiting Americans," *Journal of Divorce and Remarriage* 24-3/4 (1995): 91–108.

7. Stephen L. Nock, "A Comparison of Marriages and Cohabiting Relationships," *Journal of Family Issues* 16-1 (1995): 53–76. See also: Robert Schoen and Robin M. Weinick, "Partner Choice in Marriages and Cohabitations," *Journal of Marriage and the Family* 55 (1993): 408–414; and Scott M. Stanley, Sarah W.

Whitton and Howard Markman, "Maybe I Do: Interpersonal Commitment and Premarital and Non-Marital Cohabitation," unpublished manuscript, University of Denver, 2000.

8. Catherine L. Cohan and Stacey Kleinbaum, "Toward A Greater Understanding of the Cohabitation Effect: Premarital Cohabitation and Marital Communication," *Journal of Marriage and the Family*, 64 (2002): 180–192.

9. William G. Axinn and Jennifer S. Barber, "Living Arrangements and Family Formation Attitudes in Early Adulthood," *Journal of Marriage and the Family* 59 (1997): 595–611. See also Marin Clarkberg, "Family Formation Experiences and Changing Values: The Effects of Cohabitation and Marriage on the Important Things in Life," in Ron Lesthaeghe, ed., *Meaning and Choice: Value Orientations and Life Course Decisions*, NIDI Monograph 38, (The Hague: Netherlands, Netherlands Interdisciplinary Demographic Institute, forthcoming). Axinn and Thornton, 1992, op. cit., and Elizabeth Thomson and Ugo Colella, 1992, op. cit.

10. DeMaris and McDonald, 1993, op. cit.; Jan E. Stets, "The Link Between Past and Present Intimate Relationships." *Journal of Family Issues* 14–2 (1993): 236–260.

11. Susan L. Brown and Alan Booth, "Cohabitation Versus Marriage: A Comparison of Relationship Quality," *Journal of Marriage and the Family* 58 (1996): 668–678.

12. Lynne N. Casper and Suzanne M. Bianchi, *Continuity and Change in the American Family* (Thousand Oaks, CA: Sage Publications, 2002) Ch. 2. Surprisingly, only 52% of those classified as "precursors to marriage" had actually married after five to seven years and 31% had split up!

13. Albert Chevan, "As Cheaply as One: Cohabitation in the Older Population," *Journal of Marriage and the Family* 58 (1996): 656–666. According to calculations by Chevan, the percentage of noninstitutionalized, unmarried cohabiting persons 60 years of age and over increased from virtually zero in 1960 to 2.4 in 1990, p. 659. See also R. G. Hatch, *Aging and Cohabitation.* (New York: Garland, 1995).

14. Nock, 1995; Brown and Booth, 1996; Linda J. Waite and Kara Joyner, "Emotional and Physical Satisfaction with Sex in Married, Cohabiting, and Dating Sexual Unions: Do Men and Women Differ?" Edward O. Laumann and Robert T. Michaels, eds., *Sex, Love, and Health in America* (Chicago: University of Chicago Press, 2001) 239–269; Judith Treas and Deirdre Giesen, "Sexual Infidelity Among Married and Cohabiting Americans" *Journal of Marriage and the Family* 62 (2000): 48–60; Renate Forste and Koray Tanfer, "Sexual Exclusivity Among Dating, Cohabiting, and Married Women," *Journal of Marriage the Family* 58 (1996): 33–47; Paul R. Amato and Alan Booth, *A Generation at Risk.* (Cambridge, MA: Harvard University Press, 1997) Table 4–2, p. 258.

15. Larry L. Bumpass, James A. Sweet, and Andrew Cherlin, "The Role of Cohabitation in Declining Rate of Marriage," *Journal of Marriage the Family* 53 (1991): 913–927.

16. Casper and Bianchi, 2002, op. cit.

17. Lee A. Lillard and Linda J. Waite, "Till Death Do Us Part: Marital Disruption and Mortality," *American Journal of Sociology* 100 (1995): 1131–1156; R. Jay Turner and Franco Marino, "Social Support and Social Structure: A Descriptive Epidemiology," *Journal of Health and Social Behavior* 35 (1994): 193–212; Linda J. Waite, "Does Marriage Matter?" *Demography* 32–4 (1995): 483–507; Sanders Korenman and David Neumark "Does Marriage Really Make Men More Productive?" *The Journal of Human Resources* 26–2 (1990): 282–307; George A. Akerlof "Men Without Children." *The Economic Journal* 108 (1998): 287–309.

18. Allan V. Horwitz and Helene Raskin White, "The Relationship of Cohabitation and Mental Health: A Study of a Young Adult Cohort," *Journal of Marriage and the Family* 60 (1998): 505–514; Waite, 1995.

19. Linda J. Waite, "Social Science Finds: 'Marriage Matters,'" *The Responsive Community* (Summer 1996): 26–35 See also: Linda J. Waite and Maggie Gallagher, *The Case for Marriage* (New York: Doubleday, 2000).

20. Lee Robins and Darrel Reiger, *Psychiatric Disorders in America.* (New York: Free Press, 1990) 72. See also: Susan L. Brown, "The Effect of Union Type on Psychological Well-Being: Depression among Cohabitors versus Marrieds," *Journal of Health and Social Behavior* 41-3 (2000).

21. Jan E. Stets, "Cohabiting and Marital Aggression: The Role of Social Isolation," *Journal of Marriage and the Family* 53 (1991): 669–680. Margo I. Wilson and Martin Daly, "Who Kills Whom in Spouse Killings? On the Exceptional Sex Ratio of Spousal Homicides in the United States," *Criminology* 30-2 (1992): 189–215. One study found that, of the violence toward women that is committed by intimates and relatives, 42% involves a close friend or partner whereas only 29% involves a current spouse. Ronet Bachman, "Violence Against Women." (Washington, DC: Bureau of Justice Statistics. 1994) p. 6. A New Zealand study compared violence in dating and cohabiting relationships, finding that cohabitors were twice as likely to be physically abusive toward their partners after controlling statistically for selection factors. Lynn Magdol, T.E. Moffitt, A. Caspi, and P.A. Silva: "Hitting Without a License," *Journal of Marriage and the Family* 60-1 (1998): 41–55.

22. Todd K. Shackelford, "Cohabitation, Marriage and Murder," *Aggressive Behavior* 27 (2001): 284–291; Margo Wilson, M. Daly and C. Wright, "Uxoricide in Canada: Demographic Risk Patterns," *Canadian Journal of Criminology* 35 (1993): 263–291.

23. Nicky Ali Jackson, "Observational Experiences of Intrapersonal Conflict and Teenage Victimization: A Comparative Study among Spouses and Cohabitors," *Journal of Family Violence* 11 (1996): 191–203.

24. U. S. Census Bureau. Current Population Survey, March 2000.

25. Wendy D. Manning and Daniel T. Lichter, "Parental Cohabitation and Children's Economic Well-Being," *Journal of Marriage and the Family* 58 (1996): 998–1010.

26. Bumpass and Lu, 2000, op.cit. Using a different data set, however, Deborah R. Graefe and Daniel T. Lichter conclude that only about one in four children will live in a family headed by a cohabiting couple sometime during childhood. "Life Course Transitions of American Children: Parental Cohabitation, Marriage, and Single Motherhood," *Demography* 36-2 (1999): 205–217.

27. Research on the instability of cohabiting couples with children is discussed in Wendy D. Manning, "The Implications of Cohabitation for Children's Well-Being," in Alan Booth and Ann C. Crouter, eds., *Just Living Together: Implications for Children, Families, and Public Policy* (Hillsdale, NJ: Lawrence Erlbaum Associates, 2002) It seems to be the case, however, that—just as with married couples—cohabiting couples with children are less likely to break up than childless couples. Zheng Wu, "The Stability of Cohabitation Relationships: The Role of Children," *Journal of Marriage and the Family* 57 (1995): 231–236.

28. Bumpass and Lu, 2000, op.cit.

29. Elizabeth Thompson, T. L. Hanson and S. S. McLanahan, "Family Structure and Child Well-Being: Economic Resources versus Parental Behaviors," *Social Forces* 73-1 (1994): 221–242; Rachel Dunifon and Lori Kowaleski-Jones, "Who's in the House? Effects of Family Structure on Children's Home Environments and Cognitive Outcomes," *Child Development*, forthcoming; and Susan L. Brown,

"Parental Cohabitation and Child Well-Being," unpublished manuscript, Department of Sociology, Bowling Green State University, Bowling Green, OH.

30. By one estimate, 63%. Deborah R. Graefe and Daniel Lichter, 1999, op.cit.

31. Andrea J. Sedlak and Diane Broadhurst, *The Third National Incidence Study of Child Abuse and Neglect* (Washington, DC: HHS-National Center on Child Abuse and Neglect, 1996).

32. See, for example, Margo Wilson and Martin Daly, "Risk of Maltreatment of Children Living with Stepparents," in R. Gelles and J. Lancaster, eds. *Child Abuse and Neglect: Biosocial Dimensions,* (New York: Aldine de Gruyter, 1987); Leslie Margolin "Child Abuse by Mothers' Boyfriends: Why the Overrepresentation?" *Child Abuse and Neglect* 16 (1992): 541–551. Martin Daly and Margo Wilson have stated: "stepparenthood per se remains the single most powerful risk factor for child abuse that has yet been identified." *Homicide* (New York: Aldine de Gruyter, 1988) p. 87–88.

33. One study in Great Britain did look at the relationship between child abuse and the family structure and marital background of parents and, although the sample was very small, the results are disturbing. It was found that, compared to children living with married biological parents, children living with cohabiting but unmarried biological parents are 20 times more likely to be subject to child abuse, and those living with a mother and a cohabiting boyfriend who is not the father face an increased risk of 33 times. In contrast, the rate of abuse is 14 times higher if the child lives with a biological mother who lives alone. Robert Whelan, *Broken Homes and Battered Children: A Study of the Relationship Between Child Abuse and Family Type,* (London: Family Education Trust, 1993). See especially Table 12, p. 29. (Data are from the 1980s.) See also Patrick F. Fagan and Dorothy B. Hanks, *The Child Abuse Crisis: The Disintegration of Marriage, Family and The American Community.* (Washington, DC: The Heritage Foundation, 1997).

34. Wendy D. Manning and Daniel T. Lichter "Parental Cohabitation and Children's Economic Well-Being," *Journal of Marriage and the Family* 58 (1996): 998–1010.

35. Wendy D. Manning and Daniel T. Lichter, 1996.

36. Sanders Korenman and David Neumark, "Does Marriage Really Make Men More Productive?" *The Journal of Human Resources* 26-2 (1990): 282–307; George A. Akerlof "Men Without Children," *The Economic Journal* 108 (1998): 287–309; Steven L. Nock, *Marriage in Men's Lives* (New York: Oxford University Press, 1998).

37. Lingxin Hao, "Family Structure, Private Transfers, and the Economic Well-Being of Families with Children," *Social Forces* 75-1 (1996): 269–292.

38. R. Rindfuss and A. VanDenHeuvel, "Cohabitation: A Precursor to Marriage or an Alternative to Being Single?" *Population and Development Review* 16 (1990): 703–726; Wendy D. Manning, "Marriage and Cohabitation Following Premarital Conception," *Journal of Marriage and the Family* 55 (1993): 839–850.

39. Larry L. Bumpass, "What's Happening to the Family?" *Demography* 27-4 1990): 483–498.

40. Arland Thornton, William G. Axinn and Jay D. Treachman, "The Influence of School Enrollment and Accumulation on Cohabitation and Marriage in Early Adulthood," *American Sociological Review* 60-5 (1995): 762–774; Larry L. Bumpass, James A. Sweet, and Andrew Cherlin, "The Role of Cohabitation in Declining Rates of Marriage," *Journal of Marriage and the Family* 53 (1991): 913–927.

41. Wendy D. Manning and Pamela J. Smock, "Why Marry? Race and the Transition to Marriage among Cohabitors," *Demography* 32-4 (1995): 509–520;

Wendy D. Manning and Nancy S. Landale, "Racial and Ethnic Differences in the Role of Cohabitation in Premarital Childbearing," *Journal of Marriage and the Family* 58 (1996): 63–77; Laura Spencer Loomis and Nancy S. Landale, "Nonmarital Cohabitation and Childbearing Among Black and White American Women," *Journal of Marriage and the Family* 56 (1994): 949–962; Robert Schoen and Dawn Owens "A Further Look at First Unions and First Marriages," in S. J. South and Stewart E. Tolnay, eds., *The Changing American Family* (Boulder, CO: Westview Press, 1992) 109–117.

42. Daniel T. Lichter, Diane K. McLaughlin, George Kephart, and David J. Landry, "Race and the Retreat from Marriage: A Shortage of Marriageable Men?" *American Sociological Review* 57-6 (1992): 781–789; Pamela J. Smock and Wendy D. Manning, "Cohabiting Partners' Economic Circumstances and Marriage," *Demography* 34-3 (1997): 331–341; Valerie K. Oppenheimer, Matthijs Kalmijn and Nelson Lim, "Men's Career Development and Marriage Timing During a Period of Rising Inequality," *Demography* 34-3 (1997): 311–330.

43. Arland Thornton, W. G. Axinn and D. H. Hill, "Reciprocal Effects of Religiosity, Cohabitation and Marriage," *American Journal of Sociology* 98-3 (1992): 628–651.

44. Arland Thornton, "Influence of the Marital History of Parents on the Marital and Cohabitational Experiences of Children," *American Journal of Sociology* 96-4 (1991): 868–894; Kathleen E. Kiernan, "The Impact of Family Disruption in Childhood on Transitions Made in Young Adult Life," *Population Studies* 46 (1992): 213–234; Andrew J. Cherlin, Kathleen E. Kiernan, and P. Lindsay Chase-Lansdale, "Parental Divorce in Childhood and Demographic Outcomes in Young Adulthood," *Demography* 32-3 (1995): 299–318.

POSTSCRIPT

Should Society Support Cohabitation Before Marriage?

There is a common misperception that premarital sex is a cultural phenomenon that was introduced to American society during the sexual revolution of the 1960s and 1970s. Sexologist Robert T. Francoeur dispels this myth by commenting on the prevalence of premarital sex dating back to colonial American times. As an example, Francoeur describes the courtship ritual of "bundling," which helped frontier farmers know that a bride-to-be was fertile and could produce children to work the farm: A courting couple was permitted to sleep together, fully dressed, in a small bed in the corner of a small, often single-room log cabin or sod house. A bundling board between the couple or a bundling bag for the woman was not an insurmountable obstacle to sexual intercourse. When the prospective bride became pregnant, the marriage was announced. This is but one example of historically positive and functional attitudes toward premarital sexual intercourse in the United States.

Other countries have experienced growing trends in relationship patterns that contrast with the U.S., rise in cohabitation. In Sweden and other Scandinavian countries, for example, a concept called "LAT" (living alone together) has become increasingly popular. Adult couples who "LAT" maintain a committed interpersonal relationship but also maintain separate households. In Italy, mammoni (literally, "mama's boys") are adult men who continue to live at home with their parents. While calling a man a "mama's boy" may be an insult in American culture, it is not so in Italy, where more and more men are avoiding marriage into their later adult years, regardless of whether or not they are involved in a committed relationship. Not surprisingly, this growing trend has resulted in a drastic lowering of the Italian birth rate.

In the United States, why would a couple want to choose cohabitation before marriage, or as a relationship option instead of marriage? The following reasons have been identified:

- Some couples are not legally allowed to marry because they are members of the same sex, and some heterosexual couples avoid marriage in objection to an institution that is not legally available to all.
- Some couples believe that one's intimate relationship does not require the endorsement of government or religion.
- Some people are troubled by the divorce rate, or have experienced a divorce themselves, and wish to avoid the risk (or stigma) of divorce.
- Some people believe that a relationship does not need to be a lifelong commitment.

- Some people are not sure if their current partner is the one they would select for a lifetime commitment. They might try cohabitation as a precursor to marriage.
- Some people feel their relationship is working fine without marriage.
- Some people might lose financial benefits if they decide to marry (such as from the pension of a prior spouse).
- Some people are uncomfortable with marriage's historical view toward women as property.

Some opponents of cohabitation before marriage are concerned primarily about the sexual aspect of these relationships; namely, they believe that sexual intercourse before marriage is impermissible. However, sexual and marital trends indicate that most young people begin having intercourse in their mid-to-late teens, about *seven to nine* years before they marry. Is it better for young people to begin having sex later, or consider marrying earlier? Are the main issues the timing of sex and the marital decision, or the health and happiness of the couple?

Suggested Readings

R. T. Francoeur, "Challenging Common Religious/Social Myths of Sex, Marriage, and Family," *Journal of Sex Education and Therapy* (vol. 26, no. 4, 2001).

T. Ihara, R. Warner, and F. Hertz, *Living Together: A Legal Guide for Unmarried Couples* (Nolo Press, 2001).

L. M. Latham, "Southern Governors Declare War on Divorce," http://www.salon.com (January 24, 2000).

K. S. Peterson, "Changing the Shape of the American Family," *USA Today* (April 18, 2000).

K. S. Peterson, "Wedded to Relationship but Not to Marriage," *USA Today* (April 18, 2000).

D. Popenoe and B. Dafoe Whitehead, *Ten Important Research Findings on Marriage and Choosing a Marriage Partner: Helpful Facts for Young Adults* (National Marriage Project, Rutgers University, 2004).

R. Schoen, "The Ties That Bind: Perspectives on Marriage and Cohabitation," *Journal of Marriage and Family* (August 1, 2001).

P. J. Smock, "Cohabitation in the United States: An Appraisal of Research, Themes, Findings, and Implications," *Annual Review of Sociology* (2000).

D. Solot and M. Miller, "Ten Problems (Plus One Bonus Problem) with the National Marriage Project's Cohabitation Report," *A Report of the Alternatives to Marriage Project* (2001).

ISSUE 15

Is Pedophilia Always Harmful?

YES: Laura Schlessinger, from "Evil Among Us," *Dr. Laura Perspective* (June 1999)

NO: David L. Riegel, from *Understanding Loved Boys and Boylovers* (SafeHaven Foundation Press, 2000)

ISSUE SUMMARY

YES: Radio commentator Laura Schlessinger denounces a study, published by the American Psychological Association (APA), that reexamined the results and conclusions from 59 earlier studies of child sexual abuse (CSA) in more than 35,000 college students. Schlessinger views this study as a "pseudo-scientific" attempt to convince people to accept pedophilia as normal.

NO: Author David L. Riegel summarizes the major findings of the research in question, and criticizes the dismissal of scientific research that challenges common assumptions about CSA and its effects on children.

In 1998, *Psychological Bulletin,* the official publication of the American Psychological Association (APA), contained a research report entitled "A Meta-Analytic Examination of Assumed Properties of Child Sexual Abuse Using College Samples." This report was written by three respected researchers with solid publication records, Bruce Rind (Temple University), Robert Bauserman (Maryland State Health Department), and Philip Tromovitch (University of Pennsylvania). It received some discussion and notice in the academic world, but nothing unusual.

However, a few people alerted Laura Schlessinger, a conservative radio and television commentator. Schlessinger immediately launched a campaign to "rally the troops to fight the enemy at the barricades and save our nation" from being turned into a nation of pedophiles. Joined by The Family Research Council and the National Association for the Research and Therapy of Homosexuality (NARTH), Schlessinger enlisted the aid of a few conservative Washington lawmakers, who prepared a bill condemning the report. On July 12, 1999, Representative Matt Salmon (R-Arizona) called on members of the House of Representatives to condemn what had become known for brevity's sake as "the Rind research or report." The purpose of this study, Salmon maintained, was to make pedophilia normal and acceptable. The representatives unanimously voted to condemn the report. Only a handful of representatives abstained, suspecting that the editors of the *Psychological Bulletin* would not publish a report endorsing and promoting pedophilia, and concerned about the wisdom of condemning a scholarly publication that none of them had seen or read in its full form.

Some believe that the conclusions of the Rind research is good news for some sexual abuse victims. If it is true that many (or even a few) victims do not suffer lifelong consequences from child sexual abuse, and that many victims are not traumatized, permanently damaged, or wounded for life, we might view such findings in a positive insight. But many Americans find this possibility totally unacceptable as it would also require us to rethink the basic assumption that pedophilia is harmful all the time.

While the APA endured harsh public criticism from Congress and media commentators, it also received a letter of support from the Society for the Scientific Study of Sexuality (SSSS), in which the past and present officers urged the APA "to staunchly support the right of sexual scientists to engage in free intellectual inquiry—especially in the area of 'controversial' research," such as the sexuality of children and the long-term consequences of child sexual abuse, incest, and adult-child sex.

In the following selections, Schlessinger maintains that the release of the APA study results is harmful because the findings can be interpreted as validating and "normalizing" pedophilia. David L. Riegel summarizes the major findings of the research and criticizes those who would summarily dismiss research findings.

YES

Laura Schlessinger

Evil Among Us

[You may have] heard me on the air lambasting a recent article published in the *Bulletin* of the American Psychological Association, called "A Meta-Analytic Examination of Assumed Properties of Child Sexual Abuse Using College Samples."

In short: The three researchers claim that child sexual abuse does not necessarily cause intense, lasting harm—and go on to suggest that when there is a "willing" sexual encounter between an adult and a child, it be given the "value-neutral" term "adult-child sex!"

I've read and re-read this report until I'm sick to my stomach, and still, putting these words into print leaves me practically speechless—and you know how rare that is.

When I first heard about this, I wanted to disbelieve it. But I've done my research, and I cannot stress strongly enough how deadly serious this is.

This study is the first step on the road toward normalizing pedophilia—just as homosexuality has been mainstreamed, to the point where tolerance is no longer sufficient: We now have to "embrace" it.

I want to recap for you my own journey of discovery in this horrifying story: as I first learned of this study, examined it further, spoke with experts in the field who have excoriated the authors' methodology and their conclusions, and as I received hundreds of outraged, appalled and heartbroken letters from listeners who know all too well the "lasting, pervasive" harm of child sexual abuse—and that it is *never* a "willing," "value-neutral" experience.

The Warning Bell Sounds

It began with a letter.

I was in the middle of my show one day when I received a fax from Don, a father of two, who had just heard Dom Giordano, morning talk show host on my Philadelphia affiliate, WWDB, interview one of the authors of this study. Don wrote:

> "[The author] stated that not all children who engage in sexual contact willingly with an adult show any lasting damage. He further stated that to call this sexual contact 'abuse' is a mistake, because it's consensual . . ." [I believe the researchers had] an agenda that should scare all decent people.

> The next time some pervert gets caught with a child, I'm sure this is the first study his scum lawyer will drag out to defend his actions."

I immediately thought, "This is a very intelligent letter, but this can't be happening." I didn't believe it. So we started to track it down.

Next we received a fact sheet from NARTH, an organization I respect: the National Association for Research and Therapy of Homosexuality. The name of NARTH's report was: "The Problem of Pedophilia: Adult-Child Sex Is Not Necessarily Abuse, Say Some Psychologists."

The NARTH article pointed out that one of the authors of the *Bulletin* article had earlier co-authored an article in a special issue of the respected *Journal of Homosexuality* entitled "Male Intergenerational Intimacy." That issue was essentially an advertisement for the "benefits" of pedophilia—asserting that the loving pedophile can offer a child "companionship, security and protection" that neither peers nor parents can provide, and that parents should look on the pedophile "as a partner in the boy's upbringing, someone to be welcomed into their home . . ."!

Here are some excerpts from NARTH's report; I'd like to thank Dr. Joseph Nicolosi, director of NARTH, for giving us permission to quote from it. (I've **boldfaced** some important points.)

> "The American Psychological Association did not denounce the positions advanced within the *Journal of Homosexuality*. In fact, just recently, the APA published a new major study written by one of those same *Journal of Homosexuality* writers. The latest article appears in the APA's own prestigious *Psychological Bulletin*. It provides an overview of all of the research studying the harm resulting from childhood sexual abuse.
>
> **"The authors' conclusion? That childhood sexual abuse is, on the average, only slightly associated with psychological harm, and that the harm may not even be due to the sexual experience, but to the negative family factors in the children's backgrounds. When the sexual contact is not coerced, especially when it is experienced by a boy and enjoyed, it may not be harmful at all. . . .**
>
> **"In fact, the authors of the *Psychological Bulletin* article propose another way of understanding pedophilia: That it may be abuse if the child feels bad about the relationship. They are in effect suggesting a repetition of the steps by which homosexuality was normalized.** In its first step toward removing homosexuality from the Diagnostic Manual, the APA said the condition was normal as long as the person didn't feel bad about it. . . .
>
> "According to the latest diagnostic manual (DSM-IV), a person no longer has a psychological disorder simply because he molests children. To be diagnosed as disordered, he must feel anxious about the molestation, or be impaired in his work or social relationships. **Thus, the APA has left room for the psychologically 'normal' pedophile."**

Now, I have to reiterate a point here that I've tried to make several times on the air. Psychology has become some kind of holy writ to the general public. It's not. *Psychology is not hard science.* Just because a bunch of psychologists make intellectual-sounding pronouncements about the way things are—it ain't necessarily so!

꿍⦿꿍

So, let me ask a question of the psychologists and psychiatrists of the world: If pedophilia is not a mental disorder, then what is it? Is it normal?

When homosexuality was dropped from the *DSM*, the agenda became, "Homosexuality is normal." If you said anything to the contrary, that meant you were hateful and bigoted. Deviance became redefined as diversity, and tolerance became defined as acceptance, then celebration. It sounds like we're taking the next step with pedophilia.

To return to the NARTH fact sheet:

> "If psychology indeed recognizes consensual pedophilia as harmless, then civil law and social norms will be under pressure to follow the lead of so-called social science, as indeed they did in the issue of homosexuality. **When psychiatry declared homosexuality normal, our courts and theologians began to rewrite civil law and moral theology based upon what psychiatry said it had discovered through empirical science.**"

Later, Joe Nicolosi sent me a memo that makes some very salient additional points:

1. "The study used a *college-age* sample, which implies that most subjects were likely single. Would the results of this study have been different if they had been conducted with these same subjects ten years later? Would those subjects have been more prone to divorce, alcoholism, and child abuse? Would their spouses agree that they were well-adjusted, sexually and emotionally? We doubt it.
2. "The authors of the study try to make a case for separating 'wrongfulness' (social-moral norms) from 'harmfulness' (psychological damage). We believe that social norms of wrongfulness are not *arbitrary*, but they *evolved* out of the great religious philosophers' time-honored observations of 'harmfulness'—i.e., their finding of psychological damage to the person and society.
3. "The study makes a distinction between *forced* and *consensual* child-adult or adult-teen sex. What minor-age child can make an informed decision to consent to sex?"

The Truth Comes Out

Much as I still didn't want to believe this could be happening, I realized it was time to examine this for myself.

So I got the actual article, published [in July 1998] by the American Psychological Association, in their *Psychological Bulletin*. This is a peer-reviewed publication, which means that some number of clinicians had to read and approve this article for publication. While this may not be a statement of the

APA's official position, I hold them accountable for what I have been told by *numerous* professionals is garbage research.

- First of all, let's look at the title of the report: "A Meta-Analytic Examination . . .": Meta-analysis means you don't do any of your own work; you go into the literature, grab a lot of papers, all done by different people, put them all together, do a lot of math, and publish.
- The researchers chose 59 studies to review. Of these, 38 percent have not been published. They are unpublished master-degree or doctoral dissertations. So 23 of the 59 studies used were not even subject to any kind of peer review—that is, to the technical scrutiny of the psychological community.
- These 59 studies all used self-reporting from college students, who were questioned about the effects of child sexual abuse as they felt them. Think about that term, "self-reporting": That's a brilliant way to do research, right? You have a lot of objectivity there.
- The researchers claim that according to some of these college students' own descriptions, the negative effects of child sexual abuse "were neither pervasive nor typically intense, and that men reacted much less negatively than women." Is this anybody's personal experience? Does this bear any resemblance to anyone you know who was molested as a child?
- According to their findings, two-thirds of sexually abused men and more than one-quarter of sexually abused women "reported neutral or positive reactions." So even in their own study—again keeping in mind the dubious nature of their methods—one-third of the guys and 75 percent of the women were harmed. Aren't statistics a wonderful thing?

•❦•

What really frightens me is the idea that this study will now be used to normalize pedophilia—to change the legal system, and further destroy what I feel has been an ongoing plot against the family.

I'm not alone in this view. I had a discussion with Dr. Gerard van den Aardweg of Holland, who has seen firsthand the inroads made in his country by pedophilia activists.

Dr. van den Aardweg has a Ph.D. in psychology, did his dissertation on homosexuality, has been in private practice for many years, and has written several books and articles on homosexuality, pedophilia, neuroses and family issues.

"Their argument is that scores on some tests do not indicate harm—that if harm is not demonstrated by their way of testing, then harm does not exist," Dr. van den Aardweg says.

"I think these people are so eager to propagate the normality of adult-child sexual contact that they are blind to the obvious alternative: 'If my test did not show harm, maybe my test did not measure harm.'"

"These tests are sample questionnaires or short interview questions. At best, they can give a very rude indication of subjectively perceived discomfort. But in very many cases they not even do that. Harm is much more than 'I do or do not feel okay,' or 'I didn't like that experience.' Harm after child sexual abuse is often an increased distress with respect to adults; a distorted and unhealthy view of sexuality; a distorted view of their own or the opposite sex. It can be subsequent sexual abnormalities. It can be marriage and other relational problems later in life; problems functioning as a parent; sometimes later promiscuity; and in many cases, inferiority complexes, because children who have been misused often feel worthless.

"In short, what these psychologists offer us here is an insult to any really credible scientist of true scientific thinking. It is bogus psychology."

A Global Crisis

Now here's a further discussion that Dr. van den Aardweg and I had on the telephone:

Dr. van den Aardweg: I think the sexual reform movements of the Western world have as one of their goals to liberate sexuality in all its forms. And so there is a silent—not so silent here in Holland—cooperation of the sexual reform organizations with the cause of the militant pedophiles. Here it is very clear. For example, our Dutch Association for Sexual Reform has special meetings for pedophiles every week in most Dutch cities.

Dr. Laura: This is scary. In this country, such groups gain power and authority by attacking the opposition as phobic, intolerant of diversity, bigoted and mean.

VDA: You will do a wonderful thing if you make people aware of this, and say to them, "Don't let yourself be intimidated. Don't doubt your own commonsense judgment of these things." Because people are overruled and overwhelmed with all kinds of pseudo-science. They think "Who am I? Perhaps I'm wrong, I'm old-fashioned, I'm a victim of my Western culture." But they have to be supported as to their own convictions.

DL: So the point of liberating the sexual mores in general is, ultimately, to have access to kids.

VDA: Yes.

DL: That's what it's for: getting the kids sexually active and then getting sexually active with the kids. So there are a number of ways for people to take our kids. They can recruit them for the Fatherland's master race, they can take them out of villages and force them to become soldiers, or they can support safe-sex education in schools starting in kindergarten, and have them become active and liberated and available and open to new sexual experiences—like sex with an adult.

VDA: Pedophiles have an obsession. It's not a normal kind of sexual drive, it's a pathological obsession. It is the nucleus of their whole life. Like many disturbed people, their attitude is not that "I have to change," but that "the world has to change." And so, they are the ones to crusade to change the world, and really think that they can eventually get normal fathers and mothers to give their children to pedophiles for educational or enlightenment motivations.

Here in Holland, one of the advocates of pedophilia who just died had received royal distinction some years ago for his work to "liberate" homosexuality, as they say. He was in the Dutch senate as a very esteemed and respected senator.

Be aware: The public does not know what is happening. The pedophile network is worldwide.

Outrage and Anguish

You can imagine the firestorm I set off by devoting an entire hour of my radio show to this topic—as well as follow-ups on several subsequent days.

I hadn't even finished speaking when the faxes began pouring in. Listeners were horrified by what they were hearing. . . . The article—and my outspoken opposition to it—received a great deal of media attention. . . .

And, what a surprise, the American Psychological Association was quick to disassociate itself from the article in its own publication, according to a press release they put out:

> "As a publisher of psychological research, APA publishes thousands of research reports every year.
>
> "But, publication of the findings of a research project within an APA journal is in no way an endorsement of a finding by the Association. . .
>
> "Unfortunately, the findings of this meta-analysis . . . are being misreported by some in the media. The actual findings are that for this segment of the population (college students) being the victim of childhood sexual abuse was found to be less damaging to them than generally believed. However, one overall statement of the results was that students who were the victims of child sexual abuse were, on average, slightly less well-adjusted than students who were not victimized as children . . .
>
> "Those who are reporting that the study says that childhood sexual contact with adults is not harmful to children are misreporting the findings."

Perhaps they hadn't read their own publication: The researchers specifically say that "this poorer adjustment *could not be attributed to CSA [child sexual abuse]* [italics mine—DL] because family environment was consistently confounded with CSA. . . ."

Furthermore, the authors clearly state at the end of their report: *"A willing encounter with positive reactions would be labeled simply* adult-child *sex, a value-neutral term. . . . Moreover, the term* child *should be restricted to nonadolescent children"*—as if a nonadolescent child has the intellectual, psychological or emotional maturity to "willingly" engage in a sexual encounter with an adult!

I'm still flabbergasted by this logic.

David L. Riegel  **NO**

The Real Evil Among Us

In the spring and summer of 1999, a raging academic and public debate erupted over the July 1998 publication of "A Meta-Analytic Examination of Assumed Properties of Child Sexual Abuse Using College Samples" by Doctors Bruce Rind and Robert Bauserman and graduate student Philip Tromovitch. This fracas, which continues right up to the present, is reminiscent of that which ensued when Doctor Edward Wilson published "Sociobiology" some three decades ago. Dr. Wilson was the first to formalize the idea that social behavior could be explained evolutionarily. Biologists, psychologists, sociologists, and others quickly split into two camps, the battle was joined, accusations and personal attacks flew, and on one occasion a group of disgruntled graduate students snuck up behind Dr. Wilson at a conference, dumped a bucket of water on his head, and shouted "You're all wet!" When careful scientific research shows that time honored and revered "wisdom" is not based in fact, but that a different point of view actually is, there is often a strong and vocal reaction involving misinformation and innuendo in an attempt to discredit the research.

And yet the truths pointed out by Rind *et al.* are nothing new. In 1942 Dr. Karl Menninger, speaking of the effects of sexual experiences of children with older persons in *Love against Hate* (Harcourt, Brace & World, New York), noted: "The assumption is, of course, that children are irreparably ruined by such experiences. . . . I may . . . point out that in the cold light of scientific investigation no such devastating effects usually follow. . ."(p. 284) Over the intervening decades such respected sexologists as Frits Bernard, Larry Constantine, Paul Okami, Theo Sandfort, and many others have investigated these experiences and have generally arrived at the same conclusions as Dr. Menninger.[1] Unfortunately, these findings are still waiting for understanding and acceptance by the general public.

Rind *et al.* and the American Psychological Association (APA), which published the article in one of their journals (*Psychological Bulletin*), have been repeatedly castigated by right wing organizations such as the Family Research Council and the National Association for the Research and Therapy of Homosexuality, as well as by ultraconservative individuals like "Dr. Laura" Schlessinger. There have been indignant news conferences and outraged responses from the child sexual abuse industry; even the United States House of Representatives entered the fray by passing a resolution condemning the research, despite the fact that few, if any, of the congresspersons ever read it.

Many of these detractors invoked "morality" in their attacks. But morality is at best a very subjective issue; that which is considered grossly immoral in one society and time can be very acceptable in a different society and/or time. In our own society, masturbation, homosexuality, and premarital cohabitation were all at one time considered immoral, but only a few diehards hold these discredited positions today. The mentoring relationships between pubescent boys and older males in ancient Greece included a sexual component which was accepted in that society. Other societies today have moral expectations that allow for sexual experiences between children and older persons, and there is the possibility that our own society may some day view these matters differently. But, as Rind *et al.* and the APA found out, resistance to enlightenment can be fierce and dogged.

So what actually is this modern day heresy committed by Rind *et al.*, this latest target of witch hunters and book burners? To begin with, the authors took exception to the indiscriminate use of such value-laden terms as "perpetrator," "victim," and "child sexual abuse" (CSA).[2] However, after considering alternatives, they decided to retain these throughout their article simply for convenience, and attend to at least the last of these three terms in their conclusion. Then, simply put, they took 59 previous investigations of "CSA," subjected them to rigorous statistical analyses, and showed that, based on responses from some 35,000 college students, commonly held beliefs in four areas were highly inaccurate: (1) that "CSA" causes harm, (2) that this harm occurs in all cases, (3) that this harm is likely to be intense, and (4) that the effects of "CSA" are equivalent for boys and girls.

These cherished tenets are foundational for the enormously profitable and well entrenched child sexual abuse industry. They are also mainstays for those who are determined to preserve the archaic concept of asexual and innocent children, sexually uninformed robotic chattel property who are to be manipulated, molded, and used however their owners see fit, until they reach an arbitrary age at which they are to be suddenly and magically transformed into intelligent, responsible, and sexually competent adults.

There is no attempt in Rind's research to say that significant psychological damage can never result from non-consensual and coerced sexual relationships between a child and an older person. Rather, the main premises are that the consequences of actual "CSA" are grossly exaggerated, that inadequate consideration has been given to the vast differences in responses of boys versus girls and consensual versus non-consensual experiences, that the clinical terminology is inaccurate and highly biased, and that a revision in attitudes, terminology, perceptions, conclusions, and applications is long since past due.

For most people, large portions of the thirty-two full size double column pages of this research are a nightmare of incomprehensible statistical gibberish. But careful reading and re-reading of the non-statistical portions will give the average reader an understanding of the data, methods, and conclusions. To wit, here is a summary of the authors' findings, using their own paragraph headings, with respect to four common myths:

- *"CSA" causes harm:*

Most of the 59 sets of data used in the study indicated that people who had experienced "CSA" as children developed more emotional and psychological problems than those who said they had not been exposed to "CSA." But there are several problems here which need to be dealt with, not the least of which is that this correlation is exactly what too many of those 59 investigators expected and wanted to find. Neglect, and such factors as physical, emotional, and mental abuse were either scrambled in with "CSA" or were largely ignored, since there was no perceived need to look any further once the preconceived and desired results had been obtained.

But when these studies were sorted out and properly examined under the microscope of computerized statistical analysis, the assumed relationship between "CSA" and "maladjustment," as emotional and psychological problems are known, diminished almost to the vanishing point. There was some correlation remaining for females, but for males it was so small as to be insignificant. On the other hand, "family environment," which is a catchall for the other forms of abuse described above, had a markedly higher correlation with maladjustment than did "CSA."

The net effect of this aspect of the research was to disprove, in the vast majority of cases, and especially with males, that there is any reason whatsoever to ascribe any significant amount of maladjustment to the occurrence of "CSA."

- *Harm caused by "CSA" occurs in all cases:*

Much of the research done in years past on "CSA" was based on data from clinical populations, i.e., people who sought help for emotional and/or psychological problems. The inevitable result was that the pervasiveness of harm was greatly exaggerated, since only those who perceived themselves as needing treatment were included. Not to mention that clinical psychologists are predisposed to specifically inquire about possible "CSA," and, if there is even a vague hint that it may have occurred, they immediately seize on that "CSA" as the probable cause of any and all maladjustment they can find. There have also been many cases where a "memory" has been elicited simply from the persistent questioning by the psychologist, a memory that was later determined to be based on circumstances that, in fact, never occurred.

Analyses of the data from the non-clinical samples used in the Rind *et al.* study show that this supposed pervasiveness is not the case, since only a small minority of females, and a minuscule number of males, reported that they perceived they had been permanently harmed by their childhood or adolescent sexual encounters. Many of the women reported temporary harm, but many did not. The majority of the men did not even report temporary harm.

- *Harm caused by "CSA" is likely to be intense:*

In the case of a small boy or girl who is forcibly and repeatedly raped by an older man that they had previously loved and trusted, there is good reason to believe that intense psychological harm is likely to result. This is most definitely an extreme and rare example, although, sadly, it does occur. But the data do not support the presupposition that "CSA" causes intense harm except in such rare cases. However, as one author has put it, "children are amazingly resilient," so it cannot be assumed that a severe maladjustment is the inevitable outcome of even this extreme example.

- *The effects of "CSA" are equivalent in boys and girls:*

This position is especially espoused by those who have yet to be convinced that there are very real cognitive, emotional, and behavioral differences between boys and girls. This study continues to demolish any remnants of this concept by demonstrating the completely different attitudes, approaches, and experiences that boys and girls report about sexual activities with significantly older persons. In simple and understandable numbers, the study notes that two thirds of the men who reported "CSA" experiences viewed them at the time as other than negative, and three eighths remembered them as positive. These figures do not take consensuality into account, and it is reasonable to believe that there would be a much larger proportion of positive memories if the non-consensual experiences were eliminated from the computation.

Over two thirds of the women, on the other hand, reported negative feelings, and only one tenth had positive recollections.

Only when unwanted sex is considered separately do the male versus female findings tend toward being equivalent, and even in these cases the association with harm is, on average, small.

The issue of pejorative, value laden, and inflammatory terminology that Rind *et al.* addressed in their closing paragraphs is also nothing new. In 1990 Okami wrote "Sociopolitical Biases in the Contemporary Scientific Literature on Adult Human Sexual Behavior with Children and Adolescents," which was a chapter in *Pedophilia: Biosocial Dimensions* edited by Feierman and published by Springer-Verlag. Okami notes:

> . . . use of negatively loaded terminology such as "abuse," "assault," . . . "molestation," . . . or "victimization" to refer generically to all adult human sexual behavior with children and adolescents, confounds attempts to understand such interactions and may reflect . . . a serious conflict of interest between scientific inquiry on the one hand and enforcement of social norms or propagation of political ideology on the other (p. 99).

As noted earlier, the adverse reactions to this study were swift and vehement. Some were successfully manipulative, as when Representative Matt Salmon hoodwinked the United States House of Representatives into unanimously approving a hasty resolution denouncing both the research and the researchers.

It goes without saying that it would have been political suicide for any member of Congress to vote against condemning what Mr. Salmon trumpeted as "the emancipation proclamation of pedophiles." By approving this absurdity, these congresspersons showed themselves to be politically astute, but totally devoid of any understanding of, or respect for, science, scientists, or scientific principles.

The "Family Research Council" also made a feeble attempt to discredit the research on an imagined procedural blunder reported by an ex-president of the American Psychiatric Association, but wound up with considerable egg on their collective faces when they stated "Of the 59 studies included in the analysis, over 60% of the data are drawn from a single study done 40 years ago." An examination shows, instead of being 60% of the some 35,000 respondents to the 59 studies, that particular study comprised only 4%. Furthermore, because it used somewhat outmoded subjective techniques, and was completed before child abuse researchers began collecting objective data on the effects of "CSA," that study was not used at all in the primary analyses upon which the researchers based their conclusions.

"Dr. Laura" Schlessinger, a talk show host, published a lengthy tirade in her now defunct magazine *Dr. Laura Perspective*, referring to Rind *et al.* as the "Evil Among Us." She began by claiming, but not substantiating, that she has received "hundreds" of letters about the "lasting, pervasive" harm of child sexual abuse. Since her stated positions on these issues effectively solicits such letters, it is not surprising that she receives them. But it is surprising that her claims are in direct opposition to a huge amount of empirical data. She then quoted one of her trusted correspondents as saying that any attorney who would dare represent a "pervert" is "scum," prime examples of the pejorative and inflammatory language that is discussed earlier. Shortly before noting that "because . . . psychologists make intellectual-sounding pronouncements . . . it ain't necessarily so!," she quoted at great length from clinical psychologist Joseph Nicolosi, whose anti-gay agenda is well known. She presented his observations as if they were logical conclusions based on empirical data, when they are actually nothing more than personal and unsupported opinions. One of these is his assertion that no "minor-age child can make an informed decision to consent to sex," which, although it is a position held by some, is the subject of ongoing debate.

After citing more of Nicolosi's misleading and unsupported assertions that were previously refuted in Rind *et al.*, she took aim at the concept of meta-analysis as meaning that "you don't do any of your own work," then contradicted herself by saying that a lot of math—which certainly is "work"— was done! The analyses, discussion, and conclusions in Rind *et al.* also represent a monumental amount of work. Her next targets were masters theses and doctoral dissertations, which she complained are not peer reviewed. Since she holds a doctorate in physiology (but not in the social sciences), she should have been well aware of the fact that such papers are scrutinized by faculty examiners much more thoroughly than most peer reviews. She then took a swipe at "self-reported" behavioral data, failing to take note that the vast majority of human behavioral data are self-reported, whether it be in a personal interview or a questionnaire. Observational data, especially of children, adolescents and adults, are used much less frequently.

She went on to cite a telephone conversation—which she inflated to the status of dealing with a "Global Crisis"—with one Dr. van den Aarweg, yet another member of the psychological discipline she previously dismissed as unscientific. In her part of the conversation, she launched into some very unprofessional and pejorative rhetoric, comparing any attempt at intelligent sex education for children with the Hitler youth groups. In everything she had to say she missed the point that the world view she espouses is only a recent and localized development, and there are many other world views which are or were considered valid by a majority of mankind. Just because a radio talk show host makes intellectual-sounding pronouncements about the way she thinks things ought to be, it doesn't follow that she necessarily is correct.

It is interesting to note that those who have truth and facts on their side are pleased to invite the whole world to investigate both their deliberations and their conclusions. But those who are perpetuating lies and misrepresentations, since they have nothing of substance to say in response, so often resort to innuendo, emotional appeals, irrelevant accusations, and attempts to suppress any discussion of the real issues.

There is no way of accurately determining the inner mindset of the majority of people. Polls tend to get answers on controversial subjects such as childhood sexuality that agree mostly with what people believe they are expected to say, rather than what is actually going on in their minds. And the perceptions perpetuated by the media are mostly derived from the minority of radicals who do the most and loudest screaming. So we can only hope, or perhaps be cautiously optimistic, that beyond the blaring sirens and roaring cannons there is a quiet revolution brewing, a revolution of thinking people who are at long last beginning to realize that for decades they have been spoon fed a diet of misinformation and lies about a very critical factor of human emotional life, that of the sexuality, sexual needs, and the sexual nature of their own precious children.

It took nearly twenty years for Ed Wilson's pioneering work to begin to be accepted and recognized for the insights and wisdom it really contained, but he is now revered as one of the outstanding scientists in sociobiology. How long will it take this time for the dark clouds of the *real* evil among us to be dispelled by the bright sunshine of reason and truth?

Notes

1. See, for example, Bernard, F. (1985). *Paedophilia: A Factual Report*. Rotterdam: Enclave.

2. The term "child sexual abuse" is a pejorative argument in and of itself; however, because so much of the literature is permeated with this term and its acronym, and because Rind *et al.* also reluctantly used it, it is used in this essay for convenience. Such usage does not in any way sanction or endorse the term.

POSTSCRIPT

Is Pedophilia Always Harmful?

In 1986, after examining 300 incest relationships, Warren Farrell, a psychologist teaching at the University of California School of Medicine, concluded that the effects of incest "are perhaps best described as a magnifying glass—magnifying the worst in a poor family environment and the best in a caring and loving family environment." However, in his report titled "The Last Taboo? The Complexities of Incest and Female Sexuality," published in *The Handbook of Sexology, vol. 7* (Elsevier Science, 1991), Farrell noted that "in most family environments it exposes the family fabric to rays of confusion and guilt of such intensity that the magnifying glass burns a hole in all but the strongest."

Whether or not all, most, or only some children who have been involved in adult-child sexual relationships are emotionally and/or psychologically damaged for life, it is clear that adult-child sexual relationships are regarded as socially unacceptable in American culture. There are currently other societies where noncoercive, consensual sexual relations between adults and minors are quite acceptable. In some countries, boys and girls can be given legal consent to sexual relations if they are 12 years old. In the South Pacific, adolescent Melanesian boys and girls are not allowed to have sex with each other before marriage, but the boys are expected to have sex both with an older male and with a boy of their own age. Their first heterosexual experience comes with marriage. In the Cook Islands, Mangaian boys are expected to have sex with many girls but only after an older woman teaches them about the art of sexual pleasuring. But norms regarding sexual readiness that are acceptable in other cultures are widely rejected by U.S. culture. Still, the United States does not have a firm grasp on what it collectively believes about sexual readiness, including sexual contact between adults and minors. The age of consent varies greatly state-to-state, with a low range of 14 (Hawaii) to 18 in several states, including California. As recently as the last century, many states maintained ages of consent of 10 and 12.

Obviously, this is a serious issue that raises important questions. Do you believe adult-child sexual relationships have lifelong damaging effects on the minors involved? Where are the facts, and how should we discover them?

Suggested Readings

J. Duin, "Controversies Cloud APA Convention. Premier Psychological Body's Reports on Child Abuse Still Draw Criticism," *The Washington Times* (August 12, 1999).

G. Goslinga, "Radical Reconsideration of the Concept of Child Sexual Abuse: New Findings by Mauserman, Rind, and Tromovitch," *Koinos* (April 1998).

H. Mirkin, "Sex, Science, and Sin: The Rind Report, Sexual Politics, and American Scholarship," *Sexuality & Culture* (vol. 4, no. 2, 2000).

S. Lamb, "Some Victims Don't Need Pity," *The Boston Globe* (August 1, 1999).

S. Lilienfeld, "When Worlds Collide: Social Science, Politics, and Rind et al. (1998) Child Sexual Abuse Meta-Analysis," *American Psychologist* (vol. 57, no. 3, 2002).

T. Oellerich, "Rind, Tromovitch, and Bauserman: Politically Incorrect—Scientifically Correct," *Sexuality & Culture* (vol. 4, no. 2, 2000).

K. Parker, "Adult-Child Sex Is Abuse, Plain and Clear," *The Orlando Sentinel* (March 28, 1999).

D. Riegel, *Understanding Loved Boys and Boylovers* (SafeHaven Foundation Press, 2000).

B. Rind and P. Tromovitch, "A Meta-Analytic Review of Findings from National Samples on Psychological Correlates of Child Sexual Abuse," *Journal of Sex Research* (1997).

B. Rind, P. Tromovitch, and R. Bauserman, "A Meta-Analytic Examination of Assumed Properties of Child Sexual Abuse Using College Samples," *Psychological Bulletin* (1998).

B. Rind, P. Tromovitch, and R. Bauserman, "The Validity and Appropriateness of Methods, Analyses, and Conclusions in Rind *et al.* (1998): A Rebuttal of Victimological Critique from Ondersma *et al.* (2001) and Dallam *et al.* (2001)," *Psychological Bulletin* (vol. 127, 2001).

ISSUE 16

Should Female Circumcision Be Banned?

YES: Loretta M. Kopelman, from "Female Circumcision/Genital Mutilation and Ethical Relativism," *Second Opinion* (October 1994)

NO: P. Masila Mutisya, from "A Symbolic Form of Female Circumcision Should Be Allowed for Those Who Want It," An Original Essay Written for This Volume (November 1997)

ISSUE SUMMARY

YES: Loretta M. Kopelman, a professor of medical humanities, argues that certain moral absolutes apply to all cultures and that these, combined with the many serious health and cultural consequences of female circumcision, require that all forms of female genital mutilation be eliminated.

NO: P. Masila Mutisya, a professor of multicultural education, contends that we should allow the simplest form of female circumcision, nicking the clitoral hood to draw a couple of drops of blood, as part of the rich heritage of rite of passage for newborn and pubertal girls in those cultures with this tradition.

$\mathbf{E}$ach year in central and northern Africa and southern Arabia, 4–5 million girls have parts of their external genitals surgically removed in ceremonies intended to honor and welcome the girls into their communities or into womanhood. About 80 million living women have had this surgery performed sometime between infancy and puberty in ancient rituals said to promote chastity, religion, group identity, cleanliness, health, family values, and marriage goals. Female circumcision (FC) is deeply embedded in the cultures of many countries, including Ethiopia, Sudan, Somalia, Sierra Leone, Kenya, Tanzania, Chad, Gambia, Liberia, Mali, Senegal, Eritrea, Ivory Coast, Upper Volta, Mauritania, Nigeria, and Egypt.

Opponents of FC call it female genital mutilation (FGM) because the usual ways of performing FC frequently cause serious health problems, such as hemorrhaging, urinary and pelvic infection, painful intercourse (for both partners), infertility, delivery complications, and even death. Besides denying women orgasm, the health consequences of FC also strain the overburdened, limited health care systems in the developing nations in which it is practiced.

In Type 1 FC, the simplest form, the clitoral hood is pricked or removed. Type 1 FC should not preclude orgasms in later life, but it can when performed on the tiny genitals of infants with the pins, scissors, and knives that traditional practitioners commonly use. In Type 2 (intermediate) FC, the clitoris and most or all of the minor labia are removed. In Type 3 FC, known as pharonic circumcision, or infibulation, the clitoris, minor labia, and parts of the major labia are removed. The vulval wound is stitched closed, leaving only a small opening for passage of urine and menstrual flow. Traditional practitioners often use sharpened or hot stones or unsterilized razors or knives, frequently without anesthesia or antibiotics. Thorns are sometimes used to stitch up the wound, and a twig is often inserted to keep the passage open. Healing can take a month or more. In southern Arabia, Sudan, Somalia, Ethiopia, and other African nations, more than three-quarters of the girls undergo Type 2 or 3 FC.

Impassioned cultural clashes erupt when families migrate from countries where FC is customary to North America and Europe. In their new homes immigrant parents use traditional practitioners or ask local health professionals to perform FC. Some doctors and nurses perform FC for large fees; others do it because they are concerned about the unhygienic techniques of traditional practitioners. In the United Kingdom about 2,000 girls undergo FC each year, even though it is legally considered child abuse. Many international agencies, such as UNICEF, the International Federation of Gynecology and Obstetrics, and the World Health Organization (WHO), openly condemn and try to stop FC. France, Canada, and the United Kingdom have banned FC; the American Medical Association has denounced it; and the U.S. Congress has made all FC illegal.

The question discussed here is whether or not the traditional pluralism and openness of American culture can make some accommodation that would allow thousands of immigrants to maintain the essence of their ancient, traditional rites of passage for young girls in some symbolic way. Some commentators argue that we should prohibit Types 2 and 3 circumcision for health reasons but allow some symbolic ritual nicking of the clitoral hood as a major element in the extensive ceremonies and educational rites of passage that surround a girl's birth into her family and community or her passage to womanhood in these African and Arabic cultures. In the following selections, Loretta M. Kopelman advocates a ban on all female circumcision. P. Masila Mutisya advocates allowing a symbolic female circumcision, similar to the removal of the male foreskin (prepuce), with modern medical safeguards.

YES

Loretta M. Kopelman

Female Circumcision/Genital Mutilation and Ethical Relativism

Reasons Given for Female Circumcision/Genital Mutilation

According to four independent series of studies conducted by investigators from countries where female circumcision is widely practiced (El Dareer 1982; Ntiri 1993; Koso-Thomas 1987; Abdalla 1982), the primary reasons given for performing this ritual surgery are that it (1) meets a religious requirement, (2) preserves group identity, (3) helps to maintain cleanliness and health, (4) preserves virginity and family honor and prevents immorality, and (5) furthers marriage goals including greater sexual pleasure for men.

El Dareer conducted her studies in the Sudan, Dr. Olayinka Koso-Thomas in and around Sierra Leone, and Raquiya Haji Dualeh Abdalla and Daphne Williams Ntiri in Somalia. They argue that the reasons for continuing this practice in their respective countries float on a sea of false beliefs, beliefs that thrive because of a lack of education and open discussion about reproduction and sexuality. Insofar as intercultural methods for evaluating factual and logical statements exist, people from other cultures should at least be able to understand these inconsistencies or mistaken factual beliefs and use them as basis for making some judgments having intercultural *moral* authority.

First, according to these studies the main reason given for performing female circumcision/genital mutilation is that it is regarded as a religious requirement. Most of the people practicing this ritual are Muslims, but it is not a practice required by the Koran (El Dareer 1982; Ntiri 1993). El Dareer writes: "Circumcision of women is not explicitly enjoined in the Koran, but there are two implicit sayings of the Prophet Mohammed: 'Circumcision is an ordinance in men and an embellishment in women' and, reportedly Mohammed said to Om Attiya, a woman who circumcised girls in El Medina, 'Do not go deep. It is more illuminating to the face and more enjoyable to the husband.' Another version says, 'Reduce but do not destroy. This is enjoyable to the woman and preferable to the man.' But there is nothing in the Koran to suggest that the Prophet commanded that women be circumcised. He advised that it was important to both sexes that very little should be taken" (1992:72). Female

From Loretta M. Kopelman, "Female Circumcision/Genital Mutilation and Ethical Relativism," *Second Opinion*, vol. 20, no. 2 (October 1994). Copyright © 1994 by The Park Ridge Center for the Study of Health, Faith, and Ethics, 211 East Ontario, Suite 800, Chicago, IL 60611. Reprinted by permission. Notes and references omitted.

circumcision/genital mutilation, moreover, is not practiced in the spiritual center of Islam, Saudi Arabia (Calder et al. 1993). Another reason for questioning this as a Muslim practice is that clitoridectomy and infibulation predate Islam, going back to the time of the pharaohs (Abdalla 1982; El Dareer 1992).

Second, many argue that the practice helps to preserve group identity. When Christian colonialists in Kenya introduced laws opposing the practice of female circumcision in the 1930s, African leader Kenyatta expressed a view still popular today: "This operation is still regarded as the very essence of an institution which has enormous educational, social, moral and religious implications, quite apart from the operation itself. For the present, it is impossible for a member of the [Kikuyu] tribe to imagine an initiation without clitoridectomy . . . the abolition of IRUA [the ritual operation] will destroy the tribal symbol which identifies the age group and prevent the Kikuyu from perpetuating that spirit of collectivism and national solidarity which they have been able to maintain from time immemorial" (Scheper-Hughes 1991:27). In addition, the practice is of social and economic importance to older women who are paid for performing the rituals (El Dareer 1982; Koso-Thomas 1987; Abdalla 1982; Ginsberg 1991).

Drs. Koso-Thomas, El Dareer, and Abdalla agree that people in these countries support female circumcision as a good practice, but only because they do not understand that it is a leading cause of sickness or even death for girls, mothers, and infants, and a major cause of infertility, infection, and maternal-fetal and marital complications. They conclude that these facts are not confronted because these societies do not speak openly of such matters. Abdalla writes, "There is no longer any reason, given the present state of progress in science, to tolerate confusion and ignorance about reproduction and women's sexuality" (1982:2). Female circumcision/genital mutilation is intended to honor women as male circumcision honors men, and members of cultures where the surgery is practiced are shocked by the analogy of clitoridectomy to removal of the penis (El Dareer 1982).

Third, the belief that the practice advances health and hygiene is incompatible with stable data from surveys done in these cultures, where female circumcision/genital mutilation has been linked to mortality or morbidity such as shock, infertility, infections, incontinence, maternal-fetal complications, and protracted labor. The tiny hole generally left for blood and urine to pass is a constant source of infection (El Dareer 1982; Koso-Thomas 1987; Abdalla 1982; Calder et al. 1993; Ntiri 1993). Koso-Thomas writes, "As for cleanliness, the presence of these scars prevents urine and menstrual flow escaping by the normal channels. This may lead to acute retention of urine and menstrual flow, and to a condition known as *hematocolpos*, which is highly detrimental to the health of the girl or woman concerned and causes odors more offensive than any that can occur through the natural secretions" (Koso-Thomas 1987:10). Investigators completing a recent study wrote: "The risk of medical complications after female circumcision is very high as revealed by the present study [of 290 Somali women, conducted in the capital of Mogadishu]. Complications which cause the death of the young girls must be a common occurrence especially in the rural areas. . . . Dribbling urine incontinence, painful menstruations, haematocolpos and painful intercourse are facts that Somali women have to live with—facts that strongly motivate attempts to change the practice of female circumcision" (Dirie and Lindmark 1992:482).

Fourth, investigators found that circumcision is thought necessary in these cultures to preserve virginity and family honor and to prevent immorality. Type 3 circumcision [in which the clitoris and most or all of the labia minora are removed] is used to keep women from having sexual intercourse before marriage and conceiving illegitimate children. In addition, many believe that Types 2 [in which the clitoris, the labia minora, and parts of the labia majora are removed] and 3 circumcision must be done because uncircumcised women have excessive and uncontrollable sexual drives. El Dareer, however, believes that this view is not consistently held—that women in the Sudan are respected and that Sudanese men would be shocked to apply this sometimes-held cultural view to members of their own families. This reason also seems incompatible with the general view, which investigators found was held by both men and women in these cultures, that sex cannot be pleasant for women (El Dareer 1982; Koso-Thomas 1987; Abdalla 1982). In addition, female circumcision/genital mutilation offers no foolproof way to promote chastity and can even lead to promiscuity because it does not diminish desire or libido even where it makes orgasms impossible (El Dareer 1982). Some women continually seek experiences with new sexual partners because they are left unsatisfied in their sexual encounters (Koso-Thomas 1987). Moreover, some pretend to be virgins by getting stitched up tightly again (El Dareer 1982).

Fifth, interviewers found that people practicing female circumcision/ genital mutilation believe that it furthers marriage goals, including greater sexual pleasure for men. To survive economically, women in these cultures must marry, and they will not be acceptable marriage partners unless they have undergone this ritual surgery (Abdalla 1982; Ntiri 1993). It is a curse, for example, to say that someone is the child of an uncircumcised woman (Koso-Thomas 1987). The widely held belief that infibulation enhances women's beauty and men's sexual pleasure makes it difficult for women who wish to marry to resist this practice (Koso-Thomas 1987; El Dareer 1992). Some men from these cultures, however, report that they enjoy sex more with uncircumcised women (Koso-Thomas 1987). Furthermore, female circumcision/genital mutilation is inconsistent with the established goals of some of these cultures because it is a leading cause of disability and contributes to the high mortality rate among mothers, fetuses, and children. Far from promoting the goals of marriage, it causes difficulty in consummating marriage, infertility, prolonged and obstructed labor, and morbidity and mortality.

Criticisms of Ethical Relativism

Examination of the debate concerning female circumcision suggests several conclusions about the extent to which people from outside a culture can understand or contribute to moral debates within it in a way that has moral force. First, the fact that a culture's moral and religious views are often intertwined with beliefs that are open to rational and empirical evaluation can be a basis of cross-cultural examination and intercultural moral criticism (Bambrough 1979). Defenders of female circumcision/genital mutilation do not claim that this practice is a moral or religious requirement and end the discussion; they are willing to give and defend reasons for their views. For example, advocates of female circumcision/genital mutilation claim that it benefits women's health and well-being. Such claims are open to cross-cultural examination because information is available to determine whether the practice promotes health or cause morbidity or mortality. Beliefs that the practice enhances fertility and promotes health, that women cannot have orgasms, and that allowing the baby's head to touch the clitoris during delivery causes death to the baby are incompatible with stable medical data (Koso-Thomas 1987). Thus an opening is allowed for genuine cross-cultural discussion or criticism of the practice.

Some claims about female circumcision/genital mutilation, however, are not as easily open to cross-cultural understanding. For example, cultures practicing the Type 3 surgery, infibulation, believe that it makes women more beautiful. For those who are not from these cultures, this belief is difficult to understand, especially when surveys show that many women in these cultures, when interviewed, attributed to infibulation their keloid scars, urine retention, pelvic infections, puerperal sepsis, and obstetrical problems (Ntiri 1993; Abdalla 1982). Koso-Thomas writes: "None of the reasons put forward in favor of circumcision have any real scientific or logical basis. It is surprising that aesthetics and the maintenance of cleanliness are advanced as grounds for female circumcision. The scars could hardly be thought of as contributing to beauty. The hardened scar and stump usually seen where the clitoris should be, or in the case of the infibulated vulva, taut skin with an ugly long scar down the middle, present a horrifying picture" (Koso-Thomas 1987:10). Thus not everyone in these cultures believes that these rituals enhance beauty; some find such claims difficult to understand.

Second, the debate over female circumcision/genital mutilation illustrates another difficulty for defenders of this version of ethical relativism concerning the problem of differentiating cultures. People who brought the practice of female circumcision/genital mutilation with them when they moved to another nation still claim to be a distinct cultural group. Some who moved to Britain, for example, resent the interference in their culture represented by laws that condemn the practice as child abuse (Thompson 1989). If ethical relativists are to appeal to cultural approval in making the final determination of what is good or bad, right or wrong, they must tell us how to distinguish one culture from another.

How exactly do we count or separate cultures? A society is not a nation-state, because some social groups have distinctive identities within nations. If we do not define societies as nations, however, how do we distinguish among cultural groups, for example, well enough to say that an action is child abuse in one culture but not in another? Subcultures in nations typically overlap and have many variations. Even if we could count cultural groups well enough to say exactly how to distinguish one culture from another, how and when would this be relevant? How big or old or vital must a culture, subculture, group, or cult be in order to be recognized as a society whose moral distinctions are self-contained and self-justifying?

A related problem is that there can be passionate disagreement, ambivalence, or rapid changes within a culture or group over what is approved or disapproved. According to ethical relativism, where there is significant disagreement within a culture there is no way to determine what is right or wrong. But what disagreement is significant? As we saw, some people in these cultures, often those with higher education, strongly disapprove of female circumcision/genital mutilation and work to stop it (El Dareer 1982; Koso-Thomas 1987; Ntiri 1993; Dirie and Lindmark 1992; Abdalla 1982). Are they in the same culture as their friends and relatives who approve of these rituals? It seems more accurate to say that people may belong to various groups that overlap and have many variations. This description, however, makes it difficult for ethical relativism to be regarded as a helpful theory for determining what is right or wrong. To say that something is right when it has cultural approval is useless if we cannot identify the relevant culture. Moreover, even where people agree about the rightness of certain practices, such as these rituals, they can sometimes be inconsistent. For example, in reviewing reasons given within cultures where female circumcision/genital mutilation is practiced, we saw that there was some inconsistency concerning whether women needed this surgery to control their sexual appetites, to make them more beautiful, or to prevent morbidity or mortality. Ethical relativists thus have extraordinary problems offering a useful account of what counts as a culture and establishes cultural approval or disapproval.

Third, despite some clear disagreement such as that over the rightness of female circumcision/genital mutilation, people from different parts of the world share common goals like the desirability of promoting people's health, happiness, opportunities, and cooperation, and the wisdom of stopping war, pollution, oppression, torture, and exploitation. These common goals make us a world community, and using shared methods of reasoning and evaluation, we can discuss how well they are understood or how well they are implemented in different parts of our world community. We can use shared goals to assess whether female circumcision/genital mutilation is more like respect or oppression, more like enhancement or diminishment of opportunities, or more like pleasure or torture. While there are, of course, genuine differences between citizens of the world, it is difficult to comprehend how they could be identified unless we could pick them out against a background of our similarities. Highlighting our differences, however useful for some purposes, should not eclipse the truth that we share many goals and values and are similar enough that we can assess each other's views as rational beings in a way that has moral force. Another way to express this is to say that we should recognize universal human rights or be respectful of each other as persons capable of reasoned discourse.

Fourth, this version of ethical relativism, if consistently held, leads to the abhorrent conclusion that we cannot make intercultural judgments with moral force about societies that start wars, practice torture, or exploit and oppress other groups; as long as these activities are approved in the society that does them, they are allegedly right. Yet the world community believed that it was making a cross-cultural judgment with moral force when it criticized the Communist Chinese government for crushing a pro-democracy student protest rally, the South Africans for upholding apartheid, the Soviets for using psychiatry to suppress dissent, and the Bosnian Serbs for carrying out the siege of Sarajevo. And the judgment was expressed without anyone's ascertaining whether the respective actions had widespread approval in those countries. In each case, representatives from the criticized society usually said something like, "You don't understand why this is morally justified in our culture even if it would not be in your society." If ethical relativism were convincing, these responses ought to be as well.

Relativists who want to defend sound social cross-cultural and moral judgments about the value of freedom and human rights in other cultures seem to have two choices. On the one hand, if they agree that some cross-cultural norms have moral authority, they should also agree that some intercultural judgments about female circumcision/genital mutilation may have moral authority. Some relativists take this route (see, for example, Sherwin 1992), thereby abandoning the version of ethical relativism being criticized herein. On the other hand, if they defend this version of ethical relativism yet make cross-cultural moral judgments about the importance of values like tolerance, group benefit, and the survival of cultures, they will have to admit to an inconsistency in their arguments. For example, anthropologist Scheper-Hughes (1991) advocates tolerance of other cultural value systems; she fails to see that she is saying that tolerance between cultures is *right* and that this is a crosscultural moral judgment using a moral norm (tolerance). Similarly, relativists who say it is wrong to eliminate rituals that give meaning to other cultures are also inconsistent in making a judgment that presumes to have genuine cross-cultural moral authority. Even the sayings sometimes used by defenders of ethical relativism—such as "When in Rome do as the Romans" (Scheper-Hughes 1991)—mean it is *morally permissible* to adopt all the cultural norms in operation wherever one finds oneself. Thus it is not consistent for defenders of this version of ethical relativism to make intercultural moral judgments about tolerance, group benefit, intersocietal respect, or cultural diversity.

The burden of proof, then, is upon defenders of this version of ethical relativism to show why we cannot do something we think we sometimes do very well, namely, engage in intercultural moral discussion, cooperation, or criticism and give support to people whose welfare or rights are in jeopardy in other cultures. In addition, defenders of ethical relativism need to explain how we can justify the actions of international professional societies that take moral stands in adopting policy. For example, international groups may take moral stands that advocate fighting pandemics, stopping wars, halting oppression, promoting health education, or eliminating poverty, and they seem to have moral authority in some cases. Some might respond that our professional groups are themselves cultures of a sort. But this response raises the . . . problem of how to individuate a culture or society. . . .

Comment

We have sufficient reason, therefore, to conclude that these rituals of female circumcision/genital mutilation are wrong. For me to say they are wrong does not mean that they are disapproved by most people in my culture but wrong for reasons similar to those given by activists within these cultures who are working to stop these practices. They are wrong because the usual forms of the surgery deny women orgasms and because they cause medical complications and even death. It is one thing to say that these practices are wrong and that activists should be supported in their efforts to stop them; it is another matter to determine how to do this effectively. All agree that education may be the most important means to stop these practices. Some activists in these cultures want an immediate ban (Abdalla 1982). Other activists in these cultures encourage Type 1 circumcision (pricking or removing the clitoral hood) in order to "wean" people away from Types 2 and 3 by substitution. Type 1 has the least association with morbidity or mortality and, if there are no complications, does not preclude sexual orgasms in later life. The chance of success through this tactic is more promising and realistic, they hold, than what an outright ban would achieve; and people could continue many of their traditions and rituals of welcome without causing so much harm (El Dareer 1982). Other activists in these countries, such as Raquiya Abdalla, object to equating Type 1 circumcision in the female with male circumcision: "To me and to many others, the aim and results of any form of circumcision of women are quite different from those applying to the circumcision of men" (1982:8). Because of the hazards of even Type 1 circumcision, especially for infants, I agree with the World Health Organization and the American Medical Association that it would be best to stop all forms of ritual genital surgery on women. Bans have proven ineffective: this still-popular practice has been illegal in most countries for many years (Rushwan 1990; Ntiri 1993; El Dareer 1982). Other proposals by activists focus on education, fines, and carefully crafted legislation (El Dareer 1982; Abdalla 1982; Ozumba 1992; Dirie and Lindmark 1992; WHO 1992).

The critique of the reasons given to support female circumcision/genital mutilation in cultures where it is practiced shows us how to enter discussions, disputes, or assessments in ways that can have moral authority. We share common needs, goals, and methods of reasoning and evaluation. Together they enable us to evaluate many claims across cultures and sometimes to regard ourselves as part of a world community with interests in promoting people's health, happiness, empathy, and opportunities as well as desires to stop war, torture, pandemics, pollution, oppression, and injustice. Thus, ethical relativism—the view that to say something is right means it has cultural approval and to say it is wrong means it has cultural disapproval—is implausible as a useful theory, definition, or account of the meaning of moral judgments. The burden of proof therefore falls upon upholders of this version of ethical relativism to show why criticisms of other cultures always lack moral authority. Although many values are culturally determined and we should not impose moral judgments across cultures hastily, we sometimes know enough to condemn practices approved in other cultures. For example, we can understand enough of the debate about female circumcision/genital mutilation to draw some conclusions: it is wrong, oppressive, and not a voluntary practice in the sense that the people doing it comprehend information relevant to their decision. Moreover, it is a ritual, however well-meant, that violates justifiable and universal human rights or values supported in the human community, and we should promote international moral support for advocates working to stop the practice wherever it is carried out.

P. Masila Mutisya  **NO**

A Symbolic Form of Female Circumcision Should Be Allowed for Those Who Want It

In recent years, the issue of female circumcision has provoked heated discussion here in the United States and far from its cultural origins in Africa. As controversial as it is, the issue of female circumcision raises a very important point that needs attention across the board when we are dealing with cultural behaviors, traditions, and practices that are brought by immigrants into a foreign culture. Whether we are dealing with a sexual practice like female circumcision, parentally arranged marriages, child marriages, or a non-sexual custom, we must deal clearly with the implications of cross-cultural, intercultural and multicultural education. This need for cross-cultural sensitivity and understanding is fairly obvious from the blanket condemnations of all forms of female circumcision as a brutalization of women, and the parallel silence about its cultural meaning as an important rite of passage for women. There is certainly a lot of ignorance about African cultures among Americans, both in the general population with its vocal feminist advocacy groups as well as among our legislators and health care professionals. There is a real need for better understanding of these rich cultural traditions.

The issue here is not one of cultural relativism, or the lack of it. What I am concerned about is that it is all too easy to misinterpret the symbolism and meaning of a traditional cultural rite. Unless we understand the various forms of female circumcision and its cultural importance as part of a girl's rite of passage to womanhood we run the serious risk of doing more harm than good. Lack of understanding of the values of one culture leads to the imposition of the views and interpretations of the cultural majority on new minorities within a nation. This has often been the case in the United States with the miseducation and misinterpretation of many aspects of African cultures, as well as other cultures in this nation. This in turn leads to conflicts in social and psychological awareness that affect the identities of different people in our multicultural society. People of African descent seem to be more affected by this than others.

Loretta Kopelman's call for the abolition of all forms of female circumcision is a clear example of this cultural imperialism. This misunderstanding is also evident in ongoing discussions of female circumcision on the internet and in various journals.

In her discussion of female circumcision, Kopelman, a professor of medical humanities, attacks the cultural relativism theory. She argues that certain moral absolutes apply across the board to all cultures and that these principles clearly dictate that all forms of female circumcision should be banned regardless of its particular form and its symbolic role as a rite of passage in some African cultures. She maintains that the reasons given to explain why these rituals exist have no validity or value. For her, female circumcision falls in the same category as murder of the innocent and therefore should be totally banned.

I speak as an educator who understands the symbolism of the African rites of passage very well because I am part of one African culture in which this educational rite of passage is practiced. I find no evidence in Kopelman's arguments to indicate that she has any understanding of or appreciation for objective cross-cultural, intercultural, and multicultural interpretations. Her arguments are a classic example of how most westerners, rooted in the cultures of Europe and North America, so easily assume the role of dictating and imposing their morality on non-westerners without offering any viable alternative or accommodation. I think this is a way of saying that the people who have practiced these and other rituals for thousands of years before and after coming in contact with westerners, must abolish their culture and be assimilated into the dominant western Euro-American value and moral system, even though—and this is one of my major arguments—the western Euro-American culture which she seeks to impose on all others has very few if any educational culturally-based rites of passage for their youth. Barring marriage and death rituals, it is practically devoid of all rites of passage.

Most of the traditional education of African boys and girls for adulthood is informal. However, initiation rites, such as female circumcision, can be considered formal because they occur in a public community setting with specific symbolic activities and ceremonies, which differ according to the individual society. In those cultures where female circumcision is practiced, this community-based ritual is a formal recognition that the girl has successfully completed her preparation for womanhood and is ready for marriage. (The examples I cite below are mostly from the Kamba and Gikuyu people and Bantu ethnic groups.)

An African child's education for adulthood is matched with its cognitive development and readiness, and may begin anywhere between ages 4 and 12. Young girls are taught the skills of a woman, learning to cook, manage a home and handle other chores related to their domestic responsibilities. They are also taught the social importance of these responsibilities in terms of women's role as the pillars of society. They learn respect for their elders and their lineage, how to communicate without being offensive, an appreciation of their tribal or clan laws and their ethnic identity. An African child's education for adult responsibilities includes learning about their sexuality and the taboos of their culture related to sexual relationships. Such taboos include sexual abstinence until marriage and ways of dealing with temptations. Girls learn who they should and should not marry, how to make love to a man while enjoying themselves, how to avoid pregnancy because there are terrible consequences if one becomes pregnant before marriage, and also how to avoid divorce for irresponsible reasons. In our cultures, grandparents and aunts are usually responsible for educating girls for womanhood. Boys are given similar gender appropriate education in their youthful years.

Depending on the particular tribal culture, completion of this educational process is certified by a formal ritual such as female circumcision. Both the educational process and the formal ritual are essential because together they prepare the boy or girl for marriage. Without this education and a declaration of adulthood provided by a formal ritual capping the education, one is not eligible for marriage and is still considered a child.

I strongly disagree with Kopelman's position that *all* forms of female circumcision should be banned. I do agree, however, with her call for a ban on any mutilation and/or infibulation that involves cutting or severing of any part of a female genitalia for whatever reasons given, when this is known to result in any health or fertility complication or disorder whether minor or major.

My proposed solution stems from an understanding of the symbolic function female circumcision plays in the passage of an African girl into womanhood, and the reinforcement this ritual cutting plays in affirming the responsibilities of the African male. Kopelman's argument is based on a total distortion of the vital function female circumcision plays in the education girls from some African traditions need in their transition to womanhood. The reasons Kopelman cites are widely accepted by non-Africans (and some Africans) who do not truly understand or appreciate the depths of African rites of passage. I have provided details on this distortion elsewhere, in an article published in the *Journal of Black Studies* on "Demythologization and Demystification of African Initiation Rites: A Positive and Meaningful Education Aspect Heading for Extinction." In that article I pointed out the stereotypes critics of the African rites of passage use in misinterpreting this practice. Most of the stereotyped arguments do not acknowledge the considerable education that precedes the circumcision ceremony. This education provides an essential base of knowledge for the young woman to make the transition from childhood to adulthood. This education incorporates sex education, discipline, moral foundation, and gender awareness, a rare aspect in the socialization of today's youth in the United States of America.

My argument is that the education that precedes female circumcision enhances the psychological and social aspects that help shape the identity of African womanhood. This will be lost if the ritual is discontinued. These rites of passage provide a foundation of one's entire life which involves the awareness of the rules of the society and philosophy that guides such rules. This foundation provides young women—and men—with the essence of who they are and the framework of what they aspire to be. It provides the young person with confidence, efficacy and self-respect, which enhances the capacity to respect and value others as human beings. After this lesson, it is hard for the young person to take someone else's life or his/her own, a common occurrence in western societies. It also establishes ownership of property, beginning with the gifts the initiates receive. This leads to developing responsible management skills needed to survive throughout a woman's life. The initiation and the knowledge achieved before and after circumcision give a young woman (or man) a sense of belonging or permanence. Consequently, one is very unlikely to find a young initiate feeling alienated from her or his society as we see in today's societies where children and teens find their identity in joining gangs or cults. Even in Africa today teenage pregnancies and youth violence, which were unheard of in precolonial times, are on the rise. Unfortunately these pregnancies are mostly caused by older men with teenage girls. Before the colonial powers began their campaign against African rites of passage, teen pregnancies were rare because both the teenagers and the older men knew that it was taboo to have sex before marriage and to have children one is not going to be responsible for.

Stereotypical Reasons Given by Kopelman and Others

Kopelman begins her argument for banning all female circumcision by citing several studies conducted by people who come from places where female infibulation and genital mutilation are widely practiced. Using these studies, she lists five reasons she attributes to those seeking to justify this practice: (1) This ritual satisfies a religious requirement, (2) It preserves group identity, (3) It helps maintain cleanliness, (4) It preserves virginity and family honor and prevents immorality, and (5) It furthers marriage goals, including greater sexual pleasure. Invalid as these reasons may be in supporting the morality and acceptability of female circumcision, the problem is that they are common "straw men" arguments set up by opponents of all female circumcision because they are easily refuted. In focusing on these stereotyped and culturally biased reasons, Kopelman and other critics totally ignore and fail to deal with the main purpose of why the circumcision ritual is performed by most Africans.

Of course, anyone who is presented with these five superficial arguments and is not informed about the true core meaning of female circumcision would be easily convinced that the ritual is barbarous and should be stopped immediately. Kopelman fails to point out why this ritual has prevailed for such a long time. Instead, she focuses on the most brutal and inhumane aspects (infibulation and mutilation), which are practiced by just a few African groups. She refers to these groups as Islamic-influenced peoples, even though she admits that among the few people who practice the extreme version, their practice predates the Islamic era. Nor does she explain which particular group of people or pharonic era first practiced these extremes. This careless reference leads people to forget that there are many other forms of the ritual which have the same symbolic meaning but do not involve the extremes of infibulation or clitoridectomy. These practices are performed safely. Some do not even involve circumcision but scarification for the purpose of shedding a little blood, a symbol of courage that is a universal component of male adolescent rites of passage. It is easy for someone like Kopelman not too see the importance of this symbolism, especially when she does not have any similar positive educational experience with which to compare it. Her argument therefore paints with a broad brush on the diversity within the African continent, and her position takes away the very essence of being of most Africans. Also, like other insensitive commentators on African cultures, she fails to point out how the influence of chastity and preservation of virginity for "man's pleasure" has been introduced in both cultural and religious perspectives from outside black Africa. European missionaries and colonialists, preceded by Arabs, followed the same pattern she adopts. Such attitudes have resulted in many Africans abandoning their traditional ways of life. This has created the many identity crises that Africans experience today.

As Africans have adopted attitudes alien to their culture when they interact with the non-Africans who reject and penalize their practice of traditional rites of passage, identity crises have gripped African societies. Examples of such crises are the increase of violence, teen pregnancies, and genocide, which were rare when the rites of passage were in effect. These crises have culminated in the destruction of the base foundation that guides Africans in conceptualizing who they are as human beings. This destruction of traditional cultures and their rites of passage has also resulted in Africans being viewed as objects of exploitation marginal to European culture, and becoming subjects to be acted upon rather than actors of their own way of life, for example, defining who they are as opposed to being defined by others. Kopelman adds wounds to the deep destruction of African cultures that has been imposed on them through miseducation. Like the colonialists before her, she is driven by hegemony in her value system and judgments of other cultures.

A Culturally Sensitive Alternative

In calling for the total abolition of all forms of female circumcision, Kopelman fails to offer any alternative that might be culturally accepted by both African immigrants and those adhering to the dominant Euro-American values of the United States. Instead of suggesting a substitute ritual that would fulfill the main purpose of female circumcision, Kopelman describes all forms of this varied cultural practice, even the most simple and symbolic, as a brutal ritual. She obviously does not think the people who practice this ritual are capable of making adjustments to end the atrocities and sometimes deadly consequences that frequently accompany this rite when practiced in lands where the majority of people have little or no knowledge of sterile techniques or access to modern medical care. She ignores the possibility that an alternative ritual might be accepted by peoples who have practiced female circumcision for centuries.

Let me cite an example of what I mean by a mutually acceptable form of female circumcision that would respect the ancient traditions of some African immigrants and at the same time avoid all the negative consequences of genital mutilation and infibulation. This simple but elegant alternative emerged from discussions between the staff at one American hospital and a group of Somali and other African refugees who have recently settled in Seattle, Washington, clinging to their traditions and insisting that their daughters undergo the ritual of genital cutting.

The staff at Seattle's Harborview Medical Center faced this problem when refugee mothers were asked before delivery if they wanted their baby circumcised if it was a boy. Some mothers responded, "Yes, and also if it is a girl." The hospital, which has a long history of sensitivity to diverse cultures and customs, convened a committee of doctors to discuss what to do about the requests. The hospital staff proposed a compromise, a simple, symbolic cut in the clitoral hood to draw a couple of drops of blood, which could be used in the ritual to bond the girl with the earth, her family and clan. Despite the sensationalized publicity given to the more brutal forms of genital mutilation and infibulation, this symbolic nicking of the clitoral hood to shed a few drops of blood is in fact what most Africans outside Somalia, the Sudan, and Ethiopia do in their female circumcisions.

However, when this suggested alternative became public knowledge, it threw the liberal city of Seattle into turmoil.

Mazurka Ramsey, an Ethiopian immigrant whose San Jose–based group, Forward USA, seeks to eliminate the ritual completely, asked: "How dare it even cross their mind? What the Somali, what the immigrants like me need is an education, not sensitivity to culture." Unlike Ramsey, who is eager to cast off her cultural heritage and adopt American values, other refugee parents continue to press to have their daughters circumcised, even though the Seattle Somali community has essentially agreed that the practice should be ended.

"You cannot take away the rights of families and women," Hersi Mohamed, a Somali elder, said. "As leaders and elders of the community we cannot force a mother to accept the general idea of the community. She can say, 'I want my girl to have letting of blood.'"

Though this is an issue physicians and hospitals across the country are facing with increasing regularity, Harborview is the only hospital so far to discuss the problem openly as a public health issue, rather than treating it simply as an outdated barbaric rite that should be wiped out and totally banned.

A new federal law, in effect since April 1997, sets a prison sentence of up to 5 years for anyone who "circumcises, excises, or infibulates" the genitals of girls under age 18. With some 150,000 females of African origin in the United States having already been cut or facing the possibility of being cut, the compromise suggested by Harborview Hospital makes good sense as an attempt to save girls from the most drastic forms of this ritual.

As the *Chicago Tribune* reported:

> "It would be a small cut to the prepuce, the hood above the clitoris, with no tissue excised, and this would be conducted under local anesthetic for children old enough to understand the procedure and give consent in combination with informed consent of the parents," said Harborview spokeswoman Tina Mankowski.
>
> "We are trying to provide a relatively safe procedure to a population of young women who traditionally have had some horrendous things done to them," she said, but added, "We are not now doing female circumcisions at Harborview, nor are we considering doing female circumcisions."

Whether the proposal would be prohibited by the new law is one of the legal questions being reviewed by the Washington state attorney general. The hospital's medical director will make no final decision on the proposal until the legal review is completed and a community-wide discussion is held, Mankowski said.

The Seattle area is home to about 3,500 members of a fast-growing Somali community. Some Somali and other African immigrants here have made it clear how deeply ingrained the practice is in their cultural and religious views.

Somali men and women told *The Seattle Times* their daughters would be shamed, dishonored and unmarriageable if they were not cut, an act they believe shows their purity.

They also said that if they could not get it done in the U.S. they would pay the $1,500 fare to fly their daughters to their homeland, where they face the extreme version of the cutting ritual. Some, but not all, of them said a symbolic cut on their daughters would be enough.

Unfortunately, the compromise collapsed when a group of feminists threatened to file a lawsuit charging the hospital staff with violation of the new federal law.

Instead of being creative and flexible like the staff at Harborview Hospital, Kopelman takes a dogmatic culturally-biased stance and calls on us to get rid of a cultural practice that predates European cultures, a custom that provides a foundation for many Africans' cultural identity. In essence, she suggests that Africans should abandon their way of life and become culture-less or ritualless societies just as American society is. When a culture has no meaningful rites of passage for its youth, the young grow up without a sense of belonging, continuity and permanence, an experience of many youth and adults in both contemporary Africa and present American societies. As a result, psychologists and other mental health professionals are needed to provide a substitute ritual and rite of passage for many youth and adults looking for their identity. This search was unnecessary and rare in traditional African societies because they had meaningful rites of passage. Without a good foundation of identity development based on meaningful traditional rites of passage, many recent young immigrants from Africa try to cope or compensate with facial reconstructions, liposuctions, changing of skin color or bleaching (melanin) destruction, self-hate, bulimia, obesity, suicides and other types of self-abuse. Without rituals to confirm their respect for women, immigrant African males may come to treat women as objects as opposed to equal human beings.

The alternative I propose is a careful interpretation of the meaning of other peoples' cultures and examining them from their own perspective before jumping to judgments. Failure to take this approach only makes the situation worse. I therefore propose an alternative of just nicking the clitoris enough to perform the symbolic rituals. This would be preceded by the most important part, the education of a girl for the responsibilities of womanhood and a full explanation of the importance of the practice. This nicking would of course be done in a sanitized condition by a licensed physician. A careful analysis, as free of cultural bias as possible, should allow the continuation of many rites of passage that are an ancient part of immigrant cultures.

I also suggest that before we make sweeping generalizations about cultural practices, we should try to look into the perspective of the people we are trying to critique. Some practices may be a little difficult to understand, but with a careful, sensitive approach, it may be simpler than one might think. A great way to attempt to understand others is to learn their language as an avenue to a better understanding of the values and philosophical perspective. This is close to "walking in someone else's shoes," the best practice in cross-cultural and inter-cultural awareness.

POSTSCRIPT

Should Female
Circumcision Be Banned?

Sociologists and cultural anthropologists talk about "enculturation" as the process whereby people from one society and culture migrate from their homeland to another place where they have to adjust to a new culture with different values, attitudes, and behaviors.

Enculturation is a two-sided process. The obvious side involves the adjustments that the immigrants must make as they become acquainted with and part of the new society. The immigrants slowly, sometimes painfully, adjust their attitudes, behaviors, and values to accommodate the dominant majority society in which they are one of perhaps many minorities. They also gradually adopt some of the majority values and behaviors, even as they modify their own traditions. Sometimes, to avoid conflict, they may conceal from outsiders some of their more "unusual" attitudes and behaviors— "unusual" meaning unfamiliar to the majority—to avoid being singled out and discriminated against.

The less obvious side of enculturation is the inevitable adjustments that occur among people in the majority culture as they encounter and interact with minority immigrants who are in the process of moving into the mainstream and becoming part of the general culture. The issue of female genital cutting is typical of this process.

In late 1997 a report from Kenya illustrated the advantages of cultural sensitivity and the need to avoid imposing our values on other cultures. This report was published by Maendeleo ya Wanawake, the Kenyan national women's organization, and the Seattle, Washington–based Program for Appropriate Technology in Health, a nonprofit international organization for women's and children's health. They reported that a growing number of rural Kenyan families are turning to a new ritual called *Ntanira na Mugambo,* or "Circumcision Through Words." Developed by several Kenyan and international nongovernmental agencies working together for six years, "Circumcision Through Words" brings young girls together for a week of seclusion during which they learn traditional teachings about their coming roles as women, parents, and adults in the community, as well as more modern messages about personal health, reproductive issues, hygiene, communications skills, self-esteem, and dealing with peer pressure. A community celebration of song, dance, and feasting affirms the girls and their new place in the community.

As more and more immigrants enter the United States and become part of its ethnic and cultural diversity, the challenges of enculturation are likely to become more complex and demanding. Hence the importance of understanding the current debate over female circumcision. Most articles on the subject denounce the practice and call for a complete ban on any form of female circumcision. This side has now been canonized by enactment of the federal ban. As of late 1997 only P. Masila Mutisya has dared to raise the possibility of some kind of accommodation. What do you think of this seemingly one-sided debate?

Suggested Readings

R. Abcaria, "Rite or Wrong: Female Circumcisions Are Still Performed on African Continent," *Fayetteville Observer Times* (June 14, 1993).

A. M. A'Haleem, "Claiming Our Bodies and Our Rights: Exploring Female Circumcision as an Act of Violence," in M. Schuler, ed., *Freedom From Violence: Women's Strategies From Around the World* (Widbooks, 1992).

M. B. Assad, "Female Circumcision in Egypt: Social Implications, Current Research, and Prospects for Change," *Studies in Family Planning* (January 1980).

T. Brune, "Compromise Plan on Circumcision of Girls Gets Little Support," *Chicago Tribune* (October 28, 1996).

E. Dorkenoo, *Cutting the Rose: Female Genital Mutilation—The Practice and Its Prevention* (Minority Rights Group, 1994).

O. Koso-Thomas, *The Circumcision of Women: A Strategy for Eradication* (Zed Books, 1992).

M. Mutisya, "Demythologization and Demystification of African Initiation Rites: A Positive and Meaningful Educational Aspect Heading for Extinction," *Journal of Black Studies* (September 1996).

C. M. Nangoli, *No More Lies About Africa: Here Is the Truth From an African* (African Heritage Publishers, 1986).

ISSUE 17

Should the FCC Restrict Broadcast "Indecency"?

YES: Federal Communications Commission, from *FCC Consumer Facts: Obscene, Profane, and Indecent Broadcasts,* http://www.fcc.gov/eb/ Orders/2001/fcc01090.doc (2001)

NO: Judith Levine, from "Is 'Indecency' Harmful to Minors?" An Adaptation of an Article from *Extra! Fairness in Accuracy and Reporting (FAIR)* (October 2004)

ISSUE SUMMARY

YES: The Federal Communications Commission (FCC), a U.S. government agency charged with regulating the content of the broadcast airways, including television and radio, outlines what it defines as "indecent" broadcast material and describes its enforcement policy.

NO: Author Judith Levine traces the history of censorship in the United States, and argues that much of what the FCC has determined is "indecent" sexual speech is not, in fact, harmful to children.

In January 2004, about 100 million viewers tuned in to CBS to watch the New England Patriots defeat the Carolina Panthers in Superbowl XXXVIII. But talk at water coolers, breakfast tables, and classrooms around the country the next day had little to do with the heroics of quarterback Tom Brady, nor about Adam Vinatieri's 41-yard field goal with four seconds left. Instead, the nation was talking about performer Janet Jackson's breast. During the half-time performance, Jackson's breast was exposed by co-star Justin Timberlake, revealing a nearly bare breast, with her nipple covered by a star-shaped pastie. The incident caused a national uproar. Nielson ratings estimated that about one in five children between the ages of 2 and 11 witnessed the event. (And those who did not see it live had ample time so see the incident ad infinitum in the news media coverage that followed.) It remained a feature news story for days and then weeks, as commentators and news analysts examined who was responsible, and how severely they should be punished. CBS and Jackson apologized, Timberlake called it an unfortunate "wardrobe malfunction," and much of America wondered what effect the incident would have on children.

Meanwhile, the Federal Communications Commission (FCC) was not amused. The governmental agency charged with enforcing "indecency" violations reported having received more than a half million complaints. The FCC began holding hearings about increasing the monetary fines and proceeded to scrutinize the alleged violations of other performers and media outlets. When the FCC fined Clear Channel Communications $495,000 for sexual content aired in six Howard Stern shows, Clear Channel dropped Stern from all its radio outlets. The fine was significant as it marked a departure from the FCC's standard practice of fining. In this case, each "indecent" utterance was fined individually; previously, the FCC would fine an entire program the maximum $27,500, regardless of the number of violations on each show.

What is "indecent"? The FCC defines it as "language or material that, in context, depicts or describes, in terms patently offensive as measured by contemporary community broadcast standards for the broadcast medium, sexual or excretory organs or activities." Such material is protected as free speech by the First Amendment. However, the FCC is empowered to restrict the times of day that such material can be aired, under the premise that children need to be protected from indecency. Indecent material may not be aired between 6 a.m. and 10 p.m. Likewise, "profanity" may not be aired during these times. "Profane" material includes "personally reviling epithets naturally tending to provoke violent resentment or denoting language so grossly offensive to members of the public who actually hear it as to amount to a nuisance."

Still, the definitions of "indecency" and "profanity" are quite subjective and may require further clarification. The same is true for material that is "obscene," which may not be aired at all. In the following essays, the FCC elaborates on its definitions of indecency, profanity, and obscenity, giving case examples to illustrate its enforcement policy more clearly. In response, Judith Levine argues that the very premise of restricting indecent material is flawed, as there is no evidence that sexual speech harms children.

YES

**Federal Communications
Commission**

Enforcement Policies Regarding
Broadcast Indecency

I. Introduction

The Commission issues this Policy Statement to provide guidance to the broadcast industry regarding our case law and our enforcement policies with respect to broadcast indecency. This document is divided into five parts. Section I gives an overview of this document. Section II provides the statutory basis for indecency regulation and discusses the judicial history of such regulation. Section III describes the analytical approach the Commission uses in making indecency determinations. This section also presents a comparison of selected rulings intended to illustrate the various factors that have proved significant in resolving indecency complaints. The cited material refers only to broadcast indecency actions and does not include any discussion of case law concerning indecency enforcement actions in other services regulated by this agency such as cable, telephone, or amateur radio. Section IV describes the Commission's broadcast indecency enforcement process. Section V is the conclusion.

II. Statutory Basis/Judicial History

It is a violation of federal law to broadcast obscene or indecent programming. Specifically, Title 18 of the United States Code, Section 1464 (18 U.S.C. § 1464), prohibits the utterance of "any obscene, indecent, or profane language by means of radio communication." Congress has given the Federal Communications Commission the responsibility for administratively enforcing 18 U.S.C. § 1464. In doing so, the Commission may revoke a station license, impose a monetary forfeiture, or issue a warning for the broadcast of indecent material.

The FCC's enforcement policy has been shaped by a number of judicial and legislative decisions. In particular, because the Supreme Court has determined that obscene speech is not entitled to First Amendment protection, obscene speech cannot be broadcast at any time. In contrast, indecent speech is protected by the First Amendment, and thus, the government must both identify a compelling interest for any regulation it may impose on indecent speech and choose the least restrictive means to further that interest. Even under this restrictive standard, the courts have consistently upheld the Commission's authority to regulate indecent speech, albeit with certain limitations.

From the *FCC Consumer Facts: Obscene, Profane, and Indecent Broadcasts,* 2001. Federal Communications Commission. Notes omitted.

FCC v. Pacifica Foundation provides the judicial foundation for FCC indecency enforcement. In that case, the Supreme Court held that the government
could constitutionally regulate indecent broadcasts. In addition, the Court
quoted the Commission's definition of indecency with apparent approval.
The definition, "language or material that, in context, depicts or describes, in
terms patently offensive as measured by contemporary community standards
for the broadcast medium, sexual or excretory activities or organs," has
remained substantially unchanged since the time of the *Pacifica* decision.
Moreover, the definition has been specifically upheld against constitutional
challenges in the *Action for Children's Television (ACT)* cases in the D.C. Circuit
Court of Appeals. Further, in *Reno v. ACLU*, the U.S. Supreme Court struck
down an indecency standard for the Internet but did not question the constitutionality of our broadcast indecency standard. Rather, the Court recognized
the "special justifications for regulation of the broadcast media that are not
applicable to other speakers."

Although the D.C. Circuit approved the FCC's definition of indecency in
the *ACT* cases, it also established several restrictive parameters on FCC
enforcement. The court's decisions made clear that the FCC had to identify
the compelling government interests that warranted regulation and also
explain how the regulations were narrowly tailored to further those interests.
In *ACT I*, the court rejected as inadequately supported the Commission's
determination that it could reach and regulate indecent material aired as late
as 11:00 p.m., and remanded the cases involved to the Commission for proceedings to ascertain the proper scope of the "safe harbor" period, that is, the
time during which indecent speech may be legally broadcast. Before the Commission could comply with the court's remand order, however, Congress inter-
vened and instructed the Commission to adopt rules that enforced the
provisions on a "24 hour per day basis." The rule adopted to implement this
legislative mandate was stayed and was ultimately vacated by the court in *ACT II*
as unconstitutional. In 1992, responding to the decision in *ACT II*, Congress
directed the Commission to adopt a new "safe harbor"—generally 12 midnight
to 6:00 a.m., but 10:00 p.m. to 6:00 a.m. for certain noncommercial stations.
The Commission implemented this statutory scheme in January 1993. Before
this rule could become effective, however, the court stayed it pending judicial
review. In 1995, the D.C. Circuit, *en banc*, held in *ACT III* that there was not a
sufficient justification in the record to support a preferential "safe harbor"
period for noncommercial stations and that the more restrictive midnight to
6:00 a.m. "safe harbor" for commercial stations was therefore unconstitutional. The court concluded, however, that the less restrictive 10:00 p.m. to
6:00 a.m. "safe harbor" had been justified as a properly tailored means of
vindicating the government's compelling interest in the welfare of children
and remanded the case to the Commission "with instructions to limit its ban
on the broadcasting of indecent programs to the period from 6:00 a.m. to
10:00 p.m." The Commission implemented the court's instructions by appropriately conforming. These changes became effective on August 28, 1995.

Thus, outside the 10:00 p.m. to 6:00 a.m. safe harbor, the courts have
approved regulation of broadcast indecency to further the compelling

government interests in supporting parental supervision of children and more generally its concern for children's well being. The principles of enforcement articulated below are intended to further these interests.

III. Indecency Determinations

A. Analytical Approach

Indecency findings involve at least two fundamental determinations. First, the material alleged to be indecent must fall within the subject matter scope of our indecency definition—that is, the material must describe or depict sexual or excretory organs or activities.

Second, the broadcast must be *patently offensive* as measured by contemporary community standards for the broadcast medium. In applying the "community standards for the broadcast medium" criterion, the Commission has stated:

The determination as to whether certain programming is patently offensive is not a local one and does not encompass any particular geographic area. Rather, the standard is that of an average broadcast viewer or listener and not the sensibilities of any individual complainant.

In determining whether material is patently offensive, the *full context* in which the material appeared is critically important. It is not sufficient, for example, to know that explicit sexual terms or descriptions were used, just as it is not sufficient to know only that no such terms or descriptions were used. Explicit language in the context of a *bona fide* newscast might not be patently offensive, while sexual innuendo that persists and is sufficiently clear to make the sexual meaning inescapable might be. Moreover, contextual determinations are necessarily highly fact-specific, making it difficult to catalog comprehensively all of the possible contextual factors that might exacerbate or mitigate the patent offensiveness of particular material. An analysis of Commission case law reveals that various factors have been consistently considered relevant in indecency determinations. By comparing cases with analogous analytical structures, but different outcomes, we hope to highlight how these factors are applied in varying circumstances and the impact of these variables on a finding of patent offensiveness.

B. Case Comparisons

The principal factors that have proved significant in our decisions to date are: (1) the *explicitness or graphic nature* of the description or depiction of sexual or excretory organs or activities; (2) whether the material *dwells on or repeats at length* descriptions of sexual or excretory organs or activities; (3) *whether the material appears to pander or is used to titillate*, or *whether the material appears to have been presented for its shock value*. In assessing all of the factors, and particularly the third factor, the overall context of the broadcast in which the disputed material appeared is critical. Each indecency case presents its own particular mix of these, and possibly other, factors, which must be balanced to ultimately determine whether the material is patently offensive and therefore indecent. No single factor generally provides the basis for an indecency finding. To illustrate the noted factors, however, and to provide a sense of the weight these considerations have carried in specific factual contexts, a comparison of cases has been organized to provide examples of decisions in which each of these factors has played a particularly significant role, whether exacerbating or mitigating, in the indecency determination made.

It should be noted that the brief descriptions and excerpts from broadcasts that are reproduced in this document are intended only as a research tool and should not be taken as a meaningful selection of words and phrases to be evaluated for indecency purposes without the fuller context that the tapes or transcripts provide. The excerpts from broadcasts used in this section have often been shortened or compressed. In order to make the excerpts more readable, however, we have frequently omitted any indication of these ellipses from the text. Moreover, in cases where material was included in a complaint but not specifically cited in the decision based on the complaint, we caution against relying on the omission as if it were of decisional significance. For example, if portions of a voluminous transcript are the object of an enforcement action, those portions not included are not necessarily deemed not indecent. The omissions may be the result of an editing process that attempted to highlight the most significant material within its context. No inference should be drawn regarding the material deleted.

1. Explicitness/Graphic Description Versus Indirectness/Implication
The more explicit or graphic the description or depiction, the greater the likelihood that the material will be considered patently offensive. Merely because the material consists of double entendre or innuendo, however, does not preclude an indecency finding if the sexual or excretory import is unmistakable.

Following are examples of decisions where the explicit/graphic nature of the description of sexual or excretory organs or activities played a central role in the determination that the broadcast was indecent.

WYSP(FM), Philadelphia, PA: "Howard Stern Show"

> *God, my testicles are like down to the floor . . . you could really have a party with these . . . Use them like Bocci balls.*
> *(As part of a discussion of lesbians) I mean to go around porking other girls with vibrating rubber products . . .*
> *Have you ever had sex with an animal? Well, don't knock it. I was sodomized by Lambchop.*

Indecent—Warning Issued. Excerpted material (only some of which is cited above) consisted of "vulgar and lewd references to the male genitals and to masturbation and sodomy broadcast in the context of . . . 'explicit references to masturbation, ejaculation, breast size, penis size, sexual intercourse, nudity, urination, oral-genital contact, erections, sodomy, bestiality, menstruation and testicles.'". . .

KROQ(FM), Los Angeles, CA: "You Suck" Song

I know you're really proud cause you think you're well hung but I think its time you learn how to use your tongue. You say you want things to be even and you want things to be fair but you're afraid to get your teeth caught in my pubic hair. If you're lying there expecting me to suck your dick, you're going to have to give me more than just a token lick. . . . Go down baby, you suck, lick it hard and move your tongue around. If you're worried about babies, you can lower your risk, by giving me that special cunnilingus kiss. . . . you can jiggle your tongue on my clit. Don't worry about making me have an orgasm. . . . You asshole, you shit. I know it's a real drag, to suck my cunt when I'm on the rag. . . . You tell me it's gross to suck my yeast infection. How do you think I feel when I gag on your erection.

Indecent—NAL Issued. (graphically and explicitly describes sexual and excretory organs or activities).

. . . Less explicit material and material that relies principally on innuendo to convey a sexual or excretory meaning have also been cited by the Commission as actionably indecent where the sexual or excretory meaning was unmistakable. . . .

KGB-FM, San Diego, CA: "Candy Wrapper" Song

I whipped out my Whopper and whispered, Hey, Sweettart, how'd you like to Crunch on my Big Hunk for a Million Dollar Bar? Well, she immediately went down on my Tootsie Roll and you know, it was like pure Almond Joy. I couldn't help but grab her delicious Mounds, . . . this little Twix had the Red Hots. . . . as my Butterfinger went up her tight little Kit Kat, and she started to scream Oh, Henry! Oh, Henry! Soon she was fondling my Peter Paul, and Zagnuts and I knew it wouldn't be long before I blew my Milk Duds clear to Mars and gave her a taste of the old Milky Way. . . . I said, Look . . . why don't you just take my Whatchamacallit and slip it up your Bit-O-Honey. Oh, what a piece of Juicy Fruit she was too. She screamed Oh, Crackerjack. You're better than the Three Musketeers! as I rammed my Ding Dong up her Rocky Road and into her Peanut Butter Cup. Well, I was giving it to her Good'n Plenty, and all of a sudden, my Starburst. . . . she started to grow a bit Chunky and . . . Sure enough, nine months later, out popped a Baby Ruth.

Indecent—NAL Issued. ("While the passages arguably consist of double entendre and indirect references, the language used in each passage was understandable and clearly capable of a specific sexual meaning and, because of the context, the sexual import was inescapable."); ("notwithstanding the use of candy bar names to symbolize sexual activities, the titillating and pandering nature of the song makes any thought of candy bars peripheral at best"). . . .

KMEL(FM), San Francisco, CA: "Rick Chase Show"; "Blow Me" Song

Blow me, you hardly even know me, just set yourself below me and blow me, tonight. Hey, a handy would certainly be dandy, but it's not enough to slow (unintelligible) me, hey, you gotta blow me all night. Hey, when you pat your lips that way, I want you night and day, when you squeeze my balls so tight. I want to blow my love, hey, with all my might.

Indecent—NAL Issued.   Commission found that the language dwelled on descriptions of sexual organs and activities, "was understandable and clearly capable of a specific sexual meaning and, because of the context, the sexual import was inescapable."

Compare the following case in which the material aired was deemed not to be actionably indecent.

WFBQ(FM)/WNDE(AM), Indianapolis, IN: "Elvis" and "Power, Power, Power"

As you know, you gotta stop the King, but you can't kill him . . . So you talk to Dick Nixon, man you get him on the phone and Dick suggests maybe getting like a mega-Dick to help out, but you know, you remember the time the King ate mega-Dick under the table at a 095 picnic . . . you think about getting mega-Hodgie, but that's no good because you know, the King was a karate dude . . .

Power! Power! Power! Thrust! Thrust! Thrust! First it was Big Foot, the monster car crunching 4x4 pickup truck. Well, move over, Big Foot! Here comes the most massive power-packed monster ever! It's Big Peter! (Laughter) Big Peter with 40,000 Peterbilt horsepower under the hood. It's massive! Big Peter! Formerly the Big Dick's Dog Wiener Mobile. Big Peter features a 75-foot jacked up monster body. See Big Peter crush and enter a Volvo. (Laughter) . . . strapped himself in the cockpit and put Big Peter through its paces. So look out Big Foot! Big Peter is coming! Oh my God! It's coming! Big Peter! (Laughter)

Not Indecent.   The licensee provided a fuller transcript of the cited "Elvis" excerpt and explained the context in which it was aired, arguing that no sexual meaning was intended and that no such meaning would be reasonably understood from the material taken as a whole. The licensee also explained the regional humor of the Power, Power, Power excerpt and the context in which it was broadcast. The Mass Media Bureau held that the material was not indecent because the "surrounding contexts do not appear to provide a background against which a sexual import is inescapable."

In assessing explicitness, the Commission also looks to the audibility of the material as aired. If the material is difficult or impossible to understand, it may not be actionably indecent. However, difficulty in understanding part of the material or an attempt to obscure objectionable material will not preclude a finding of indecency where at least some of the material is recognizable or understandable.

KGB-FM, San Diego, CA: "Sit on My Face" Song

Sit on my face and tell me that you love me. I'll sit on your face and tell you I love you, too. I love to hear you moralize when I'm between your thighs. You blow me away. Sit on my face and let me embrace you. I'll sit on your face and then I'll love you (?) truly. Life can be fine, if we both sixty-nine. If we sit on faces (?) the ultimate place to play (?). We'll be blown away.

Indecent—NAL Issued. The song was found to be actionably indecent despite English accent and "ambient noise" because the lyrics were sufficiently understandable.

WWKX(FM), Woonsocket, RI: "Real Deal Mike Neil Show"

Douche bag, hey what's up, fu(Bleep)ck head? . . . You his fuck (Bleep) ho or what? You his fuck (Bleep) bitch man, where you suck his dick every night? . . . Suck some di(Bleep)ck make some money for Howard and pay your pimp okay?

Indecent—NAL Issued. Material was found to be actionably indecent despite attempt to obscure objectionable language because "editing was ineffective and merely resulted in a "bleep" in the middle of clearly recognizable words (or in some cases a "bleep" after the word)." The Mass Media Bureau held that "[b]ecause the words were recognizable, notwithstanding the editing," they were indecent within the context used in this broadcast.

2. Dwelling/Repetition versus Fleeting Reference

Repetition of and persistent focus on sexual or excretory material have been cited consistently as factors that exacerbate the potential offensiveness of broadcasts. In contrast, where sexual or excretory references have been made once or have been passing or fleeting in nature, this characteristic has tended to weigh against a finding of indecency.

WXTB(FM), Clearwater, FL: "Bubba, The Love Sponge"

Could you take the phone and rub it on you Chia Pet? Oh, let me make sure nobody is around. Okay, hang on a second (Rubbing noise). Okay I did it. . . . Now that really your little beaver? That was mine. Your what? That was my little beaver? Oh I love when a girl says beaver. Will you say it again for me honey please? It was my little beaver. . . . Will you say, Bubba come get my beaver? Bubba, would come get my little beaver? . . . tell me that doesn't do something for you. That is pretty sexy. . . . bring the beaver. It will be with me. We got beaver chow. I can't wait, will you say it for me one more time? Say what? My little beaver or Bubba come get my little beaver? Okay, Bubba come get my beaver. Will you say, Bubba come hit my beaver? Will you say it? Bubba, come hit my beaver. That is pretty sexy, absolutely. Oh, my God, beaver.

Indecent—NAL Issued.

WXTB(FM), Clearwater, FL: "Bubba, The Love Sponge"

Well, it was nice big fart. I'm feeling very gaseous at this point but there, so far has been no enema reaction, as far as. There's been no, there's been no expelling? No expelling. But I feel mucus rising. . . . Can't go like. (Grunting sound) Pushing, all

I keep doing is putting out little baby farts. . . . on the toilet ready to go. . . . Push it, strain it. It looks normal. Just average, average. Little rabbit one. Little rabbit pellets. I imagine maybe, we'll break loose. Push hard Cowhead. I'm pushing, I got veins popping out of my forehead. Go ahead, those moles might pop right off. You can tell he's pushing. I'm out of breath. One more, last one. One big push.

Indecent—NAL Issued.   The cited material dwells on excretory activities and the Commission found it to be patently offensive.

Compare the following cases where material was found not indecent because it was fleeting and isolated.

WYBB(FM), Folly Beach, SC: "The Morning Show"

The hell I did, I drove mother-fucker, oh. Oh.

Not Indecent.   The "broadcast contained only a fleeting and isolated utterance which, within the context of live and spontaneous programming, does not warrant a Commission sanction."

KPRL(AM)/KDDB(FM), Paso Robles, CA: News Announcer Comment

Oops, fucked that one up.

Not Indecent.   The "news announcer's use of single expletive" does not "warrant further Commission consideration in light of the isolated and accidental nature of the broadcast."

In contrast, even relatively fleeting references may be found indecent where other factors contribute to a finding of patent offensiveness. Examples of such factors illustrated by the following cases include broadcasting references to sexual activities with children and airing material that, although fleeting, is graphic or explicit.

3. . . . *Presented in a Pandering or Titillating Manner or for Shock Value*

The apparent purpose for which material is presented can substantially affect whether it is deemed to be patently offensive as aired. In adverse indecency findings, the Commission has often cited the pandering or titillating character of the material broadcast as an exacerbating factor. Presentation for the shock value of the language used has also been cited. As Justice Powell stated in his opinion in the Supreme Court's decision affirming the Commission's determination that the broadcast of a comedy routine was indecent, "[T]he language employed is, to most people, vulgar and offensive. It was chosen specifically for this quality, and it was repeated over and over as a sort of verbal shock treatment." On the other hand, the manner and purpose of a presentation may well preclude an indecency determination even though other factors, such as explicitness, might weigh in favor of an indecency finding. In the following cases, the decisions looked to the manner of presentation as a factor supporting a finding of indecency.

KLOL(FM), Houston, TX: "Stevens & Pruett Show"

Sex survey lines are open. Today's question, it's a strange question and we hope we have a lot of strange answers. What makes your hiney parts tingle? When my husband gets down there and goes (lips noise). . . . I love oral sex. . . . Well, my boyfriend tried to put Hershey kisses inside of me and tried to lick it out and it took forever for him to do it.

Indecent—NAL Issued. Explicit description in a program that focused on sexual activities in a lewd, vulgar, pandering and titillating manner.

WEBN(FM), Cincinnati, OH: "Bubba, The Love Sponge"

All I can say is, if you were listening to the program last night you heard Amy and Stacy . . . come in here, little lesbians that they are. Little University of Cincinnati ho's and basically that we could come over and watch them. We got over to the house. . . . They start making out a little bit. They go to bed. They get, they start, they're starting like a mutual 69 on the bed. Guido all of a sudden whips it out. . . . Rather than take care of each other . . . Guido is like knee deep with the butch bitch and all of a sudden here is the fem bitch looking at me. Hot. I get crazy. I hook up a little bit. Then Guido says, hey, I done got mine, how about we switching? So I went into the private bedroom with the butch bitch and then got another one.

Indecent—NAL Issued. . . . In determining whether broadcasts are presented in a pandering or titillating manner, the context of the broadcast is particularly critical. Thus, even where language is explicit, the matter is graphic, or where there is intense repetition of vulgar terms, the presentation may not be pandering or titillating, and the broadcast may not be found actionably indecent.

. . . WABC-TV, New York, NY: "Oprah Winfrey Show" (How to Make Romantic Relations with Your Mate Better)

Okay, for all you viewers out there with children watching, we're doing a show today on how to make romantic relations with your mate better. Otherwise known as s-e-x. . . . I'm very aware there are a number of children who are watching and so, we're going to do our best to keep this show rated "G" but just in case, you may want to send your kids to a different room. And we'll pause for a moment while you do that. . . . According to experts and recent sex surveys the biggest complaints married women have about sex are . . . their lovemaking is boring . . . American wives all across the country have confessed to using erotic aids to spice up their sex life and . . . thousands of women say they fantasize while having sex with their husbands. . . . And most women say they are faking it in the bedroom.

    [Quiz:] I like the way my partner looks in clothing. . . . I like the way my partner looks naked. . . . I like the way my partner's skin feels. . . . I like the way my partner tastes. . . .

    [Psychologist and panelists:] Do you know that you can experience orgasm, have you experienced that by yourself? No, I have not . . . Okay, one of

the things that, well, you all know what I'm talking about. . . . You need to at least know how to make your body get satisfied by yourself. Because if you don't know how to do it, how is he going to figure it out? He doesn't have your body parts, he doesn't know.

Not Indecent.   Subject matter alone does not render material indecent. Thus, while material may be offensive to some people, in context, it might not be actionably indecent.

. . . WSMC-FM, Collegedale, TN: "All Things Considered" [National Public Radio]

Mike Schuster has a report and a warning. The following story contains some very rough language. [Excerpt from wiretap of telephone conversation in which organized crime figure John Gotti uses "fuck" or "fucking" 10 times in 7 sentences (110 words).]

Not Indecent.   Explicit language was integral part of a bona fide news story concerning organized crime; the material aired was part of a wiretap recording used as evidence in Gotti's widely reported trial. The Commission explained that it did "not find the use of such [coarse] words in a legitimate news report to have been gratuitous, pandering, titillating or otherwise "patently offensive" as that term is used in our indecency definition."
    . . . Compare the following cases where licensees unsuccessfully claimed that, because of the context of the broadcasts (*i.e.,* alleged news stories), the broadcasts were not pandering.

KSD-FM, St. Louis, MO: "The Breakfast Club"

I've got this Jessica Hahn interview here in Playboy. I just want to read one little segment . . . the good part.
    "[Jim Bakker] has managed to completely undress me and he's sitting on my chest. He's really pushing himself, I mean the guy was forcing himself. He put his penis in my mouth . . . I'm crying, tears are coming, and he is letting go. The guy came in my mouth. My neck hurts, my throat hurts, my head feels like it's going to explode, but he's frustrated and determined, determined enough that within minutes he's inside me and he's on top and he's holding my arms. He's just into this, he's inside me now. Saying, when you help the shepherd, you're helping the sheep."
    (followed by air personality making sheep sounds) This was rape. Yeah, don't you ever come around here Jim Bakker or we're going to cut that thing off.

Indecent—NAL Issued.   The broadcast contained excerpts from a *Playboy* magazine account of the alleged rape of Jessica Hahn by the Rev. Jim Bakker. The licensee explained the broadcast was newsworthy "banter by two on-air personalities reflecting public concern, criticism, and curiosity about a public figure whose reputedly notorious behavior was a widespread media issue at the time." Responding to the licensee's argument, the Mass Media Bureau stated that "although the program . . . arguably concerned an incident that was at the time 'in the news,' the particular material broadcast was not only exceptionally explicit and vulgar, it was . . . presented in a pandering manner. In short, the rendition of the details of the alleged rape was, in context, patently offensive."

. . . KSJO(FM), San Jose, California: Lamont & Tonelli Show

> ". . . she should go up and down the shaft about five times, licking and sucking and on the fifth swirl her tongue around the head before going back down. . . . "
> "Show us how its done" (evidently the guest had some sort of a prop).
> "Well, if this was a real penis, it would have a ****ridge, I would like (sic) around the ridge like this. . . . "
> [laughter, comments such as 'oh yeah, baby'].

Indecent—NAL Issued. The licensee claimed that the program was a clinical discussion of oral sex. The Enforcement Bureau rejected this argument on the grounds that the disc jockeys' comments on her material showed that the material was offered in a pandering and titillating manner. "The disc jockeys' invitation to have Dr. Terry use a prop on a radio program, and their laughter and statements (such as "oh yeah, baby") while she conducted that demonstration showed that the material was intended to be pandering and titillating as opposed to a clinical discussion of sex."

The absence of a pandering or titillating nature, however, will not necessarily prevent an indecency determination, as illustrated by the following case.

WIOD(AM), Miami, FL: "Penis Envy" Song

> If I had a penis, . . . I'd stretch it and stroke it and shove it at smarties . . . I'd stuff it in turkeys on Thanksgiving day. . . . If I had a penis, I'd run to my mother, Comb out the hair and compare it to brother. I'd lance her, I'd knight her, my hands would indulge. Pants would seem tighter and buckle and bulge. (Refrain) A penis to plunder, a penis to push, 'Cause one in the hand is worth one in the bush. A penis to love me, a penis to share, To pick up and play with when nobody's there. . . . If I had a penis, . . . I'd force it on females, I'd pee like a fountain. If I had a penis, I'd still be a girl, but I'd make much more money and conquer the world.

Indecent—NAL Issued. The Mass Media Bureau found the material to be patently offensive. In response to the licensee's assertion that this song was not pandering or titillating and therefore should not be considered indecent, the Bureau stated: "We believe . . . that it is not necessary to find that the material is pandering or titillating in order to find that its references to sexual activities and organs are patently offensive. (Citations omitted.) Moreover, humor is no more an absolute defense to indecency . . . than is music or any other one component of communication."

IV. Enforcement Process

The Commission does not independently monitor broadcasts for indecent material. Its enforcement actions are based on documented complaints of indecent broadcasting received from the public. Given the sensitive nature of these cases and the critical role of context in an indecency determination, it is important that the Commission be afforded as full a record as possible to evaluate allegations of indecent programming. In order for a complaint to be considered, our practice is that it must generally include: (1) a full or partial tape or transcript or significant excerpts of the program; (2) the date and time of the broadcast; and (3) the call sign of the station involved. Any tapes or other documentation of the programming supplied by the complainant, of necessity, become part of the Commission's records and cannot be returned. Documented complaints should be directed to the FCC, Investigations and Hearings Division, Enforcement Bureau, 445 Twelfth Street, S.W., Washington, D.C. 20554.

If a complaint does not contain the supporting material described above, or if it indicates that a broadcast occurred during "safe harbor" hours or the material cited does not fall within the subject matter scope of our indecency definition, it is usually dismissed by a letter to the complainant advising of the deficiency. In many of these cases, the station may not be aware that a complaint has been filed.

If, however, the staff determines that a documented complaint meets the subject matter requirements of the indecency definition and the material complained of was aired outside "safe harbor" hours, then the broadcast at issue is evaluated for patent offensiveness. Where the staff determines that the broadcast is not patently offensive, the complaint will be denied. If, however, the staff determines that further enforcement action might be warranted, the Enforcement Bureau, in conjunction with other Commission offices, examines the material and decides upon an appropriate disposition, which might include any of the following: (1) denial of the complaint by staff letter based upon a finding that the material, in context, is not patently offensive and therefore not indecent; (2) issuance of a Letter of Inquiry (LOI) to the licensee seeking further information concerning or an explanation of the circumstances surrounding the broadcast; (3) issuance of a Notice of Apparent Liability (NAL) for monetary forfeiture; and (4) formal referral of the case to the full Commission for its consideration and action. Generally, the last of these alternatives is taken in cases where issues beyond straightforward indecency violations may be involved or where the potential sanction for the indecent programming exceeds the Bureau's delegated forfeiture authority of $25,000.

Where an LOI is issued, the licensee's comments are generally sought concerning the allegedly indecent broadcast to assist in determining whether the material is actionable and whether a sanction is warranted. If it is determined that no further action is warranted, the licensee and the complainant will be so advised. Where a *preliminary* determination is made that the material was aired and was indecent, an NAL is issued. If the Commission previously determined that the broadcast of the same material was indecent, the subsequent broadcast constitutes egregious misconduct and a higher forfeiture amount is warranted.

The licensee is afforded an opportunity to respond to the NAL, a step which is required by statute. Once the Commission or its staff has considered any response by the licensee, it may order payment of a monetary penalty by issuing a Forfeiture Order. Alternatively, if the preliminary finding of violation in the NAL is successfully rebutted by the licensee, the NAL may be rescinded. If a Forfeiture Order is issued, the monetary penalty assessed may either be the same as specified in the NAL or it may be a lesser amount if the licensee has demonstrated that mitigating factors warrant a reduction in forfeiture.

A Forfeiture Order may be appealed by the licensee through the administrative process under several different provisions of the Commission's rules. The licensee also has the legal right to refuse to pay the fine. In such a case, the Commission may refer the matter to the U.S. Department of Justice, which can initiate a trial *de novo* in a U.S. District Court. The trial court may start anew to evaluate the allegations of indecency.

V. Conclusion

The Commission issues this Policy Statement to provide guidance to broadcast licensees regarding compliance with the Commission's indecency regulations. By summarizing the regulations and explaining the Commission's analytical approach to reviewing allegedly indecent material, the Commission provides a framework by which broadcast licensees can assess the legality of airing potentially indecent material. Numerous examples are provided in this document in an effort to assist broadcast licensees. However, this document is not intended to be an all-inclusive summary of every indecency finding issued by the Commission and it should not be relied upon as such. There are many additional cases that could have been cited. Further, as discussed above, the excerpts from broadcasts quoted in this document are intended only as a research tool. A complete understanding of the material, and the Commission's analysis thereof, requires review of the tapes or transcripts and the Commission's rulings thereon.

OBSCENE, PROFANE, AND INDECENT BROADCASTS: FCC CONSUMER FACTS

It's Against the Law

It is a violation of federal law to broadcast **obscene** programming at any time. It is also a violation of federal law to broadcast **indecent** or **profane** programming during certain hours. Congress has given the Federal Communications Commission (FCC) the responsibility for administratively enforcing the law that governs these types of broadcasts. The Commission may revoke a station license, impose a monetary forfeiture, or issue a warning, for the broadcast of obscene or indecent material.

Obscene Broadcasts Are Prohibited at All Times

Obscene speech is not protected by the First Amendment and cannot be broadcast at any time. To be obscene, material must meet a three-prong test:

- An average person, applying contemporary community standards, must find that the material, as a whole, appeals to the prurient interest;
- The material must depict or describe, in a patently offensive way, sexual conduct specifically defined by applicable law; and
- The material, taken as a whole, must lack serious literary, artistic, political, or scientific value.

Indecent Broadcast Restrictions

The FCC has defined broadcast indecency as "language or material that, in context, depicts or describes, in terms patently offensive as measured by contemporary community broadcast standards for the broadcast medium, sexual or excretory organs or activities." Indecent programming contains patently offensive sexual or excretory references that do not rise to the level of obscenity. As such, the courts have held that indecent material is protected by the First Amendment and cannot be banned entirely. It may, however, be restricted in order to avoid broadcast during times of the day when there is a reasonable risk that children may be in the audience.

Consistent with a federal statute and federal court decisions interpreting the indecency statute, the Commission adopted a rule pursuant to which broadcasts—both on television and radio—that fit within the indecency definition and that are aired between 6:00 a.m. and 10:00 p.m. are subject to indecency enforcement action.

Profane Broadcast Restrictions

The FCC has defined profanity as including language that "denot[es] certain of those personally reviling epithets naturally tending to provoke violent resentment or denoting language so grossly offensive to members of the public who actually hear it as to amount to a nuisance."

Like indecency, profane speech is prohibited on broadcast radio and television between the hours of 6 a.m. to 10 p.m.

Enforcement Procedures and Filing Complaints

Enforcement actions in this area are based on documented complaints received from the public about indecent, profane, or obscene broadcasting. The FCC's staff reviews each complaint to determine whether it has sufficient information to suggest that there has been a violation of the obscenity, profanity, or indecency laws. If it appears that a violation may have occurred, the staff will start an investigation by sending a letter of inquiry to the broadcast station. Otherwise, the complaint will be dismissed or denied.

Context

In making indecency and profanity determinations, context is key! The FCC staff must analyze what was actually said during the broadcast, the meaning of what was said, and the context in which it was stated. Accordingly, the FCC asks complainants to provide the following information:

- *Information regarding the details of what was actually said (or depicted) during the allegedly indecent, profane or obscene broadcast.* There is flexibility on how a complainant may provide this information. Complainant may submit a significant excerpt of the program describing what was actually said (or depicted) or a full or partial recording (e.g., tape) or transcript of the material.

  In whatever form the complainant decides provide the information, it must be sufficiently detailed so the FCC can determine the words and language actually used during the broadcast and the context of those words or language. Subject matter alone is not a determining factor of whether material is obscene, profane, or indecent. For example, stating only that the broadcast station "discussed sex" or had a "disgusting discussion of sex" during a program is not sufficient. Moreover, the FCC must know the context when analyzing whether specific, isolated words are indecent or profane. The FCC does not require complainants to provide recordings or transcripts in support of their complaints. Consequently, failure to provide a recording or transcript of a broadcast, in and of itself, will not lead to automatic dismissal or denial of a complaint.
- *The date and time of the broadcast.* Under federal law, if the FCC assesses a monetary forfeiture against a broadcast station for violation of a rule, it must specify the date the violation occurred. Accordingly, it is important that complainants provide the date the material in question was broadcast. A broadcaster's right to air indecent or profane speech is protected between the hours of 10 p.m. and 6 a.m. Consequently, the FCC must know the time of day that the material was broadcast.
- The call sign of the station involved.

Of necessity, any documentation you provide the FCC about your complaint becomes part of the FCC's records and may not be returned. Complaints containing this information should be directed to:

Federal Communications Commission

Enforcement Bureau

Investigations and Hearings Division

445 12th St., SW, Room 3-B443

Washington, DC 20554

You may also file a complaint electronically using the FCC Form 475 (complaint form) . . . or by e-mail. . . .

Judith Levine

Is "Indecency" Harmful to Minors?

"For more than 75 years . . . Congress has entrusted the FCC with protecting children from broadcast indecency," the Federal Communications Commission's chief enforcer David H. Solomon declared in April, 2004. "There's no question that the FCC is taking indecency enforcement very seriously these days."

No question indeed. Solomon was referring to the commission's new regulatory enthusiasm—some would call it a crusade—spearheaded by Chairman Michael Powell, seconded by President Bush, and toughened by two GOP bills to raise fines from the current maximum of $27,500 to as high as a half-million dollars; the laws would also revoke licenses after "three strikes." Solomon crowed about enlivening the definition of indecency—"language or material that, in context, depicts or describes, in terms patently offensive as measured by contemporary community standards for the broadcast medium, sexual or excretory organs or activities"—with a broader subset of "profanity." In addition to blasphemy (an already questionable concept in a secular nation), the commission would prohibit as profane any "personally reviling epithets naturally tending to provoke violent resentment" or language "so grossly offensive. . . . as to amount to a nuisance." The "F-word," as the commission delicately refers to it, would hereafter be considered such a violently resentment-provoking nuisance.

And, oh yes, the FCC "remain[ed] strongly committed" to the First Amendment.

Powell had been itching to act. In January, 2003, his enforcers ruled that the Bono's exclamation on NBC's Golden Globe awards—"Fucking brilliant!"—was not profane. All year on Clear Channel radio, Bubba the Love Sponge nattered on about "waxing [his] carrot," Howard Stern discussed cum with porn stars.

But the last straw was half-time, Superbowl 2004. During a song-and-dance duet, a scripted bodice-rip by Justin Timberlake resulted in the momentary baring of Janet Jackson's right breast, bedecked with a sunburst-shaped "nipple shield." Organized conservatives predicted the end of civilization and helped mobilize a half-million complaints to CBS. Powell told the press of his cozy family "celebration" being ambushed by this "classless, crass, and deplorable stunt," and vowed to investigate. Rejecting Timberlake's claim of a "wardrobe malfunction," the FCC in July found the performance indecent—to the tune of $550,000 in fines against Viacom Inc., parent company to the 20 CBS affiliates that aired the show.

While civil libertarians protested the supersized penalties and the ever-vaguer regulations, media companies sped to adopt failsafe policies. Scripts from *NYPD Blue* to *Masterpiece Theatre* were scrubbed, on-air personalities were muzzled and non-compliers canned. Clear Channel dumped Stern, and at Santa Monica-based KCRW-FM, Sandra Tsing Loh lost her $150-a-week job when the "F-word" slipped by un-bleeped during a commentary on knitting (the station later offered the position back, but Loh declined). The FCC praised such "voluntary action." Many producers called it scared s—less self-censorship.

The concept of indecency is inextricably linked to protecting children, which is why most sexual speech is prohibited on radio and commercial television between 6 a.m. and 10 p.m., when minors might be in the audience. According to veteran civil liberties attorney Marjorie Heins, laws are routinely passed and upheld in court based on the notion that witnessing sexual words and images is harmful to minors. Even among those who challenge the laws' free-speech infringements, few question this truism.

But there is no evidence that sexual speech harms children.

The idea that young (or female or feeble) minds are vulnerable to media-induced bad thoughts, which might lead to bad acts, might be called the founding principle of obscenity law. In 1868, an English anti-clerical pamphlet called "The Confessional Unmasked" was deemed punishably obscene because its text might "suggest to the minds of the young of either sex, and even to persons of more advanced years, thoughts of a most impure and libidinous character."

The worry that mobilizes the law, while neither pan-historic nor universal, is nonetheless old and enduring. In 1700, an English anti-masturbation treatise called *Onania, or the Heinous Sin of Self-Pollution, And All its Frightful Consequences, in Both Sexes consider'd, &c* became a best-seller with such warnings as "*Dogs* in the Streets and *Bulls* in the Fields may do mischief to Debauch's Fancy's, and it is possible that either Sex may be put in mind of Lascivious Thoughts, by their own *Poultry*."

In the late 19th century, while Anthony Comstock scoured daily newspapers for censorable "traps for the young," the New York Society for the Prevention of Cruelty to Children "kept a watchful eye upon the so-called Museums of the City," whose advertisements were "like magnets to curious children." According to one of the society's reports, a play featuring "depravity, stabbing, shooting, and blood-shedding" so traumatized a 10-year-old girl that she was found "wander[ing] aimlessly along Eighth Avenue as if incapable of ridding herself of the dread impressions that had filled her young mind."

By 1914, essayist Agnes Repellier was inveighing against a film and publishing industry "coining money" creating a generation hypersophisticated in sin. "[Children's] sources of knowledge are manifold, and astoundingly explicit," she wrote in *The Atlantic*. Perhaps the first to propose a movie-rating system, Repellier asked "the authorities" to bar children "from all shows dealing with prostitution." And in 1934, Dr. Ira S. Wile indicted "lurid movies, automobiles, speed, jazz, [and] literature tinged with pornography," among the causes of "The Sexual Problems of Adolescence."

After jazz came comic books, then rock 'n' roll, hip-hop, videogames, Internet porn—it's a miracle anyone has survived childhood with sufficient morality to protect the next generation from corruption.

In spite of all this hand-wringing, though, evidence of the harm of exposure to sexually explicit images or words in childhood is inconclusive, even nonexistent. The 1970 U.S. Commission on Obscenity and Pornography, the "Lockhart Commission," failed to find harm to children in viewing erotica, and even suggested such exposure could "facilitate much needed communication between parent and child over sexual matters."

In a survey of 3,200 elementary school kids in the 1970s (before MTV!), "the most productive responses were elicited with the instructions, 'Why children shouldn't be allowed to see R and X rated movies'; or 'What is in R and X rated movies that children are too young to know about?' Here, the children proceeded with aplomb to tell all that they knew but were not supposed to know," wrote the study's authors. The conclusion: Children are sexual, they know about sex, and this does not harm them. Their "innocence" is an adult fantasy.

Assembled to overturn the 1970 findings, the Reagan Administration's 1985 Commission on Pornography (the "Meese Commission") could not establish factual links between sexual explicit materials and antisocial behavior either. The lion's share of the testimony it heard concerned adult consumers, yet the commission pitched its pro-restriction recommendations to popular fears about children: "For children to be taught by these materials that sex is public, that sex is commercial, and that sex can be divorced from any degree of affection, love, commitment, or marriage," the report read, "is for us the wrong message at the wrong time."

Indeed, some research suggests that *less* exposure to sexual materials may be worse for children than more. Interviews of sex criminals including child molesters reveal that the children who eventually became rapists were usually less exposed to pornography than other kids. In general, according to Johns Hopkins University sexologist John Money, "the majority of patients with paraphilias"—deviant sexual fantasies and behaviors—"described a strict anti-sexual upbringing in which sex was either never mentioned or was actively repressed or defiled." On a less criminal note, students who attend sex ed classes in which a wide range of sexual topics are discussed do far better than those in abstinence-only classes in protecting themselves against pregnancy and disease and negotiating their sexual relationships.

So what about these fresh corrupting "indecencies"? Anecdotal evidence suggests the breast, the F-word, or anything Bubba says are not news to any child who isn't Amish. Eighth-graders interviewed after the Superbowl evinced only mild concern—for their younger siblings. "I thought the end was a little bit inappropriate," commented one girl, "being that kids of all ages were watching it."

And Bono's outburst? In a successful appeal of NBC's exoneration, Parents Television Coalition argued that the singer could "enlarge a child's vocabulary. . . in a manner that many, if not most, parents would find highly detrimental and objectionable."

To test this thesis, I googled "swearing and children." A hundred-fifty-five thousand hits proved PTC right on one claim: parents object to their kids' swearing. On the other, though, the evidence is shaky. Kent State psychologist Timothy Jay, an expert on cursing, told NPR that as soon as kids can speak, they start to cuss—because everyone around them does. Nevertheless, every online "expert" predicts parental surprise: "What a shock [when] a foul word escapes your little angel's lips!"

As with much objection to victimless crimes, a circular logic emerges. Kids curse, often in "inappropriate" settings like Grandma's house or kindergarten, to gain attention, to shock. This works (see above) because, well, cursing is inappropriate. Cursing is inappropriate because it is shocking and shocking because it is inappropriate.

Older kids curse to be like other kids, say the experts. Which came first, the kids cursing or the other kids cursing, is never clear. As for harms to children, the worst one mentioned is that cursing elicits punishment. Cursing is bad because it is shocking and shocking because bad; bad because inappropriate and inappropriate because bad; punishable because harmful and harmful because punished.

But cursing can be reined in with gentle discipline (aka punishment). Since it is a minor offense, mouth-washing with soap is not recommended. Adult cursing, on the other hand, is "highly detrimental" to children; thus, fines up to $500,000 are recommended.

When discussing sexual speech, child-development experts often invoke "age-appropriateness," a determination of high sensitivity, with miscalculations carrying grave consequences (Penelope Leach: "Although secrecy makes for dangerous ignorance, too much openness can turn on what is meant to stay turned off until later"). This leads to movie and TV ratings indicating that this film is okay for 13-year-olds but not 12-year-olds, that one for 17-year-olds but only when accompanied by an adult (who could be 18).

Given the gradual and idiosyncratic nature of children's maturation, the timing mechanism of a sexual education probably resembles a sundial more than the IBM Olympic stopwatch. Parents needn't worry so much. But efforts to delineate the boundary between child and adolescent, adolescent and adult, express an anxiety far greater than whether a breast that is appropriate at 10:30 p.m. is inappropriate at 9:30.

What scares us is that these boundaries, if they ever existed, are disappearing.

Philippe Ariès, founder of childhood history, famously proposed that before the 18th Century, there was no such thing as childhood. At seven, a 17th Century person might become a maid or shoemaker's apprentice; by 14 he could be a soldier, a king, or a parent; by 40, he'd likely be dead. The 18th Century Romantics gave us the Innocent Child, uncorrupted by adult knowledge; the following century, the Victorians figured childhood innocence sexual in nature, even as the dangers and pleasures of the Industrial Revolution gave the lie to this wishful invention.

We have not left off trying to fortify the official wall between childhood and adulthood. Twentieth-century innovations from Freudian psychology to child labor laws laid heavy bricks in it. But in our century, globalized economies and proliferating communications technologies are kicking that wall down. Worldwide, children work in sweatshops, invest in stocks, commit crimes, join armies. Even "sheltered" children watch the same videos, listen to the same music, and surf the same Web sites as adults. They know about sex and they engage in sex.

While we locate them in a separate political category, a medical specialty, a market niche—and an FCC-patrolled time slot. But children in the 21st Century may be more like adults than they have been since the 17th Century.

It is unlikely the air will get less dense with information, or with sex—and no law, no Internet filter or vigilant parent can keep tabs on every pixel that passes before a child's eyes. All adults can do is help kids understand and negotiate the sexual world.

But the campaign against indecency is bigger than children. Parents Television Council and their allies in and outside government would like to Bowdlerize the public sphere entirely. So far, the courts have limited attempts, such as numerous online decency statutes, that would reduce all communications to a level appropriate to the Teletubbies.

Still, it is wrong to see censorship as bad for adults and good for children. Everyone can benefit from abundant accurate, realistic sexual information and diverse narratives and images of bodies and sex. In sex as in politics, only more speech can challenge bad speech. We won't all agree on what is bad, but it is time to wrest those definitions from the hands of radical moralists.

POSTSCRIPT

Should the FCC Restrict Broadcast "Indecency"?

All broadcast outlets are responsible for knowing the FCC's policies regarding obscenity, indecency, and profanity. Ironically, station managers who carefully read the FCC's own publication, with all its vivid case studies, could reasonably determine the document itself to be obscene, indecent, and profane. Indeed, portions of the FCC's Enforcement Policies were too obscene to include in this text, as they cited crude jokes about pedophilia, for example. One must wonder how professionals in radio and television respond when such an obscene document arrives in the mail from the FCC. On the other hand, explicit guidance is necessary for station managers to fully understand what may and may not be aired.

The examples cited in the FCC's Enforcement Policies may not always seem congruous. Further, some argue that the FCC has not been even-handed in its enforcement. Howard Stern, a frequent target of the FCC, routinely directs listeners to lodge complaints against other shows, like the *Oprah Winfrey Show,* when it features graphic discussions of sex, or *60 Minutes* when a singer missed a lyric and said, "Shit!"

On Veterans Day in November 2004, ABC aired the movie *Saving Private Ryan* in prime time, uncut with all its expletives and graphic violent war imagery. Sixty-six ABC affiliates refused to air the film, uncertain about whether the FCC would levy substantial fines for every single expletive uttered throughout the film, or if it would regard the film's airing as a patriotic way to honor veterans of World War II. To date, the FCC has taken no action against ABC or the affiliates who aired it, despite clear violations of the FCC policy on indecency.

If the FCC were to take action on the airing of *Saving Private Ryan,* it could only fine ABC based on its airing of expletives. No portion of the FCC policy restricts airing violent imagery. Thus, scenes in which soldiers are maimed are deemed acceptable for viewing, but any utterance of "fuck" would be categorically harmful to children.

What is harmful to children? Is sexual speech and sexual imagery inherently harmful as the FCC policy suggests? Do you agree with Levine when she rejects the idea that sexual material is harmful to children? What do you make of the various cases cited by the FCC? Would you decide differently for any of those cases? Which ones? What other content, if any, do you believe should be restricted as "indecent," or as harmful to children? What penalties would you impose for stations that violate these restrictions?

Suggested Readings

J. Levine, *Harmful to Minors: The Perils of Protecting Children from Sex* (University of Minnesota Press, 2002).

Parents' Television Council, "Basic Cable Awash in Raunch," http://www.parentstv.org/PTC/publications/reports/2004cablestudy/main.asp (November 2004).

Parent's Television Council, "Dereliction of Duty: How the Federal Communications Commission has Failed the Public," http://www.parentstv.org/PTC/publications/reports/fccwhitepaper/main.asp (February 3, 2004).

R. Pugh, "Decency Advocate: ABC's Ryan Broadcast Flouted FCC Rules—What Now?," http://headlines.agapepress.org/archive/11/afa/172004b.asp (November 17, 2004).

F. Rich, "The Great Indecency Hoax," *New York Times* (November 28, 2004).

T. Shales, "Michael Powell Exposed! The FCC Chairman Has No Clothes," *Washington Post* (November 21, 2004).

United States Government Printing Office, *Can You Say That on TV?: An Examination of the FCC's Enforcement with Respect to Broadcast Indecency: Hearing Before the Subcommittee on Teleco* (2004).

ISSUE 18

Should Sexual Content on the Internet Be Restricted?

YES: Stephen G. Breyer, from the Dissenting Opinion in *Ashcroft v. American Civil Liberties Union* (June 29, 2004)

NO: Anthony M. Kennedy, from the Court's Opinion in *Ashcroft v. American Civil Liberties Union* (June 29, 2004)

ISSUE SUMMARY

YES: In a dissenting opinion, United States Supreme Court Justice Stephen G. Breyer argues that the Child Online Protection Act does not impose an unreasonable burden on free speech, and should have been upheld by the high court.

NO: Explaining the Supreme Court's decision to strike down the Child Online Protection Act, Justice Anthony M. Kennedy says that filtering software is a better and less restrictive alternative for protecting children from sexual content on the Internet.

Sexual content is available *everywhere* on the Internet. A search for the word "sex" on the popular search engine google.com yields 181 million results. Many of these links will direct Internet travelers to erotic or pornographic sites, but many of the links will also lead to useful information sites. Among the first sites listed in a Google search will be sxetc.org, a reliable sexuality information Web site by teens for teens. Another site, safersex.org, will give viewers helpful hints about protection from sexually transmitted infections. Other non-pornographic sites returned in such a search include links to the Kinsey Institute and the Sexuality Information and Education Council of the United States (SIECUS), not to mention fan sites for HBO's popular *Sex and the City* and one for the punk rock band, the Sex Pistols! (One can even find a link for this book in such a search!)

Despite the many useful and "legitimate" Web sites that are returned when searching for "sex" online, there are also many that concern people. Erotic, obscene, or pornographic material is a click away for anyone who looks for it. Sometimes sexual material finds Web surfers, even when they aren't looking. Instant messages may pop up on one's screen offering unsolicited links to view erotic pictures. Unwelcome e-mail may offer discounts on Viagra or penis and breast enhancements. Most adults will navigate the Internet through unwanted material without worrying too much about it, but passions heat up when it comes to sexual material that arrives on the computer screens of children.

The Child Online Protection Act (COPA) was drafted by Congress to address the high volume of sexual content to which children may be routinely exposed when connected to the Internet. Other media have governmentally imposed restrictions on sexual content. Television and radio are limited in the sexual content it can depict or discuss. Newspapers and magazines also limit sexual content. When sexual content is their trade (such as *Playboy* or other erotic magazines), age and access restrictions apply.

COPA was conceptualized to address unregulated sexual content online deemed "harmful to minors" by requiring Web sites with such material to have their patrons give their credit card information for entry (or to otherwise employ technology to prevent minors from accessing the Web site). COPA would impose penalties of $50,000 and six months in prison for those who would knowingly post material that is "harmful to minors" without such mechanisms to prevent minors from entering.

Free speech advocates challenged COPA in court. The American Civil Liberties Union (ACLU) argued that sexual content could already be regulated by concerned parents using filtering software to prevent their children from viewing sexual material online. Such technology, the ACLU argued, would protect minors from material their parents did not want them to see, while not imposing any new burdens on providers or legitimate consumers of erotic materials. The challenge eventually made its way to the United States Supreme Court, in the form of a "writ of certiorari" (or a request for the Supreme Court to review a lower court's decision). After reviewing the case, the Supreme Court upheld the decisions of lower courts, effectively striking down COPA.

In the following essays, Supreme Court Justices Stephen G. Breyer and Anthony M. Kennedy explain their differing perspectives on this decision. Justice Breyer argues that the high court should have upheld COPA, since it did not impose unreasonable expectations on Web site providers. In speaking for the court majority, Justice Kennedy argues that Internet filtering software is less restrictive than COPA, and likely more effective in restricting children's access to material that may cause harm.

YES

Stephen G. Breyer

John D. Ashcroft, Attorney General, Petitioner v. American Civil Liberties Union et al.

Justice Breyer, with whom The Chief Justice and Justice O'Connor join, dissenting.

The Child Online Protection Act (Act), seeks to protect children from exposure to commercial pornography placed on the Internet. It does so by requiring commercial providers to place pornographic material behind Internet "screens" readily accessible to adults who produce age verification. The Court recognizes that we should "'proceed . . . with care before invalidating the Act,'" while pointing out that the "imperative of according respect to the Congress . . . does not permit us to depart from well-established First Amendment principles." I agree with these generalities. Like the Court, I would subject the Act to "the most exacting scrutiny," requiring the Government to show that any restriction of nonobscene expression is "narrowly drawn" to further a "compelling interest" and that the restriction amounts to the "least restrictive means" available to further that interest.

Nonetheless, my examination of (1) the burdens the Act imposes on protected expression, (2) the Act's ability to further a compelling interest, and (3) the proposed "less restrictive alternatives" convinces me that the Court is wrong. I cannot accept its conclusion that Congress could have accomplished its statutory objective—protecting children from commercial pornography on the Internet—in other, less restrictive ways.

I

Although the Court rests its conclusion upon the existence of less restrictive alternatives, I must first examine the burdens that the Act imposes upon protected speech. That is because the term "less restrictive alternative" is a comparative term. An "alternative" is "less restrictive" only if it will work less First Amendment harm than the statute itself, while at the same time similarly furthering the "compelling" interest that prompted Congress to enact the statute. Unlike the majority, I do not see how it is possible to make this comparative determination without examining both the extent to which the Act regulates

Ashcroft v. American Civil Liberties Union, United States Supreme Court, No. 03-218 (June 29, 2004).

protected expression and the nature of the burdens it imposes on that expression. That examination suggests that the Act, properly interpreted, imposes a burden on protected speech that is no more than modest.

A

The Act's definitions limit the material it regulates to material that does not enjoy First Amendment protection, namely legally obscene material, and very little more. A comparison of this Court's definition of unprotected, "legally obscene," material with the Act's definitions makes this clear.

Material is legally obscene if

> "(a) . . . 'the average person, applying contemporary community standards' would find that the work, taken as a whole, appeals to the prurient interest . . . ; (b) . . . the work depicts or describes, in a patently offensive way, sexual conduct specifically defined by the applicable state law; and (c) . . . the work, taken as a whole, lacks serious literary, artistic, political, or scientific value."

The present statute defines the material that it regulates as material that meets all of the following criteria:

> "(A) the average person, applying contemporary community standards, would find, taking the material as a whole *and with respect to minors*, [that the material] is designed to appeal to, or is designed to pander to, the prurient interest;
> "(B) [the material] depicts, describes, or represents, in a manner patently offensive *with respect to minors,* an actual or simulated sexual act or sexual contact, an actual or simulated normal or perverted sexual act, or a lewd exhibition of the genitals or postpubescent female breast; and
> "(C) [the material] taken as a whole, lacks serious literary, artistic, political, or scientific value *for minors*."

Both definitions define the relevant material through use of the critical terms "prurient interest" and "lacks serious literary, artistic, political, or scientific value." Insofar as material appeals to, or panders to, "the prurient interest," it simply seeks a sexual response. Insofar as "patently offensive" material with "no serious value" simply seeks that response, it does not seek to educate, it does not seek to elucidate views about sex, it is not artistic, and it is not literary. Compare, *e.g., Erznoznik* v. *Jacksonville* (invalidating an ordinance regulating nudity in films, where the ban was not confined to "sexually explicit nudity" or otherwise limited), with *Ginzburg* v. *United States* (finding unprotected material that was "created, represented, and sold solely as a claimed instrument of the sexual stimulation it would bring"). That is why this Court, in *Miller [v. California]*, held that the First Amendment did not protect material that fit its definition.

The only significant difference between the present statute and *Miller's* definition consists of the addition of the words "with respect to minors," and "for minors." But the addition of these words to a definition that would otherwise cover only obscenity expands the statute's scope only slightly. That is because the material in question (while potentially harmful to young children) must, first, appeal to the "prurient interest" of, *i.e.*, seek a sexual response from, some group of adolescents or postadolescents (since young children normally do not so respond). And material that appeals to the "prurient interest[s]" of some group of adolescents or postadolescents will almost inevitably appeal to the "prurient interest[s]" of some group of adults as well.

The "lack of serious value" requirement narrows the statute yet further—despite the presence of the qualification "for minors." That is because one cannot easily imagine material that has serious literary, artistic, political, or scientific value for a significant group of adults, but lacks such value for any significant group of minors. Thus, the statute, read literally, insofar as it extends beyond the legally obscene, could reach only borderline cases. And to take the words of the statute literally is consistent with Congress' avowed objective in enacting this law; namely, putting material produced by professional pornographers behind screens that will verify the age of the viewer.

These limitations on the statute's scope answer many of the concerns raised by those who attack its constitutionality. Respondents fear prosecution for the Internet posting of material that does not fall within the statute's ambit as limited by the "prurient interest" and "no serious value" requirements; for example: an essay about a young man's experience with masturbation and sexual shame; "a serious discussion about birth control practices, homosexuality, . . . or the consequences of prison rape"; an account by a 15-year-old, written for therapeutic purposes, of being raped when she was 13; a guide to self-examination for testicular cancer; a graphic illustration of how to use a condom; or any of the other postings of modern literary or artistic works or discussions of sexual identity, homosexuality, sexually transmitted diseases, sex education, or safe sex, let alone Aldous Huxley's Brave New World, J. D. Salinger's Catcher in the Rye, or, as the complaint would have it, "Ken Starr's report on the Clinton-Lewinsky scandal."

These materials are *not* both (1) "designed to appeal to, or . . . pander to, the prurient interest" of significant groups of minors *and* (2) lacking in "serious literary, artistic, political, or scientific value" for significant groups of minors. Thus, they fall outside the statute's definition of the material that it restricts, a fact the Government acknowledged at oral argument.

I have found nothing elsewhere in the statute's language that broadens its scope. Other qualifying phrases, such as "taking the material as a whole" and "for commercial purposes" limit the statute's scope still more, requiring, for example, that individual images be considered in context. In sum, the Act's definitions limit the statute's scope to commercial pornography. It affects unprotected obscene material. Given the inevitable uncertainty about how to characterize close-to-obscene material, it could apply to (or chill the production of) a limited class of borderline material that courts might ultimately find is protected. But the examples I have just given fall outside that class.

B

The Act does not censor the material it covers. Rather, it requires providers of the "harmful to minors" material to restrict minors' access to it by verifying age. They can do so by inserting screens that verify age using a credit card, adult personal identification number, or other similar technology. In this way, the Act requires creation of an internet screen that minors, but not adults, will find difficult to bypass.

I recognize that the screening requirement imposes some burden on adults who seek access to the regulated material, as well as on its providers. The cost is, in part, monetary. The parties agreed that a Web site could store card numbers or passwords at between 15 and 20 cents per number. And verification services provide free verification to Web site operators, while charging users less than $20 per year. According to the trade association for the commercial pornographers who are the statute's target, use of such verification procedures is "standard practice" in their online operations.

In addition to the monetary cost, and despite strict requirements that identifying information be kept confidential, the identification requirements inherent in age-screening may lead some users to fear embarrassment. Both monetary costs and potential embarrassment can deter potential viewers and, in that sense, the statute's requirements may restrict access to a site. But this Court has held that in the context of congressional efforts to protect children, restrictions of this kind do not automatically violate the Constitution. And the Court has approved their use. See, *United States* v. *American Library Assn., Inc.* ("[T]he Constitution does not guarantee the right to acquire information at a public library without any risk of embarrassment"). (O'Connor, J., concurring in judgment in part and dissenting in part) (calling the age-verification requirement similar to "a bouncer [who] checks a person's driver's license before admitting him to a nightclub").

In sum, the Act at most imposes a modest additional burden on adult access to legally obscene material, perhaps imposing a similar burden on access to some protected borderline obscene material as well.

II

I turn next to the question of "compelling interest," that of protecting minors from exposure to commercial pornography. No one denies that such an interest is "compelling." Rather, the question here is whether the Act, given its restrictions on adult access, significantly advances that interest. In other words, is the game worth the candle?

The majority argues that it is not, because of the existence of "blocking and filtering software." The majority refers to the presence of that software as a "less restrictive alternative." But that is a misnomer—a misnomer that may lead the reader to believe that all we need do is look to see if the blocking and filtering software is less restrictive; and to believe that, because in one sense it is (one can turn off the software), that is the end of the constitutional matter.

But such reasoning has no place here. Conceptually speaking, the presence of filtering software is not an *alternative* legislative approach to the problem of protecting children from exposure to commercial pornography. Rather, it is part of the status quo, *i.e.,* the backdrop against which Congress enacted the present statute. It is always true, by definition, that the status quo is less restrictive than a new regulatory law. It is always less restrictive to do *nothing* than to do *something*. But "doing nothing" does not address the problem Congress sought to address—namely that, despite the availability of filtering software, children were still being exposed to harmful material on the Internet.

Thus, the relevant constitutional question is not the question the Court asks: Would it be less restrictive to do nothing? Of course it would be. Rather, the relevant question posits a comparison of (a) a status quo that includes filtering software with (b) a change in that status quo that adds to it an age-verification screen requirement. Given the existence of filtering software, does the problem Congress identified remain significant? Does the Act help to address it? These are questions about the relation of the Act to the compelling interest. Does the Act, compared to the status quo, significantly advance the ball? (An affirmative answer to these questions will not justify "[a]ny restriction on speech," as the Court claims, for a final answer in respect to constitutionality must take account of burdens and alternatives as well.)

The answers to these intermediate questions are clear: Filtering software, as presently available, does not solve the "child protection" problem. It suffers from four serious inadequacies that prompted Congress to pass legislation instead of relying on its voluntary use. First, its filtering is faulty, allowing some pornographic material to pass through without hindrance. Just last year, in *American Library Assn.,* Justice Stevens described "fundamental defects in the filtering software that is now available or that will be available in the foreseeable future." He pointed to the problem of underblocking: "Because the software relies on key words or phrases to block undesirable sites, it does not have the capacity to exclude a precisely defined category of images." That is to say, in the absence of words, the software alone cannot distinguish between the most obscene pictorial image and the Venus de Milo. No Member of this Court disagreed.

Second, filtering software costs money. Not every family has the $40 or so necessary to install it. By way of contrast, age screening costs less.

Third, filtering software depends upon parents willing to decide where their children will surf the Web and able to enforce that decision. As to millions of American families, that is not a reasonable possibility. More than 28 million school age children have both parents or their sole parent in the work force, at least 5 million children are left alone at home without supervision each week, and many of those children will spend afternoons and evenings with friends who may well have access to computers and more lenient parents.

Fourth, software blocking lacks precision, with the result that those who wish to use it to screen out pornography find that it blocks a great deal of material that is valuable. As Justice Stevens pointed out, "the software's reliance on words to identify undesirable sites necessarily results in the blocking of thousands of pages that contain content that is completely innocuous for both adults and minors, and that no rational person could conclude matches the filtering companies' category definitions, such as pornography or sex."

Indeed, the American Civil Liberties Union (ACLU), one of the respondents here, told Congress that filtering software "block[s] out valuable and protected information, such as information about the Quaker religion, and web sites including those of the American Association of University Women, the AIDS Quilt, the Town Hall Political Site (run by the Family Resource Center, Christian Coalition and other conservative groups)." The software "is simply incapable of discerning between constitutionally protected and unprotected speech." It "inappropriately blocks valuable, protected speech, and does not effectively block the sites [it is] intended to block."

Nothing in the District Court record suggests the contrary. No respondent has offered to produce evidence at trial to the contrary. No party has suggested, for example, that technology allowing filters to interpret and discern among images has suddenly become, or is about to become, widely available. Indeed, the Court concedes that "[f]iltering software, of course, is not a perfect solution to the problem."

In sum, a "filtering software status quo" means filtering that underblocks, imposes a cost upon each family that uses it, fails to screen outside the home, and lacks precision. Thus, Congress could reasonably conclude that a system that relies entirely upon the use of such software is not an effective system. And a law that adds to that system an age-verification screen requirement significantly increases the system's efficacy. That is to say, at a modest additional cost to those adults who wish to obtain access to a screened program, that law will bring about better, more precise blocking, both inside and outside the home.

The Court's response—that 40% of all pornographic material may be of foreign origin—is beside the point. Even assuming (I believe unrealistically) that *all* foreign originators will refuse to use screening, the Act would make a difference in respect to 60% of the Internet's commercial pornography. I cannot call that difference insignificant.

The upshot is that Congress could reasonably conclude that, despite the current availability of filtering software, a child protection problem exists. It also could conclude that a precisely targeted regulatory statute, adding an age-verification requirement for a narrow range of material, would more effectively shield children from commercial pornography.

Is this justification sufficient? The lower courts thought not. But that is because those courts interpreted the Act as imposing far more than a modest burden. They assumed an interpretation of the statute in which it reached far beyond legally obscene and borderline-obscene material, affecting material that, given the interpretation set forth above, would fall well outside the Act's scope. But we must interpret the Act to save it, not to destroy it. So interpreted, the Act imposes a far lesser burden on access to protected material. Given the modest nature of that burden and the likelihood that the Act will significantly further Congress' compelling objective, the Act may well satisfy the First Amendment's stringent tests. Indeed, it does satisfy the First Amendment unless, of course, there is a genuine alternative, "less restrictive" way similarly to further that objective.

III

I turn, then, to the actual "less restrictive alternatives" that the Court proposes. The Court proposes two real alternatives, *i.e.,* two potentially less restrictive ways in which Congress might alter the status quo in order to achieve its "compelling" objective.

First, the Government might "act to encourage" the use of blocking and filtering software. The problem is that any argument that rests upon this alternative proves too much. If one imagines enough government resources devoted to the problem and perhaps additional scientific advances, then, of course, the use of software might become as effective and less restrictive. Obviously, the Government could give all parents, schools, and Internet cafes free computers with filtering programs already installed, hire federal employees to train parents and teachers on their use, and devote millions of dollars to the development of better software. The result might be an alternative that is extremely effective.

But the Constitution does not, because it cannot, require the Government to disprove the existence of magic solutions, *i.e.,* solutions that, put in general terms, will solve any problem less restrictively but with equal effectiveness.

Otherwise, "the undoubted ability of lawyers and judges," who are not constrained by the budgetary worries and other practical parameters within which Congress must operate, "to imagine *some* kind of slightly less drastic or restrictive an approach would make it impossible to write laws that deal with the harm that called the statute into being." As Justice Blackmun recognized, a "judge would be unimaginative indeed if he could not come up with something a little less 'drastic' or a little less 'restrictive' in almost any situation, and thereby enable himself to vote to strike legislation down." Perhaps that is why no party has argued seriously that additional expenditure of government funds to encourage the use of screening is a "less restrictive alternative."

Second, the majority suggests decriminalizing the statute, noting the "chilling effect" of criminalizing a category of speech. To remove a major sanction, however, would make the statute less effective, virtually by definition.

IV

My conclusion is that the Act, as properly interpreted, risks imposition of minor burdens on some protected material—burdens that adults wishing to view the material may overcome at modest cost. At the same time, it significantly helps to achieve a compelling congressional goal, protecting children from exposure to commercial pornography. There is no serious, practically available "less restrictive" way similarly to further this compelling interest. Hence the Act is constitutional.

V

The Court's holding raises two more general questions. First, what has happened to the "constructive discourse between our courts and our legislatures" that "is an integral and admirable part of the constitutional design"? After eight years of legislative effort, two statutes, and three Supreme Court cases the Court sends this case back to the District Court for further proceedings. What proceedings? I have found no offer by either party to present more relevant evidence. What remains to be litigated? I know the Court says that the parties may "introduce further evidence" as to the "relative restrictiveness and effectiveness of alternatives to the statute." But I do not understand what that new evidence might consist of.

Moreover, Congress passed the current statute "[i]n response to the Court's decision in *Reno [v. American Civil Liberties Union]*" striking down an earlier statutory effort to deal with the same problem. Congress read *Reno* with care. It dedicated itself to the task of drafting a statute that would meet each and every criticism of the predecessor statute that this Court set forth in *Reno*. It incorporated language from the Court's precedents, particularly the *Miller* standard, virtually verbatim. And it created what it believed was a statute that would protect children from exposure to obscene professional pornography without obstructing adult access to material that the First Amendment protects. What else was Congress supposed to do?

I recognize that some Members of the Court, now or in the past, have taken the view that the First Amendment simply does not permit Congress to legislate in this area. ("[T]he Federal Government is without any power whatever under the Constitution to put any type of burden on speech and expression of ideas of any kind"). Others believe that the Amendment does not permit Congress to legislate in certain ways, *e.g.*, through the imposition of criminal penalties for obscenity. There are strong constitutional arguments favoring these views. But the Court itself does not adopt those views. Instead, it finds that the Government has not proved the nonexistence of "less restrictive alternatives." That finding, if appropriate here, is universally appropriate. And if universally appropriate, it denies to Congress, in practice, the legislative leeway that the Court's language seem to promise. If this statute does not pass the Court's "less restrictive alternative" test, what does? If nothing does, then the Court should say so clearly.

As I have explained, I believe the First Amendment permits an alternative holding. We could construe the statute narrowly—as I have tried to do—removing nearly all protected material from its scope. By doing so, we could reconcile its language with the First Amendment's demands. We would "save" the statute, "not . . . destroy it." And in the process, we would permit Congress to achieve its basic child-protecting objectives.

Second, will the majority's holding in practice mean greater or lesser protection for expression? I do not find the answer to this question obvious. The Court's decision removes an important weapon from the prosecutorial arsenal. That weapon would have given the Government a choice—a choice other than "ban totally or do nothing at all." The Act tells the Government that, instead of prosecuting bans on obscenity to the maximum extent possible (as respondents have urged as yet another "alternative"), it can insist that those who make available material that is obscene or close to obscene keep that material under wraps, making it readily available to adults who wish to see it, while restricting access to children. By providing this third option—a "middle way"—the Act avoids the need for potentially speech-suppressing prosecutions.

That matters in a world where the obscene and the nonobscene do not come tied neatly into separate, easily distinguishable, packages. In that real world, this middle way might well have furthered First Amendment interests by tempering the prosecutorial instinct in borderline cases. At least, Congress might have so believed. And this likelihood, from a First Amendment perspective, might ultimately have proved more protective of the rights of viewers to retain access to expression than the all-or-nothing choice available to prosecutors in the wake of the majority's opinion.

For these reasons, I dissent.

Anthony M. Kennedy  **NO**

John D. Ashcroft, Attorney General, Petitioner *v.* American Civil Liberties Union et al.

Justice Kennedy delivered the opinion of the Court.

This case presents a challenge to a statute enacted by Congress to protect minors from exposure to sexually explicit materials on the Internet, the Child Online Protection Act (COPA). We must decide whether the Court of Appeals was correct to affirm a ruling by the District Court that enforcement of COPA should be enjoined because the statute likely violates the First Amendment.

In enacting COPA, Congress gave consideration to our earlier decisions on this subject, in particular the decision in *Reno* v. *American Civil Liberties Union* (1997). For that reason, "the Judiciary must proceed with caution and . . . with care before invalidating the Act." The imperative of according respect to the Congress, however, does not permit us to depart from well-established First Amendment principles. Instead, we must hold the Government to its constitutional burden of proof.

Content-based prohibitions, enforced by severe criminal penalties, have the constant potential to be a repressive force in the lives and thoughts of a free people. To guard against that threat the Constitution demands that content-based restrictions on speech be presumed invalid, and that the Government bear the burden of showing their constitutionality. This is true even when Congress twice has attempted to find a constitutional means to restrict, and punish, the speech in question.

This case comes to the Court on certiorari review of an appeal from the decision of the District Court granting a preliminary injunction. The Court of Appeals reviewed the decision of the District Court for abuse of discretion. Under that standard, the Court of Appeals was correct to conclude that the District Court did not abuse its discretion in granting the preliminary injunction. The Government has failed, at this point, to rebut the plaintiffs' contention that there are plausible less restrictive alternatives to the statute. Substantial practical considerations, furthermore, argue in favor of upholding the injunction and allowing the case to proceed to trial. For those reasons, we affirm the decision of the Court of Appeals upholding the preliminary injunction, and we remand the case so that it may be returned to the District Court for trial on the issues presented.

Ashcroft v. American Civil Liberties Union, United States Supreme Court, No. 03-218 (June 29, 2004).

I

A

COPA is the second attempt by Congress to make the Internet safe for minors by criminalizing certain Internet speech. The first attempt was the Communications Decency Act of 1996. The Court held the CDA unconstitutional because it was not narrowly tailored to serve a compelling governmental interest and because less restrictive alternatives were available.

In response to the Court's decision in *Reno*, Congress passed COPA. COPA imposes criminal penalties of a $50,000 fine and six months in prison for the knowing posting, for "commercial purposes," of World Wide Web content that is "harmful to minors." Material that is "harmful to minors" is defined as:

"any communication, picture, image, graphic image file, article, recording, writing, or other matter of any kind that is obscene or that—

> "(A) the average person, applying contemporary community standards, would find, taking the material as a whole and with respect to minors, is designed to appeal to, or is designed to pander to, the prurient interest;
> "(B) depicts, describes, or represents, in a manner patently offensive with respect to minors, an actual or simulated sexual act or sexual contact, an actual or simulated normal or perverted sexual act, or a lewd exhibition of the genitals or post-pubescent female breast; and
> "(C) taken as a whole, lacks serious literary, artistic, political, or scientific value for minors."

"Minors" are defined as "any person under 17 years of age." A person acts for "commercial purposes only if such person is engaged in the business of making such communications." "Engaged in the business," in turn, "means that the person who makes a communication, or offers to make a communication, by means of the World Wide Web, that includes any material that is harmful to minors, devotes time, attention, or labor to such activities, as a regular course of such person's trade or business, with the objective of earning a profit as a result of such activities (although it is not necessary that the person make a profit or that the making or offering to make such communications be the person's sole or principal business or source of income)."

While the statute labels all speech that falls within these definitions as criminal speech, it also provides an affirmative defense to those who employ specified means to prevent minors from gaining access to the prohibited materials on their Web site. A person may escape conviction under the statute by demonstrating that he "has restricted access by minors to material that is harmful to minors—

> "(A) by requiring use of a credit card, debit account, adult access code, or adult personal identification number;

"(B) by accepting a digital certificate that verifies age, or

"(C) by any other reasonable measures that are feasible under available technology."

Since the passage of COPA, Congress has enacted additional laws regulating the Internet in an attempt to protect minors. For example, it has enacted a prohibition on misleading Internet domain names in order to prevent Web site owners from disguising pornographic Web sites in a way likely to cause uninterested persons to visit them (giving, as an example, the Web site "white-house.com"). It has also passed a statute creating a "Dot Kids" second-level Internet domain, the content of which is restricted to that which is fit for minors under the age of 13.

B

Respondents, Internet content providers and others concerned with protecting the freedom of speech, filed suit in the United States District Court for the Eastern District of Pennsylvania. They sought a preliminary injunction against enforcement of the statute. After considering testimony from witnesses presented by both respondents and the Government, the District Court issued an order granting the preliminary injunction. The court first noted that the statute would place a burden on some protected speech. The court then concluded that respondents were likely to prevail on their argument that there were less restrictive alternatives to the statute: "On the record to date, it is not apparent . . . that [petitioner] can meet its burden to prove that COPA is the least restrictive means available to achieve the goal of restricting the access of minors" to harmful material. In particular, it noted that "[t]he record before the Court reveals that blocking or filtering technology may be at least as successful as COPA would be in restricting minors' access to harmful material online without imposing the burden on constitutionally protected speech that COPA imposes on adult users or Web site operators."

The Government appealed the District Court's decision to the United States Court of Appeals for the Third Circuit. The Court of Appeals affirmed the preliminary injunction, but on a different ground. The court concluded that the "community standards" language in COPA by itself rendered the statute unconstitutionally overbroad. We granted certiorari and reversed, holding that the community-standards language did not, standing alone, make the statute unconstitutionally overbroad. We emphasized, however, that our decision was limited to that narrow issue. We remanded the case to the Court of Appeals to reconsider whether the District Court had been correct to grant the preliminary injunction. On remand, the Court of Appeals again affirmed the District Court. The Court of Appeals concluded that the statute was not narrowly tailored to serve a compelling Government interest, was overbroad, and was not the least restrictive means available for the Government to serve the interest of preventing minors from using the Internet to gain access to materials that are harmful to them. The Government once again sought review from this Court, and we again granted certiorari.

II

A

"This Court, like other appellate courts, has always applied the abuse of discretion standard on the review of a preliminary injunction." *Walters* v. *National Assn. of Radiation Survivors.* "The grant of appellate jurisdiction does not give the Court license to depart from established standards of appellate review." If the underlying constitutional question is close, therefore, we should uphold the injunction and remand for trial on the merits. Applying this mode of inquiry, we agree with the Court of Appeals that the District Court did not abuse its discretion in entering the preliminary injunction. Our reasoning in support of this conclusion, however, is based on a narrower, more specific grounds than the rationale the Court of Appeals adopted. The Court of Appeals, in its opinion affirming the decision of the District Court, construed a number of terms in the statute, and held that COPA, so construed, was unconstitutional. None of those constructions of statutory terminology, however, were relied on by or necessary to the conclusions of the District Court. Instead, the District Court concluded only that the statute was likely to burden some speech that is protected for adults, which petitioner does not dispute. As to the definitional disputes, the District Court concluded only that respondents' interpretation was "not unreasonable," and relied on their interpretation only to conclude that respondents had standing to challenge the statute, which, again, petitioner does not dispute. Because we affirm the District Court's decision to grant the preliminary injunction for the reasons relied on by the District Court, we decline to consider the correctness of the other arguments relied on by the Court of Appeals.

The District Court, in deciding to grant the preliminary injunction, concentrated primarily on the argument that there are plausible, less restrictive alternatives to COPA. A statute that "effectively suppresses a large amount of speech that adults have a constitutional right to receive and to address to one another . . . is unacceptable if less restrictive alternatives would be at least as effective in achieving the legitimate purpose that the statute was enacted to serve." When plaintiffs challenge a content-based speech restriction, the burden is on the Government to prove that the proposed alternatives will not be as effective as the challenged statute.

In considering this question, a court assumes that certain protected speech may be regulated, and then asks what is the least restrictive alternative that can be used to achieve that goal. The purpose of the test is not to consider whether the challenged restriction has some effect in achieving Congress' goal, regardless of the restriction it imposes. The purpose of the test is to ensure that speech is restricted no further than necessary to achieve the goal, for it is important to assure that legitimate speech is not chilled or punished. For that reason, the test does not begin with the status quo of existing regulations, then ask whether the challenged restriction has some additional ability to achieve Congress' legitimate interest. Any restriction on speech could be justified under that analysis. Instead, the court should ask whether the challenged regulation is the least restrictive means among available, effective alternatives.

In deciding whether to grant a preliminary injunction stage, a district court must consider whether the plaintiffs have demonstrated that they are likely to prevail on the merits. (The court also considers whether the plaintiff has shown irreparable injury but the parties in this case do not contest the correctness of the District Court's conclusion that a likelihood of irreparable injury had been established.) As the Government bears the burden of proof on the ultimate question of COPA's constitutionality, respondents must be deemed likely to prevail unless the Government has shown that respondents' proposed less restrictive alternatives are less effective than COPA. Applying that analysis, the District Court concluded that respondents were likely to prevail. That conclusion was not an abuse of discretion, because on this record there are a number of plausible, less restrictive alternatives to the statute.

The primary alternative considered by the District Court was blocking and filtering software. Blocking and filtering software is an alternative that is less restrictive than COPA, and, in addition, likely more effective as a means of restricting children's access to materials harmful to them. The District Court, in granting the preliminary injunction, did so primarily because the plaintiffs had proposed that filters are a less restrictive alternative to COPA and the Government had not shown it would be likely to disprove the plaintiffs' contention at trial.

Filters are less restrictive than COPA. They impose selective restrictions on speech at the receiving end, not universal restrictions at the source. Under a filtering regime, adults without children may gain access to speech they have a right to see without having to identify themselves or provide their credit card information. Even adults with children may obtain access to the same speech on the same terms simply by turning off the filter on their home computers. Above all, promoting the use of filters does not condemn as criminal any category of speech, and so the potential chilling effect is eliminated, or at least much diminished. All of these things are true, moreover, regardless of how broadly or narrowly the definitions in COPA are construed.

Filters also may well be more effective than COPA. First, a filter can prevent minors from seeing all pornography, not just pornography posted to the Web from America. The District Court noted in its factfindings that one witness estimated that 40% of harmful-to-minors content comes from overseas. COPA does not prevent minors from having access to those foreign harmful materials. That alone makes it possible that filtering software might be more effective in serving Congress' goals. Effectiveness is likely to diminish even further if COPA is upheld, because the providers of the materials that would be covered by the statute simply can move their operations overseas. It is not an answer to say that COPA reaches some amount of materials that are harmful to minors; the question is whether it would reach more of them than less restrictive alternatives. In addition, the District Court found that verification systems may be subject to evasion and circumvention, for example by minors who have their own credit cards. Finally, filters also may be more effective because they can be applied to all forms of Internet communication, including e-mail, not just communications available via the World Wide Web.

That filtering software may well be more effective than COPA is confirmed by the findings of the Commission on Child Online Protection, a blue-ribbon commission created by Congress in COPA itself. Congress directed the Commission to evaluate the relative merits of different means of restricting minors' ability to gain access to harmful materials on the Internet. It unambiguously found that filters are more effective than age-verification requirements (assigning a score for "Effectiveness" of 7.4 for server-based filters and 6.5 for client-based filters, as compared to 5.9 for independent adult-id verification, and 5.5 for credit card verification). Thus, not only has the Government failed to carry its burden of showing the District Court that the proposed alternative is less effective, but also a Government Commission appointed to consider the question has concluded just the opposite. That finding supports our conclusion that the District Court did not abuse its discretion in enjoining the statute.

Filtering software, of course, is not a perfect solution to the problem of children gaining access to harmful-to-minors materials. It may block some materials that are not harmful to minors and fail to catch some that are. Whatever the deficiencies of filters, however, the Government failed to introduce specific evidence proving that existing technologies are less effective than the restrictions in COPA. The District Court made a specific factfinding that "[n]o evidence was presented to the Court as to the percentage of time that blocking and filtering technology is over- or underinclusive." In the absence of a showing as to the relative effectiveness of COPA and the alternatives proposed by respondents, it was not an abuse of discretion for the District Court to grant the preliminary injunction. The Government's burden is not merely to show that a proposed less restrictive alternative has some flaws; its burden is to show that it is less effective. It is not enough for the Government to show that COPA has some effect. Nor do respondents bear a burden to introduce, or offer to introduce, evidence that their proposed alternatives are more effective. The Government has the burden to show they are less so. The Government having failed to carry its burden, it was not an abuse of discretion for the District Court to grant the preliminary injunction.

One argument to the contrary is worth mentioning—the argument that filtering software is not an available alternative because Congress may not require it to be used. That argument carries little weight, because Congress undoubtedly may act to encourage the use of filters. We have held that Congress can give strong incentives to schools and libraries to use them. It could also take steps to promote their development by industry, and their use by parents. It is incorrect, for that reason, to say that filters are part of the current regulatory status quo. The need for parental cooperation does not automatically disqualify a proposed less restrictive alternative. ("A court should not assume a plausible, less restrictive alternative would be ineffective; and a court should not presume parents, given full information, will fail to act"). In enacting COPA, Congress said its goal was to prevent the "widespread availability of the Internet" from providing "opportunities for minors to access materials through the World Wide Web in a manner that can frustrate parental supervision or control." COPA presumes that parents lack the ability, not the will, to monitor what their children see. By enacting programs to promote use of filtering software, Congress could give parents that ability without subjecting protected speech to severe penalties.

The closest precedent on the general point is our decision in *Playboy Entertainment Group*. *Playboy Entertainment Group*, like this case, involved a content-based restriction designed to protect minors from viewing harmful materials. The choice was between a blanket speech restriction and a more specific technological solution that was available to parents who chose to implement it. Absent a showing that the proposed less restrictive alternative would not be as effective, we concluded, the more restrictive option preferred by Congress could not survive strict scrutiny. In the instant case, too, the Government has failed to show, at this point, that the proposed less restrictive alternative will be less effective. The reasoning of *Playboy Entertainment Group*, and the holdings and force of our precedents require us to affirm the preliminary injunction. To do otherwise would be to do less than the First Amendment commands. "The starch in our constitutional standards cannot be sacrificed to accommodate the enforcement choices of the Government."

B

There are also important practical reasons to let the injunction stand pending a full trial on the merits. First, the potential harms from reversing the injunction outweigh those of leaving it in place by mistake. Where a prosecution is a likely possibility, yet only an affirmative defense is available, speakers may self-censor rather than risk the perils of trial. There is a potential for extraordinary harm and a serious chill upon protected speech. The harm done from letting the injunction stand pending a trial on the merits, in contrast, will not be extensive. No prosecutions have yet been undertaken under the law, so none will be disrupted if the injunction stands. Further, if the injunction is upheld, the Government in the interim can enforce obscenity laws already on the books.

Second, there are substantial factual disputes remaining in the case. As mentioned above, there is a serious gap in the evidence as to the effectiveness of filtering software. For us to assume, without proof, that filters are less effective than COPA would usurp the District Court's factfinding role. By allowing the preliminary injunction to stand and remanding for trial, we require the Government to shoulder its full constitutional burden of proof respecting the less restrictive alternative argument, rather than excuse it from doing so.

Third, and on a related point, the factual record does not reflect current technological reality—a serious flaw in any case involving the Internet. The technology of the Internet evolves at a rapid pace. Yet the factfindings of the District Court were entered in February 1999, over five years ago. Since then, certain facts about the Internet are known to have changed. Compare (36.7 million Internet hosts as of July 1998) with Internet Systems Consortium, Internet Domain Survey, Jan. 2004, . . . (as visited June 22, 2004, and available in the Clerk of Court's case file) (233.1 million hosts as of Jan. 2004). It is reasonable to assume that other technological developments important to the First Amendment analysis have also occurred during that time. More and better filtering alternatives may exist than when the District Court entered its findings. Indeed, we know that after the District Court entered its factfindings, a congressionally appointed commission issued a report that found that filters are more effective than verification screens.

Delay between the time that a district court makes factfindings and the time that a case reaches this Court is inevitable, with the necessary consequence that there will be some discrepancy between the facts as found and the facts at the time the appellate court takes up the question. We do not mean, therefore, to set up an insuperable obstacle to fair review. Here, however, the usual gap has doubled because the case has been through the Court of Appeals twice. The additional two years might make a difference. By affirming the preliminary injunction and remanding for trial, we allow the parties to update and supplement the factual record to reflect current technological realities.

Remand will also permit the District Court to take account of a changed legal landscape. Since the District Court made its factfindings, Congress has passed at least two further statutes that might qualify as less restrictive alternatives to COPA—a prohibition on misleading domain names, and a statute creating a minors-safe "Dot Kids" domain. Remanding for trial will allow the District Court to take into account those additional potential alternatives.

On a final point, it is important to note that this opinion does not hold that Congress is incapable of enacting any regulation of the Internet designed to prevent minors from gaining access to harmful materials. The parties, because of the conclusion of the Court of Appeals that the statute's definitions rendered it unconstitutional, did not devote their attention to the question whether further evidence might be introduced on the relative restrictiveness and effectiveness of alternatives to the statute. On remand, however, the parties will be able to introduce further evidence on this point. This opinion does not foreclose the District Court from concluding, upon a proper showing by the Government that meets the Government's constitutional burden as defined in this opinion, that COPA is the least restrictive alternative available to accomplish Congress' goal.

⚜

On this record, the Government has not shown that the less restrictive alternatives proposed by respondents should be disregarded. Those alternatives, indeed, may be more effective than the provisions of COPA. The District Court did not abuse its discretion when it entered the preliminary injunction. The judgment of the Court of Appeals is affirmed, and the case is remanded for proceedings consistent with this opinion.

It is so ordered.

POSTSCRIPT

Should Sexual Content on the Internet Be Restricted?

The Supreme Court's rejection of COPA may not be the final word on the subject. As Justice Kennedy noted, the high court does not outright reject Congress's ability to legislate to limit minors' access to sexual material; it only rejects their attempt in this case as too restrictive.

Although Justice Kennedy championed the benefits of Internet filtering software, they also have limits. Such software is of varying quality, and while it might block out the pornography that is of concern, some programs are overambitious, also restricting access to some very helpful sexual information, like Planned Parenthood's teenwire.com, Web sites that provide information for gay and lesbian young people (like youthresource.com), or even the federal government's own iwannaknow.org.

If the burden of restricting material that is "harmful to minors" is placed on individuals, should they also bear the expense of filtering software? New televisions are required to have a "v-chip" installed—a device that when activated restricts sexual or violent content. Should new computers similarly be required to have filtering software bundled with other software? And what settings should apply? Or should that be left up to the individuals who use—or do not use—the software? What about public facilities like libraries, universities, and hotel lobbies?

Further, what do you think of COPA's definition of what is "harmful to minors"? It specifically describes sexual content but does not address violence. If the purpose of legislation is truly to protect minors from harm, should it also restrict access to violent imagery? And if so, what would the implications of such legislation be? Would news information Web sites like cnn.com and msnbc.com need to obtain one's credit card data before permitting access to stories and images about war or a murder investigation? What material, if any, would you want to see restricted, either through a credit card entry system or through filtering software?

Finally, the inexact nature of cyberspace also raises the question of jurisdiction. Where exactly *is* a person when they are downloading or uploading something on the Web? Do the laws of the physical place apply? Take, for example, a person who creates a Web site from his or her home in one city, and then uploads (adds) material to that Web site from another city—or from another country. Whose laws apply? If legislation like COPA were upheld, would providers of sexual material seek to establish foreign universal resource locators (URLs) where such laws do not apply, in order to maintain their Web sites without restrictions?

Suggested Readings

W. Adamson, "Sex in the City: What Happened at the Minneapolis Public Library," *Off Our Backs* (May–June 2004).

Associated Press, "Justices Block Internet Porn Law," msnbc.com (June 29, 2004).

A. Beeson, "Online Porn Law—COPA Opponent," *Washington Post* (June 30, 2004).

P. Brick and B. Taverner, "Savvy Websites: In Search of Accurate Sexuality Information on the 'Net," *Positive Images: Teaching Abstinence, Contraception, and Sexual Health* (Planned Parenthood of Greater Northern, New Jersey, 2001).

M. Heins, "The Right Result; The Wrong Reason," *The Free Expression Policy Project* (July 1, 2004).

K. Lehmann, "Avoiding Pornography Landmines While Traveling the Information Superhighway: Adult Content, You Must be at Least 18 Years of Age to Enter," *Multimedia Schools* (May–June 2002).

B. Mears, "Supreme Court Affirms Use of Computer Filters in Public Libraries," http://www.cnn.com/2003/LAW/06/24/scotus.internetporn.library/index.html (January 13, 2004).

J. Schwartz, "Antipornography Law Keeps Crashing Into First Amendment," *New York Times* (June 30, 2004).

Contributors to This Volume

EDITOR

WILLIAM J. TAVERNER, M.A., was named "one of the country's pre-eminent sex educators, trainers of sex educators, and sex education theorists" (*Sexual Intelligence*, 2006). He is the co-founding editor of the *American Journal of Sexuality Education*, and director of The Center for Family Life Education, the acclaimed education department of Planned Parenthood of Greater Northern New Jersey. Taverner is the author or co-author of numerous sex education manuals, including *All Together Now: Teaching about Contraception and Safer Sex, Making Sense of Abstinence, Sex Ed 101,* and *Streetwise to Sex-Wise: Sexuality Education for High-Risk Youth.* Taverner is also the editor of several editions of *Taking Sides: Clashing Views on Controversial Issues in Human Sexuality,* and a contributing author to the *International Encyclopedia of Sexuality.* In 2006, Taverner was honored with the "Golden APPLE Award," given for leadership in the field of sexuality education by the Association for Planned Parenthood Leaders in Education (APPLE), and also received a national award given by the electronic journal *Sexual Intelligence.* A year earlier, he became the first recipient of the "AASECT Founder's Award," given by the American Association of Sex Educators, Counselors, and Therapists (AASECT) for the best workshop demonstrating interactive approaches to learning about sexuality.

An adjunct professor of human sexuality at Fairleigh Dickinson University, currently on sabbatical, Taverner has trained sexual health professionals throughout the nation. He received his Master of Arts degree in human sexuality from New York University, and can be reached at Taverner@ptd.net.

STAFF

Larry Loeppke	Managing Editor
Jill Peter	Senior Developmental Editor
Susan Brusch	Senior Developmental Editor
Beth Kundert	Production Manager
Jane Mohr	Project Manager
Tara McDermott	Design Coordinator
Nancy Meissner	Editorial Assistant
Julie Keck	Senior Marketing Manager
Mary Klein	Marketing Communications Specialist
Alice Link	Marketing Coordinator
Tracie Kammerude	Senior Marketing Assistant
Lori Church	Pemissions Coordinator

CONSULTING EDITOR

RYAN W. MCKEE, M.S., is an adjunct professor of human sexuality at Montclair State University and Fairleigh Dickinson University. He also works as a sexuality education consultant and program evaluator. He has written for Columbia University Health Services' renowned GoAskAlice! Web page (www.goaskalice.columbia.edu) and is a member of the American Association of Sex Educators, Counselors, and Therapists (AASECT).

He received his Master of Science degree in Sociology from Virginia Commonwealth University (VCU). He was a Research Assistant at VCU's Survey Evaluation Research Laboratory where he worked on numerous projects including the Virginia Transgender Health Initiative, the Virginia Teen Pregnancy Prevention Initiative, the Youth Risk Behavior Survey, the Virginia Community Youth Survey, and the Virginia Youth Tobacco Survey. He can be reached at mckeer@mail.montclair.edu.

AUTHORS

STEPHEN G. BREYER is an Associate Justice of the United States Supreme Court, appointed by President Bill Clinton in 1994.

JANE E. BRODY is the personal health columnist for the *New York Times,* and author of several bestselling books on health and nutrition.

MICHAEL BRUNO writes press releases for Edelman, an independent global public relations firm.

GEORGE W. BUSH is the 43rd president of the United States and was formerly the governor of Texas.

PATRICK J. CARNES is a nationally known speaker on the topic of sex addiction. He is the author of numerous books, including *Facing the Shadow: Starting Sexual and Relationship Recovery* and *In the Shadows of the Net: Breaking Free of Compulsive Online Sexual Behavior.*

RHONDA CHITTENDEN is a regional educator for Planned Parenthood of Greater Iowa, and is a regular columnist for *Sexing the Political,* an online journal of Gen X feminists on sexuality.

JOHN CORNYN is a United States Senator from Texas, who chairs the Senate Judiciary subcommittee on the Constitution, Civil Rights and Property Rights. He is a former state supreme court justice and state attorney general.

CYNTHIA DAILARD is a senior public policy associate at the Guttmacher Institute's Washington, DC office and is responsible for issues related to domestic family planning programs, sex education, and teenager's sexual behavior.

JENS ALAN DANA is a student at Brigham Young University, where he is also an editor for the student newspaper, *The Daily Universe.*

MARCY DARNOVSKY is the associate executive director of the Center for Genetics and Society in Oakland, California.

NORA GELPERIN is the director of training and education for Answer at Rutgers University and has presented workshops at local, state, and national conferences.

TERENCE M. HINES is a professor of psychology at Pace University in Pleasantville, New York.

PAUL JOANNIDES is a research psychoanalyst. He is the author of *The Guide To Getting It On!* which has won four awards and has been translated into fourteen languages.

MAUREEN A. KELLY is the vice president for education and training for Planned Parenthood of the Southern Finger Lakes, in Ithaca, New York.

ANTHONY M. KENNEDY is an associate justice of the United States Supreme Court, appointed by President Ronald Reagan in 1988.

JUDITH KLEINFELD is a professor of psychology at the University of Alaska at Fairbanks and author of *Gender Tales: Tensions in the Schools.*

LORETTA M. KOPELMAN is a professor and chair of the Department of Medical Humanities in the School of Medicine at East Carolina University. She is coeditor of *Children and Health Care: Moral and Social Issues.*

JUDITH LEVINE is the author of *Harmful to Minors: The Perils of Protecting Children From Sex,* which won the 2002 Los Angeles Times Book Prize.

MARSHALL MILLER is the co-founder of the Alternatives to Marriage Project (www.unmarried.org) and co-author of *Unmarried to Each Other: The Essential Guide to Living Together as an Unmarried Couple.*

DOUGLAS F. MUNCH is founder and president of DFM, Ltd., a strategic management consulting firm specializing in the health care industry. He has more than 20 years of senior health care experience encompassing pharmaceuticals, medical products, and diagnostics.

P. MASILA MUTISYA is an assistant professor in the Department of Curriculum and Instruction in the School of Education at Fayetteville State University. He teaches courses on foundations of education, human development, and multicultural education.

DAVID POPENOE is co-director of the National Marriage Project and a professor of sociology at Rutgers University. He is the author of several books, including *Life Without Father: Compelling New Evidence that Fatherhood and Marriage are Indispensable for the Good of Children and Society.*

RONI RABIN is a journalist whose work has appeared in *Newsday* and the *New York Times.*

DAVID L. RIEGEL is the author of *Understanding Loved Boys and Boylovers* and *Beyond Hysteria: Boy Erotica on the Internet.* He has also published articles in

Archives of Sexual Behavior, the *Journal of Psychology and Human Sexuality,* and *Sexuality and Culture.*

JOHN A. ROBERTSON holds the Vinson & Elkins Chair at The University of Texas School of Law at Austin. A graduate of Dartmouth College and Harvard Law School, he has written and lectured widely on law and bioethical issues.

STEPHANIE ANN SANDERS is an associate director and associate scientist for the Kinsey Institute for Research in Sex, Gender, and Reproduction at Indiana University.

LAURA SCHLESSINGER is the host of the radio talk show "The Dr. Laura Schlessinger Show." She is also the author of *The Ten Commandments: The Significance of God's Laws in Everyday Life.*

GARY SCHUBACH is a sex educator, lecturer, writer, and an associate professor for the Institute for the Advanced Study of Human Sexuality in San Francisco. He moderates the Web site www.DoctorG.com.

LAWRENCE A. SIEGEL is the president and CEO of the Sage Institute for Family Development in Boynton Beach, Florida.

RICHARD M. SIEGEL is the vice president of education, training, and counseling services for Planned Parenthood of South Palm Beach & Broward Counties, Inc. in Boca Raton, Florida.

DORIAN SOLOT is the executive director of the Alternatives to Marriage Project (www.unmarried.org) and co-author of *Unmarried to Each Other: The Essential Guide to Living Together as an Unmarried Couple.*

CAROLYN SUSMAN is a reporter for the *Palm Beach Post.*

JANICE WEINMAN is the executive director of the American Association of University Women.

Index

virginity: female circumcision and, 271; oral sex and, 30–31; pledges of, 114

Walsh, William, 226
Warren, Mary Anne, 163
Waskow, Arthur, 226
Watson, James, 164
websites, college: sexual health information available on, 85
Weinman, Janice, on gender bias in schools, 138–41
Whelihan, Maureen, 71
Whipple. Beverly, on female sexual response anatomy and physiology, 56–65
Whitehead, Barbara Dafoe, on recent research on cohabitation, 234–48
Wilson, Edward, 259

Wilson, Susie, 113
withdrawal, in addiction, 13
women. *See also* girls: anatomy and physiology of sexual response of, 56–65; circumcision of (*See* female circumcision); computer skills of, 142–43; low libido in, testosterone patch for, 70–74; misinformed about sexuality, 54; "missing," 165; paraurethral glands of, 52; professional equality of, 140, 143; prostate gland in, 51–54; research focused on, 61–62; sexual response of, 37–39; vaginal orgasm in, 57–58; views on cohabitation and marriage, 231–33

"You Suck" Song, 293